Frontiers of Economics

This book is based on a symposium organized by the
Yrjö Jahnsson Foundation

Frontiers of Economics

Edited by Kenneth J. Arrow
and Seppo Honkapohja

Basil Blackwell

First published 1985

Basil Blackwell Ltd
108 Cowley Road, Oxford OX4 1JF, UK

Basil Blackwell Inc.
432 Park Avenue South, Suite 1505,
New York, NY 10016, USA

British Library Cataloguing in Publication Data

Frontiers of economics.
1. Economics
I. Arrow, Kenneth J. II. Honkapohja, Seppo
III. Yrjö Jahnsson Foundation
330 HB171

ISBN 0-631-13408-5
ISBN 0-631-14599-0 Pbk

Library of Congress Cataloging in Publication Data

Frontiers of economics.
Papers presented at a symposium honoring Hilma Gabriella Jahnsson.
Includes index.
1. Economics – Congresses. 2. Jahnsson, Hilma Gabriella. I. Arrow, Kenneth Joseph, 1921–
II. Honkapohja, Seppo, 1951– . III. Jahnsson, Hilma Gabriella.
HB21.F76 1985 330 84-21610
ISBN 0-631-13408-5
ISBN 0-631-14599-0

Typeset by Unicus Graphics Ltd, Horsham
Printed in Great Britain by TJ Press Ltd, Padstow

Contents

Foreword

Hilma Gabriella Jahnsson, whose centenary was commemorated by this symposium, was a remarkable personality. She was the daughter of a prison guard who became one of the greatest philanthropists in Finland. She held two academic degrees and participated actively in Finnish cultural and political life together with her husband Yrjö, professor of economics at the Institute of Technology in Helsinki. For several years the Jahnssons strongly criticized the economic policies pursued in the 1930s. In their opinion, the monetary policy of the time was far too tight.

Yrjö Jahnsson also put his theory into practice, and the Jahnssons accumulated considerable wealth. In 1954 Hilma Jahnsson established the Yrjö Jahnsson Foundation in memory of her husband, who died in 1936. As early as the 1920s the Jahnssons had laid down the principles guiding the Foundation and had decided that it should support economic and medical research. Apart from making grants, the Foundation has arranged scientific seminars to train young economists, at which many renowned scholars have served as speakers or teachers. Since 1963 it has also arranged a series of lectures, called the Yrjö Jahnsson Lectures, and has published them in English.

As was indicated by its title, the general aim of this symposium was to survey selected areas of economic research, where fruitful theoretical or empirical developments have recently taken place. I would like to take this opportunity to express our gratitude to Professor Kenneth Arrow, who acted as the programme chairman and selected an excellent set of topics and speakers. I would also like to thank the local organizing committee consisting of Dr Seppo Honkapohja, Dr Vesa Kanniainen, Professor Arvi Leponiemi, Mr Antti Suvanto and Professor Esko Vuorela for their work in making the symposium possible. There is no need to say anything about the importance or relevance of the topics chosen because the authors do that eloquently. I would rather thank all six speakers – Robert Aumann,

Jerry Green, Oliver Hart, Mervyn King, Jean-Jacques Laffont and John Taylor – as well as all the persons who acted as discussants at the seminar.

I hope not only that this symposium in Sannäs offered the opportunity for fruitful discussion, but that it will be remembered by our foreign visitors as an enjoyable and memorable sojourn in Finland.

Pentti Vartia

Introduction

KENNETH J. ARROW AND SEPPO HONKAPOHJA

1 BACKGROUND

This book consists of the proceedings of the symposium with the same title which was held in Sannäs near Helsinki in Finland on 27–30 June 1983 under the auspices of the Yrjö Jahnsson Foundation to celebrate the centenary of Mrs Hilma Jahnsson, who created the Foundation in 1954. The Foundation decided a few years ago to use the occasion as an opportunity to organize a conference, in which the object would be to survey, discuss and evaluate the current state of research in several important areas of economics among a very distinguished group of participants. This was seen to be a valuable service to the field of economics not only in Finland, but also at the international level, through the publication of the proceedings.

The choice of the topics for the symposium was guided by three principles. First, significant results and advances in the area have taken place in the past 10–15 years, and the area is subject to continued extensive research effort at present. Second, some emphasis was placed on theoretical developments, in particular inasmuch as they have contributed improvements to current research in more applied areas of economics, or are likely to do so in the future. Third, in order to permit coverage in sufficient depth we had to be very selective, with the unfortunate consequence that many important topics had to be completely left out. Needless to say, these criteria were far from complete, and the final choice of topics also reflects our personal preferences, judgement and interests.

Looking back to the last decade, we saw several important developments in economics that led us to include those areas in the agenda of the symposium. After the initial outburst of research activity and the subsequent temporary disenchantment in the 1950s, the theory of games has become an increasingly prominent and widely used analytical tool in economics, though naturally its significance extends to many other sciences as well. We only need to mention the relationships between perfectly competitive equilibrium and some of the cooperative solution concepts of game theory, the vital role of the theory of games with incomplete information in the economics of information, and the close relationship between game theory and oligopoly theory, though these are just a few examples of the numerous applications. Hence we chose to include game theory and economics in the agenda.

The perennial topic of imperfect competition has received a great deal of fruitful research effort in the 1970s. Among the important developments one may perhaps list the attempts to build general equilibrium models with imperfect competition, the extensions of oligopoly theory to include aspects of dynamics and uncertainty, the refinement and clarification of the notion of entry barriers, and improvements in the analysis of advertising, product differentiation, entry, research and development and other phenomena. To these primarily theoretical advances one has to add to the whole extensive applied literature in the field of industrial organization. Imperfect competition was thus a natural selection as a topic for the symposium.

The economics of information has experienced an extremely rapid growth during the past decade and into the present. A large part of recent research has focused on the consequences of incomplete and asymmetric information on the forms of economic organization in different fields, ranging from trading activities to problems of income taxation. Various sophisticated trading arrangements, incentive contracts, signalling devices and nonlinear regulating schemes are used when the contingent markets of the Arrow–Debreu model of general equilibrium under uncertainty fail to exist and facilitate efficient risk-sharing. A related development has been the formulation of the concept of an equilibrium with rational or consistent expectations for price-mediated markets. Consequently, we picked differential information, the market and incentive compatibility as the third topic for the symposium.

The economics of savings behavior has been subject to a lot of both empirical and theoretical research during the 1970s. Much of it has been stimulated directly by policy considerations such as the problems of social security, but more generally the area is of prime importance in the wider context of the study of wealth accumulation and distribution over time. The life-cycle and permanent income hypotheses, which were developed in the 1950s, are still widely used frameworks, but other aspects such as the potentially important bequest motive have also been coming to the forefront of research effort. We felt that it would be quite useful to have an overview of the main issues in the area, and we thus selected the economics of saving as the fourth topic.

In macroeconomics the 1970s can be seen primarily as a period of reformulation and search for a more solid foundation, after the growing dissatisfaction with the so-called orthodox Keynesian doctrine. Many of the controversies still continue, and different approaches or schools of thought exist. One of the innovative developments has been the formulation of rigorous models of general equilibrium under price rigidity and quantity rationing, which has led to the wide use of fixed-price models in the analysis of short-run macroeconomic questions. After the theoretical advances, econometric methodology has also been developed for these kinds of models. Fixed-price models were therefore added to the agenda.

A fundamental innovation in macroeconomic theory was achieved through the use of the notion of rational expectations in macroeconomic models with flexible prices. Clearly, the agenda would have been deficient if rational expectations models had not been included in it. Though the area is closely interwoven with general equilibrium theory and the economics of information, we decided to emphasize the significance of rational expectations modelling in the field of macroeconomics, in which it has also been studied intensively. Rational expectations models in macroeconomics concluded the roster.

In the symposium, each of the six topics was first surveyed in a major lecture, after which two invited comments were delivered. The surveys and the comments make up the body of the volume. Needless to say, each topic is broad, and quite often the surveys take particular viewpoints which were left to the authors' choosing. In many cases the comments not only reflect on the survey, but also provide supplementary material that was left uncovered. In the symposium a significant amount of time was available for general discussion of each topic, and a separate session was held to provide an opportunity for additional reflections on the topics and for suggestions and remarks on other currently important related areas and problems for research. In this Introduction we try to provide a guide to the contents of the book by taking up briefly some of the major issues considered by the authors. In doing so we have relied on the discussions at the symposium, and we try to point out at least some matters in which different opinions exist at present, and on which further research would be valuable. We also try to provide an account of the discussions in the final session on open problems and future tasks of research.

Given the nature of the material, this Introduction is organized as follows. Section 2 is confined to game theory and methodology, since Robert Aumann's lecture was on a broad philosophical level, discussing not only game theory but also general issues of importance to economic theory. In section 3, under the heading of 'Resource allocation', we introduce the material on three of the topics: imperfect competition, differential information and incentives, and savings. In section 4, under the title of 'Macroeconomics', we have included the material dealing with fixed-price models and rational expectations models in macroeconomics. Finally, in section 5 we try to provide our interpretation of the open problems and topics for further research that came up in the concluding session of the symposium.

2 GAME THEORY AND METHODOLOGY

A large part of economic theory is awesomely dependent on game theory, borrowing from it the conceptual apparatus for the analysis of various economic problems. To give some examples, the symposium included sessions on imperfect competition, incentive compatibility and perhaps rational expectations. The first part of Robert Aumann's lecture (chapter 1) contains a beautiful broad philosophical essay stating his viewpoint for assessing the usefulness, validity and 'truthness' of game theory, though in fact his arguments can be applied to much of the current contents of mathematical economics, which is based on the hypothesis of rational behavior, and of social equilibrium arising from the interaction of strategically behaving agents.

According to Aumann, the success of game theory should not be judged by innate plausibility, but rather by its ability to facilitate comprehension of the different phenomena under study, in its three components: relationship or 'fitting things together,' unification ('I am not thinking of validity in the usual sense of truth, but rather in the sense of applicability or usefulness; I am measuring validity of an idea by the amount that people use it' (p. 30)) and simplicity. This viewpoint also leads him to argue that the concept of truth applies to observations, not to theories, so that, for example, the pluralism or multiplicity of solution concepts in game theory is an advantage, not a handicap. When applied to the role of the hypothesis of rationality and utility maximization, this viewpoint vitiates much of the critique such as 'Do individuals really maximize utility?' In Aumann's own words, 'it [the significance of utility maximization] derives from its being the underlying postulate that pulls together most of economic theory; it is the major component of a certain way of thinking, with many important and familiar implications, which have been part of economics for decades and even centuries. Alternatives such as satisficing have proved next to useless in this respect' (p. 35). Aumann also points out that in evolutionary biology the doctrine of the survival of the fittest takes the form of maximizing behavior of genes, though 'we know that genes don't "really" maximize anything' (p. 36).[1]

This viewpoint implies a particular way of looking at game theory and economic theory as descriptive sciences, since in reality human beings are motivated and influenced by other factors apart from rationality: 'the criterion for judging our theories cannot be rigid; we cannot ask, is it right or wrong? Rather we must ask, *how often* has it been useful, *how* useful has it been?' (p. 37). Aumann also concludes that the distinction between normative and descriptive models is not as sharp as is often thought, and that normative aspects of game theory are multidimensional.

While Aumann's systematic discussion of methodology has many attractive ideas, it may be felt to be somewhat extreme in that it leaves little or no role for empiricism and falsification of theories by means of experimentation and empirical work. It should be a challenge to economics and game theory to find ways of formulating such tests that face the real world. In his comments Reinhard Selten discusses various viewpoints on the question of empirical relevance of game theory, and more generally the hypothesis of rationality, opting for 'methodological dualism,' which makes a sharp distinction between normative theories based on rationality and descriptive ones. He bases this on recent work studying learning processes, and emphasizes, as Martin Shubik does in his comments, the importance of the recent experimental work. The use of money rewards in designing experiments has been a particularly important innovation, as was emphasized by Aumann and others at the symposium. When learning situations and the consequent possibilities for convergence to rational behavior are not possible, Selten advocates theories of limited rationality based on experimental research. In this he is supported by Shubik's emphasis on the need to develop satisfactory concepts of limited rationality.

The second part of Aumann's lecture consists of an assessment of the most important solution concepts of game theory: Nash equilibrium, the core, the stable set and the Shapley value. Both Aumann and Shubik stress that the multitude of solution concepts do not provide a basis for criticism of game theory. Each one of the solution concepts focuses on different aspects of rational decision-making and play. Nash equilibrium and its numerous variants and refinements stress individual incentives, i.e. economic agents simultaneously maximize their utility. The core is a cooperative solution concept emphasizing the outcome of unlimited competition in economic situations in which the competition can lead to a stable outcome in that the core is non-empty. Aumann points out that this interpretation of the core is not apparent from the definition, but emerges from the application and existing results. The von Neumann–Morgenstern stable set refines the idea of stability with respect to blocking coalitions of the core: the blocking coalition of a given one should itself have a stability property. Aumann's lecture emphasizes that, somewhat surprisingly, this feature leads, via its applications, to the view that the stable set is a solution concept expressing the idea of social organization, its forms being endogenous and quite subtle. The last of the solutions discussed by Aumann is the Shapley value, which, again through the applications, can be interpreted as describing power, reasonable compromise or outcome of arbitration.

Most of Martin Shubik's commentary concentrates on the use of the apparatus of game theory as a tool of modelling social, economic and other phenomena; and in particular he emphasizes modelling problems encountered prior to the formulation of the solution concept: 'there is a considerable distinction in the level of detail and nature of aggregation provided in the extensive, strategic, and coalitional forms [of games]' (p. 89), the first being detailed, and the last one becoming pre-institutional in its nature. Shubik provides a schematic summary of this modelling choice and then illustrates it by looking briefly at the theory of competitive equilibrium, market games, oligopoly and financial institutions.

3 RESOURCE ALLOCATION

Different problems of resource allocation or microeconomics were the subject matter of three of the sessions in the symposium, namely those dealing with imperfect competition, incentive compatibility and differential information, and savings behavior. The first two concentrate on recent theoretical work, while the focus of the third is primarily on models used for empirical proposes.

Imperfect competition

In his survey (chapter 2) Oliver Hart provides an extensive review of the general equilibrium models of imperfect competition that have been developed in the recent literature. The starting point is a synthesis of the so-called subjective demand approach, originally due to Negishi (1961), in which the monopolistically competitive firms have perceived demand functions for their products. These functions go through the status quo point but are otherwise subjective or arbitrary. As Hart points out, this approach is quite general, but its main difficulty is that no justification is provided for the subjective conjectures, so that 'to an outside observer who is asked to predict the market outcome but who does not know what these conjectures are, almost anything could be an equilibrium; i.e., the set of allocations that are a monopolistically competitive equilibrium for *some* conjectures ... is very large' (p. 107).

The second set of general equilibrium models with monopolistic competition discussed by Hart is more specific than the Negishi approach in that the conjectures of the firms are required to be correct: 'objective demands' are assumed, in Hart's terminology. Hart first surveys the Cournot-type models with quantity-setting firms, pointing out some important problems concerning the existence of equilibria; the currently known conditions guaranteeing existence are 'extraordinarily strong' (p. 112). Moreover, 'once one departs from relatively simple cases the [Cournot–Nash] formulation itself becomes unsatisfactory' (p. 114), in the sense that it is not evident what constitutes a plausible conjecture, and the approach requires that each firm make a full general equilibrium calculation in order to make its decisions.

For the second class of models with objective demands discussed by Hart, the starting point is the preceding observation that full general equilibrium calculations for decision-making by imperfectly competitive firms are not very plausible. Rather, it seems more likely that an individual firm takes as given some relevant variables, for example the wealth of the consumers. Hart provides a very interesting and novel justification for this by means of limiting and replication arguments, and he then proves an existence theorem for such imperfectly competitive equilibria, though in part the Roberts–Sonnenschein (1977) problem regarding the nature of the primitive assumptions still remains. As Hart emphasizes, the absence of these feedback effects, or 'Henry Ford effects,' as dubbed by Jean Jaskold Gabszewicz in his comments, leads to a more tractable model, though a less general one.

Hart's general conclusion about these models is that 'the objective demand approach ties equilibrium down to a much greater extent than the subjective demand approach, given particular assumptions about reactions. However, as we vary the assumptions about reactions the number of equilibria that the objective demand approach generates can be very large. . . . which of these equilibria is the "right" one?' (p. 123). This argument is the basis for the recent research about rational or reasonable conjectures, which attempts to study situations in which strategies are observable, so that underlying conjectures can be considered. In a partial equilibrium context Hart provides an account of the recent results and shows that in many circumstances the requirement of rationality or reasonableness is not sufficient to tie down the indeterminacies that are characteristic in oligopoly theory.

The final part of Hart's survey focuses on the meaning of the economists' favorite notion, perfect competition, in the light of the general equilibrium models of imperfect competition. After rejecting the validity of the ideas that perfect competition is a special case of Negishi's model, or that it arises out of Bertrand-type price-setting behavior, Hart turns to the view that the Arrow–Debreu model corresponds to the case, where each agent is small relative to the markets in which it operates. In other words, perfect competition is a limiting result for some imperfectly competitive economies, when the number of agents is replicated *ad infinitum*, so that each agent becomes small relative to the markets. The recent results discussed by Hart are based on the non-cooperative viewpoint, in contrast to the well-known theorems about the core and perfect competition in which the apparatus is taken from cooperative game theory. The latter support, of course, the same interpretation of perfect competition as a limiting case.[2]

One of the major simplifying assumptions in the general equilibrium models of imperfect competition surveyed by Hart is that products are homogeneous, so that issues related to the choice of product quality and product differentiation are not considered. In his comments Jean Jaskold Gabszewicz discusses the recent research on product differentiation and relates it to the problem of entry and exit, which is another major topic in the analysis of oligopoly and imperfect competition. On the basis of recent results, he suggests that properties and characteristics of demand can be an important determinant of the nature of equilibrium in an industry.

In his commentary Hugo Sonnenschein takes up some microeconomic aspects of monopolistically competitive situations. First, he suggests that the recent research on auctions and some experimental settings can provide a useful perspective on the use of different strategic variables: 'I understand the game defined by "the monopolist announces a price and each buyer decides whether or not to buy at that price." However, I see no clear game associated with "the monopolist announces a quantity." ... Why should a monopolist not consider labeling his product with two or more different prices?' Sonnenschein goes on to venture that 'monopolistically competitive theory will not go too far until we supply a similar degree of institutional detail [to that of auction theory]' (pp. 171–3). He also suggests that the recent experimental work may provide a lot of insight for future research on imperfect competition.

The opinions about the amount of institutional detail that should be present in modelling monopolistic and oligopolistic competition varied a great detail in the discussions at the symposium. Some of them echoed Sonnenschein in emphasizing the need for it, while others felt that the basis for monopolistic competition theory should be in the presence of increasing returns and the resulting non-convexities, without specifying too far the precise institutional characteristics.

Both Gabszewicz and Sonnenschein point out the need to model the circumstances leading to cooperation and collusion, the former emphasizing the use of cooperative notions such as the core, atoms and syndicates, and the latter focusing on the possibilities for repeated play which are conducive for cooperation. Repetition creates new issues in using game theory, auctions theory and experimental work in modelling oligopolies.

Differential information, the market and incentive compatibility

Jerry Green's lecture (chapter 3) does not try to provide a complete survey of the area, which, as he points out, has experienced an 'explosion of research' in the past decade. Instead, Green seeks to formulate the common foundations of the diverse literature by viewing it from the perspective of games of incomplete information which is the natural theoretical foundation for many of the economic models involving differential information among the individual agents.

The first distinction made by Green is that of games and generalized games, originally proposed by Debreu (1952). The latter is characterized by the interdependence of individuals' strategy sets and by the presence of 'player O,' who sets the values of certain endogenous variables to achieve a consistent outcome. After summarizing the main features of games of incomplete information, Green points out some potential difficulties in extending that theory to generalized games: one has to specify the information of 'player O' and its communication to other players as part of the equilibrium. This point is related to the important issues in giving better justifications for models of rational expectations. They are much less decentralized than the classical competitive model, since it appears that one is forced to assume that the individuals have a correctly specified structural model, making possible convergence via learning in a stationary environment, or else that they have the same information at the outset.

After this Green develops the main elements of the welfare analysis of games of incomplete information. He discusses the three viewpoints for welfare evaluation, based respectively on *ex ante*, interim and *ex post* utilities of the individuals with respect to the information on which the utilities are conditioned, and he then outlines the main features of the normative aspect of the welfare analysis, usually called mechanism design, emphasizing the significance of the revelation principle in simplifying the analysis. He also points out that the study of the design problems without a mediator is a nearly unstudied area.

In the classification of some of the important economic models, Green stresses that, formally, in many of them the corresponding game is supplemented by further constraints arising from the specific circumstance under study, and these can be classified as 'participation constraints,' expressing constraints on utilities and arising from the partial equilibrium nature of the models, and 'auxiliary equilibrium conditions,' which relate to dependencies among endogenous variables not in the form of constraints on expected utilities. The classifying material is then concluded by an emphasis on the potential problems arising from dimensionality considerations with respect to both observable and unobservable variables, many of the economic models being one- or zero-dimensional in both. Green concludes his lecture by discussing the most important results of the welfare analysis of some economic models.

Bengt Holmström's commentary is a general appraisal of the literature in its focus on illustrative applications, central economic issues and limitations and challenges of the research. According to him, the most important accomplishments have to do with the multitude of non-market organizational structures that can arise from asymmetric information, but which the complete information competitive model is unable to account for. The examples include cost-sharing contracts, bonus payments, monitoring practices, incidence of strikes and the like. Holmström stresses that 'these naturally occurring inefficiencies ... reflect nothing more than legitimate costs of information transfer,' or that 'they may also be viewed as stemming from rents that accrue to parties who hold an informational monopoly' (p. 204). Holmström goes on to suggest that the main difficulty of the 'new institutional economics' is that it is too easy to explain many of the institutions, and empirical work should be developed to discriminate between the alternative theories. Another difficulty emphasized by him and others at the symposium is that, so far, the nature of information costs is not comprehensive enough. The inefficiencies relate to strategic costs, but information has other aspects that should be considered as well. One of them concerns the costs of observations and information-gathering which is technological and not due to strategic behavior of parties possessing pieces of it. Holmström also discusses the complications to efficiency concepts caused by private information.

In his comments, John Riley develops the economics of competitive and monopolistic self-selection as another concrete illustration of the recent research. After discussing the main implications of the signalling model, initially due to Spence (1974) and others, Riley points out the problem of the non-existence of equilibria and the refined equilibrium concepts that have been proposed to resolve the issue. As examples of monopolistic self-selection mechanisms he first outlines the case of a public monopoly in which the mechanism design leads to the problem of finding information-constrained Pareto optima, with the basic result of d'Aspremont and Gérard-Varet (1979) concerning cases in which the full-information optimum can be attained. Second, Riley considers a private monopoly in which the natural criterion is to maximize the gain of the monopolist. As an illustration he outlines the derivation of the revenue equivalence theorem of auction theory and discusses the recent efforts studying the weakening of the basic assumptions about the symmetry of beliefs, independent valuations and risk neutrality. On the basis of the apparent complications, Riley ventures the speculation that 'even in relatively simple and highly specialized models, we may be asking too much in the search for non-cooperative equilibria in order to explain observed behavior. Perhaps the best we can hope for in some cases is to identify a set of logically consistent strategies' (p. 224).

Savings behavior

The object of Mervyn King's lecture on savings behavior (chapter 4) is to provide a detailed account of the recent work on consumption and savings decisions of households and their application to econometric analysis. The determinants of savings have been an important element in a number of topical debates, and King focuses on the different variants of the well-known life-cycle hypothesis, which he interprets broadly to mean that 'individual behavior is forward-looking, that individuals optimize over their expected remaining lifetime, and that the cost of acquiring information about the future is not so prohibitive that only current observations are used to determine current consumption' (p. 228).

The first part of King's survey deals with the various theoretical elements of the life-cycle model, and he discusses both the deterministic and stochastic variants, laying special emphasis on the various parametric specifications that have been used in empirical analysis. A particularly important one of these is the often-used separability condition on preferences, both over time and within the period with respect to consumption and labor supply. King suggests that 'tests of the life-cycle model ... are unlikely to be conclusive because they are tests of the joint hypothesis that (a) individuals are life-cycle savers, and (b) preferences are parametrized in a particular way' (p. 239). King also reports some simulations concerning the profile of assets over a lifetime, as predicted by a life-cycle model and compared with empirical evidence, based on King and Dicks-Mireaux (1982) and other work. The main difficulty of the model is that in reality the pattern of wealth decumulation at old age is far less pronounced than is predicted by the model, though King suggests that this might perhaps be reconciled by extending the model to include a stochastic date of death. Mordecai Kurz and Peter Diamond point out, in their comments, that this idea would also have other implications, such as market provision of insurance against it, with the appearance of the consequent demand for indexed annuities.

In the discussion on alternative models to the life-cycle hypothesis, King focuses on the potential significance of unemployment and quantity constraints in capital markets, relegating the treatment of bequests to a later section. He points out that problems of aggregation are likely to be very difficult, when some individuals are subject to these constraints while others are not. He also mentions the recent literature pointing out difficulties in expected utility theory and rational decision-making in the presence of major uncertainties. Diamond also stresses this issue in his comments.

In reviewing the empirical studies of savings behavior, King discusses first those that have employed aggregate time-series data. He points out that such data are likely to contain aggregation biases which make testing of the life-cycle model hazardous, as 'almost any set of aggregate data could be consistent with underlying rational individual behavior' (p. 271), and that the tests 'have been rather disappointing' (p. 272), though they seem to provide some support to the view that consumption is rather more sensitive to current income than is predicted by the simple life-cycle model.

The second class of studies reviewed by King has utilized household data, and King stresses that its accuracy can often be a major problem. This obstacle was emphasized by many others in the conference, and it would be desirable in future studies to have a more detailed explanation and assessment of the data used. Cross-section data also bring into relief the basic issue of heterogeneity in the population, and King concludes that 'support for the life-cycle model is mixed' (p. 282) at best. In this he is supported by Diamond, whose comments provide some further information on wealth accumulation from the study by himself and Hausman (1984) suggesting great diversity in behavior. Kurz also agrees with the need to account for heterogeneity, though his focus is primarily on bequest motives in savings decisions.

King devotes some space for a review of problems encountered in studying bequests and assessing their significance, and the topic is discussed in great detail by Kurz in his comments. Kurz argues that the interpretation of the life-cycle hypothesis as meaning that agents are 'forward-looking' in their behavior is too broad, since it does not distinguish between the life-cycle motive and the bequest motive. After an account of the theoretical elements of the latter, which he calls the 'intergenerational hypothesis,' Kurz discusses first the empirical evidence on social security and life-cycle savings and the evidence on the bequest motive, pointing out as a general conclusion that neither hypothesis appears to be in agreement with the empirical results, even if one takes notice of several severe methodological problems, especially in studies using cross-section data. Second, Kurz discusses evidence from several studies concerned with the quantitative significance of life-cycle motives, which suggest that only a small share of the US wealth stock can be accounted for by them. He concludes that other motives for wealth accumulation are very diverse and complex, so that 'research should concentrate on studying statistical regularities of the stochastic process that results from aggregating over a heterogenous population' (p. 325) and less on estimating parameters of hypothetical utility functions.

In the discussions, many participants felt that there was a great need for further work, but that in it one should carefully specify one's objectives and the questions addressed. Clearly, a good deal of population heterogeneity in motives for wealth accumulation exists, and polar hypotheses probably cannot account for them. On the other hand, it is possible in principle that a large fraction of the households behave in a way not too far removed from the life-cycle model and its extensions, as they do not have large estates and significant amounts of wealth. For some policy considerations, studies of behavior of these households may provide important empirical information. This is an open field, with much controversy, in which the benefits from clear statements of purpose can be substantial in narrowing down the points of disagreement.

4 MACROECONOMICS

Two of the topics of the symposium belong to the domain of macroeconomics, as they survey important developments of the last decade, namely fixed-price models and rational expectations models in macroeconomics. In both lectures the emphasis is to a large extent empirical, so that problems and issues of econometric research in the areas is discussed, together with an overview of the underlying basic theory.

Fixed-price models

Fixed-price models, often called disequilibrium or non-Walrasian models, attempt to provide a unified framework for the analysis of circumstances in which, owing to price rigidities, markets do not clear, and discrepancies between demands and supplies can prevail at least in the short run. In his survey (chapter 5) Jean-Jacques Laffont first outlines a prototype of the macroeconomic models used in the literature, and then summarizes the main features of the four empirical macro-models that have been developed so far.

Laffont emphasizes four empirical and methodological issues that each of the four studies have had to resolve in econometric implementation. The first of these is the lack of countercyclical variation in labor productivity, which is in contrast to the implication of the basic theoretical model. According to Laffont, in all four studies this difficulty is resolved in a fairly *ad hoc* way, and there is 'need for a better analysis of labor hoarding from a theoretical point of view' (p. 337). The second major empirical problem is the presence of frictional unemployment in the available data. The remaining two problems are methodological. First, one has to decide the link between realized transactions and demand and supplies, the so-called 'min' condition, for which different specifications have been used. Second, there is the problem of obtaining restrictions that guarantee the existence of a well-defined reduced form, sometimes called the coherency constraints. Laffont points out that these conditions imply restrictions on the size of the spillover effects in piecewise linear models, while for nonlinear models 'the question of uniqueness is more difficult' (p. 340).

After the overview of existing macroeconometric work Laffont turns to recent developments beyond the standard prototype models. First, 'the treatment of inventories as an exogenous variable in models where, by the logic of fix-price equilibria, they are playing an important role as a buffer stock' (p. 341) is a serious weakness in the existing empirical work. Laffont comments that little work has been done in this area, but the existing studies 'suggest that the price dynamics will not be seriously disturbed by the inventories–money holdings dynamics' (p. 346). This takes up the critical issue in fixed-price models, namely the lack of convincing explanations of price rigidity and price adjustment over time. Laffont surveys the existing models, which are based on mechanistic adjustment rules, and stresses that improvements are necessary before reliable conclusions can be made. In this he is supported by Frank Hahn's comments, which suggest that one needs to formulate models with monopolistic competition before such resolutions are obtainable. (Hahn also outlines a framework of this kind.)

The issue of price determination is related to the recent literature on implicit labor contracts, which has sometimes been suggested as a justification for rigid wages. Laffont provides a synopsis of the theory in an appendix, and Hahn comments on the area in detail. In the general discussion it was stressed that the distinction between nominal and real-price rigidities is important, the contract theory providing an explanation only for real-price rigidity.

When price dynamics are interrelated with investment and growth, various intermediate or long-run tendencies for the economy can emerge, but Laffont cites Malinvaud (1980) and suggests that the foundations of the models are very insecure in two respects: first, the behavioral rules of the economic agents are not derived satisfactorily; and second, the influence of expectations has not been considered in any detail, but is likely to be of fundamental importance. Laffont then concludes with a discussion of problems of aggregation; he reports on some preliminary results using survey data and suggests that 'fix-price theory enables us to look at data from a different point of view which might prove to be useful to economic policy in the short run' (p. 358).

In contrast to Hahn's commentary, which deals with the main problems of fixed-price theory and the related research on labor contracts, János Kornai's discussion provides a brief survey of the recent research on another class of non-Walrasian models, namely those by him and his colleagues that have been designed to analyze the chronic shortage phenomena of the socialist economies. Kornai emphasizes that this work is not within the fixed-price literature but rather is an independent area of studies, of which the major characteristic is that it is concerned with permanent or chronic situation, in contrast to alterations between different regimes.

Kornai also ventures an important conjecture about the nature of unemployment in market economics: 'chronic unemployment is systemic in a market economy . . . and theorists do not pay great attention to the long-term institutional–structural aspects of the problem' (pp. 380–1). Indeed, many participants felt that the economics profession cannot at present provide a reliable non-controversial explanation for the apparently persistent unemployment in the Western world. In any case, in addition to its weaknesses, the fixed-price models are capable of explaining only temporary unemployment, but not its persistence.

Rational expectations models in macroeconomics

In the beginning of his survey (chapter 6) John Taylor emphasizes that the basic aim of most of the current macroeconomic models with rational expectations is the analysis of business cycles in market economies, and that the hypothesis of rational expectations seems natural for this recurrent phenomenon. Taylor identifies two distinct branches of the recent literature. First, there are the pioneering macroeconomic models by Robert E. Lucas Jr, Thomas Sargent, Neil Wallace and Robert Barro, in which the primary source for the output–price relationships is informational in that certain informational constraints on suppliers exist: 'the constraints give rise to a perception of a relative price increase [and consequent quantity response] when in reality there is none' (p. 397). These models explicitly make the assumption that in each period prices are perfectly flexible and clear the markets. The second class of models identified by Taylor relies on explicit wage and price-setting behavior and consequent rigidity, so that the markets do not clear. Taylor terms the latter 'sticky price models'.

After a careful outline of the basic elements of both types of models, Taylor provides a summary of the empirical work that has tried to test the validity of the two approaches. The information-based models have been subject to a lot of testing, and Taylor points out that the results give reasons to be doubtful about the models. He is supported by Laurence Weiss, who in his comments states that 'I find the evidence on price surprises and output compelling. . . . [The Lucas model] must be judged a failure' (p. 442). The sticky price models have not been tested so extensively, and Taylor suggests that the first results indicate reasonably favorable results, though some problems concerning the explanation of the observed intertemporal correlations seem to emerge.

In the remaining part of the lecture Taylor reviews rational expectations models of consumption and investment, techniques for estimation and policy analysis, and open problems, stressing in particular questions about agents' learning of their environment and the problem of non-uniqueness of rational expectations equilibria. The latter issue is taken up by Seppo Honkapohja in his comments, in which he demonstrates the existence of non-stationary equilibria in a version of Taylor's models of staggered contracts, concluding with a strong opinion: 'the existence of a continuum of solutions to many rational expectations models, whether of "new classical" or "Keynesian" variety, is a fundamental difficulty in this research' (p. 433).

Honkapohja also takes up the basic characteristics of the rational expectations models with sticky prices, suggesting that they are problematic in two basic aspects. First, the existing justifications for the assumed price adjustment equations are not fully satisfactory in that at best they can be defended on some basis of limited rationality. Laurence Weiss also points out this questionable feature of the models with sticky prices. The second difficulty is that, since markets do not clear in these models, they should provide an account of the influence of quantity constraints on the behavior of economic agents, with the possibility of several types of equilibria. The existing models postulate that the economy is always in the region of Keynesian unemployment, in the terminology of the fixed-price models.

Laurence Weiss in his comments stresses that the rational expectations models have been an important extension to the existing microeconomic general equilibrium theory, with its emphasis on the role of prices in transmitting information. Weiss also points out that the rational expectations hypothesis has been quite useful in the study of the behavior of interest rates and volatility in asset markets. These innovations in microeconomics have been quite significant, and they may eventually lead to 'strong implications for aggregate economic activity' (p. 442). On the other hand, the debate about the significance of business cycles is far from being resolved, and Weiss suggests that successful models will be based on the assumption of maximizing behavior.

5 OPEN PROBLEMS AND FUTURE RESEARCH TOPICS

The concluding session of the symposium was devoted to an exploration of open problems in economics and suggestions for future research. Edmund Phelps, Jouko Paunio, Eytan Sheshinski and Carl Christian von Weizsäcker started with prepared statements, which were followed by comments by most of the participants in the symposium. What follows is a slightly organized list of the participants' visions of fruitful and needed research topics.

One general statement was made several times: both at this symposium and among economists in general, there was a tendency to shy away from the grandest themes. The fundamental questions of economic change, the theme of Schumpeter's work, are not discussed. It was suggested that economists displayed strong risk aversion in their own choice of research topics.

Despite this admonition, the actual topics proposed tended to be relatively specific and at least apparently researchable. Indeed, there was some question as to whether a theory of innovation was not a contradiction in terms. An innovation that can be predicted is no longer an innovation. Not surprisingly, the topics covered in the survey lectures and the comments on them were given little weight in proposals for future research. It was felt that they had already been given adequate expression.

For convenience, the topics of suggested high research priority are grouped under several headings.

Macroeconomics

As is not surprising, the dilemmas of unemployment and inflation received the most discussion. The chief emphasis was on providing a foundation in some variant of microeconomic theory for understanding macroeconomic phenomena. It may fairly be said that, among those at the conference, there was very little defence of those rational expectations theories that assume that all markets clear at all times.

One macroeconomic topic suggested was in the class of grand questions otherwise neglected: why are unemployment and excess capacity characteristics of capitalist economies? Equilibrium theory implies equality of supply and demand on all markets, including those for labor and capital goods. Even if the economy departs from equilibrium from time to time, standard theory has no reason why the deviation should be more often in one direction rather than another. Yet it appears to be obvious that periods of excess demand are rare indeed (except perhaps in wartime conditions) compared with periods of underutilization. Thus, as noted earlier in Taylor's sticky price models, the supply is always adequate to meet demand. Only one hypothesis to explain the systematic preference for unemployment was offered: employers keep wages above the market-clearing level so that dismissing an employee is an effective sanction against shirking.

The phenomenon of wage and price stickiness was discussed from several viewpoints. One stressed that some prices, particularly wages, were revised only periodically; this could explain failure to clear markets. One question was to explain the length of the revision period, to make it endogenous to the system. A possible explanatory variable is the cost of changing prices. A price will change only when the gain to the controlling agent exceeds the cost of the change. This model is parallel to inventory models and leads to the conclusion that the period from one change to another is not constant but depends on the shifts in input prices and shifts in the production function, which determine the relation between price and profit. Analysis so far has been carried out only for single markets.

A somewhat different explanation for wage stickiness is the concept of implicit contracts; risk-averting workers are willing to accept some probability of unemployment in exchange for wage stability. This model explains stickiness in real wages, whereas, it was felt, the phenomenon of stickiness of wages in nominal terms also needs explanation.

Another question raised for research was the cause and effect of occasional collapses of market institutions, such as bank failures or breakdowns of securities and commodity markets. Older literature spoke often of commercial and financial 'crises.' There was no agreement as to the empirical significance or frequency of such collapses.

General equilibrium updated

It was fully agreed that standard general equilibrium theory needed to be extended to cover more adequately incomplete information on the part of individual agents and incomplete markets. Of course, there is already considerable literature in these fields, but it has not yet received a consistent overall formulation comparable in generality to standard general equilibrium theory as set forth, for example, in Gerard Debreu's (1959) *Theory of Value*.

A problem that has proved difficult is to derive rational expectations by optimal learning from the market. If individual agents do not know the probability distributions of parameters observed by others, it is conceivable that they may acquire this knowledge by Bayesian updating through observing what they can of the market outcomes in successive realizations. However, the behavior observed is itself influenced by the fact that others are learning at the same time. It is possible that this process does not converge even under strong assumptions, for example that everyone's prior is the same.

Finally, it was urged that integration of capital asset pricing models into general equilibrium theory was a step that was both useful and likely not to be too difficult. The point is that the probability distribution of asset returns, which is taken as given in the capital asset pricing model, is endogenous to the general equilibrium under uncertainty, and is itself undoubtedly affected by the prices of assets and the distribution of their ownership.

Efficiency and transaction costs

The topics under this heading aroused a good deal of attention at the conference.

One starting point was the emphasis on adaptation to change as a major source of transaction costs. Suppose the world were actually stationary: the Coase theorem suggests that a fully efficient allocation of resources would be attained. Even though there might be costs of acquiring information and other kinds of transaction costs, they would need to be incurred only once, while the benefits would accrue for ever. Hence, it would always pay to incur the costs. (In this extreme form, it is implicitly assumed that the rate of interest in a stationary world is zero. However, even with discounting it would follow that stationary optimal resource allocations would be much cheaper to arrive at than non-stationary allocations, which have to be renegotiated from time to time or even continuously.) If the world is in fact non-stationary, economic institutions will evolve to minimize the costs of transactions. Therefore, understanding change and its consequences is basic to achieving efficiency and to understanding the particular economic institutions we have.

Hart, in his survey, assumes throughout the law of one price; he does not discuss the case of price discrimination. Hence, at least in the models of imperfect competition that he discusses, price is greater than marginal cost, and there is an inefficient allocation of resources. If it is true that stationary economic systems are efficient, as just argued, then it follows that the inefficiency of imperfect competition must be attributed to the incomplete information associated with economic change.

Fixed and sticky prices typically imply an excess of price over marginal cost; the firm would like to sell more at the going price but faces a sales constraint. Again, there is inefficiency. These remarks suggest that price stickiness may actually be the result of economic change!

Costly search and the achievement of search equilibria provide a basis for analyzing transactions costs. In these models, the expected cost of achieving a sale, for example, depends on the number of buyers who are searching, and this in turn depends on the probability of finding a seller. Hence, transaction costs become endogenous to the model.

If transaction costs are in major part the costs of acquiring information, then it would follow that a sharp reduction in these costs would improve the allocation of resources. Thus, another research topic is the effects of the current information revolution on the general efficiency of the economic system.

At a more technical level, the costs of transactions can be related to communications games, games in which one individual sends messages to another who uses them. The first individual incurs costs in making the information more accurate. The problem is to design a reward system to achieve as efficient an allocation as possible given the informational inequality between the parties. The results suggest implications for the existence and structure of hierarchical economic and other organizations. Typically, they have many equilibria.

Political economy

A more extended theory would have to include the workings of the political system. One approach is to assume that the agents are the same in the political and economic systems and that they are rational and express the same preferences in both. This general remark has of course been the basis of a large body of research over the last 25 years. The importance of this work was stressed at the conference, but only a few specific suggestions emerged.

It was urged that the economic and political systems could both be regarded as games but as operating on very different time scales. The economic game could be regarded as nested into the political; that is, at any moment, the political rules are taken as given, and the economic game is played out under those rules. But over a longer period the political rules themselves are subject to choice as the result of game-playing.

It was also observed, as it had been in Aumann's paper, that the core is typically empty for political games. This suggests that different solution concepts may be appropriate for such games, i.e. those in which a majority (ordinary or extraordinary) can allocate all resources. On the other hand, it was noted that, if the rules of the game required some protection for minority interests, the core need not be empty.

The modelling of political as well as economic games gives rise to a philosophical problem: in what sense can there be a meaningful welfare economics if political actions are themselves determined? The statement that economic welfare analysis implies that a state of affairs A should be preferred to state B becomes uninteresting if the playing of the political game according to the preferences of individuals will predictably determine the state of affairs. This problem is not far from the theological difficulties of reconciling free will with divine omniscience (or, in more secular form, with scientific predictability).

Alternative models of economic behavior

The economists' assumptions that individuals behave rationally has been under attack at least since the days of Thomas Carlyle. There are many specific dimensions on which criticism can be made, only some of which were raised in the discussions at this symposium.

One point raised and not generally discussed in the current literature is that individuals may have limited knowledge about themselves and about their assets. This was a specific form of a more general observation that there is a tendency in economic theory to attribute too much information to agents. This point is a serious criticism of rational expectations models.

A closely related, if not virtually identical, point is that the complexity of strategies proposed as equilibria for games is more than can be considered reasonable for an individual to understand and use. The ideas of complexity and computability that have been developed in computer science and mathematical logic may be relevant here.

A different, though possibly related, criticism of standard economic behavior assumptions is that tastes are not invariant but are altered by factors endogenous to the economic system. Tastes may alter as a result of past consumption or the consumption of others. Although some models have been suggested in this area, the theory is underdeveloped and the empirical work very limited (except for the much earlier work on relative income hypotheses of savings behavior, advanced by Dorothy Brady and Rose Friedman (1947) and by James Duesenberry (1949)). If tastes are endogenous, then, again, the basis for welfare economic propositions is undermined.

Finally, it can also be argued that preferences extend beyond individual consumption to the consumption of others. There are non-profit institutions, aimed at the general welfare and motivated and operating without the spur of the profit motive; the Yrjö Jahnsson Foundation may be taken as an example. The law is administered and enforced, however imperfectly, in such a way that the agents concerned do not maximize immediate self-interest. We also observe giving to others, even individuals not personally known to the donor, as exemplified in charities and blood donation. A theory of behavior should also explain these phenomena, which it can be argued have implications even in the more usual fields of economic behavior.

Specific microeconomic issues

As will have been seen, the bulk of the suggestions for future research directions dealt with issues of great generality in economics. There were two questions raised with regard to financial markets specifically. The first was for an explanation of the observed volatility of the securities markets, a degree of variation in prices that seems much too great to be explained by changes in rationally held expectations. One possible line of explanation is based on incomplete rationality in revising expectations on the basis of new information, specifically an experimentally observed over-emphasis on current information as compared with past observations.

A second aspect of financial markets that has received little attention in the theoretical literature is an explanation of the volume of trade. All attention has been concentrated on price changes. In the usual models of the financial markets (intentionally simplified), all agents are assumed to be alike. Then, indeed, there will never be any trade whatever, though prices will fluctuate so as to just barely induce each individual to retain his or her holdings. Since trade does take place, a more sophisticated analysis based on heterogeneity of the securities holders is needed.

A very different point urged in the discussion was a repetition of the demand for greater use of game theory in the analysis of imperfect competition, raised in the discussion of Hart's survey (see p. 7 above).

Methodological suggestions

Two general suggestions about the methodology of economic theory were made. The first was that, in view of the number of cases in which theoretical results were non-existent or too difficult to find, reliance should be placed to a greater extent on numerical simulation of models for various values of the parameters. Simulation would also give a greater feel for the sensitivity of results to specific numerical assumptions. Closely related was the urging that, when theorists model a specific area, they should give some indication of the range of parameter values they would regard as basically consistent with the intended applicability of the model.

Discussion time was limited; doubtless more topics would have been raised had there been more time. The title and orientation of the symposium certainly oriented the thinking of its participants to broad and fundamental questions rather than those in more specific fields of economic analysis. We may take these suggestions as at least among the more promising possibilities for extending the frontiers of economics.

NOTES

We are grateful to the participants of the symposium for lively discussions which provided the basis for some of the remarks in this essay, though the views expressed are solely our responsibility. Juha Kähkönen and Arja Turunen deserve thanks for assistance. Mika Pantzar and Timo Rajakangas prepared the index.

1 It should be pointed out that this doctrine is based on fairly strong hypotheses, and modelling reproduction as maximizing fitness is valid only under these restrictions. Fitness is viewed as a short-run maximization, and its relation to long-run survival and evolution is the basic issue. There also exist evolutionary changes that have no adaptive motives.

2 The definitive work is, of course, the treatise by Hildenbrand (1974), which contains detailed references to the limit theorems.

REFERENCES

Brady, D. and Friedman, R. (1947), 'Savings and the Income Distribution', *Studies in Income and Wealth X*, National Bureau of Economic Research, New York, pp. 247–65.

d'Aspremont, C. and Gérard-Varet, L. A. (1979), 'Incentives and Incomplete Information', *Journal of Public Economics*, **16**, 25–45.

Debreu, G. (1952), 'A Social Equilibrium Existence Theorem', *Proceedings of the National Academy of Sciences*, **38**, 886–93.

Debreu, G. (1959), *Theory of Value: an Axiomatic Analysis of Economic Equilibrium*, Yale University Press, New Haven, Conn.

Diamond, P. A. and Hausman, J. (1984). 'Individual Retirement and Savings Behavior', *Journal of Public Economics*, **23**, 81–114.

Duesenberry, J. (1949), *Income, Saving, and the Theory of Consumer Behavior*, Harvard University Press, Cambridge, Mass.

Hildenbrand, W. (1974), *Core and Equilibria of a Large Economy*, Princeton University Press.

King, M. A. and Dicks-Mireaux, L. (1982), 'Asset Holdings and the Life Cycle', *Economic Journal*, **92**, 247–67.

Malinvaud, E. (1980), *Profitability and Unemployment*, Cambridge University Press.

Negishi, T. (1961), 'Monopolistic Competition and General Equilibrium', *Review of Economic Studies*, **28**, 196–201.

Roberts, J. and Sonnenschein, H. (1977), 'On the Foundations of the Theory of Monopolistic Competition', *Econometrica*, **45**, 101–13.

Spence, M. A. (1974), *Market Signaling*, Harvard University Press, Cambridge, Mass.

1

What is Game Theory Trying to Accomplish?

ROBERT J. AUMANN

1 INTRODUCTION

The language of game theory – coalitions, payoffs, markets, votes – suggests that it is not a branch of abstract mathematics; that it is motivated by and related to the world around us; and that it should be able to tell us something about that world. Most of us have long realized that game theory and the 'real world' (it might better be called the complex world) have a relationship that is not entirely comfortable; that it is not clear just what it is that we are trying to do when we build a game-theoretic model and then apply solution concepts to it. This is the subject I would like to explore in this paper. I might add that much the same questions apply to economic theory, at least the kind that those of us working in mathematical economics see most often; and that much of my paper will apply, *mutatis mutandis*, to economic theory as well. There is a branch of philosophy that deals with theory in the social sciences, so some of the things I have to say are unquestionably old hat. But I am not trying to be particularly original: I am only trying to open this topic, which I think concerns all of us, for discussion, and to suggest a particular point of view. No doubt others have thought about these questions more thoroughly and deeply than I have, and are better versed in the history and philosophy of science in general. I will be grateful to anybody who sets me straight when I err, and who gives me references for the things I get right.

My main thesis is that a solution concept should be judged more by what it does than by what it is; more by its success in establishing relationships and providing insights into the workings of the social processes to which it is applied than by considerations of *a priori* plausibility based on its definition alone.

The first eight sections of the paper are concerned with generalities; sections 9–17 illustrate my point of view; and the last section summarizes and concludes.

2 COMPREHENSION

To come to grips with the question of what we are trying to do in game theory, we must first back off a little and ask ourselves what science in general is trying to do. The 'man in the street' may answer this question in terms of practical applications: light bulbs, plastic, computers, atom bombs, preventing depression, and so on. He concedes that, in the long run, applications and inventions require a broad infrastructure of 'basic' science; but (according to this view) the *purpose* of science is the development of the practical application.

More sophisticated observers, including many scientists themselves, answer the question in terms of predictive power. The theory of relativity was a success, they believe, because it predicted the precession of the perihelion of Mercury and the displacement of the images of the stars in a solar eclipse. If a theory has no predictive power – if it is not 'falsifiable' – then it is not science.

Both these views miss the main point, I think. On the most basic level, what we are trying to do in science is to understand our world. Predictions are an excellent means of testing our comprehension, and once we have the comprehension, applications are inevitable; but the basic aim of scientific activity remains the comprehension itself.

3 THREE COMPONENTS OF COMPREHENSION: RELATIONSHIPS, UNIFICATION, SIMPLICITY

Comprehension is a complex concept, with several components. Perhaps the most important component has to do with fitting things together, relating them to each other. To 'understand' an idea or a phenomenon – or even something like a piece of music – is to relate it to familiar ideas or experiences, to fit it into a framework in which one feels 'at home'. When one first listens to Bach, one feels attacked by a discordant jumble of meaningless, disconnected sounds. But eventually one begins to hear patterns; the horn takes up what the violin said, groups of sound recur in minor and major keys, passages are repeated. Things jell, and one begins to feel 'at home.' After a while one recognizes the style, and even if one is listening to an unfamiliar piece one can relate it to other pieces by the same composer or of the same period. One understands the music.

I would like to emphasize that I am not talking merely about familiarity; while it is important, it is not the main point. I am talking about relating, associating, *recognizing patterns*. Snowflakes are hexagonal; the shells of certain snails are logarithmic spirals; buses on busy routes arrive in bunches; in their orbits around the sun, the planets sweep out equal areas in equal times; waves and ripples occur in the ocean as well as on sand dunes; fever is associated with infections; E predominates as the Deity's name in some parts of the bible, J in others; even total randomness has its patterns (normal and Poisson distributions, etc.). After a while, a pattern becomes so familiar that it itself is viewed as an observation, and then we begin seeking – and finding – patterns in the patterns. The law of gravitation is a pattern that one can discern both in the motion of the planets and in the form of a water wave or a sand wave. And there are also different kinds of waves – electromagnetic or sound waves, which seem to have nothing to do with gravity. Crystalline form is observed not only in snow, but in many other materials. And so on.

This brings us to the second component of comprehension, which is really part of the first: unification. The broader the area that is covered by a theory, the greater is its 'validity'. I am not thinking of 'validity' in the usual sense of truth, but rather in the sense of applicability or usefulness; I am measuring the validity of an idea by the amount that people (directly or indirectly) use it. Part of the greatness of theories like gravitation or evolution, or the atomic theory of matter, is that they cover so much ground, that they 'explain' so many different things.

Of course, a unificatory theory is really a special case of a relationship; many different phenomena are pulled together – related to each other – by means of it. The idea of gravitation in itself, in the abstract, is rather mysterious; it is important because it enables us to relate the tides to the motion of the planets and to the trajectories of shells and missiles.

The third component of comprehension that I would like to discuss is *simplicity*. What I mean is mostly the opposite of complexity, though the other meaning of 'simple' – the opposite of 'difficult' – also plays a role. Here there are several sub-components. One is spareness; as few as possible exogenous parameters should be used to account for any particular phenomenon. Ptolemy's theory of epicycles is in a certain sense correct; it cannot be rejected on the basis of the evidence. But to describe the motion of a heavenly body one needs many exogenous parameters, whereas in Newton's theory one needs just two (mass and velocity).

In addition to spareness in exogenous parameters, one would like spareness in the basic structure of the theory. Here again Newton's theory is an apt example, because it can be derived from his three basic laws of motion plus the inverse square law of gravitation, all of which are very simple. The theory of evolution or the atomic theory of matter are other apt examples of spareness, or relative spareness, in basic structure. An example of complexity – the opposite of what we want – is modern elementary particle theory. It is clear that nobody is particularly happy with this, and that it is considered an intermediate stage on the way to a more satisfactory theory.

We come finally to the matter of simplicity in the sense that is opposite to difficulty. For a theory to be useful, working with it must be practical. If you cannot figure out what it implies, it won't unify anything, it won't establish relationships. If the chief problems of celestial mechanics had been 3-body (or n-body) problems, then the theory of gravitation would not have been very important, because we could not have used it to calculate any results. All other things being equal, the simpler a theory is, the more useful it is – and hence the more valid.

4 SCIENCE AND TRUTH

Most readers will by now have understood that, in my view, scientific theories are not to be considered 'true' or 'false.' In constructing such a theory, we are not trying to get at the truth, or even to approximate to it: rather, we are trying to organize our thoughts and observations in a useful manner.

One rough analogy is to a filing system in an office operation, or to some kind of complex computer program. We do not refer to such a system as being 'true' or 'untrue'; rather, we talk about whether it 'works' or not, or, better yet, how well it works. As an office operation grows, filing systems change and evolve; at some points, completely new and different systems may be introduced, to accommodate to the evolution of the kind and amount of material to be filed.

Similarly, scientific theories must be judged by how well they enable us to organize and understand our observations; by how well they 'work.' As our observations increase in volume and change in character, old scientific theories are no longer as appropriate as before; they either evolve and change, or are replaced by entirely new and different theories. Truth, however, is not the issue. We discard a theory not because it has been 'disproved,' but because it no longer works, is no longer appropriate.

It is even possible for two competing theories to exist happily side by side and be used simultaneously, in much the same way that many of us file letters both chronologically and by the name of the correspondent. Two famous examples are relativistic vs Newtonian mechanics, and wave vs particle theories of light. In each case each of the theories has its areas of usefulness. I remember reading in my teens that one famous scientist considered the wave theory 'true' on Mondays, Wednesdays and Fridays, whereas he preferred the particle theory on Tuesdays, Thursdays and Saturdays (apparently he didn't work on Sundays). He used either, at convenience, on any day of the week; but the problem of which one was 'true' seems to have bothered him. Apparently he didn't subscribe to my view of science; or maybe his flippant remark was meant to indicate that he did, that the matter of 'truth' was secondary to him, and that the most important thing was to get on with his work.

The example of relativistic vs Newtonian mechanics is particularly instructive. It is probably fair to say that most of those scientists who seek the 'truth' consider relativistic mechanics a better approximation to the truth than Newtonian mechanics. Nevertheless, they continue to use Newtonian mechanics for most 'everyday' purposes. Why? Well, they say, the Newtonian theory is usually a good enough approximation to relativity. Why settle for an approximation when you can get it exactly right? Well, they might say, in many cases the relativistic theory is too cumbersome to work with; the Newtonian theory is more workable. But then, it appears, 'truth' is after all not the only criterion; Newtonian mechanics continues to be used as a model – on a much larger scale than relativity – even after it has been discredited from the point of view of 'truth.'

I vividly remember an afternoon ten or fifteen years ago when Paul Erdos, on one of his many visits to Jerusalem, was delivering a lecture at the mathematics colloquium. Though his mathematical powers were (and are) still extraordinary, he started by saying that he was now old and exhausted ('Zaken Vetashush'), and that little could be expected of him. Of course we all protested. But Erdos insisted, and finally stated flatly that he could prove that he was no less than 2 billion years old. In his childhood the earth had been 2 billion years old; now it was 4 billion years old; the conclusion about his age was inescapable.

Like many good jokes, Erdos's has a serious kernel. In the 1920s, the model that best fitted the known observations and existing theory was a 2-billion-year-old earth. By the 1970s, radioactive dating had been discovered, our ways of thought had changed in many ways, and the 4-billion-year model fitted much better. Evidence that had seemed strong and convincing 50 years ago gave way to stronger and more convincing evidence in a different direction; the older evidence had to be, and was, explained away. It would be foolhardy to think that the process has ended here, that no new evidence will be discovered, that the earth is *truly* 4 billion years old. It seems much more likely that in the course of time we will change our minds – or rather our model – again and again; indeed, the end of the process is not in sight. Why say that we were 'wrong' then, that we have discovered the errors of our ways and are 'right' now? It seems much more apt to say that when Erdos was a child, 2 billion years was right, and now 4 billion years is right. Each of these two models is the one that best fits, or organizes, or ties together, the observations available at its time, and the theories current at its time.

Here is another example. When the red shift in light from distant galaxies was first observed, two theories presented themselves. The one was that, in travelling such long distances, the light somehow gets 'tired,' the frequency of vibration decreases, and a shift to the red results; the other theory was that the galaxies are receding – the universe is expanding – and the red shift is associated with the Doppler effect. At present, the expanding universe theory appears to have won out. Most reasonable scientists will agree, however, that this area is very much in flux, and that our thinking on these matters is liable to change. Some will express this by saying that, though we now think that the universe *really is* expanding, new evidence – or new theories – may change our minds. But I prefer to say that the best model or system we can find for organizing our current observations and current theories involves an expanding universe; and that in the future we may, for one reason or another, find that other systems work better.

Some philosophies deny altogether the existence of objective truth, but for my purposes this is not necessary, and I do not wish to insist on it. The concept of truth applies to *observations*; one can say that such and such were truly the observations. It also applies to all kinds of everyday events, like whether or not one had hamburger for dinner yesterday. It does not, however, apply to *theories*.

I'd like to stress that I am not being dogmatic. What I would like to sell is a point of view, not a hard and fast position. The boundary lines are without doubt fuzzy. A conjecture about what happened next door yesterday may well be considered true or false, whereas a theory about what happened a billion years ago or a billion light-years away will not be. It can even happen that a theory graduates into a truth; whereas the roundness of the earth was a theory for the ancients, it can, I think, be considered a truth for us.

Readers may ask, why am I so insistent on making this point? What difference does it make whether we are looking for the truth or for a workable model, as long as we are not dogmatic and are willing to consider new evidence or new ways of thinking?

I think that the distinction is crucial for social science in general, and for game theory and economics in particular. For one thing, we have the matter of pluralism – the existence of parallel scientific theories side by side. We have seen that this occurs even in the natural sciences; but in our disciplines it is ubiquitous, it is very much the name of the game. People ask, since game theory offers a multiplicity of solution notions, what good can it be? Which solution notion is the right one? How do people 'truly' behave? If one takes the point of view suggested above, this question loses much of its sharpness. None of the solution notions tells us how people truly behave. They do not go about organizing blocking coalitions, as the core might suggest; they do not object and counter-object as in the bargaining set; they do not declare dividends as in Harsanyi's value;

and so on. Rather, a solution notion is the scientists' way of organizing in a single framework many disparate phenomena and many disparate ideas. And it is simply that the kind of social phenomenon that our disciplines cover has not yet proved amenable to a single overriding system of thought, and perhaps never will.

Another reason for stressing this point – that a theory should not be thought of as true or false – is to avoid the pitfalls of taking it too literally. For example, an objection that has been raised to the fundamental notion of utility maximization is that, for one reason or another, individuals do not *really* maximize utility. Alternatives such as satisficing have been proposed, which sometimes seem more appropriate as descriptions of true individual behavior. But the validity of utility maximization does not depend on its being an accurate description of the behavior of individuals. Rather, it derives from its being the underlying postulate that pulls together most of economic theory; it is the major component of a certain way of thinking, with many important and familiar implications, which have been part of economics for decades and even centuries. Alternatives such as satisficing have proved next to useless in this respect. While attractive as hypotheses, there is little theory built on them; they pull together almost nothing; they have few interesting consequences. In judging utility maximization, we must ask not 'Is it plausible?' but 'What does it tie together, where does it lead?'

5 GAME THEORY AS DESCRIPTIVE SCIENCE

Briefly put, game and economic theory are concerned with the interactive behavior of *Homo rationalis* – rational man. *Homo rationalis* is the species that always acts both purposefully and logically, has well-defined goals, is motivated solely by the desire to approach these goals as closely as possible, and has the calculating ability required to do so.

The difficulty with this definition is apparent as soon as one writes it down. *Homo rationalis* is a mythical species, like the unicorn and the mermaid. His real-life cousin, *Homo sapiens*, is often guided by subconscious psychological drives, or even by conscious ones, that are totally irrational; herd instincts play a large role in his behavior; even when his goals are well-defined, which isn't often, his motivation to achieve them may be less than complete; far from possessing infinite calculating ability, he is often downright stupid; and even when intelligent, he may be tired or hungry or distracted or cross or drunk or stoned, unable to think under pressure, able to think only under pressure, or guided more by his emotions than his brains. And this is only a very partial list of departures from the rational paradigm.

Thus we cannot expect game and economic theory to be descriptive in the same sense that physics or astronomy are. Rationality is only one of several factors affecting human behavior; no theory based on this one factor alone can be expected to yield reliable predictions.

In fact, I find it somewhat surprising that our disciplines have any relation at all to real behavior. (I hope that most readers will agree that there is indeed such a relation, that we do gain *some* insight into the behavior of *Homo sapiens* by studying *Homo rationalis*.) There is apparently some kind of generalized invisible hand at work. While in any given situation an individual may well act irrationally, there seems to be a cumulative effect of numbers and time and learning that pushes people 'in general' in the direction of rational decision-making. It doesn't make people more and more rational, but as a given setting gets more and more common and familiar, it makes them act more and more rationally *in that setting*. The descriptive power of the rationality hypothesis is nicely summed up in Abraham Lincoln's remark, 'You can fool all of the people some of the time, and some of the people all of the time, but you can't fool all of the people all of the time.' If one is careful not to expect too much, then *Homo rationalis* can serve as a *model* for certain aspects of the behavior of *Homo sapiens*. This is related to ideas in biology and evolution, in which the doctrine of survival of the fittest translates into maximizing behavior on the part of individual genes. We know that genes don't 'really' maximize anything; but the phenomena we observe, or some of them, are nicely tied together by the hypothesis that they act *as if* they were maximizing. Things are more complicated in the social sciences, first because the decisions themselves are very complex, and second because non-maximizing conduct is not as ruthlessly punished as in the jungle; but perhaps there is a similar trend.

Descriptively speaking, then, we can expect our disciplines only *sometimes* to explain or provide insights into 'real' phenomena. We cannot expect them always to do so, because they are admittedly incomplete. We cannot even say beforehand *when* we expect them to do so, because we do not yet know how to integrate rational sciences like game theory and economics with non-rational sciences like psychology and sociology to yield accurate predictions. The criterion for judging our theories cannot be rigid; we cannot ask, is it right or is it wrong? Rather, we must ask, *how often* has it been useful? *how* useful has it been?

All this may sound very slippery and unsatisfactory. There are no firm predictions, no falsifiability. If our theory appears not to work, we don't lose any sleep. 'Rationality is just one of the relevant factors,' we say blandly; 'here something else was at work.'

But for better or for worse, that is how things stand. We must get used to the fact that economics is not astronomy, and game theory is not physics. We know that, in bringing up our children, we must accept each one for what *he* is, for the good that is in *him*, and must not force him into somebody else's mold. The sciences are the children of our minds; we must allow each one of them to develop naturally, and not force them into molds that are not appropriate for them.

It should be pointed out that our fields are by no means the only ones in science that are not strong on predictions and falsifiability; in which the measure of success is 'does it enable me to gain insight?' rather than 'what will be my observations?' Similar in this respect are disciplines like psychoanalysis, archeology, evolution, meteorology and to some extent even aerodynamics. Airplanes are not designed by solving the equations of aerodynamics: they are designed by intuition and experience, and tested in wind tunnels and in test flights. The intuition that goes into the design is based partly on theory; theory provides important general principles. But it does not do anything like predicting airworthiness of a particular design.

In the end, I think that the ordinary laws of economic activity apply to our fields as well. The world will not long support us on our say-so alone. We must be doing something right, otherwise we wouldn't find ourselves in this beautiful place today.

6 NORMATIVE ASPECTS OF GAME THEORY

In the previous section we indicated in what sense game and economic theory could be considered descriptive. In this section we consider its normative aspects – game theory as engineering rather than as science.

A word of caution before starting out. The distinction between the descriptive and the normative modes is not as sharp as might appear, and often it is difficult to decide which of these two we are talking about. For example, when we use game or economic theory to analyze existing norms (e.g., law), is that descriptive or is it normative? We must also be aware that a given solution concept will often have both descriptive and normative interpretations, so that one will be talking about both aspects at the same time. Indeed, there is a sense in which the two aspects are almost tautologically the same. In the previous section we pointed out that game theory purports to describe not *Homo sapiens*, but *Homo rationalis*; and that it actually is descriptive of *Homo sapiens* only to the extent that he can be modelled by *Homo rationalis*. On the other hand, when we come to advise people, it is clear that we should give them rational, utility-maximizing advice, i.e., precisely what *Homo rationalis* would do; so that the two aspects are in this sense quite close.

Nevertheless, if not taken too rigidly the distinction is sometimes quite useful, and we shall avail ourselves of it here.

Normative aspects of game theory may be subclassified using various dimensions. One is whether we are advising a single player (or group of players) on how to act best in order to maximize payoff to himself, if necessary at the expense of the other players; and the other is advising society as a whole (or a group of players) of reasonable ways of dividing payoff among themselves. The axis I'm talking about has the strategist (or the lawyer) at one extreme, the arbitrator (or judge) at the other. Again, the distinction is often spurious; when advising what to do, you must take into account what the other players can do, and the outcome may well be a reasonable compromise. In real life, an important function of lawyers is to restrain their clients, and to press for reasonable compromises. Conversely, reasonable compromises are based, amost by definition, on the capabilities of the players. So this distinction, too, is a blurry one; but it is useful to keep in mind.

Another distinction is between advice that is precise and/or numerical, and normative insights of a general nature. An example of the former would be a specific minimax strategy in a well defined tactical situation (e.g. a destroyer-submarine hide-and-seek situation).

An example of the latter would be the insight that, in negotiating an international treaty, each side should make sure that the proposed treaty represents an equilibrium point, i.e. that it is written in such a way that it is *a priori* common knowledge that it is not worthwhile for either side to violate it.

7 THE CLASSIFYING FUNCTION OF GAME THEORY

Another important function of game theory is the classification of interactive decision situations. Perhaps this could be considered part of the descriptive theory; but it really is something different, because is describes the situations themselves rather than the behavior of the participants in them. A classification of game situations is in fact as important for the normative as for the descriptive theory.

Much of science starts out with classifications; the 'right' classification is often the key to a successful theory. Modern biology was made possible by Linnaeus's classification of all living things into species, genera, etc.; geology starts with the classification of rocks; and so on. Often classifications are to some extent spurious; we know now that the notion of species is not as central as had been thought, and that life might be more accurately considered a continuum of different individuals representing different combinations of genetic characteristics. But the classification is nevertheless indispensable to enable us to organize our thoughts.

Just making the classifications is already a form of science; it enables us to relate interactive situations to each other, to identify common features, often to draw operative conclusions. We classify games into cooperative or non-cooperative according as to whether or not there is available a mechanism that can enforce agreements. The man in the street is, I think, not aware of this distinction; certainly he is not aware of its crucial importance; therefore he may think of an international treaty as if it were much like a contract between businessmen. Having classified games by their coalitional form, we become aware that the weighted majority game [5;2,3,4] is in a sense 'the same' as [2;1,1,1]; this is far from obvious to the man in the street.

It may seem that these applications are comparatively trivial, and that one shouldn't require the whole gigantic theoretical structure of game theory to reach this kind of elementary conclusion. Nothing could be further from the truth. It is not enough formally to define concepts like cooperative or non-cooperative in order to make them conceptually meaningful. A formal definition is given meaning and content only by experience and use. Without the theoretical work that has been done over the last decades on both cooperative and non-cooperative games, the concepts themselves would be sterile, and the fundamental distinctions they embody would be overlooked.

An interesting example of this kind of process is the distinction between games of complete and incomplete information. The early development of game theory treated only complete information games, i.e., those in which the structure of the game and the payoffs are common knowledge to the players. The restrictive nature of this assumption was not overlooked; for example, Luce and Raiffa (1957) are quite explicit on this point. Nevertheless, this was the only available theory; the result was that the existing applications all used the complete information model, for better or for worse. No adequate tool for dealing with incomplete information existed; nobody knew just how the theory would have to be modified to deal with it. After muttering a few words of apology, therefore, people simply used the complete information model as an 'approximation' to the existing situation. That is, the effects of incomplete information were ignored; for all practical purposes, incomplete information games did not exist.

Then came the landmark work of Harsanyi (1967). The most important immediate effect was the realization that incomplete information games were indeed in principle no different from complete information games, that the classical game-theoretic framework applied to them as well. Without further work on the subject, it is possible that people would have continued to think mainly in terms of complete information, simply substituting a citation of Harsanyi for the muttered words of apology. But Harsanyi's work led to a stream of investigations of incomplete information models of ever-increasing volume and depth; today, incomplete information is perhaps the 'hottest' topic in economic theory. All this work led to the realization that models with incomplete information are quite different from those with complete information; that they have their own problems and their own features. To cite just one example, it became clear that disagreement was a perfectly rational outcome in incomplete information cooperative bargaining. It is the sum total of the work on incomplete information models – not the mere definition – that makes the idea meaningful and gives it content. Of course, it is Harsanyi's definition that led to the development of the theory, that made the theory possible; but it is the theory itself that is decisive, not the definition.

A case in point is the ingenious experimental work of Roth and Murnighan (1982) on bargaining under complete and incomplete information, with and without assumptions of common knowledge.[1] It is interesting to compare these experiments with those of Fouraker and Siegel (1960) carried out some 20 years earlier. Fouraker and Siegel also ran bargaining experiments in both the complete and incomplete information modes. But they did not have Harsanyi's model, and so were unable to specify the incomplete information case more than that each side 'is not informed' of the other side's payoffs. Roth and Murnighan, on the other hand, specified the incomplete information in terms of types, and made explicit use of the common knowledge variable (whether or not the description of the game was common knowledge).

In fact, Roth and Murnighan use little or no theory. In principle, it would have been possible to perform these experiments in 1960; in practice, this could not – and did not – happen before Harsanyi's 'type' model, and the related notion of common knowledge, were not only defined, but also given a chance to mature, to become part of the atmosphere, to be *understood*. And this can happen only as a result of the development of the related theory.

8 GAME THEORY AND MATHEMATICAL ECONOMICS AS ART FORMS

An alternative way of viewing game theory and mathematical economics is as art forms. The distinction between the common conceptions of science and art is in any case not sharp; perhaps our disciplines are somewhere in between. Much of art portrays the artist's subjective view of the world; art is successful when the view expressed by the artist finds an echo in the minds of his audience, when the audience empathizes with what the artist is expressing. For this to happen, the artist's statement must have some universality; it must express some insight of a general nature, must be related to the audience's experience – in brief, there must be some objectivity in it.

The case for thinking of mathematics itself as an art form is clear. Mathematics at its best possesses great beauty and harmony. The great theorems of, for example, analytic number theory are reminiscent of Baroque architecture or Baroque music, both in their intricacy and in their underlying structure and drive. Other sides of mathematics are reminiscent of modern art in their simplicity, spareness and elegance; the most lasting and important mathematical ideas are often also the simplest.

A characterization of art that I find very apt is 'expression through a difficult (or resistive) medium.' (I heard this from my friend M. Brachfeld; he said he had read it somewhere, but could not remember where.) The medium may be stone or rhyme or meter or a musical instrument or canvas and paint, or the less well-defined but no less demanding medium of the novel. The resistiveness of the medium imposes a kind of discipline that enables – or perhaps forces – the artist to think carefully about what he wants to express, and then to make a clear, forthright statement.

In game theory and mathematical economics, the resistive medium is the mathematical model, with its definitions, axioms, theorems and proofs. Because we must define our terms, state our axioms and prove our theorems precisely, we are forced into a discipline of thought that is absent from, say, verbal economics.

If one thinks of mathematics as art, then one can think of pure mathematics as abstract art, like a Bach fugue or a Pollock canvas (though often even these express an emotion of some kind); whereas game theory and mathematical economics would be expressive art, like a cubist painting or Tolstoy's *War and Peace*. We strive to make statements that, while perhaps not falsifiable, do have some universality, do express some insight of a general nature; we discipline our minds through the medium of the mathematical model; and at their best, our disciplines do have beauty, simplicity, force and relevance.

9 SOME SOLUTION CONCEPTS

The point of view I shall take in the next few sections was set forth at the end of the introductory section: that a solution concept should be judged by its performance in the applications, by the quantity and quality of the relations that it engenders, not by 'armchair' philosophizing about its definition. From this point of view we will consider four of the most important solution concepts of game theory – the Nash equilibrium, the core, the N–M stable set (or 'solution') and the Shapley value. The idea is not to give an exhaustive survey of game theory or even of these four solution concepts, but to illustrate our ideas by *some* examples of *some* solution concepts. In addition to mentioning applications of these concepts, we will try to get some feel for what each of them expresses – not from its definition, but from the applications themselves.

10 THE NASH EQUILIBRIUM

This is certainly the game-theoretic solution concept that is most frequently applied in economic theory. Born more than a century ago in connection with Cournot's (1838) study of duopoly, it is now extremely common in many different applications. In perfectly competitive markets, it is closely associated with the competitive equilibrium.[2] Novshek, Sonnenschein and others have used it to study entry and exit.[3] It is commonly used for search,[4] location[5] and product quality[6] problems. In incomplete information set-ups it has been used to study auctions,[7] insurance,[8] principal–agent problems,[9] again entry and exit,[10] health,[11] higher education,[12] discrimination[13] and a host of other particular models. In social choice theory it is ubiquitous. It is probably safe to say that it impinges significantly on every area in which incentives are important – and this includes just about all of economic theory.

The Nash equilibrium is the embodiment of the idea that economic agents are rational; that they simultaneously act to maximize their utility. If there is any idea that can be considered *the* driving force of economic theory, that is it. Thus in a sense, Nash equilibrium embodies the most important and fundamental idea of economics, that people act in accordance with their incentives.

There is a beautiful theorem of John Harsanyi (1973) relating to mixed strategy equilibria that illuminates and underscores this idea. Mixed strategy equilibria have always been intuitively problematic because they are not 'strict' (cf. the discussion of strictness below):

a player will not lose if he abandons the randomization and uses instead any arbitrary one of the pure strategy components of the randomization. Harsanyi gets around this by subjecting the payoff function of each player to a slight random perturbation. Each player is privately informed of the true value of his payoff function, but the other players know only the mean. The result is that each player will be motivated to choose a particular one of the pure strategy components of his equilibrium mixed strategy. An outside observer sees the game as one of complete information, with the players playing mixed strategies. In fact, the game is of incomplete information, and the players are playing pure strategies. The mixed strategy models the ignorance of the outside observer and of the other players, not a conscious randomization.

The beauty of this model is that it rings so true. No game can really be of complete information; there are always nuances in tastes and whims of the other players of which we cannot be aware.

Nash equilibrium has spawned a number of variants and related concepts. In the applications the most significant of these to date have been Selten's 'perfection' concepts: first the subgame variety (Selten, 1965), later the more general 'trembling hand' variety (Selten, 1975). Many of the economic applications mentioned above in fact use perfect rather than ordinary equilibrium points (EPs). Related to perfection are the notions of subgame symmetry proposed by Kalai and Samet (1983), Selten (1980) and others, the Kreps–Wilson (1982a) sequential equilibrium, Kalai and Samet's (1982) persistency, Myerson's (1978) properness, and recent concepts developed by Kohlberg and Mertens (1982) which are based on topological properties of the equilibrium correspondence.

The *definitions* of these concepts usually express a certain robustness or continuity; if the game is changed a little, the equilibrium won't change much. In *practice*, they express a more subtle idea, a sort of forward-lookingness. Nash equilibrium may take threats into account; i.e., it allows the players to knuckle under to threats even when it would hurt the threatener to carry them out. The above concepts do not; in a sense, they say 'no matter what happens, do what is best for the future, and assume that it is common knowledge that everybody will do so.' The problem remains as to how to resolve uncertainties about the past that affect optimal behavior in the future; this is where the above concepts differ, the 'forward-lookingness' being a kind of common denominator.

Several other kinds of variants of the Nash concept appear in the literature. An equilibrium is *strict* if the inequalities appearing in its definition are strict, i.e., if each player's equilibrium strategy is the *unique* best reply to the other players' strategies. This implies stability of the equilibrium; i.e., if some or all players use strategies slightly different from the equilibrium strategies, all are motivated to return to the equilibrium. It thus expresses robustness in a different sense than that expressed by perfection: robustness as a function of the strategies rather than of the game. Harsanyi (1974, 1975) and Selten have used this kind of stability, together with Pareto domination and many other ideas, in constructing an elaborate theory that chooses a unique equilibrium point for each game. This theory has been applied to several specific game-theoretic models, most of them bargaining models with either complete or incomplete information (e.g. Selten and Guth, 1982).

An equilibrium is *strong* if no coalition of players can all gain by a simultaneous deviation (while the players outside the coalition maintain their strategies). Strong equilibria have significant applications in repeated games, as we will see below; they are also important in social choice theory, where they appear, e.g., in the context of manipulations of elections.

Two other variants that have been proposed are the subjective and the correlated equilibrium (Aumann, 1974). In subjective equilibria, the players use uncertain events for which they have differing subjective probabilities to do their randomizing; in correlated equilibria, the randomizations of the players need not be independent. Correlated equilibria have been applied to various contexts, including repeated games (Forges, 1985a, 1985b). Subjective equilibria have to date found little direct application to specific economic or other models, though various general theorems have been proved relating them to objective equilibria. But there has been one very interesting spinoff: they led to the notion of *common knowledge*, and to the subsequent development of the theory in this area. This notion was originally defined by the philosopher Lewis (1969) and found its way into the decision sciences as a result of an investigation of the properties of subjective equilibria (Aumann, 1976).

Let us now return to the applications. A surprising and beautiful application of Nash equilibrium points is to evolutionary biology (cf. the discussion in section 3 above). Maynard Smith's (1982) Evolutionarily Stable Strategy (ESS) represents a kind of Nash equilibrium point. Recently Selten (1980) has combined Maynard Smith's ESS with the perfection notion and developed a comprehensive game-theoretic approach to animal conflicts and similar biological contexts. This has not remained in the purely theoretical sphere; there are applications to empirical investigations of the behavior of specific animals (speckled wood butterflies, etc.).

Another wide area of application that we have not yet mentioned is that of cooperative games. It will be recalled that cooperative games differ from non-cooperative games only in that, in the former, agreements can be enforced. In his 1951 *Annals of Mathematics* paper, Nash suggested that EPs could be applied to cooperative games if the pre-play bargaining procedure by which players form coalitions and agree on payoffs were formalized, and made a proper part of the game. Once this is done it is no longer necessary to specify that the players may make enforceable agreements, since these are possible within the framework of the game. The game is therefore non-cooperative, and may be analyzed by means of equilibrium points.

For a time this program had only limited success. In most bargaining procedures, a very large number of equilibrium points is possible; there may also be considerable dependence on the specific form of the bargaining procedure. Nash himself (1950) proposed a way of getting around some of these problems in the case of his two-person bargaining problem, but it was fraught with difficulties and he never managed to carry it out explicitly.

As often happens, the first successes in this area were indirect. Rather than using specific bargaining procedures, repeated games were used as a paradigm for bargaining procedures. Underlying and justifying this approach is the famous 'Folk Theorem,' according to which *any* individually rational feasible outcome of a game can be achieved as an equilibrium outcome of an infinite repetition of that game; as shown by Rubinstein (unpublished) and others, this holds also for perfect equilibria. As early as 1959 it was shown that strong equilibria of the repeated games are associated with the core of the one-shot game (Aumann, 1959).

Later attention shifted to incomplete information repeated games. In such games, bargaining involves a subtle interplay of concealing and revealing information: concealing, to prevent the other players from using the information to your disadvantage; revealing, to use the information yourself, and to permit the other players to use it to your advantage. In order to study these phenomena, attention was first concentrated on two-person zero-sum repeated games. A large, subtle and deep literature on this subject was spawned, which spilled over into related fields such as stochastic games. Two-person zero-sum games certainly cannot give us any insight into bargaining, but here again we see the importance of not taking too narrow an approach. In order to understand cooperative games of incomplete information, we study non-zero-sum repeated games of incomplete information; and for this purpose, it is necessary first to understand zero-sum repeated games of incomplete information. After zero-sum repeated games were studied intensively for about 15 years, a major breakthrough in the area of non-zero-sum repeated games was recently achieved by Sergiu Hart (1985), who gave a complete characterization of equilibrium outcomes in such games when there are just two players and there is complete information on one side. The characterization is not just technical; it gives important qualitative insights into the nature of incomplete information bargaining.

Complete information repeated games have also been taken up again in recent years. Important applications of equilibrium points in repeated games have been made in economic contexts such as altruism, principal–agent problems, insurance, oligopoly and the development of reputations by several authors.[14] The repeated prisoner's dilemma has always been an object of considerable theoretical as well as experimental interest; this has led in recent years to the development of several additional variants on the equilibrium concept. Worthy of special mention here is Axelrod's (1984) beautiful computer experiment.

Quite recently it has been shown that the more direct approach to the Nash program for attacking cooperative games can prove fruitful after all. Using a bargaining procedure in which time is costly, Rubinstein (1982) showed that perfect equilibrium outcomes lead to equal division in a two-person bargaining problem with a flat efficient frontier; later Binmore (1982) extended Rubinstein's result by showing that, in any two-person bargaining problem, Nash equilibrium outcomes are associated with Nash's product maximization solution (which coincides with the non-transferable utility value). The Rubinstein–Binmore results are particularly beautiful because they express an important practical insight: impatience is an important component in reaching a compromise; the players are more likely to reach a reasonable compromise if delay is costly to them, if the value of the product that is being bargained for deteriorates with time.

11 NASH EQUILIBRIUM: SUMMARY AND CONCLUSIONS

Nash equilibrium is without a doubt the most 'successful' – i.e., widely used and applied – solution concept of game theory. It touches almost every area of economic theory, as well as social choice, politics and many other areas of application. Within game theory itself it engenders a host of relationships. Basically a non-cooperative concept, it has nevertheless been applied with considerable success to cooperative models.

Conceptually, the Nash equilibrium and most of its variants express the idea that each player individually maximizes his utility; it is a simple expression of the rationality of the individual player. Two of its variants, though – the strong equilibrium and the Harsanyi-Selten unique equilibrium – go beyond this to express some form of cooperation or joint rationality.

The definition of the Nash equilibrium is in form extremely simple. Moreover, the concept is mathematically very tractable and easy to work with. But there are problems with its intuitive interpretation. In games of perfect information, perfect equilibria can be arrived at by a sort of dynamic-programming, backwards-induction procedure whose intuitive content is very clear and compelling. In other games it is by no means clear how the players would arrive at an equilibrium, why they should play equilibrium strategies, and how a specific equilibrium would be chosen from among the set of all equilibria. There are indeed games in which the Nash equilibrium looks very strange and counterintuitive. For a long time it was thought that a Nash equilibrium could be thought of as a self-enforcing agreement, but recently it has been shown that this, too, is incorrect: there are games with multiple Nash equilibria, in which an *agreement* to play a certain one of them does not increase the chance of its *actually* being played (Aumann, 1985).

Nash equilibrium therefore is an example *par excellence* of our basic thesis. On the one hand, philosophical analysis of the definition itself leads to difficulties, and it has its share of counterintuitive examples. On the other hand, it is conceptually simple and attractive, and mathematically easy to work with. As a result, it has led to many important insights in the applications, and has illuminated and established relations between many different aspects of interactive decision situations. It is these applications and insights that lend it validity.

12 THE CORE

An outcome x of a game *dominates* another outcome y if there is a coalition S that can achieve x by its own efforts, each of whose members prefers x to y. The *core* of the game is the set of all undominated outcomes.

The 'core' applies to cooperative games; it is the cooperative solution concept that is perhaps best known to economists. Most famous among its applications is the core equivalence principle, which states that the core coincides with the set of competitive (price equilibrium or Walras) outcomes in perfectly competitive markets with many traders, each individual one of whom is insignificant. First demonstrated by Edgeworth (1881) more than a century ago, it was forgotten, then exhumed and reformulated by Shubik (1959) about 25 years ago. Since then an amazingly rich and deep literature has sprung up, all of it focusing on this one basic principle. It has been expressed as a limit theorem[15] for markets with n traders as $n \to \infty$, in the context of a non-atomic continuum of traders,[16] and in the context of non-standard analysis, in which individual traders formally appear as infinitesimal.[17] Among the aspects that have been discussed in one or more of these forms or modes are rates of convergence,[18] extension to productive economies,[19] continuity as the utility functions or initial bundles vary,[20] and the extent to which the result remains true when one restricts the family of 'permitted' coalitions (coalitions via which domination may take place).[21] Considerable effort has also gone into carefully determining the boundaries of the core equivalence principle, i.e., just where it ceases to hold. For example, in general, the principle no longer holds when there is a continuum of goods (qualities, locations) as well as traders.[22]

It should be mentioned that in any market – even one with a small number of traders – each competitive outcome is in the core. It is the converse that requires a large number of individually insignificant traders.

While the lion's share of the literature on the core has been devoted to the equivalence principle, there has been significant work on other applications. One area in which much work has been done is oligopoly or syndication; in the continuum framework, one would express this by saying that the space of traders has atoms (the oligopolists or syndicates) as well as a non-atomic part (the 'small' agents).[23] One typical result is that, when all the oligopolists are similar in utility and endowment (although they may differ in size), the equivalence principle continues to hold (Shitovitz, 1973). This relates to Bertrand's (1883) classical approach to duopoly theory, in which the duopolists compete until a perfectly competitive outcome is reached.

The core has also been applied to public goods; it has been shown that the Lindahl equilibrium is always in the core (Foley, 1970). The equivalence principle, however, does not hold in public goods economies with a continuum of agents; there may be core points that are not Lindahl equilibria.

An area that is currently very active is the study of the core in discrete markets (e.g. private homes) with a fixed finite number of traders.[24] The classic paper in this area is Gale and Shapley's (1962) 'College Admissions and the Stability of Marriage.' The main issue in those cases is the non-emptiness of the core; there need be no price equilibrium in these markets, and the core becomes the expression of competition.

There is no general existence (or rather non-emptiness) theorem for the core, and if one strays too far from classical market models, it is indeed often empty. In voting games, for example, the core is always empty unless there are veto players (in which case the core shares all the payoff among the veto players). Economies with S-shaped production curves (initially increasing returns, then decreasing) also have empty cores. Non-emptiness of the core expresses a situation in which there is no disincentive for the all-player coalition to form, in which each set of players can do at least as well in the framework of the all-player coalition as it could by itself – a kind of consumer surplus from the formation of the all-player coalition. In transferable utility games v, it is related to superadditivity of the coalitional worth function, or more specifically to local superadditivity 'at' the all-player coalition N (i.e. the worth of N is at least as great as the sum of the worths of the coalitions in any partition of N). In fact, the Bondareva–Shapley necessary and sufficient condition for the non-emptiness of the core ('balancedness') can be thought of as a strong kind of superadditivity at N, as follows. Suppose we extend the game to include 'part-time' coalitions. That is, each player may split his time into several parts, each of which he devotes to a different coalition; if the players in a coalition S each devote a proportion θ of their time to S, then the resulting 'part-time' coalition θS has worth $\theta v(S)$. Then the core is non-empty if and only if the worth of N is at least as great as the sum of the worths in any partition of N into 'part-time' coalitions (Bondareva, 1962, 1963; Shapley, 1967).

We noted above the loose association between non-empty cores and markets. In the case of transferable utility (TU) games this was made precise by Shapley and Shubik (1969): a game is associated with a market if and only if it *and* all its subgames have non-empty cores. And this happens if and only if the *extended* game is superadditive in the ordinary sense; i.e., the worth of *each* (part- or full-time) coalition S is at least as great as the sum of the worths of the (part- or full-time) coalitions in any partition of S. (This is what is called a 'totally balanced game.')

As far as non-transferable utility (NTU) games are concerned, the situation is roughly as follows. H. Scarf (1967) has extended the notion of balancedness to such games, has shown that balanced games have non-empty cores (but not conversely), and that markets are balanced. Billera and Bixby (1973a, 1973b, 1974), Mas-Colell (1975) and others have extended the characterization of market games to the NTU case; the subject is, however, a difficult one, and the results are not as complete as in the TU case.

One cannot complete the discussion of the core without mentioning computation. Using his definition of balancedness, Scarf (1967) developed an algorithm for finding a point in the core. This algorithm was the forerunner of the algorithms later developed by Scarf (1973) for finding competitive equilibria and, more generally, fixed points of mappings. Here again is an unexpected spinoff: investigation of the core eventually led to the creation of a whole new branch of numerical mathematics, the calculation of fixed points.

Like the Nash equilibrium, the core is subject to puzzling counter-intuitive examples. In a market with two complementary goods – e.g. right and left gloves – suppose m traders are endowed with one right glove each and $m+1$ traders with one left glove each: then the core consists of a unique point, under which the owners of the left gloves must simply give all their merchandise, for nothing, to the owners of the right gloves. This might perhaps be viewed as an extreme expression of cut-throat competition.

More puzzling, though, is the case in which two traders hold one right glove each, one trader holds a left glove, and one trader holds *two* left gloves. In this case, too, the holders of the left gloves must give their merchandise, for nothing, to the owners of the right gloves. This is more difficult to understand: by the simple expedient of throwing away a glove – an action that he can take by himself, without consulting anybody – the holder of the two left gloves can make the situation completely symmetric. Yet the unique core point assigns him nothing.

We have already mentioned that the core (more precisely, the β-core) of a game coincides with the strong equilibrium payoffs in an infinite repetition of that game. Some relations with other solution concepts are as follows. The core is included in each von Neumann–Morgenstern (N–M) stable set (see section 14) as well as in the bargaining set (Davis and Maschler, 1967; Peleg, 1967); when non-empty it intersects the kernel (Davis and Maschler, 1965) and contains the nucleolus (Schmeidler, 1969b). There are in fact some beautiful geometric characterizations of the kernel and the nucleolus as 'central' points in the core (Maschler, Peleg and Shapley, 1979). There is no clear general relationship with the value; but in non-atomic market games the core contains the value, and coincides with it if the market is sufficiently smooth (Aumann, 1975). A convex TU game always has a non-empty core (Shapley, 1971); it contains the value, includes the kernel (which coincides with the nucleolus for such games) and coincides with the bargaining set and the N–M stable set (there is only one stable set in such games) (Maschler, Peleg and Shapley, 1979). From all this there emerges a picture of the core as being a 'central' solution concept, one with significant relations with many other concepts. Conceptually, too, one may think of the core as a sort of starting point or first approximation, with other solution concepts overcoming shortcomings in the core in various different ways.

13 THE CORE: SUMMARY AND CONCLUSIONS

Most applications of the core are to economic contexts, more specifically to market contexts of one form or another. The outstanding application is embodied in the core equivalence principle, which relates the core of a perfectly competitive market to its competitive equilibria.

Conceptually, the core expresses the idea of unbridled competition; non-emptiness of the core expresses the idea that such competition can lead to stability, that there is an outcome consistent with it. In practice, this happens chiefly in economic contexts of the kind described above. Political contexts are inherently less stable, and for them the core is often empty; they are covered by concepts such as the value, which express compromise or average outcome, or the von Neumann–Morgenstern (N–M) stable set, which expresses a weaker and more complex kind of stability than the core. In a game with both political and economic aspects, the core often is not sensitive to the political aspects even when it is not empty (e.g. in the voting model of Aumann and Kurz, 1977, or, more generally, Neyman's 1985 political–economic games).

It should be stressed that this image of the core as expressing competition emerges from the applications; it is not in any sense obvious from the definition. The relationship between the core and competition is indeed a two-way street; several investigations of the core – most notably the equivalence principle itself, but also Ostroy's investigations of the equivalence principle with a continuum of goods, or the study of the core in one-homogeneous non-atomic superadditive games – have shed light on the nature of competition, and have sharpened our idea of what we mean when we talk about a perfectly competitive set-up.

The definition of the core is in form extremely simple, and the concept is mathematically fairly tractable and easy to work with. Intuitively, it is perhaps the clearest and most transparent concept in the theory of games. Its main fault is that it is often empty; therefore, unlike the Nash equilibrium, the von Neumann–Morgenstern stable set and the value, it cannot serve as a unifying theory for the rational social sciences, or even for all of economics. It is closely associated with the competitive side of economics, and there it gives important insights.

There are important relationships between the core and almost all other solution concepts. In a sense, the extremely simple and transparent definition of the core may be considered a starting point for the reasoning leading to more sophisticated concepts like the N–M stable set, the nucleolus, and so on. Thus, in more senses than one, the core occupies a central position in cooperative game theory.

14 THE VON NEUMANN–MORGENSTERN STABLE SET

The definition of the core of a game as the set of all undominated outcomes is subject to the following conceptual query. Suppose we think of outcomes in the core as 'good' or 'stable.' Then we should not exclude an outcome just because it is dominated by *some* other outcome; we should demand that the dominating outcome itself be 'stable.' If the outcome y is dominated by an outcome x that is not itself 'stable,' then the argument for excluding y is rather weak; proponents of y can argue with some justice that replacing it with x would not lead to a more stable situation, so we may as well stay where we are. If the core were the set of all outcomes not dominated by any element of the core, then there would be no difficulty: this, however, is not the case.

We are led to the following definition: a set K of outcomes is called *stable* if it is the set of all outcomes not dominated by any element of K. The stable sets are precisely the *solutions* of von Neumann and Morgenstern (1944).

In two-person bargaining games, there is a unique stable set, which consists of all efficient (i.e., Pareto-optimum) and individually rational outcomes. Usually, however, there is more than one stable set. For example, in the three-person majority game there is a unique symmetric stable set; it consists of three outcomes, each of which provides for formation of one of the three possible two-person coalitions, which then divides the available payoff equally. But there are many non-symmetric stable sets, called 'discriminatory.' Each of these specifies that some fixed two-person coalition forms, assigns to the remaining player a fixed amount (which must be less than half the total payoff), then divides the remaining amount in an arbitrary fashion between the two players in the coalition. Geometrically, therefore, each such stable set is an interval.

Intuitively, the symmetric solution represents a situation in which, *a priori*, each of the three players is a possible coalition partner; which coalition will form is determined by negotiations between the players, based on payoff. The three outcomes in the solution are stable as a set, not individually; in a sense, each is 'right' only because the others are also there. Von Neumann and Morgenstern use the term 'standard of behavior;' the idea is that, since each coalition knows or expects that the other coalitions will divide 50–50 if they form, it too is motivated to divide 50–50. It represents a form of social organization that, together with corresponding norms of dividing the payoff, is stable as a whole.

The discriminatory solutions also represent stable forms of social organization, of a different kind. One player is excluded *a priori* from the negotiations. He may or may not be given a certain sum 'to keep him quiet,' but this sum is fixed and not subject to negotiation, and neither of the other players considers it a real possibility that the excluded player will enter the negotiations. As a consequence, there is no constraint on them; the negotiations between them turn into a two-person bargaining game, and the solution of this, as we have seen, is the entire efficient individually rational interval.

Consider next the 'glove market' of section 12. Take the very simple case in which $m = 1$; i.e., there are just three players, two holding left gloves and one holding a right glove. It is convenient to think of the former as 'sellers,' the latter as a 'buyer' (of left gloves). The core says that the sellers simply give their merchandise to the buyer: they get nothing out of it. This corresponds to unbridled competition, in which each seller tries to underbid the other. The N–M stable sets, on the other hand, have the two sellers colluding, i.e., forming a single bargaining unit, to bargain with the buyer. Between this bargaining unit and the buyer we again have a two-person bargaining game, which leads to an interval. How the two sellers divide what they get depends on the particular stable set under consideration. Some stable sets have them dividing it in a fixed proportion, e.g., 50–50; in others they may divide 50–50 up to a certain amount, with the remainder going to the first seller; and so on. There are many possible arrangements. The important thing is that the sellers must agree beforehand on a definite way of dividing whatever they get, and it must be worthwhile for each seller that the coalition of sellers get as much as possible from the buyer, so that there is no possibility of the sellers entering into competition with each other during negotiations with the buyer.

Note that, unlike in the three-person majority game, in this game all the stable sets involve essentially the same form of social organization: the sellers organize in a unit that bargains with the buyer. The different stable sets differ only in the internal arrangement that the sellers may have for dividing what they get from the buyer.

A good chunk of stable set theory is devoted to weighted majority voting games. These may be thought of as parliaments; the 'players' are the parties rather than individual members. The interesting cases are those in which no single party has a majority. Such a game is called *homogeneous* if each minimal winning coalition has total 'weight' equal to the 'quota' (the 'weight' of a party is the number of members it has; the 'quota' is the minimum total weight needed to 'win' – i.e., to form a government or pass a bill). It is called *strong* if the quota is a simple majority and the total weight is odd. It would seem that strong homogeneous voting games are few and far between; but in fact there are many games that are equivalent to strong homogeneous games, though this is not apparent from the given numbers. For example, this is the case for every strong game with fewer than six players (von Neumann and Morgenstern, 1944).

Every strong homogeneous game has a stable set which predicts that some minimal winning coalition will form, and will divide the payoff among the parties in the coalition in proportion to their representation in parliament. This generalizes the symmetric solution in the three-person majority game.

When the game is not strong, as for example in American political conventions in the first half of the century, the social organization predicted by stable set theory is not in terms of minimal winning coalitions, but in terms of minimal blocking coalitions. A coalition S is *blocking* if it can prevent a win, i.e., if each winning coalition must intersect S. In the convention example, any coalition with more than one-third of the members is blocking.

This is a nice example of the kind of insight that game theory affords. All the evidence from strong games – and this includes far more than the simple homogeneous weighted majority case cited above – indicated that the important coalitions were the winning ones. Then came Bott's (1953) analysis of the simplest symmetric voting games that are not strong, which pointed to the blocking coalitions, and indicated that in strong games the winning coalitions are important because they coincide with the blocking ones. As soon as one realizes that in non-strong games the players organize themselves into blocking coalitions, one understands much better what went on in those political conventions, the deals that were made in the smoke-filled back rooms, the payoffs to special interest groups that were, in fact, blocking coalitions.

In brief, the outcome is unexpected, but once there, it sounds right and natural; it clicks into place. This is game theory at its best.

The literature is full of dozens of applications of the N–M theory, each with its own stable set or class of stable sets, each with its own story and interpretation involving some particular form of social organization. There is no space here even to mention all these results; indeed, we are not trying to survey the field, but only to give the flavor of the kind of insight that is afforded by the theory.

We mention only one more outstanding application, of a more recent vintage than the foregoing ones. This is S. Hart's (1974) analysis of the formation of cartels in large markets. The market has a continuum of traders, divided into disjoint types (traders of the same type have the same endowments and utility functions). Each type has a monopoly on some commodity; more precisely, each commodity is held by only one type. Then the symmetric stable sets of the market correspond to the stable sets of the market in which there is only one trader of each type. (A stable set is *symmetric* if it treats traders of the same type in the same way, i.e., if it is invariant under permutations of each type separately. It is not required *a priori* that individual outcomes be symmetric.)

The interpretation, of course, is that the types organize themselves into cartels, each of which acts as a single player.

Consider, for example, a *two-type* market of this kind. Hart's theorem says that each of the two types will bargain as a unit. The result is a two-person bargaining game, which as we know has only one solution, consisting of all efficient individually rational outcomes. In the original game, therefore, there is a unique symmetric solution, consisting of all efficient individually rational outcomes that assign the same bundle to traders of the same type. In contrast, the core of the two-type non-atomic market is very different from that of its two-person cousin; in the non-atomic case it contains only the competitive outcome (or outcomes), in the two-person case it contains the whole bargaining range.

Most of stable set theory deals with TU games; Hart's theorem is one of the few instances of a successful NTU analysis.

There is no general existence theorem for stable sets. The existence problem was open for many years. R. Stearns (1965) found a seven-person NTU game without a stable set, and W. Lucas (1969) made headlines by finding a ten-person TU game without a stable set. Recently Lucas and Rabie (1982) have found a coreless 14-person TU game without a stable set.

But non-existence is not nearly as serious a problem for stable sets as for the core. The counter-examples are ingenious, difficult and deep; but there is no question that they are contrived. They do not appear to correspond to any economic, political or social reality; there is no broad class of games known to have no stable sets. Lucas's examples are of great importance because they show that it is hopeless to look for a general existence theorem; in practice, though, one can usually find a stable set if one tries hard enough.

15 N–M STABLE SETS: SUMMARY AND CONCLUSION

Conceptually, stable sets express the idea of social organization – minimal winning coalitions, blocking coalitions, systematic discrimination against players or groups of players, cartel formation, groups within groups and so on. The organizational forms are often of great subtlety; they are endogenous, they spring from the analysis. This is quite different from other game-theoretic approaches to social organization, in which the forms (e.g., partitions into coalitions) are exogenous, and one looks for a structure of the given form possessing one or another kind of stability. In this sense the N–M theory is of a subtlety and depth unparalleled in game theory.

As in the case of the core, it should be stressed that this image of stable sets emerges from the applications. It is not in any sense obvious from the definition; indeed, there is no hint in the definition of organizational forms – the definition refers only to outcomes. The conceptual connection with organizational forms is in the interpretation only and has no formal status; and it is a matter of some mystery that this particular definition should lead so frequently and consistently to this kind of interpretation.

A stable set is stable as a whole; unlike core outcomes or Nash equilibria, individual outcomes in a stable set possess little or no stability by themselves. This, too, emerges from the applications; one would not have expected it from the definition as such, which in form very much resembles that of the core.

Stable set theory has been moderately 'successful.' It has a large number of applications. They are not limited to one area, but are spread over the whole gamut of applications of game theory – political, economic, production with constant or increasing or S-shaped returns (Hart, 1973) and so on. As we have seen, the applications often yield important insights; and while the insights usually have to do with organizational forms, they are, other than that, often quite different from each other. In an important sense, therefore, the N–M theory can be considered unifying.

What has prevented the theory from being more successful is that it is so difficult to work with. Finding stable sets involves a new *tour de force* of mathematical reasoning for each game or class of games that is considered. Other than a small number of very elementary truisms (e.g., that the core is contained in every stable set), there is no theory, no tools, certainly no algorithm. There are perhaps some rough methods, ideas that recur here and there, tricks of the trade; people with experience are better at it than newcomers. But basically you just have to slug it out anew every time. And because stable sets do not always exist, you cannot even be sure that you are looking for something that is there. NTU games are even more difficult to solve than TU games. This has led to the paucity of NTU results; and, because of the central importance of NTU games in the applications, this is another factor limiting the 'success' of the theory.

But while there is no mathematical theory that will help one to find stable sets, there is a sort of qualitative classificatory theory in the interpretations. Similar qualitative phenomena pop up in solutions of many different games. Minimal winning and minimal blocking coalitions occur in many stable sets; in interpreting the solutions of a three-person market game we make use of the solution of two-person bargaining games; 'bargaining curves' appear in stable sets; and so on. Other than hinting at what to look for, this perhaps is not of much use in finding stable sets. But it does lend coherence and unity to the qualitative theory.

16 THE SHAPLEY VALUE

Like the core and the N–M stable set, the Shapley value (Shapley, 1953) is a cooperative solution concept; i.e., it applies to cooperative games only. In finite TU games, it assigns a unique outcome to each game, which can be thought of as a sort of average or expected outcome, or an *a priori* measure of power. Other interpretations will be discussed below.

The Shapley value has a very broad spectrum of applications. Voting games have been studied thoroughly. In the UN Security Council, the 'Big Five' hold more than 98 per cent of the total power (i.e., value) (Shapley and Shubik, 1954). In a parliament with one large party and many small parties, the large party holds a disproportionately large proportion of the power (Shapiro and Shapley, 1978; Milnor and Shapley, 1978). For example, if the large party has more than half the seats, it has all the power; if it has one-third of the seats, it has approximately half the power. In the American Electoral College, the large states again have a disproportionately large share of the power; a state like California, for example, has about 10 per cent more power than could be expected from its proportion in the Electoral College (Riker and Shapley, 1968).

These phenomena correspond well with our experience, and also with our intuitions (which are, of course, the creation of our experience). Perhaps the disproportionate strength of the Big Five in the UN Security Council comes as somewhat of a surprise to the casual observer; but the careful student will have realized that nothing can be done without them, and once they do all agree, then enough of the other countries will also. That a party with a majority in parliament has all the power is obvious. Perhaps the statement about a party with a third of the seats having half the power is less obvious; but it will not sound so strange to some of the older Israelis, who may remember the disproportionate power of the Labor Party in the long years when it held only one-third of the seats in parliament. Altogether this corresponds nicely to the dictum 'Unity is power' ('L'Union fait la force'). As for the Electoral College, presidential candidates spend most of their campaign time in 'key states,' and these rarely include Nevada.

Let us next consider a parliament with *two* large parties and many small ones. Suppose, for example, that each of the large parties has one-third of the seats, the remaining seats being spread among many small parties. Then unity is *weakness*! The large parties have only about one-quarter of the power each, and the small parties have half the power between them (Milnor and Shapley, 1978). It would be foolish for the small parties to form a 'common front.'

This may sound paradoxical, but, again, students of the Israeli scene will not be surprised. In the presence of the two large parties – the Likud and Labor – there seems to be no tendency for the smaller parties (e.g., the four religious parties) to form a common front.

This curious phenomenon can be understood as follows. If the two large parties form a coalition with each other, they will have between them two-thirds of the vote, which is much more than needed, and they will have to share power equally. There is therefore a tendency for the large parties to seek coalition partners among the smaller parties; only half the smaller parties will be needed. However, competition will develop among the two large parties for the favors of the small parties; this will drive up the 'price' of the latter until the point is reached where it is hardly more worthwhile for either large party to go with small parties than for it to join forces with the other large party (as has, in fact, happened in Israel).

The 'competitive price of a vote' is an idea that appears in the intuitive interpretation of results about the value in several voting contexts. Another example is in voting for non-exclusive public goods, in which under certain circumstances the choice of public goods is not affected by who is allowed to vote; what is happening is that, because of the non-exclusivity, the 'price of a vote' is next to nothing, and so the vote becomes insignificant (Aumann, Kurz and Neyman, 1983, 1985).

Normatively, values have been used to analyze weighted voting in connection with the US Supreme Court 'one-man, one-vote' decision. According to this decision, equal representation in the legislature for districts with substantially different populations is unconstitutional. Rather than redistricting frequently, it was proposed to use weighted voting. Theoretically, this could lead to a situation in which a single district has a majority in the legislature; and even when this does not happen, the power conferred by weighted voting on the various representatives is by no means proportional to their weight, as we have seen. An analysis of this situation in terms of various philosophies of legislative government was carried out by Riker and Shapley (1968): it turns out that it makes a considerable difference whether the 'players' are the districts, or the individual voters in the district. Testimony on values has been an important factor in deciding court cases on re-districting.[25]

Let us turn to economics. In large markets, the value consists of competitive outcomes. In the smooth case (sufficiently differentiable utilities, no corner solutions), it consists of *all* competitive outcomes; i.e., it coincides with the core. In non-smooth situations the core may be quite large; in these cases, the value occupies a central position in the core. For example, in large TU markets in which the core has a center of symmetry, the value is that center of symmetry (Hart, 1977a, 1977b). When the core has no center of symmetry, the value is obtained by calculating, for each trader, the core point that is best for him, then averaging over all traders (Hart, 1980).

Values have also been used to analyze problems of taxation,[26] public goods,[27] monopoly,[28] increasing returns[29] and other specific economic models.

In two-person NTU games, the value coincides with the bargaining solution of Nash (1950). If one uses Harsanyi's (1959) method for deriving the coalitional worth ('characteristic function') from the strategic ('normal') form, this leads to Nash's solution (1953) for two-person cooperative games.

It is worthwhile here to point to an interesting normative implication of Nash's bargaining model, as well as of other bargaining models. A fundamental feature of these models is that, while threats are never carried out (in the complete information case), the ability to make them plays a crucial role in determining the final Pareto-optimal accommodation between the bargainers. Our ability to fight a war determines how we shall live at peace. It is a mistake to think that atomic weapons, for example, exist only for defense in case of war: on the contrary, they determine how we live on a day-to-day basis.

A surprising normative application of value theory, which has recently gathered quite a bit of momentum, is to cost allocation.

Specific applications include, for example, water management,[30] electric power,[31] pollution treatment,[32] intra-company transfer prices,[33] allocation of TVA projects,[34] allocation of taxes,[35] public utility pricing[36] and water resource development.[37] Another application, spectacular because of its depth and complexity, is to internal pricing of long-distance telephone calls in a large organization; a system of this kind, developed by Billera, Heath and Raanan (1978), was adopted by Cornell University about five years ago.

We illustrate the method with the airport landing application, due to Littlechild and Owen (1973). The runway at an airport must be large enough to accommodate the largest aircraft that will land there. But it would be absurd to charge the same fees to a Boeing 747 and a Piper. The system used at many airports is as follows. One figures the cost of a runway sufficient for the smallest plane that lands at the airport; this cost is divided equally between all landings. Next, one figures the cost *increment* necessary to build a runway long enough for the next largest plane; this increment is divided equally between all landings *except* those of the smallest planes. And so on.

Littlechild noticed that this is equivalent to charging each landing the Shapley value of a certain game. The players are individual landings; the worth of a coalition is the cost of building an airport that would accommodate those landings. The extension to more complex cost allocation problems is clear, at least in principle.

In the 2000-year-old Babylonian Talmud, the Shapley value crops up in the solution of a bankruptcy problem. Of course, the Talmud does not justify this solution by means of axioms; it does not have the general notion of a game as we know it. The problem the Talmud deals with is identical in mathematical form to the landing fee problem; its solution has independent intuitive appeal, and presumably the Talmud's choice of solution is based on this. (This is confirmed by medieval commentators.) The interesting point is that the Shapley value is able to unify so many different, apparently disparate phenomena.

Incidentally, it is this kind of legal application that I referred to in section 6 as being somewhere between descriptive and normative. It is *descriptive* of existing legal *norms*.

The Shapley value was originally axiomatized for finite TU games (Shapley, 1953); the axiomatization was later extended to games with a continuum of players (Aumann and Shapley, 1974) and to

NTU games. A. Roth (1977) used the original TU axiomatization to give a rigorous treatment of the idea that the value represents the utility to a player of participating in a game.

Existence of the value is no problem. The value exists in all finite games, and in large classes of NTU games and infinite games. J.F. Mertens (1985) has shown that all non-atomic TU market games have a value. Uniqueness is slightly more delicate. The value is unique in all finite TU games, in many infinite TU games, and in two-person NTU games; in NTU games with three or more players, however, the value is not always unique. Indeed, we have seen that, in non-atomic NTU markets that are sufficiently smooth, the value coincides with the competitive outcomes, and these are known not to be unique.

17 THE SHAPLEY VALUE: SUMMARY AND CONCLUSIONS

The Shapley value is perhaps the most 'successful' of all cooperative solution concepts. Like the N–M stable sets, it has a very broad spectrum – it almost always exists, and it applies to political as well as economic and 'mixed' contexts. It very often gives results with significant intuitive content; unlike with the core, this intuitive content is often of independent interest, not connected with the idea of value in any obvious or transparent manner. Unlike with either the N–M stable sets or the core, there are very general existence theorems, which cover essentially all the applications that one might want to consider.

A very important point is that the value is mathematically tractable. It lends itself to the application of mathematical methods from probability, measure theory, functional analysis and other areas. As a result, a very considerable body of theory has been built around the value; this theory may well be mathematically the richest and deepest in game theory. Of course this is intellectually pleasing, but that is not where its importance lies. Its importance lies in the fact that this theory enables us to deal with the applications, to attack fairly complex models in a systematic manner and to solve them. For non-atomic games there has even been developed a sort of rough calculus that enables us to calculate values 'quickly,' though often the rigorous justification takes longer.

Conceptually, the image of the value that arises from the applications is of an index of strength of a player, based on the strength of the coalitions of which he is a member and of those of which he is not a member. A closely related view of the value is as a group decision or arbitrated outcome. Unlike the Nash equilibrium, the core, or the N–M stable set, the value has little or no stability on its own.

18 GENERAL SUMMARY AND CONCLUSION

Game-theoretic solution concepts should be understood in terms of their applications, and should be judged by the quantity and quality of their applications. The solution concepts we have considered all have different kinds of applications, which reflect back on the solution concepts and yield different interpretations of them. In each case, important descriptive and normative insights result; each of the concepts unifies a different aspect of rationality in interactive decision-making.

NOTES

This work was supported by National Science Foundation Grant SES-8201373 and Contract ONR-N00014-79-C-0685 at the Institute for Mathematical Studies in the Social Sciences (Economics), Stanford University, California. The paper presents an approach to the philosophy of Game Theory; it is not a survey. The examples and references are an eclectic, largely haphazard selection – strongly skewed towards applications – from a truly enormous literature. The idea was merely to illustrate some of the points in the text; the references are neither representative nor systematically chosen, even within the particular subjects actually discussed.

1 See also Malouf and Roth (1981) and Roth, Malouf and Murnighan (1981).
2 Arrow and Debreu (1954), Debreu (1952), Hurwicz (1979a, 1979b), Schmeidler (1969a, 1980), Shapley and Shubik (1967), von Neumann (1937).
3 Novshek (1980), Novshek and Sonnenschein (1978).
4 Butters (1977), Diamond (1971).
5 d'Aspremont, Gabszewicz and Thisse (1979), Hotelling (1929), Prescott and Visscher (1977).
6 Akerlof (1970), Salop (1979).
7 Griesmer and Shubik (1963), Milgrom and Weber (1982), Myerson (1981), Vickrey (1961, 1962), Wilson (1979).
8 Rothschild and Stiglitz (1976).
9 Radner (1981), Ross (1973), Shavell (1979).
10 Milgrom and Roberts (1982a, 1982b).
11 Pauly and Satterthwaite (1981).

12 Arrow (1973b), Spence (1974, 1976).
13 Arrow (1972a, 1972b, 1973a).
14 Friedman (1977), Hammond (1975), Kreps, Milgrom, Roberts and Wilson (1982), Kreps and Wilson (1982b), Kurz (1978), Milgrom and Roberts (1982b), Radner (1980, 1981), Rosenthal (1979), Rubinstein (1979) and others.
15 Debreu and Scarf (1963).
16 Aumann (1964), Vind (1964).
17 Brown and Robinson (1975).
18 Anderson (1978), Arrow and Hahn (1971), Aumann (1979), Bewley (1973), Cheng (1981), Debreu (1975), Grodal (1975), Shapley (1975).
19 Hildenbrand (1974), Sondermann (1974).
20 Dierker and Dierker (1972), Kannai (1970, 1972).
21 Grodal (1972), Mas-Colell (1977), Schmeidler (1972), Vind (1972).
22 See Ostroy (1981).
23 Aumann (1973), Dreze, Gepts and Gabszewicz (1969), Gabszewicz and Dreze (1971), Gabszewicz and Mertens (1971), Shitovitz (1974).
24 Crawford and Knoer (1981), Dubins and Freedman (1981), Gale (1964), Kaneko (1976), Knuth (1976), Quinzii (1984), Roth (1982, 1984), Shapley and Scarf (1974), Shapley and Shubik (1972), Thompson (1980).
25 Testimony on values was heard by the Supreme Court during the following cases: Baker v. Carr, 369 US 186 [1962], Grey v. Sanders, 372 US 368 [1963], Wesberry v. Sanders, 376 US 1 [1964], Reynolds v. Sims, 377 US 533 [1964].
26 Aumann and Kurz (1977), Gardner (1981), Imai (1983), Kurz (1977, 1980), Osborne (1984).
27 Aumann, Kurz and Neyman (1983, 1985), Gardner (1975), Harsanyi (1959), Rosenmuller (1981, 1982).
28 Guesnerie (1977).
29 Mas-Colell (1980).
30 Bogardi and Szidarovsky (1978).
31 Gately (1974).
32 Loehman, Pengry and Whinston (1973).
33 Manes and Verrecchia (1982), Shubik (1963).
34 Parker (1943), Ransmeier (1942), Straffin and Heaney (1981).
35 Scott (1981), Verrecchia (1981).
36 Sharkey (1982).
37 Suzuki and Nakayama (1976).

REFERENCES

Akerlof, G. (1970), 'The Market for Lemons: Qualitative Uncertainty and the Market Mechanism', *Quarterly Journal of Economics*, **89**, 488–500.

Anderson, R. (1978), 'An Elementary Core Equivalence Theorem', *Econometrica*, **46**, 1483–7.

Arrow, K. J. (1972a), 'Models of Job Discrimination', in A. H. Pascal (ed.), *Racial Discrimination in Economic Life*, D. C. Heath, Lexington, Mass., pp. 8–102.

Arrow, K. J. (1972b), 'Some Mathematical Models of Race in the Labor Market', in A. H. Pascal (ed.), *Racial Discrimination in Economic Life*, D. C. Heath, Lexington, Mass., pp. 187–204.

Arrow, K. J. (1973a), 'The Theory of Discrimination', in O. Ashenfelter and A. Rees (eds), *Discrimination in Labor Markets*, Princeton University Press, pp. 3–33.

Arrow, K. J. (1973b), 'Higher Education as a Filter', *Journal of Public Economics*, **2**, 193–216.

Arrow, K. J. and Debreu, G. (1954), 'Existence of an Equilibrium for a Competitive Economy', *Econometrica*, **22**, 265–90.

Arrow, K. J. and Hahn, F. (1971), *General Competitive Analysis*, North Holland, New York.

Aumann, R. J. (1959), 'Acceptable Points in General Cooperative N-Person Games', in R. D. Luce and A. W. Tucker (eds), *Contributions to the Theory of Games IV*; Annals of Mathematics Studies, vol. 40, Princeton University Press, pp. 287–324.

Aumann, R. J. (1964), 'Markets with a Continuum of Traders', *Econometrica*, **32**, 39–50.

Aumann, R. J. (1973), 'Disadvantageous Monopolies', *Journal of Economic Theory*, **6**, 1–11.

Aumann, R. J. (1974), 'Subjectivity and Correlation in Randomized Strategies', *Journal of Mathematical Economics*, **1**, 67–96.

Aumann, R. J. (1975), 'Values of Markets with a Continuum of Traders', *Econometrica*, **43**, 611–46.

Aumann, R. J. (1976), 'Agreeing to Disagree', *Annals of Statistics*, **4**, 1236–9.

Aumann, R. J. (1979), 'On the Rate of Convergence of the Core', *International Economic Review*, **20**, 349–57.

Aumann, R. J. (1985), 'On the Non-transferable Utility Value': A Comment on the Roth–Shafer Examples', *Econometrica*, **53**, in press.

Aumann, R. J. and Kurz, M. (1977), 'Power and Taxes', *Econometrica*, **45**, 1137–61.

Aumann, R. J., Kurz, M. and Neyman, A. (1983), 'Voting for Public Goods', *Review of Economic Studies*, **50**, 677–93.

Aumann, R. J., Kurz, M. and Neyman, A. (1985), 'Power and Public Goods', *Journal of Economic Theory*, in press.

Aumann, R. J. and Shapley, L. S. (1974), *Values of Non-atomic Games*, Princeton University Press.

Axelrod, R. (1984), *The Evolution of Cooperation*, Basic Books, New York.

Bertrand, J. (1883), 'Theorie mathematique de la Richesse Sociale', *Journal des Savants*, **48**, 499–508.

Bewley, T. (1973), 'Edgeworth's Conjecture', *Econometrica*, **41**, 425–52.

Billera, L. J. (1974), 'On Games without Side Payments Arising from a General Class of Markets', *Journal of Mathematical Economics*, **1**, 129–39.

Billera, L. J. and Bixby, R. (1973a), 'A Characterization of Pareto Surfaces', *Proceedings of the American Mathematical Society*, **41**, 261–7.

Billera, L. J. and Bixby, R. (1973b), 'A Characterization of Polyhedral Market Games', *International Journal of Game Theory*, **2**, 253–61.

Billera, L. J. and Bixby, R. (1974), 'Market Representation of N-Person Games', *Bulletin of the American Mathematical Society*, **80**, 522–6.

Billera, L. J., Heath, D. C. and Raanan, J. (1978), 'International Telephone Billing Rates – A Novel Application of Non-Atomic Game Theory', *Operations Research*, **26**, 956–65.

Binmore, K. (1982), 'Perfect Equilibria in Bargaining Models', ICERD Discussion Paper no. 58, London School of Economics.

Bogardi, I. and Szidarovsky, F. (1978), 'Application of Game Theory in Water Management', *Applied Mathematical Modelling*, **1**, 11–20.

Bondareva, O. N. (1962), 'Teoriia iadra v igre n lits' (Theory of the core in the n-person game), *Vestnik LGU* (Leningrad State University), **13**, 141–2.

Bondareva, O. N. (1963), 'Nekotorye primeneniia metodor linejnogo programmirovaniia k teorii kooperativnykn igr' (Some applications of linear programming methods to the theory of cooperative games), *Problemy Kibernetiki*, **10**, 119–39.

Bott, R. (1953), 'Symmetric Solutions to Majority Games', in H. W. Kuhn and A. W. Tucker (eds), *Contributions to the Theory of Games II*, Annals of Mathematics Studies, vol. 28, Princeton University Press, pp. 319–23.

Brown, D. F. and Robinson, A. (1975), 'Non-standard Exchange Economies', *Econometrica*, **43**, 41–55.

Butters, G. (1977), 'Equilibrium Distribution of Sales and Advertising Prices', *Review of Economic Studies*, **44**, 465–92.

Cheng, H. C. (1981), 'What is the Normal Rate of Convergence of the Core?' (Part I), *Econometrica*, **49**, 73–84.

Cournot, A. A. (1838), *Recherches sur les principes mathematiques de la theorie des richesses*, Machette, Paris (*Researches into the Mathematical Principles of the Theory of Wealth*, trans. N. T. Bacon, Macmillan, New York, 1897.)

Crawford, V. and Knoer, E. M. (1981), 'Job Matching with Heterogeneous Firms and Workers', *Econometrica*, **49**, 437–50.

d'Aspremont, C., Gabszewicz, J. J. and Thisse, J. F. (1979), 'On Hotelling's "Stability in Competition" ', *Econometrica*, **5**, 1145–50.

Davis, M. and Maschler, M. (1965). 'The Kernel of a Cooperative Game', *Naval Research Logistics Quarterly*, **12**, 223–59.

Davis, M. and Maschler, M. (1967), 'Existence of Stable Payoff Configurations for Cooperative Games', in M. Shubik (ed.), *Essays in Mathematical Economics in Honor of Oskar Morgenstern*, Princeton University Press, pp. 39–52.

Debreu, G. (1952), 'A Social Equilibrium Existence Theorem', *Proceedings of the National Academy of Sciences*, **38**, 886–93.

Debreu, G. (1975), 'The Rate of Convergence of the Core of an Economy', *Journal of Mathematical Economics*, **2**, 1–7.

Debreu, G. and Scarf, H. (1963), 'A Limit Theorem on the Core of an Economy', *International Economic Review*, **4**, 235–46.

Diamond, P. A. (1971), 'A Model of Price Adjustment', *Journal of Economic Theory*, **3**, 156–68.

Dierker, E. and Dierker, H. (1972), 'The Local Uniqueness of Equilibria', *Econometrica*, **40**, 867–82.

Dreze, J. H., Gepts, S. and Gabszewicz, J. (1969), 'On Cores and Competitive Equilibria', in *La Decision*, CNRS, Paris, pp. 91–114.

Dubins, L. E. and Freedman, D. A. (1981), 'Machiavelli and the Gale–Shapley Algorithms', *American Mathematical Monthly*, **88**, 485–94.

Edgeworth, F. Y. (1881), *Mathematical Psychics: An Essay on the Application of Mathematics to the Moral Sciences*, London.

Foley, D. (1970), 'Lindahl's Solution and the Core of an Economy with Public Goods', *Econometrica*, **38**, 66–72.

Forges, F. (1985a), 'Correlated Equilibria in a Class of Repeated Games with Incomplete Information', *International Journal of Game Theory*, in press.

Forges, F. (1985b), 'Correlated Equilibria in Repeated Games with Lack of Information on One Side: A Model with Verifiable Types', *International Journal of Game Theory*, in press.

Fouraker, L. E. and Siegel, S. (1960), *Bargaining and Group Decision Making: Experiments in Bilateral Monopoly*, McGraw-Hill, New York.

Friedman, J. W. (1977), *Oligopoly and the Theory of Games*, North-Holland, Amsterdam and New York.

Gabszewicz, J. J. and Dreze, J. H. (1971), 'Syndicates of Traders in an Exchange Economy', in H. W. Kuhn and G. P. Szego (eds), *Differential Games and Related Topics*, North-Holland, Amsterdam, pp. 399–414.

Gabszewicz, J. J. and Mertens, J. F. (1971), 'An Equivalence Theorem for the Core of an Economy Whose Atoms Are Not "Too Big" ', *Econometrica*, **39**, 713–22.

Gale, D. (1984), 'Equilibrium in a Discrete Exchange Economy with Money', *International Journal of Game Theory*, **13**, 61–4.

Gale, D. and Shapley, L. S. (1962), 'College Admissions and the Stability of Marriage', *American Mathematical Monthly*, **69**, 9–15.

Gardner, R. (1975), 'Studies in the Theory of Social Institutions', PhD thesis, Cornell University.

Gardner, R. (1981a), 'Wealth, Prices and the Power to Requisition: The New Economic Policy in the Soviet Union', Department of Economics, Iowa State University.

Gardner, R. (1981b), 'Wealth and Power in a Collegiate Polity', *Journal of Economic Theory*, **25**, 353–66.

Gately, D. (1974), 'Sharing the Gain from Regional Cooperation: A Game Theoretic Application to Planning Investment in Electric Power', *International Economic Review*, **15**, 195–208.

Griesmer, J. H. and Shubik, M. (1963), 'Toward a Study of Bidding Processes, Parts I, II and III', *Naval Research Logistics Quarterly*, **10**, 11–21, 151–73, 199–217.

Grodal, B. (1972), 'A Second Remark on the Core of an Atomless Economy', *Econometrica*, **40**, 581–4.

Grodal, B. (1975), 'The Rate of Convergence of the Core of a Purely Competitive

Sequence of Economies', *Journal of Mathematical Economics*, **2**, 171–86.

Guesnerie, R. (1977), 'Monopoly, Syndicate and Shapley Value: About Some Conjectures', *Journal of Economic Theory*, **15**, 235–52.

Hammond, P. (1975), 'Charity: Altruism or Cooperative Egoism', in E. Phelps (ed.), *Altruism, Morality and Economic Theory*, Russel Sage Foundation, New York.

Harsanyi, J. C. (1959), 'A Bargaining Model for the Cooperative *N*-Person Game', in A. W. Tucker and R. D. Luce (eds), *Contributions to the Theory of Games IV*, Annals of Mathematics Studies, vol. 40, Princeton University Press, pp. 325–55.

Harsanyi, J. C. (1967), 'Games with Incomplete Information Played by Bayesian Players, Parts I, II and III', *Management Science*, **14**, 159–82, 320–34, 486–502.

Harsanyi, J. C. (1973), 'Games with Randomly Disturbed Payoffs: A New Rationale for Mixed Strategy Equilibrium Points', *International Journal of Game Theory*, **2**, 1–23.

Harsanyi, J. C. (1974), 'A Solution Concept for *N*–Person Noncooperative Games', *International Journal of Game Theory*, **3**, 211–25.

Harsanyi, J. C. (1975), 'The Tracing Procedure, A Bayesian Approach to Defining a Solution to *N*-Person Noncooperative Games', *International Journal of Game Theory*, **4**, 61–94.

Hart, S. (1973), 'Symmetric Solutions of Some Productive Economies', *International Journal of Game Theory*, **2**, 53–62.

Hart, S. (1974), 'Formation of Cartels in Large Markets', *Journal of Economic Theory*, **7**, 453–66.

Hart, S. (1977a), 'Values of Non-differentiable Markets with a Continuum of Traders', *Journal of Mathematical Economics*, **4**, 103–16.

Hart, S. (1977b), 'Asymptotic Value of Games with a Continuum of Players', *Journal of Mathematical Economics*, **4**, 57–80.

Hart, S. (1980), 'Measure-based Values of Market Games', *Mathematics of Operations Research*, **5**, 197–228.

Hart, S. (1985), 'Non-zero-sum Two-person Games with Incomplete Information', *Mathematics of Operations Research*, **10**, in press.

Hildenbrand, W. (1974), *Core and Equilibria of a Large Economy*, Princeton University Press.

Hotelling, H. (1929), 'Stability in Competition', *Economic Journal*, **39**, 41–57.

Hurwicz, L. (1979a), 'Outcome Functions Yielding Walrasian and Lindahl Allocations at Nash Equilibrium Points', *Review of Economic Studies*, **46**, 217–25.

Hurwicz, L. (1979b), 'On Allocations Attainable through Nash Equilibria', *Journal of Economic Theory*, **21**, 140–65.

Imai, H. (1983), 'On Harsanyi's Solution', *International Journal of Game Theory*, **12**, 161–79.

Kalai, E. and Samet, D. (1984), 'Persistent Equilibria in Strategic Games', *International Journal of Game Theory*, **13**, 129–44.

Kalai, E. and Samet, D. (1985), 'Unanimity Games and Pareto Optimality', *International Journal of Game Theory*, in press.

Kaneko, M. (1976), 'On the Core and Competitive Equilibria of a Market with Indivisible Goods', *Naval Research Logistics Quarterly*, **23**, 321–37.

Kannai, Y. (1970), 'Continuity Properties of the Core of a Market', *Econometrica*, **38**, 791–815.

Kannai, Y. (1972), 'Continuity Properties of the Core of a Market: A Correction', *Econometrica*, **40**, 955–8.

Knuth, D. E. (1976), *Mariages Stables*, Les Presses de l'Universite de Montreal.

Kohlberg, E. and Mertens, J. F. (1982), 'On the Strategic Stability of Equilibria', Center for Operations Research and Econometrics Discussion Paper no. 8248, Universite Catholique de Louvain.

Kreps, D., Milgrom, P., Roberts, J. and Wilson, R. (1982), 'Rational Cooperation in the Finitely Repeated Prisoner's Dilemma', *Journal of Economic Theory*, **27**, 245–52.

Kreps, D. and Wilson, R. (1982a), 'Sequential Equilibria', *Econometrica*, **50**, 863–94.

Kreps, D. and Wilson, R. (1982b), 'Reputation and Imperfect Information', *Journal of Economic Theory*, **27**, 253–79.

Kurz, M. (1977), 'Distortion of Preferences, Income Distribution and the Case for a Linear Income Tax', *Journal of Economic Theory*, **14**, 291–8.

Kurz, M. (1978), 'Altruism as an Outcome of Social Interaction', *American Economic Review*, **68**, 216–22.

Kurz, M. (1980), 'Income Distribution and Distortion of Preferences: The l-Commodity Case', *Journal of Economic Theory*, **22**, 99–107.

Lewis, D. K. (1969), *Convention*, Harvard University Press, Cambridge, Mass.

Littlechild, S. C. and Owen, G. (1973), 'A Simple Expression for the Shapley Value in a Special Case', *Management Science*, **20**, 370–2.

Loehman, E. T., Pengry, D. and Whinston, A. B. (1973), 'Cost Allocation for Regional Pollution Treatment Systems', in J. R. Conner and E. T. Loehman (eds), *Economics and Decision Making for Environmental Quality*, University of Florida Press, Gainesville.

Lucas, W. F. (1969), 'The Proof that a Game May Not Have a Solution', *Transactions of the American Mathematical Society*, **137**, 219–29.

Lucas, W. F. and Rabie, M. (1982), 'Games with No Solutions and Empty Cores', *Mathematics of Operations Research*, **7**, 491–500.

Luce, R. D. and Raiffa, H. (1957), *Games and Decisions*, John Wiley, New York.

Malouf, M. and Roth, A. (1981), 'Disagreement in Bargaining: An Experimental Study', *Journal of Conflict Resolution*, **25**, 329–48.

Manes, R. P. and Verrecchia, R. (1982), 'A New Proposal for Setting Intra-company Transfer Prices', *Accounting and Business Research*, **12**, 97–104.

Mas-Colell, A. (1975), 'A Further Result on the Representation of Games by Markets', *Journal of Economic Theory*, **10**, 117–22.

Mas-Colell, A. (1977), 'Competition and Value Allocations of Large Exchange Economies', *Journal of Economic Theory*, **14**, 419–38.

Mas-Colell, A. (1980), 'Remarks on the Game-theoretic Analysis of a Simple Distribution of Surplus Problem', *International Journal of Game Theory*, **9**, 125–40.

Maschler, M., Peleg, B. and Shapley, L. S. (1972), 'The Kernel and Bargaining Set for Convex Games', *International Journal of Game Theory*, **1**, 73–93.

Maynard Smith, J. (1982), *Evolution and the Theory of Games*, Cambridge University Press, Cambridge and New York.

Mertens, J. F. (1985), 'The Shapley Value in the Non-Differentiable Case', *International Journal of Game Theory*, in press.

Milgrom, P. and Roberts, J. (1982a), 'Limit Pricing and Entry Under Incomplete Information: An Equilibrium Analysis', *Econometrica*, **50**, 443–60.

Milgrom, P. and Roberts, J. (1982b), 'Predation, Reputation and Entry Deterrence', *Journal of Economic Theory*, **27**, 280–312.

Milgrom, P. and Weber, R. (1982), 'A Theory of Auctions and Competitive Bidding', *Econometrica*, **50**, 1089–122.

Milnor, J. W. and Shapley, L. S. (1978), 'Values of Large Games II: Oceanic Games', *Mathematics of Operations Research*, **3**, 290–307.

Myerson, R. (1978), 'Refinements of the Nash Equilibrium Concept', *International Journal of Game Theory*, **7**, 73–80.

Myerson, R. (1981), 'Optimal Auction Design', *Mathematics of Operations Research*, **6**, 58–73.

Nash, J. F. (1950), 'The Bargaining Problem', *Econometrica*, **18**, 155–62.

Nash, J. F. (1951), 'Non-cooperative Games', *Annals of Mathematics*, **54**, 86–295.

Nash, J. F. (1953), 'Two-person Cooperative Games', *Econometrica*, **21**, 128–40.

Neyman, A. (1985), Semi-values of Political Economic Games', *Mathematics of Operations Research*, **10**, in press.

Novshek, W. (1980), 'Cournot Equilibrium with Free Entry', *Review of Economic Studies*, **47**, 473–86.

Novshek, W. and Sonnenschein, H. (1978), 'Cournot and Walras Equilibrium', *Journal of Economic Theory*, **19**, 223–66.

Osborne, M. J. (1984), 'Why Do Some Goods Bear Higher Taxes Than Others?', *Journal of Economic Theory*, **32**, 301–16.

Ostroy, J. (1981), 'Differentiability as Convergence to Perfectly Competitive Equilibrium', *Journal of Mathematical Economics*, **8**, 59–73.

Parker, T. (1943), 'Allocation of the Tennessee Valley Authority Projects', *Transactions of the American Society of Civil Engineering*, **108**, 174–87.

Pauly, M. V. and Satterthwaite, M. A. (1981), 'The Pricing of Primary Care Physicians' Services: A Test of the Role of Consumer Information', *Bell Journal of Economics*, **12**, 488–506.

Peleg, B. (1967), 'Existence Theorem for the Bargaining Set $M_1^{(i)}$', in M. Shubik (ed.), *Essays in Mathematical Economics in Honor of Oskar Morgenstern*, Princeton University Press, pp. 53–6.

Prescott, E. C. and Visscher, M. (1977), 'Sequential Location among Firms with Foresight', *Bell Journal of Economics*, **8**, 378–93.

Radner, R. (1980), 'Collusive Behavior in Noncooperative Epsilon-equilibria of Oligopolies with Long but Finite Lives', *Journal of Economic Theory*, **22**, 136–54.

Radner, R. (1981), 'Monitoring Cooperative Agreements in a Repeated Principal–Agent Relationship', *Econometrica*, **49**, 1127–48.

Ransmeier, J. S. (1942), *The Tennessee Valley Authority: A Case Study in the Economics of Multiple Purpose Stream Planning*, Vanderbilt University Press, Nashville, Tenn.

Riker, W. and Shapley, L. S. (1968), 'Weighted Voting: A Mathematical Analysis for Instrumental Judgments', in J. R. Pennock and J. W. Chapman (eds), *Representation: Nomos X*, Atherton Press, New York, pp. 199–216.

Rosenmuller, J. (1981), 'Values of Non-sidepayment Games and Their Application in the Theory of Public Goods', in *Essays in Game Theory and Mathematical Economics in Honor of Oskar Morgenstern*, vol. 4 of *Gesellschaft, Recht Wirtschaft*, Bibliographisches Institut, Mannheim, Vienna and Zurich, pp. 111–29.

Rosenmuller, J. (1982), 'On Values, Location Conflicts, and Public Goods', in M. Deistler, E. Furst and G. Schwodianer (eds), *Proceedings of the Oskar Morgenstern Symposium at Vienna*, Physica-Verlag, Vienna, pp. 74–100.

Rosenthal, R. W. (1979), 'Sequences of Games with Varying Opponents', *Econometrica*, **47**, 1353–66.

Ross, S. (1973), 'The Economic Theory of Agency: The Principal's Problem', *American Economic Review*, **63**, 134–9.

Roth, A. E. (1977), 'The Shapley Value as a von Neumann–Morgenstern Utility', *Econometrica*, **45**, 657–64.

Roth, A. E. (1982), 'The Economics of Matching: Stability and Incentives', *Mathematics of Operations Research*, **7**, 617–28.

Quinzii, M. (1984), 'Core and Competitive Equilibria with Indivisibilities', *International Journal of Game Theory*, **13**, 41–60.

Roth, A. E. (1984), 'The Evolution of the Labor Market for Medical Interns and Residents: A Case Study in Game Theory', *Journal of Political Economy*, **92**, 991–1016.

Roth, A. E., Malouf, M. and Murnighan, J. K. (1981), 'Sociological versus Strategic Factors in Bargaining', *Journal of Economic Behavior and Organization*, **2**, 153–77.

Roth, A. E. and Murnighan, J. K. (1982), 'The Role of Information in Bargaining: An Experimental Study', *Econometrica*, **50**, 1123–42.

Rothschild, M. and Stiglitz, J. (1976), 'Equilibrium in Competitive Insurance Markets: An Essay on the Economics of Imperfect Information', *Quarterly Journal of Economics*, **90**, 629–49.

Rubinstein, A. (1979), 'An Optimal Conviction Policy for Offenses that May Have Been Committed by Accident', in S. J. Brams, A. Schotter and G. Schwodiauer (eds), *Applied Game Theory*, Physica-Verlag, Vienna, pp. 406–13.

Rubinstein, A. (1982), 'Perfect Equilibria in a Bargaining Model', *Econometrica*, **50**, 97–110.

Salop, S. C. (1979), 'Monopolistic Competition with Outside Goods', *Bell Journal of Economics*, **10**, 141–56.

Scarf, H. E. (1967), 'The Core of an *N*-Person Game', *Econometrica*, **35**, 50–69.

Scarf, H. E. (1973), *The Computation of Economic Equilibria*, Yale University Press, New Haven, Conn.

Schmeidler, D. (1969a), 'Competitive Equilibria in Markets with a Continuum of Traders and Incomplete Preferences', *Econometrica*, **37**, 578–85.

Schmeidler, D. (1969b), 'The Nucleolus of a Characteristic Function Game', *Society for Industrial and Applied Mathematics, Journal on Applied Mathematics*, **17**, 1163–70.

Schmeidler, D. (1972), 'A Remark on the Core of an Atomless Economy', *Econometrica*, **40**, 579–80.

Schmeidler, D. (1980), 'Walrasian Analysis via Strategic Outcome Functions', *Econometrica*, **48**, 1585–94.

Scott, M. (1981), 'Comments on R. E. Verrecchia's "A Question of Equity: Use of the Shapley Value to Allocate State and Local Income and Franchise Taxes" ', in S. Moriarity (ed.), *Joint Cost Allocations: Proceedings of the University of Oklahoma Conference on Cost Allocations, April 23, 24, 1981*, Center of Economic and Management Research, University of Oklahoma.

Selten, R. (1965), 'Spieltheoretische Behandlung eines Oligopolmodells mit Nachfragetragheit', *Zeitschrift für die gesammte Staatswissenschaft*, **121**, 301–24, 667–89.

Selten, R. (1973), 'A Simple Model of Imperfect Competition where 4 are Few and 6 are Many', *International Journal of Game Theory*, **2**, 141–201.

Selten, R. (1975), 'Re-examination of the Perfectness Concept for Equilibrium Points in Extensive Games', *International Journal of Game Theory*, **4**, 25–55.

Selten, R. (1980), 'A Note on Evolutionarily Stable Strategies in Asymmetric Animal Conflicts', *Journal of Theoretical Biology*, **84**, 93–101.

Selten, R. and Guth, W. (1982), 'Game Theoretic Analysis of Wage Bargaining in a Simple Business Cycle Model', *Journal of Mathematical Economics*, **10**, 177–95.

Shapiro, N. Z. and Shapley, L. S. (1978), 'Values of Large Games I: A Limit Theorem', *Mathematics of Operations Research*, **3**, 1–9.

Shapley, L. S. (1953), 'A Value for *N*-Person Games', in H. W. Kuhn and A. W. Tucker (eds), *Contributions to the Theory of Games II*, Annals of Mathematics Studies, vol. 28, Princeton University Press, pp. 307–12.

Shapley, L. S. (1967), 'On Balanced Sets and Cores', *Naval Research Logistics Quarterly*, **14**, 453–60.

Shapley, L. S. (1969). 'Utility Comparison and the Theory of Games', *La Decision*, CNRS, Paris, pp. 251–63.

Shapley, L. S. (1971), 'Cores of Convex Games', *International Journal of Game Theory*, **1**, 11–26.

Shapley, L. S. (1975), 'An Example of a Slow Converging Core', *International Economic Review*, **16**, 345–51.

Shapley, L. S. and Scarf, H. E. (1974), 'On Cores and Indivisibilities', *Journal of Mathematical Economics*, **1**, 23–8.

Shapley, L. S. and Shubik, M. (1954), 'A Method for Evaluating the Distribution of Power in a Committee System', *American Political Science Review*, **48**, 787–92.

Shapley, L. S. and Shubik, M. (1967), 'Concepts and Theories of Pure Competition', in M. Shubik (ed.), *Essays in Mathematical Economics in Honor of Oskar Morgenstern*, Princeton University Press.

Shapley, L. S. and Shubik, M. (1969), 'On Market Games', *Journal of Economic Theory*, **1**, 9–25.

Shapley, L. S. and Shubik, M. (1972), 'The Assignment Game I: The Core', *International Journal of Game Theory*, **1**, 111–30.

Sharkey, W. W. (1982), 'Suggestions for a Game Theoretic Approach to Public Utility Pricing and Cost Allocation', *Bell Journal of Economics*, **13**, 57–68.

Shavell, S. (1979), 'Risk Sharing and Incentives in the Principal and Agent Relationship', *Bell Journal of Economics*, **10**, 55–73.

Shitovitz, B. (1973), 'Oligopoly in Markets with a Continuum of Traders', *Econometrica*, **41**, 467–502.

Shitovitz, B. (1974), 'On Some Problems Arising in Markets with Some Large Traders and a Continuum of Small Traders', *Journal of Economic Theory*, **8**, 458–70.

Shubik, M. (1959), 'Edgeworth Market Games', in R. D. Luce and A. W. Tucker (eds), *Contributions to the Theory of Games IV*, Annals of Mathematics Studies, vol. 40, Princeton University Press, pp. 267–78.

Shubik, M. (1963), 'Incentives, Decentralized Control, the Assignment of Joint Costs and Internal Pricing', in C. Bonini, R. Jaedicke and M. Wagner (eds), *Management Controls*, McGraw-Hill, New York.

Sondermann, D. (1974), 'Economies of Scale and Equilibria in Coalition Production Economies', *Journal of Economic Theory*, **8**, 259–91.

Spence, M. (1974), *Market Signaling: Information Transfer in Hiring and Related Processes*, Harvard University Press, Cambridge, Mass.

Spence, M. (1976), 'Competition in Salaries and Signaling Prerequisites for Jobs', *Quarterly Journal of Economics*, **90**, 51–75.

Stearns, R. (1965), in W. F. Lucas (ed.), 'A Game without Side Payments that has No Solution', Report of the Fifth Conference on Game Theory, mimeograph, Department of Mathematics, Princeton University.

Straffin, D. D. and Heaney, J. P. (1981), 'Game Theory and the Tennessee Valley Authority', *International Journal of Game Theory*, **10**, 35–43.

Suzuki, M. and Nakayama, M. (1976), 'The Cost Assignment of Cooperative Water Resource Development: A Game Theoretic Approach', *Management Science*, **22**, 1081–6.

Thompson, G. L. (1980), 'Computing the Core of a Market Game', in A. V. Fiacco and K. O. Kortanek (eds), *External Methods and System Analysis*, Springer-Verlag, Vienna.

Verrecchia, R. E. (1981), 'A Question of Equity: Use of the Shapley Value to Allocate State and Local Income and Franchise Taxes', in S. Moriarity (ed.), *Joint Cost Allocations: Proceedings of the University of Oklahoma Conference on Cost Allocation, April 23, 24, 1981*, Center for Economic and Management Research, University of Oklahoma.

Vickrey, W. (1961), 'Counterspeculation, Auctions and Competitive Sealed Tenders', *Journal of Finance*, **16**, 8–37.

Vickrey, W. (1962), 'Auctions and Bidding Games', in *Recent Advances in Game Theory* (Conference Proceedings), Princeton University Press, pp. 15–27.

Vind, K. (1964), 'Edgeworth Allocations in an Exchange Economy with Many Traders', *International Economic Review*, **5**, 165–77.

Vind, K. (1972), 'A Third Remark on the Core of an Atomless Economy', *Econometrica*, **40**, 585–6.

von Neumann, J. (1937), 'A Model of General Economic Equilibrium', *Review of Economic Studies*, **13**, 1–9.

von Neumann, J. and Morgenstern, O. (1944), *Theory of Games and Economic Behavior*, Princeton University Press.

Wilson, R. (1979), 'Auctions of Shares', *Quarterly Journal of Economics*, **93**, 675–98.

Comment

REINHARD SELTEN

Aumann's paper not only vividly presents his methodological point of view, but it also contains an impressive description of important conceptual and mathematical developments in game theory, organized around three solution concepts: the equilibrium point, the core and the value.

I shall focus my remarks on the use of game theory in economics, commenting on Aumann's methodological position in connection with the question of empirical relevance of game theory for economics. Aumann's arguments sound like a defense of present research practices based on unquestioned strong rationality assumptions. Even if this kind of theorizing may have to go on for some time in the absence of superior alternatives, a redirection of efforts towards the development of a descriptive theory of game behavior seems to be desirable. In this respect, experimental research is of crucial importance. I shall attempt to indicate possible new directions of theory-building in the area of strategic interaction.

1 THE USE OF GAME THEORY IN ECONOMICS

Immediately after the publication of the famous book by von Neumann and Morgenstern (1944), the great significance of game theory was recognized by many economic theorists. Later, some researchers felt that game theory had disappointed their initial high hopes. This was due to the fact that rather few people had worked on the subject and its applications. Nevertheless, there has been a slow but steady increase of game-theoretical thinking in economics. Today, this influence is very strong. Some game-theoretical concepts, such as the core or the equilibrium point, are now commonly used in economic theory.

For a long time, optimization of utility or profit has been the prevalent principle of explanation in microeconomics. Strong rationality assumptions are a familiar point of departure in economic theorizing. Wherever problems of strategic interaction occur, game-theoretical reasoning is an unavoidable consequence of strong rationality assumptions. This is the reason why game theory has become more and more popular as a tool of economic analysis.

It is interesting to observe that in the last decade a parallel development has started in evolutionary biology. Since Darwin, it has been a familiar idea that natural selection results in a tendency towards optimization of individual reproductive success (fitness). The application of this idea to social interactions between animals of the same species has led to the introduction of the game-theoretical concept of an evolutionarily stable strategy by Maynard Smith and Price (1973). The approach has proved to be empirically successful. References to concrete applications can be found in a recent book by Maynard Smith (1982).

Game theory has been conceived as a mathematical method for the social sciences. It is surprising and encouraging to see that it has found its way into the natural sciences. Of course, the interpretation of game-theoretical concepts in biology is quite different from the usual one in economics. Equilibrium is seen as the outcome of a dynamic process of natural selection rather than as the necessary consequence of strategic reasoning by rational players. It is the latter point of view that prevails in economics.

2 IMPACT OF NORMATIVE GAME THEORY

Problems concerning the optimal allocation of resources can be looked upon as purely normative questions. Undoubtedly, it is of interest to ask what a decision-maker should do under idealized circumstances. The limits of human information-processing capabilities may not permit a similar approach to the real world. Nevertheless, it is of great importance to understand the conceptual and mathematical consequences of strong rationality assumptions. The logic of rational decision-making merits intensive exploration independently of its practical significance.

In game theory it is not always clear what should be considered as rational. Game theorists work towards the definition of rationality in situations of strategic interaction. Many conceptual problems remain to be solved.

Game theory already has made considerable contributions to the clarification of problems of strategic interaction in economic contexts. The older literature on oligopoly was often very confused. Theories that claimed to describe rational behavior proceeded from arbitrary assumptions on conjectures held by oligopolists concerning the behavior of their competitors. Cournot's theory (1838) was generally understood in this way. The modern game-theoretical interpretation of equilibrium points in the sense of Nash (1951) is quite different. It is based on the idea that a rational theory should not be a self-destroying prophecy which creates an incentive to deviate for those who believe in it. Among the older authors, only Erich Schneider (1932) held a view that was similar to the modern one.

Much of the confusion in oligopoly theory arose from insufficient attempts to discuss questions arising in repeated games in the framework of the one-shot game. A pioneering paper by Aumann (1959) made the difference between both types of games very clear many years ago.

The definition of an extensive game, introduced by von Neumann and Morgenstern (1944) and further refined by Kuhn (1953), has brought a tremendous conceptual progress. Unfortunately, a part of the control-theory-inspired literature on dynamic games fails to make proper use of this achievement. This has led to the misguided 'open-loop' approach, where strategies are construed as decision sequences, rather than as functions that connect past histories to decisions; a failure to distinguish between the rules of an extensive game and its solution has led to such notions as the 'Stackelberg solution.' Hopefully, the increasing popularity of game theory will help to spread its basic conceptual insights and to prevent inappropriate approaches to the logic of strategic interaction.

In the last decades cooperative game theory has had a considerable impact on modern developments in general equilibrium theory. Convergence theorems concerning various cooperative concepts have thrown new light on the notion of competitive equilibrium. In view of the illuminating discussion of the core and the value in Aumann's paper, it is not necessary to add further detail.

Surprisingly, cooperative game theory has found interesting practical applications to problems of cost accounting. It may be sufficient to mention the pioneering paper by Shubik (1962) and the work by Billera and others (1978) for the telephone system of Cornell University.

Bargaining is a subject that has been intensely explored by means of both cooperative and non-cooperative game theory. The investigation of bargaining problems has been greatly enhanced by Harsanyi's (1967–8) theory of games with incomplete information. This theory has also had a strong influence on the social choice literature concerned with incentive compatibility.

It is maybe worthwhile to mention that the use of game-theoretical models has also spread to macroeconomics and even econometrics. References and examples can be found in a recent article by Haas (1983).

These brief remarks on the impact of normative game theory on economic theory cannot do justice to the vast literature. A better impression can be gained from the survey article by Schotter and Schwödiauer (1980).

3 THE QUESTION OF EMPIRICAL RELEVANCE

Economic theory cannot restrict itself to the discussion of normative problems. Economics as an empirical science demands the attention of the theorist. This raises the question of descriptive relevance of game theory.

Aumann presents a methodological point of view that seems to de-emphasize the necessity to compare theories with empirical data. He maintains that theories are neither true nor false; they are like filing systems, which should be judged 'by how well they enable us to understand and organize our observations.' Capability to produce insight rather than empirical accuracy is seen as the main characteristic of a good theory.

The nature of scientific theories is a difficult subject, extensively studied in modern philosophy of science. The 'non-statement view' of the structural approach (Sneed, 1971; Stegmüller, 1973, 1980) also looks at theories, or more precisely at 'structural cores' of theories, as neither true nor false. Essentially, the structural core of a theory is nothing more than 'a mathematical formalism connected with the hope that it can be successfully applied to the world' (Stegmüller, 1973: 275).

However, this view, which strongly appeals to me, does not deny that statements on the range of successful applications can still be judged as true or false. A theory may have a narrower or wider range of successful applications, and it may fit these applications more or less closely. In this sense, it is meaningful to say that a descriptive theory is more or less distant from truth. The empirical scientist cannot avoid judging the truth of scientific statements in the light of empirical data. This applies to game theory, too, where it is meant to be descriptive.

Aumann does not completely reject the distinction between normative and descriptive theories, but he thinks that it is 'not as sharp as it may appear' (p. 38). I feel that a sharp distinction should be made. It is true that the same mathematical formalism may have a normative and a descriptive interpretation. However, both kinds of interpretations require completely different justifications and, therefore, should be kept separate. Descriptive theories need to be compared with reality, whereas normative theories cannot be tested empirically. The justification of normative theories of rationality must be sought in compelling intuitive arguments. Such arguments have little force as far as descriptive theories are concerned.

A methodological position that often has been implicit in the thinking of microeconomists and game theorists may be epitomized as 'naive rationalism.' The naive rationalist thinks that the logic of decision-making is so obvious that it simply cannot be violated by mentally sane human beings. A sharp distinction between normative and descriptive theories of economic behavior would not be necessary if this were true. Aumann is well aware of the evidence to the contrary and carefully avoids the pitfalls of naive rationalism.

It is perhaps fitting to use the label 'sophisticated rationalism' for the position taken by Aumann on the appropriateness of strong rationality assumptions in economic theory. He contrasts the mythical figure of *Homo rationalis* with the real-life *Homo sapiens* and invokes sophisticated arguments in order to defend absolute rationality as the basis of microeconomic theorizing. He argues that the assumption of utility maximization does not have to be empirically correct in order to serve as a useful point of departure. It is useful, since it succeeds in unifying and interconnecting a large body of economic theory, and thereby enhances our understanding of the world, in the sense that it enables us to relate a great number of empirical phenomena to each other. Unlike naive rationalism, sophisticated rationalism is a tenable position.

Like some other economists, I feel uncomfortable with an imposing construction on a shaky foundation. Even if research in the spirit of sophisticated rationalism may have to go on for some time in view of the absence of sufficiently powerful alternatives, economists should not close their eyes to basic questions in the description of human decision behavior.

As Herbert Simon (1957) pointed out long ago, human rationality is limited by severe restrictions on the complexity of information processing. Experimental results obtained by social psychologists and experimental economists clearly show that human behavior does not conform to the usual picture of rational decision-making. I have tried to convey some of the insights obtained from the experimental literature in a survey article (Selten, 1979).

In a recent book the psychologist Huber (1982) reports on the experimental literature and on his own experiments on choices between alternatives described on several dimensions. He comes to the conclusion that utility theory must be considered as falsified. This already concerns choices under certainty. As Tversky and Kahnemann have shown (1973), additional difficulties arise for decisions under uncertainty.

The discussant opts for a position of 'methodological dualism,' based on a sharp distinction between normative theories of rationality and descriptive theories of human decision-making. Bayesian rationality has its place in normative theory but a more realistic approach should be developed for descriptive purposes.

In view of the fact that human beings do not seem to maximize utility, one is tempted to jump to the conclusion that game theory has no relevance whatsoever for the description of economic reality. Of course, this conclusion would apply not only to game theory, but to most of microeconomic theory as well.

4 GAME LEARNING

The situation may not be quite as bad as it seems to be at first glance. Biological game theory is empirically successful in spite of the fact that animals like digger wasps or dung flies are not supposed to be utility maximizers. Forces of natural selection rather than rationality exert a pressure towards optimization.

To some extent, selection processes also go on in economic life – firms sometimes go bankrupt – but the tendency towards optimization produced by such events is probably a very weak one. Selection processes seem to be less important for economic behavior than learning processes.

The models of evolutionary economic theory initiated by Nelson and Winter (1982) are a very interesting step towards a more realistic formal theory of economic activity. In spite of the use of the term 'evolution,' these models rely on learning processes rather than selection processes. As Nelson and Winter have shown, competitive equilibrium can be approached by learning processes.

Psychological learning theory has some common features with utility theory. Learning is guided by rewards and punishment. In many cases learning can be expected to converge to a mode of behavior that optimizes the amount of rewards. In situations of strategic interaction, learning processes may converge to an equilibrium point of a suitably defined game.

Learning processes cannot converge to equilibrium unless there are sufficiently many repetitions of essentially the same decision situation. Moreover, the criteria of success and failure must be sufficiently clear.

Consider, for example, a flower auction held every day where the buyers are flower retailers. Over the years a buyer can obtain a considerable amount of experience. Moreover, the money earned by retailing the flowers offers a clear criterion of success. Afterwards a buyer can see whether he should have bought more or fewer flowers and whether he should have made a higher or lower bid. Under such circumstances, it may be possible to approach an equilibrium point of an auction game by a learning process.

Obviously, one cannot learn how to optimize buying a house if one does this only once or twice in one's lifetime. It is also hard to see how one could learn long-run optimization, since in the long run we are all dead – as Keynes said – before we can experience success or failure. Nevertheless, there is some scope for a descriptive application of non-cooperative game theory.

It seems to be necessary to develop a game learning theory. A theory of this kind cannot avoid looking at the question of dynamic stability. An equilibrium point cannot be approached unless it is dynamically stable with respect to the learning process.

Up to now, problems of game learning have found relatively little attention in the literature. The Brown–Robinson process of fictitious play permits an interpretation as a learning process, even if it has been introduced as a numerical method for the computation of optimal strategies in two-person zero-sum games (Brown, 1951; Robinson, 1951). As Shapley (1964) has shown, the process does not always converge for two-person non-zero-sum games, but it is quite possible that it does converge for many game models of important economic situations. Deschamps (1975) has shown that this is the case for the Cournot duopoly model under reasonable assumptions on cost and demand.

Various other learning processes have been considered in the psychological literature. The process proposed by Bush and Mosteller (1955) and other similar processes do not necessarily converge to optimum, even in one-person decision situations; they often produce the so-called phenomenon of 'probability matching,' which seemed to be observable in early experiments with animals and with human subjects. The newer literature on animal learning shows that in many experimental situations higher animals learn to optimize rather than to match probabilities (Mackintosh, 1974).

Siegel and others (1964) have shown that human subjects approach optimization behavior if monetary rewards are sufficiently high. Probability-matching is a phenomenon connected to the lack of appropriate motivation.

5 STRATEGIC INTERACTION AND LIMITED RATIONALITY

Economics as an empirical science cannot exclusively rely on learning approaches in the analysis of game situations. It is necessary to develop descriptive theories of game behavior in situations with little scope for learning. In order to do this one has to look at empirical evidence.

Experimental research on cooperative games and bargaining already has produced a number of interesting descriptive theories. A recent volume edited by Reinhard Tietz (1983) conveys an impression of the developments in this field. Typically, such descriptive theories formalize ideas on limited rationality decision-making.

Satisficing and the adaptation of aspiration levels rather than optimization play an important role.

The principle of balanced aspiration levels discovered by Tietz and Weber (1972) provides an illustrative example. This principle applies to repetitive bargaining situations similar to collective wage bargaining: the same two partners meet again and again in changing but structurally similar negotiations on a one-dimensional variable, e.g., a percentage wage increase. The rewards of both partners are not sufficiently comparable to permit equity considerations. (The principle of equal division and its variants have proved to be powerful predictors for other types of bargaining situations.)

According to the theory of Tietz and Weber, both bargainers form five 'aspiration levels': the first proposal, the planned result, the result regarded as minimally attainable, the point of conflict threat and the conflict limit. These levels (measured by questionnaires) form an ordinal five-point scale. The principle of balanced aspiration levels predicts that the highest of these levels satisfied by the agreement will be the same for both bargainers.

Actually, the theory is a little more complicated; it predicts not only the end result but also the sequence of concessions during the bargaining process. The scales are determined by past bargaining experiences.

The theory of Tietz and Weber has been supported by experiments performed by Scholz (1982), different from those that have been the original source of hypothesis construction. Obviously, a theory of this type cannot be developed by mere speculation in order to be tested afterwards. It has to be discovered as a regularity in a body of data. Later, it can be tested by other experiments.

Economic models involving collective bargaining could make use of the principle of balanced aspiration levels. For analytical convenience one could use continuous rather than discrete ordinal aspiration scales. If the goal of theory construction is descriptive rather than normative, this approach may be preferable to the use of normative game theory.

As Aumann rightly points out, theories based on utility maximization have the advantage of being connected to a 'major way of thinking, with many important and familiar implications, which have been part of economics for decades and even centuries' (p. 35). Is this really a reason to ignore theories with at least some empirical support in favor of other theories without empirical support? New ways of thinking have to be tried out, to see if they offer a better chance of descriptive success. Of course, not everybody will take part in such efforts, but at least some should feel encouraged to do so.

Perhaps many descriptive theories for specific contexts will finally grow together into a coherent theory of limited rationality. However, one cannot expect that an abstract principle of sweeping generality will be the end result of experimental research. Limited rationality decision-making seems to have a complex structure, which needs to be explored in detail.

REFERENCES

Aumann, R. J. (1959), 'Acceptable Points in General Cooperative *n*-Person Games', in: R. D. Luce and A. W. Tucker (eds), *Contributions to the Theory of Games*, vol. IV, Princeton University Press, pp. 287–324.

Billera, R. J., Heath, D. C. and Raanan, J. (1978), 'International Telephone Billing Rates: A Novel Application of Non-Atomic Game Theory', *Operations Research*, **26**, 956–65.

Bush, R. and Mosteller, F. (1955), *Stochastic Models of Learning*, John Wiley, New York.

Brown, G. W. (1951), 'Iterative Solution of Games by Fictitious Play', in *Activity Analysis of Production and Allocation*, John Wiley, New York, pp. 374–6.

Cournot, A. (1838), *Recherches sur les principes mathematiques de la theorie de richesses*, Paris.

Deschamps, R. (1975), 'An Algorithm of Game Theory Applied to the Duopoly Problem', *European Economic Review*, **6**, 187–94.

Haas, H. (1983), 'Conflict, Cooperation and Social Preference Functions', in J. Gruber (ed.), *Econometric Decision Models, Lecture Notes in Economics and Mathematical Systems*, no. 208, Springer-Verlag, Berlin, Heidelberg, New York and Tokyo.

Harsanyi, J. C. (1967–8), 'Games of Incomplete Information Played by Bayesian Players', *Management Science*, **14**, 159–82, 320–34, 486–502.

Huber, O. (1982), *Entscheiden als Problemlösen*, Verlag Hans Huber, Bern, Stuttgart and Vienna.

Kuhn, H. W. (1953), 'Extensive Games and the Problem of Information', in H. W. Kuhn and A. W. Tucker (eds), *Contributions to the Theory of Games*, vol. II, *Annals of Mathematical Studies*, **28**, 424–36.

Mackintosh, N. J. (1974), *The Psychology of Animal Learning*, Academic Press, London, New York and San Francisco.

Maynard Smith, J. (1982), *Evolution and the Theory of Games*, Cambridge University Press.

Maynard Smith, J. and Price, G. (1973), 'The Logic of Animal Conflict', *Nature*, no. 246, 15–18.

Nash, J. F. (1951), 'Non-Cooperative Games', *Annals of Mathematics*, **44**, 286–95.

Nelson, R. and Winter, S. (1982), *An Evolutionary Theory of Economic Changes*, Harvard University Press, Cambridge, Mass.

von Neumann, J. and Morgenstern, O. (1944), *Theory of Games and Economic Behavior*, Princeton University Press.

Robinson, J. (1951), 'An Iterative Model of Solving a Game', *Annals of Mathematics*, **54**, 296–301.

Schneider, E. (1932), *Reine Theorie monopolistischer Wirtschaftsformen*, Tubingen.

Scholz, R. W. (1982), *Dyadische Verhandlungen*, vol. 17 of *Mannheimer sozialwissenschaftliche Studien*, Verlag Anton Hain.

Schotter, A. and Schwödiauer, G. (1980), 'Economics and the Theory of Games', *Journal of Economic Literature*, **18**, 479–527.

Selten, R. (1979), 'Experimentelle Wirtschaftsforschung', *Rheinisch-Westfälische Akademie der Wissenschaften*, Vorträge N 287, Westdeutscher Verlag, pp. 42–57.

Shapley, L. S. (1964), 'Some Topics in Two-person Games', in M. Drescher, L. S. Shapley and A. W. Tucker (eds), *Advances in Game Theory*, Annals of Mathematics Studies no. 52, Princeton, NJ, pp. 1–28.

Shubik, M. (1962), 'Incentives, Decentralized Control, the Assignment of Joint Costs and Internal Pricing', *Management Science*, **8**, 325–43.

Siegel, S., Siegel, A.M. and Andrews, J. M. (1964), *Choice, Strategy and Utility*, McGraw-Hill, New York, San Francisco, Toronto and London.

Simon, H. A. (1957), *Models of Man*, John Wiley, New York.

Sneed, J. D. (1971), *The Logical Structure of Mathematical Physics*, Reidel, Dordrecht.

Stegmüller, W. (1973), *Probleme und Resultate der Wissenschaftstheorie und Analytischen Philosophie*, vol. II of *Theorie und Erfahrung, Studienausgabe Teil E*, Springer-Verlag, Berlin, Heidelberg and New York.

Stegmüller, W. (1980), *Neue Wege der Wissenschaftsphilosophie*, Springer-Verlag, Berlin, Heidelberg and New York.

Tietz, R. (ed.) (1983), *Aspiration Levels in Bargaining and Economic Decision Making, Lecture Notes in Economics and Mathematical Systems*, no. 213, Springer-Verlag, Berlin, Heidelberg, New York and Tokyo.

Tietz, R. and Weber, H.-J. (1972), 'On the Nature of the Bargaining Process in the KRESKO-Game', in H. Sauermann (ed.), *Beiträge zur experimentellen Wirtschaftsforschung – Contributions to Experimental Economics*, vol. III, Tübingen, pp. 305–34.

Tversky, A. and Kahnemann, D. (1973), 'Availability: A Heuristic for Judging Frequency and Probability', *Cognitive Psychology*, **5**, 207–32.

Comment

MARTIN SHUBIK

1 INTRODUCTION

The paper by Aumann is written on a broadly philosophical level, touching upon what we are trying to accomplish. He discusses our need for comprehension and the components of comprehension, the relationship between science and truth; then considers game theory as a descriptive science, as a normative device, and in its function as a means for classifying phenomena. He closes his preamble elegantly with the contemplation of game theory and mathematical economics as art forms, with a reference to the Baroque but none to the Rococo.

The second part deals with some solution concepts – the Nash equilibrium, the core, the von Neumann–Morgenstern stable set and the Shapley value. He ends with the remark that game-theoretic solution concepts should be judged and understood in terms of the quality and quantity of their applications.

I share many of Aumann's views, especially his acceptance of the utilization of a multiplicity of solution concepts as a useful way to develop game theory and its applications. My remarks are addressed primarily to the second part of his paper. They entail some change in emphasis, a supplementation of some of the comments on solutions and applications, and a few observations concerning new directions and open questions.

2 MODELS, PRESOLUTIONS AND SOLUTIONS

Rather than begin with a discussion of solution concepts, I believe that it is more fruitful to consider the modeling problems that are encountered prior to formulating the idea of a solution. In particular, game theory provides a language for the formal description of many phenomena encountered in political economy and other behavior sciences.

In general, game theory has provided a precise language for the description of conscious, goal-oriented, interactive but individualistically based behavior. The great book by von Neumann and Morgenstern contains within it four logically independent topics, each of which has been developed virtually independently: (1) a theory of measurable utility, (2) a description of a finite player game with finite choices in extensive form, (3) a description of a game in strategic form and normative theory on how to play two-person zero-sum games, and finally (4) a description of a game in coalitional form together with a stable set solution theory.

Although von Neumann and Morgenstern did not dwell upon this particular feature, there is a considerable distinction in the level of detail and nature of aggregation provided by the extensive, strategic and coalitional forms. Each can and has been used as a direct basis for modeling. The most highly aggregated is the coalitional form. In essence, it is *pre-institutional.* There are many problems in political economy where any attempt to model process in any detail would result in extremely *ad hoc* and unmanageably complicated models. Examples are provided by attempts to formalize face-to-face bargaining, or coalition formation or cartel structure. Rather than being lost in a maze of detail concerning explicit rules and institutions, the coalition form cuts straight through to the combinatorics, paying the price that the coalitions portrayed do not have an institutional equivalence, but are 'coalitions-in-being,' all being simultaneously potentially present with no costs of formation.

The coalition form either can be modeled directly from basic data such as traders, resources held and preferences, or it can be derived from a strategic form. An example of the former is the cooperative game model for exchange.

The solution concepts that have been the most used have been the *core* and the *value*. To a lesser extent the *stable set*, *bargaining set*, *nucleolus* and *kernel* have been considered.[1]

The calculation or specification of the *characteristic function* is virtually a presolution in and of itself. A great amount of modeling must be done before one can accept the characteristic function as an adequate representation of a game in coalitional form. In particular, virtually any form of externality among groups may require the modeler to modify the characteristic function as it rarely reflects the threat structure present.

Several alternatives to games in characteristic function form have been suggested; they include the Harsanyi function; a characteristic function together with a vector of n 'weights,' one for each player indicating his relative importance; and the game in *partition function* form, where the worth attached to coalition S depends upon the structure of the partition of the set $\bar{S}$ of remaining players.

The development of solutions based on the partition function has been relatively slight to date, with Lucas and Thrall considering stable sets and Myerson considering the value. It is, however, possible that a study of the partition function form will yield results in problems involving externalities.

The strategic form can be either derived from the extensive form or obtained directly as a characterization of empirical data. An example of the latter is provided by a two-person sealed bidding contest, where each player must submit a bid in units of $1 with an upper bound of $100 on bids. If we include zero, then this models immediately as a 101×101 matrix game.

The classical oligopoly analysis of Cournot can be regarded as a game in strategic form, as can the works of Bertrand, Edgeworth and Hotelling, although a dynamic 'story' appears to have accompanied some of them.

For games in strategic form, the dominant solution concept has been the non-cooperative equilibrium of Nash. As Aumann has noted, it has many manifestations and difficulties. Among the difficulties are a proliferation of equilibria, generic inefficiency (proved by Dubey and Rogawski), and little hope for finding nice stability properties for general classes of non-cooperative equilibria. Shubik (1982, chapter 10) provides a rogues' gallery of examples constructed over the years by Shapley, Shubik and others.

Among the modifications to plain non-cooperative equilibria are *proper*, *strong* and *perfect*. Various attempts have also been made to cut down on equilibria by requiring domination properties, interchangeability or other features such as Pareto optimality.

In spite of all of the pathologies that can be constructed, the non-cooperative equilibrium has had a long and central role in the study of oligopoly theory. As with all game-theoretic solution concepts, it is possible to construct examples in which the solution does not appear to be plausible and yet there may be a class of games for which a particular solution appears to be highly plausible and provides considerable insights.

Other solutions that have been applied to games in strategic form include the *maxmin* in several variations (including extreme paranoia, where everyone assumes that all others are out to get him), beat-the-average (or weighted average), and a long awaited but not yet formally published solution of Harsanyi and Selten which offers a rationale for the selection of a unique equilibrium point.

The extensive form is by far the most detailed representation of a game. All rules must be totally specified. Frequently it may require greater detail than is required for the proposed analysis. Thus, for example, in considering bilateral bargaining the economist may be content with all that can be packed into an Edgeworth box, which is the coalitional model, rather than attempting to provide a complete protocol on how bargaining takes place.

Possibly the key operational distinction between the strategic and extensive forms is that the former supresses detail concerning information, while the latter highlights this detail. The extensive form is both the most detailed game representation and the only one to provide the basis for a full process description of economic activity. A *solution* to a game in extensive form is described by a path down a game tree, and the path describes the *process*. The tree as a whole is defined by the rules of the game and provides the constraints on the set of processes. In essence, at least in the short run, the economic and other institutions of a society provide the rules of the game for the economy that enable us to define the game tree. Thus, the institutions can be viewed as the carriers of process.

In general, a game tree of large size can quickly become unmanageable, but it is my belief that, by being willing to model games with anywhere between one to ten to fifteen simultaneous moves, the essential features of most economic institutions, such as markets, firms, insurance companies and various financial markets, can be modeled and analyzed.

3 A SUMMARY OF SOME CONNECTIONS BETWEEN MODELS AND SOLUTIONS

Figure 1 presents a brief summary of some basic connections between the types of models and solutions. It must be noted, however, that in

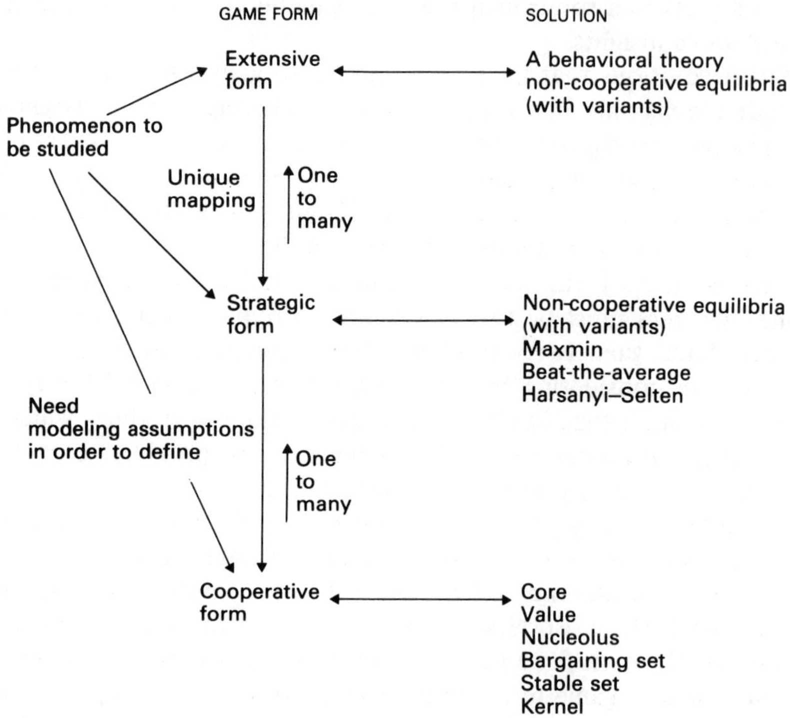

FIGURE 1

comments as brief as these it is not possible to discuss representations for important classes of games such as recursive games, stochastic games and other games involving a continuum of strategies. Going from the extensive form to the coalitional form, there is a progressive loss of detail, which explains why the upward mappings are 'one to many.'

4 SENSITIVITY ANALYSIS AND THE COMPETITIVE EQUILIBRIUM

In the game theory modeler's applied tool kit, sensitivity analysis looms large. Among the key features which must be checked are the following.

(1) Do the verbal description and the mathematics match? Examples of difficulties are provided in Debreu's Theory of Value – the

main theorem holds true independent of the number of agents (but the concept of competition depends on number) – or in the failure to rule out gambling in an exchange economy without exogenous uncertainty. (If the utility functions are not concave, gambling will arise endogenously even if the indifference curves are convex.)

(2) Should the phenomenon be modeled in extensive, strategic or cooperative form? Are there any special difficulties such as characterizing threats?

(3) What solutions are to be considered? Is there any intersolutional overlap; i.e., if we solve the same game two or more ways, do solutions overlap or coincide?

(4) How do solutions behave for (a) changes in information conditions, (b) changes in number of players, (c) changes in length of horizon (when relevant) and (d) 'natural' variations in some descriptions, assumptions or axioms?

Rather than go into further detail at this time, most of the modeling features noted above are illustrated in figure 2 for the competitive equilibrium of a differentiable exchange economy.

We may model directly in two different ways, one non-institutional, the other institutional. In the spirit of Edgeworth, we may immediately describe a game in coalitional form. Shapley and Shubik (1969) formalized this direct description of an exchange economy as a *market game*. They observed that for exchange economies the characteristic function description is adequate, as the threat possibilities are accounted for adequately.

As is shown in figure 2, we may then apply six different cooperative solution concepts to the market game. First we check for existence. Lucas (1969) showed that the stable set may not exist for a game that can be construed as a market game. Given that a solution does exist, we may now study its behavior under replication or when there is a continuum of small traders. For five different cooperative solution concepts, the solutions approach the competitive equilibrium solutions as the economies are replicated.

Starting with the same economic information, we may construct a strategic model in the style of Cournot. This type of model was formulated by Shubik (1973) as a *strategic market game*. It must contain a price formation mechanism and is more detailed and institutional than a market game.

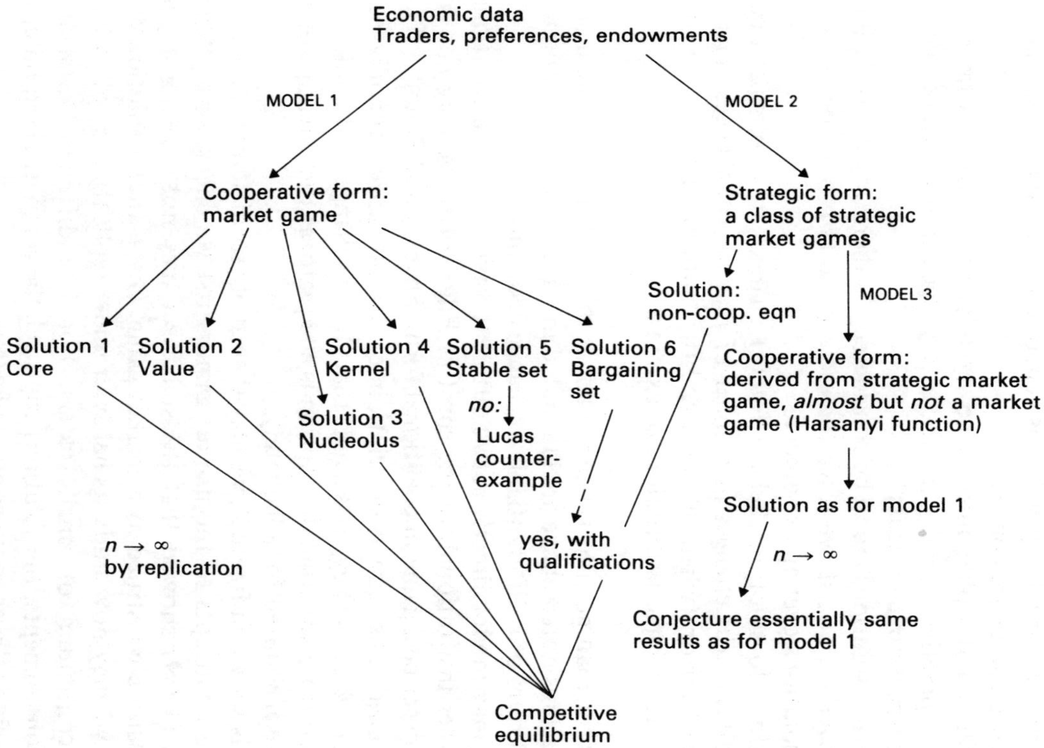

Economic data
Traders, preferences, endowments
MODEL 1
MODEL 2
Cooperative form:
market game
Strategic form:
a class of strategic
market games
Solution:
non-coop. eqn
MODEL 3
Solution 1
Core
Solution 2
Value
Solution 4
Kernel
Solution 5
Stable set
Solution 6
Bargaining
set
Cooperative form:
derived from strategic market
game, almost but not a market
game (Harsanyi function)
Solution 3
Nucleolus
no:
Lucas
counter-
example
Solution as for model 1
n → ∞
by replication
yes, with
qualifications
n → ∞
Conjecture essentially same
results as for model 1
Competitive
equilibrium

FIGURE 2

Given the strategic market game, we may establish that a pure strategy non-cooperative equilibrium exists. Then the behavior of the non-cooperative equilibria under replication may be examined. It can be shown that a subset of the non-cooperative equilibria approaches the competitive equilibria under replication.

Given the strategic market game, instead of applying a non-cooperative solution we may transform the model into a cooperative or coalitional form of a strategic market game. This will differ from a market game as the market structure and explicit price formation mechanism introduce externalities. Utilizing the coalitional form of a strategic market game, we may then consider cooperative solutions and their behavior under replication. It is suggested that any price formation mechanism satisfying the axioms of Dubey, Mas-Colell and Shubik (1980) will cause only a weak externality in large markets, and the various solutions for large games will approach the competitive equilibria.

5 STRATEGIC MARKET GAMES, OLIGOPOLY MONEY AND FINANCIAL INSTITUTIONS

In the remainder of these comments, I confine my specific remarks to two further topics – money and financial institutions and experimental gaming – then close with a few more general observations.

In the development and analysis of market games, core and value theory as applied to exchange, it was clear that, in spite of the interesting links being forged between the core and competitive equilibrium and the value and competitive equilibrium, the earliest of game-theoretic solution concepts clearly described by Cournot was missing. Cournot had presented an open model for the non-cooperative equilibrium, but a closed model that preserved the intrinsic symmetry of the players did not exist.

While attempting to construct a strategic game for equilibrium analysis, I noted that the normalization of the price of a commodity to serve as numeraire, which is an innocent assumption in general equilibrium theory, is not so for a strategic market game. This led to the conclusion that the commodity used for the numeraire in a strategic market game should enter symmetrically into all strategy sets. A way of doing this is to have it serve as the means of payment.

If we consider commodities as points, and *simple markets* in which good i is exchanged for j as a line connecting i with j, then an easy definition of a commodity money is suggested: it is a commodity for which all simple markets exist. This is illustrated in figure 3. Part (a) of the figure has commodity 1 as a money, as does part (b). In part (c) all four commodities are monies: in part (d), none.

We can use either 3(b) or 3(c) to construct a symmetric strategic market game. If we use 3(c), the strategy set of each player must be of dimension of $m(m-1)$ if there are m commodities and if the player can buy or sell in each market. If we use figure 3(b), his strategy is of size $2(m-1)$ where m is the number of commodities. This suggests that a direct strategic market game analogy to the Arrow–Debreu competitive exchange market is one with $m(m-1)/2$ markets, in which all commodities are monies and all individuals maximize utility.

A class of models different from the strategic market games with m monies, but empirically closer to the markets of a modern economy, are those with one money. These are the strategic market games analyzed by Shubik (1973), Shapley and Shubik (1977), Dubey and Shubik (1978, 1980) and others.

There is no logical imperative to choose between one or m monies (although possibly parsimony provides a reason). Transactions costs and casual empiricism suggest that one money is a better approximation to reality than m.

If only one money is considered (or for that matter any number of monies less than or equal to $m-2$), a cash flow or liquidity constraint appears in the optimization problem. In the one-trading-period game it is not possible to liquidate all resources and buy a bundle of equal value without credit. This suggests the introduction of credit. But this in turn calls for the invention of credit-granting

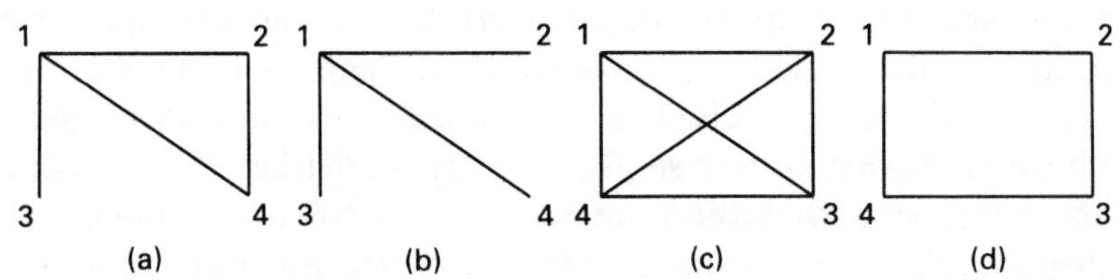

FIGURE 3

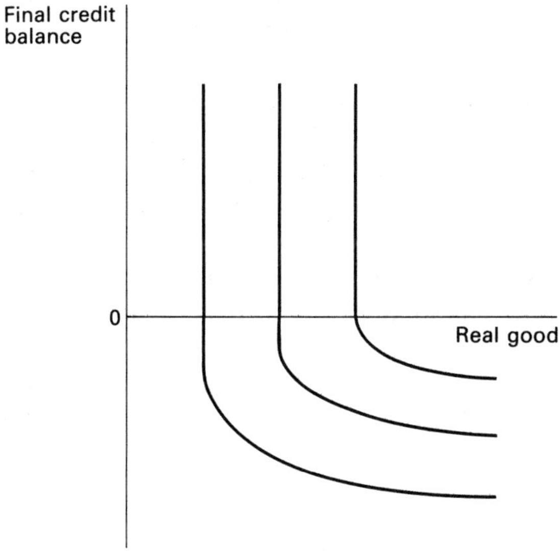

FIGURE 4

facilities and a specification of payoffs to those who are unable to pay back their credits. This calls for bankruptcy conditions. A simple way to introduce credit is to consider an $(m + 1)$st commodity in the utility functions defined on R, as indicated in figure 4. Positive credit left over at the end of the game may be of no value, but negative balances cause a loss to the individual.

Further investigations have considered fiat money, and exchange and production. The general thrust of this approach is to construct the simplest of games in extensive form which adequately portray institutions such as firms, markets, stock markets, commercial banks, insurance companies and central banks.

6 GAME THEORY, BEHAVIORAL THEORIES AND GAMING

Paradoxically, one of the most important uses of the theory of games is in making precise the limitations on rational strategic behavior. Interest in experimental gaming has grown along with game theory. In particular, experimental gaming imposes upon the game designer not only the logical consistency and completeness conditions of game theory but also simplicity and playability conditions, which are frequently the earmark of good institutional design.

Experiments have been done with games in extensive, strategic, characteristic function and other forms. An extensive literature has been generated by Siegel and Fouraker, Fouraker, Shubik and Siegel, Hoggatt, Friedman, Rapaport, Selten, Smith, Maschler, Flood, Shubik, Plott and many others.[2] No solution concept appears to be universally powerful, but several solutions, such as the core and non-cooperative equilibrium, appear as reasonably good predictors in certain contexts.

It is my belief that there will be a continued growth in experimental gaming and a fruitful interchange between the development of solution theory and experimentation and the modeling of institutions and experimental gaming.

7 CONCLUDING REMARKS

As is not uncommon with other theories, the current growth and successes of game theory have led to a deeper understanding of its weaknesses and of many of the weaknesses in economic theory. In particular, the need for further development and experimentation with solution theories is clear. There is also a considerable need to develop infinite horizon game theory. And has been indicated in the survey by Green, much work remains to be done on games with incomplete information.

The profusion of modifications to non-cooperative equilibrium solutions indicates that we are some distance from having a satisfactory theory (or theories) of multistage play. Possibly the most important problem confronting game theory, and for that matter economic theory at this time, is the development of satisfactory concepts of behavior with limited rationality. I suggest that it has been the 'super rationality' and formal precision of game-theoretic methods, together with experimental gaming experience, that have made the reasons for the necessity for the development of limited rationality solutions so clear.

NOTES

1 As no attempt is made here to provide an exhaustive survey with the needed references; the reader is referred to the coverage in Shubik (1982, 1984).

2 For bibliographic references see Shubik (1975a, 1975b) and Plott (1982).

REFERENCES

Dubey, P., Mas-Colell, A. and Shubik, M. (1980), 'Efficiency Properties of Strategic Market Games: An Axiomatic Approach', *Journal of Economic Theory*, **22**, 339–62.

Dubey, P. and Shubik, M. (1978), 'The Noncooperative Equilibria of a Closed Trading Economy with Market Supply and Bidding Strategies', *Journal of Economic Theory*, **17**, 1–20.

Dubey, P. and Shubik, M. (1980), 'A Strategic Market Game with Price and Quantity Strategies', *Zeitschrift fur Nationalokonomie*, **40**, 25–34.

Lucas, W. F. (1969), 'The Proof that a Game May Not Have a Solution', *Transactions of the American Mathematical Society*, **137**, 219–29.

Plott, C. R. (1982), 'Industrial Organization Theory and Experimental Economics', *Journal of Economic Literature*, **20**, 1485–527.

Shapley, L. S. and Shubik, M. (1969), 'On Market Games', *Journal of Economic Theory*, **1**, 9–25.

Shapley, L. S. and Shubik, M. (1977), 'Trade Using One Commodity as a Means of Payment', *Journal of Political Economy*, **85**, 937–68.

Shubik, M. (1973), 'Commodity Money, Oligopoly, Credit and Bankruptcy in a General Equilibrium Model', *Western Economic Journal*, **11**, 24–38.

Shubik, M. (1975a), *Games for Society, Business and War*, Elsevier, Amsterdam.

Shubik, M. (1975b), *The Uses and Methods of Gaming*, Elsevier, New York.

Shubik, M. (1982), *Game Theory in the Social Sciences*, vol. I, MIT Press, Cambridge, Mass.

Shubik, M. (1984), *Game Theory in the Social Sciences*, vol. II, MIT Press, Cambridge, Mass.

2

Imperfect Competition in General Equilibrium: An Overview of Recent Work

OLIVER D. HART

1 INTRODUCTION

The 1930s saw, with the publication of the books by Chamberlin (1933) and Robinson (1933), an upsurge of interest in the theory of imperfect competition. The intensive work that this inspired led some (e.g. Triffin, 1940) to hold out the hope that a general theory of monopolistic competition would be developed that would be comparable in scope to the Walrasian theory of general equilibrium under perfect competition. Unfortunately, in spite of a number of important contributions, particularly over the last 20 years or so, this has not happened. In this paper I want to consider what has been achieved and why we have fallen well short of the goal laid down by Triffin.

A truly general theory of monopolistic or imperfect competition would incorporate not only non-negligible agents, but also product differentiation and imperfect information. The latter issues have in fact been the focus of a great deal of the recent work on imperfect competition, most of it in a partial equilibrium setting. In the present paper, however, I will retain the traditional assumptions of homogeneous products and perfect information and will depart from the Walrasian model only in allowing large, non-price-taking agents. I will also confine myself to a static, 'one-shot' situation, thus ignoring much recent work on dynamic, multi-period games. These simplifications are perhaps justifiable, since my particular interest, which also seemed to be that of Triffin, will be the problems that market power raises for *general* equilibrium, as opposed to *partial* equilibrium, analysis. That is, I will be interested in models that emphasize the circular relationship between the demand facing monopolistic competitors, their price and quantity decisions, and their profits and demand (on this, see Nikaidô, 1975).

Two main approaches have been taken in the study of imperfect competition in general equilibrium. One may be called the subjective (or perceived or conjectural) demand approach; the other, for purposes of contrast, may be termed the objective demand approach.

The subjective demand approach is considered in section 2 and the objective demand approach in sections 3 and 4. In section 5, drawing on the recent literature on rational conjectures, I discuss the question of what are appropriate conjectures for each agent to have about other agents' reactions (in this section, the analysis is strictly partial equilibrium). Finally, in section 6 I consider some of the recent work on imperfectly competitive equilibria in large economies and the bearing that this work has on the old question about the meaning of perfect competition.

2 SUBJECTIVE DEMAND

The subjective demand approach to general equilibrium was developed in a seminal paper by Negishi (1961) (see also Negishi, 1972). Although some refinements have been made by other authors, his paper is still an excellent reference.

Negishi divides firms into two types: perfect competitors and monopolistic competitors. The former take prices as given, while the latter recognize that they can affect some (but not all) prices. Let $N^1 = \{1, \ldots, n'\}$ be the set of perfectly competitive firms and $N^2 = \{n'+1, \ldots, n\}$ be the set of monopolistically competitive firms, so that there are n firms in all. There are l goods. Each firm $j = 1, \ldots, n$ has a production set $Y_j \subset R^l$. Assume

$$Y_j \text{ is convex, closed and } 0 \in Y_j \, (j = 1, \ldots, n). \tag{A1}$$

As usual, negative components of $y \in Y_j$ denote inputs and positive components denote outputs. We also assume

$$\sum_j Y_j \cap \left(-\sum_j Y_j\right) = \{0\} \quad \text{(irreversible production)} \tag{A2}$$

$$\sum_j Y_j \cap R^l_+ = \{0\} \quad \text{(no free lunch).} \tag{A3}$$

There are assumed to be m consumers, each of whom is a price-taker. Each consumer has the consumption set R^l_+. Consumer i has a utility function $U_i(x)$ defined on R^l_+, and an initial endowment vector $\bar{x}_i$. We assume

$$\bar{x}_i \in R^l_{++} \text{ and } U_i \text{ is a continuous, non-decreasing, quasi-concave,}^1 \text{ unsaturated,}^2 \text{ utility function } (i = 1, \ldots, m). \qquad \text{(A4)}$$

Each consumer i has an initial shareholding $\bar{\theta}_{ij} \geqslant 0$ in each firm j, where $\Sigma_i \bar{\theta}_{ij} = 1$ for all j.

For each monopolistically competitive firm $j \in N^2$, let $J^j \subset \{1, \ldots, l\}$ denote those goods for which firm j is an imperfect competitor; that is, $k \in J^j$ means that firm j has some monopoly or monopsony power with respect to good k. Negishi assumes

$$J^j \cap J^{j'} = \phi \text{ if } j \neq j' \in N^2. \qquad \text{(A5)}$$

That is, if j is an imperfect competitor with respect to good k, then no other firm is. (A5) is a strong assumption which rules out both oligopoly and bilateral monopoly. We return to it later. Let $L = \{1, \ldots, l\}$. Given the J^j, we may compute

$$\bigcup_{j \in N^2} J^j$$

which equals the set of goods for which there is at least one imperfect competitor and

$$L \setminus \bigcup_{j \in N^2} J^j,$$

the set of 'competitive' goods. Note that the latter set may or may not be empty. We will, however, assume

$$L \setminus J^j \neq \phi \text{ for all } j. \qquad \text{(A6)}$$

That is, no firm is a price-setter for all goods.

Each firm $j \in N^2$ is assumed to have a subjective (inverse) demand curve for its outputs $k \in J^j$ and supply curve for its inputs $k \in J^j$ given by

$$P^*_{jj} = P^*_{jj}(y^*_j, p, \omega). \qquad (2.1)$$

Here, $\omega = (x_1, \ldots, x_m, y_1, \ldots, y_n)$ is some initial, status quo allocation and $p = (p_1, \ldots, p_l)$ is the corresponding status quo price vector. The interpretation of this subjective demand (or supply) curve is that, if the economy is initially in the position (p, ω), then firm j conjectures that, if it changed its production plan from y_j to y_j^*, the prices of goods $k \in J^j$ would change from p_{J^j} to $P_{J^j}^*$. Prices for goods $k \notin J^j$ are conjectured not to change. Let $l^j = \# J^j$. We assume

$P_{J^j}^*(y_j^*, p, \omega)$ is a continuous function:

$$Y_j \times R_+^l \times R_+^{ml} \times \prod_{j=1}^{n} Y_j \rightarrow R^{l^j}, \text{ which satisfies } P_{J^j}^*(y_j, p, \omega) = p_{J^j}. \tag{A7}$$

(A7) implies that each firm can form conjectures about how prices are affected by a change in its production plan given any conceivable starting point for the economy. The last part of (A7) is a consistency requirement, which says that, if the firm retains the production plan y_j in the status quo allocation, prices will not change; in other words, the phrase 'status quo' means what it says. Put another way, the firm's subjective demand curve passes through the point where it finds itself.

So far the conjectures are of a very general form. On economic grounds, it seems desirable to rule out money illusion. Therefore we assume

$P_{J^j}^*(y_j^*, p, \omega)$ is homogeneous of degree one in p. (A8)

Given their conjectures, each monopolistically competitive firm is assumed to maximize profits. This leads to the following definition of equilibrium.

Monopolistically Competitive Equilibrium (MCE) An MCE is a $(n+m+1)$-tuple $[p, (x_i)_{i=1,\ldots,m}, (y_j)_{j=1,\ldots,n}]$, where $p \in R_+^l$, such that

$$x_i \in R_+^l \text{ maximizes } U_i(x) \text{ subject to } p \cdot x \leqslant p \cdot \bar{x}_i + \sum_{j=1}^{n} \bar{\theta}_{ij} p \cdot y_j \quad (i = 1, \ldots, m) \tag{2.2}$$

$$\text{for all } j \in N^1, y_j \text{ maximizes } p \cdot y \text{ subject to } y \in Y_j \tag{2.3}$$

for all $j \in N^2$, $y_j^* = y_j$ maximizes

$$P_{J^j}^*[y_j^*, p, (x_1, \ldots, x_m, y_1, \ldots, y_n)]\, y_{J^j}^* + p_{L \setminus J^j} y_{L \setminus J^j}^*$$

subject to $y_j^* \in Y_j$ (2.4)

$$\sum_{i=1}^{m} x_i - \sum_{j=1}^{n} y_j - \sum_{i=1}^{m} \bar{x}_i = 0. \tag{2.5}$$

The interpretation of this equilibrium is straightforward. (2.3) says that perfectly competitive firms maximize profits as price-takers. (2.4) says that, given the status quo $(p, (x_1, \ldots, x_m, y_1, \ldots, y_n))$, each monopolistically competitive firm conjectures that any change in its production plan from y_j to y_j^* will lead to new prices for the goods it controls such that its profits will fall. Note that profits here are measured in some sense using the goods $L \backslash J^j$ as numeraire; i.e., their prices in (2.4) are held constant. ((A6) guarantees that the numeraire set is non-empty for each firm.)

In the literature on imperfect competition, much attention has been paid to proving the existence of an MCE. In order to establish existence in the above model, we need a further assumption:

> The function $P_{J^j}^*(y_j^*, p, \omega)\, y_{J^j}^* + p_{L\backslash J^j} y_{L\backslash J^j}^*$ is quasi-concave in y_j^* for all (p, ω) $(j = 1, \ldots, n)$. (A9)

Proposition 2.1 Assume (A1)–(A9). Then an MCE exists.

The proof is along the lines of Negishi (1961, 1972) and will be omitted. The basic idea is as follows. First, we bound the consumption and production sets as in Debreu (1959). Let S be the price simplex and F a bounded set of allocations ω. Consider a correspondence from $S \times F$ into itself defined as follows: $(p^A, \omega^A) \to (p^B, \omega^B)$, where x_i^B is a solution of (2.2) at prices p^A and production plans y_j^A but where we replace $p^A \cdot y_j^A$ by $\max(0, p^A \cdot y_j^A)$ in the budget constraint; y_j^B is a solution of (2.3) for $j \in N^1$ at prices p^A; $y_j^* = y_j^B$ is a solution of (2.4) for $j \in N^2$ given the status quo (p^A, ω^A); and p^B maximizes $p \cdot (\Sigma_i x_i^A - \Sigma_j y_j^A - \Sigma_i \bar{x}_i^A)$ over S. (A9) (and the convexity of Y_j) guarantees that this correspondence is convex-valued. It is also closed-graph. Therefore Kakutani's fixed-point theorem can be applied. The fixed point can be shown to be an MCE. Note that in equilibrium all firms make non-negative profits (by (A1)) and so $\max(0, p \cdot y_j) = p \cdot y_j$.

Negishi (1961) in fact considered the special case where the subjective demand curve $P_{J^j}^*$ satisfies

$$P_k^*(y_j^*, p, \omega) = a_k(p, \omega)\, y_{jk}^* + b_k(p, \omega) \text{ for all } k \in J^j \tag{2.6}$$

where $a_k(p, \omega) < 0$. That is to say, the price of each good is conjectured to depend only on the quantity of that good, and the dependence is linear. The condition $a_k < 0$ says that demand curves slope downwards for outputs ($y^*_{jk} > 0$) and supply curves slope upwards for inputs ($y^*_{jk} < 0$). Under these assumptions, the profit function (2.4) is quadratic and so (A9) is automatically satisified. Negishi (1961) recognized, however, that linearity of demand was a much stronger assumption than necessary, and that quasi-concavity of the profit function was the crucial assumption.

Negishi (1972) generalized the model to allow for demand interdependence, but retained the linear structure; that is, he assumed

$$P^*_{jj}(y^*_j, p, \omega) = y^*_{jj}A(p, \omega) + B(p, \omega), \tag{2.7}$$

where A is a $l^j \times l^j$ matrix and B is a l^j dimensional vector. (A9) will then be satisfied if A is negative semi-definite.

There are a number of comments and criticisms that can be made about Negishi's approach. Let me start with some minor ones. First, it is not clear to me why bilateral monopoly and oligopoly need to be ruled out. In the case of bilateral monopoly, one can imagine that both the supplier of an output and the demander of an input have subjective demand curves of the form (2.1). The formal definition of equilibrium remains the same, and existence can be established in the same way. (Below, however, we will give some economic reasons for ruling out bilateral monopoly.) Oligopoly can also, at least formally, be incorporated. Suppose that two firms are producing the same good k. Write firm j's conjectures about the price of good k as ${}^jP^*_k(y^*_j, p, \omega)$. This can be interpreted as the price that firm j thinks will rule if it changes its production plan from y_j to y^*_j. If these conjectures satisfy (A7) and (A9), existence can again be established. To make sense of these conjectures, one must assume that different firms always charge the same price for the same good, so that there is indeed a 'ruling' price. Thus, the model is closer to Cournot than to Bertrand. Note, however, that firm j does not necessarily have to suppose that other firms keep their outputs the same. The conjecture ${}^jP^*_k$ may incorporate all sorts of output reactions in response to the change from y_j to y^*_j.

Second, assumption (A9) that profit functions are quasi-concave is clearly very strong. Much of the recent literature has been concerned with this assumption, and we will return to it in the next section. The assumption of non-increasing returns to scale is also strong in the context of imperfect competition and robs the model of some of its interest. This assumption, like (A9), is made to ensure that each monopolistically competitive firm has a convex-valued reaction correspondence. Silvestre (1977a) has shown that this assumption may be weakened as follows. Rule out monopsony, and assume that each monopolistic competitor produces a single output. We may then define the total cost function $C_j^T(p; y_g)$ for firm j as the minimum cost of producing y_g units of output given the price vector p (firm j is a price-taker with respect to its inputs). Silvestre assumes that $C_j^T(p; 0) = 0$ and $C_j^T(p; y_g)$ is differentiable, so that there are no set-up costs. Let $C_j^M(p; y_g)$ equal marginal cost. Silvestre allows $C_j^M(p; y_g)$ to be decreasing in y_g, but insists that it be convex in y_g and that $C_j^M(p; 0)$ be finite. Under the additional assumptions that conjectured demand curves are linear, that the marginal revenue curve is steeper than the marginal cost curve at the origin, and that the input isoquants are convex to the origin for each value of y_g, Silvestre is able to establish the existence of an MCE.

The point is that the steepness condition plus the convexity of marginal cost guarantee that the solution of the equation, marginal revenue equals marginal cost, is unique (or is an interval). Thus, reaction correspondences are convex-valued and existence follows straightforwardly.

Silvestre's contribution is interesting in that it shows that some forms of increasing returns can be incorporated into Negishi's model. On the other hand, it clearly relies on some very strong assumptions.

A third point to note is that, in Negishi's work and most generalizations, it is assumed that all firms, both perfect competitors and monopolistic competitors, maximize profit. In a competitive framework, this is usually accepted without question as the right objective for a firm. Under imperfect competition matters are more complicated, a point noted a long time ago by Marshall (1922: 402) and emphasized more recently by Gabszewicz and Vial (1972).[3] The reason is that the owners of a firm are interested not in monetary profit *per se*, but rather in what this profit can buy. Given that a monopolistically competitive firm can influence prices, the owners may prefer low monetary profit but favourable prices for consumption goods to high monetary profit and unfavourable prices.

This argument suggests that we should substitute owner utility maximization for profit maximization as the firm's goal. Unfortunately, things are not that simple. If owners have different tastes, they will have different trade-offs concerning high monetary profit versus favourable consumption goods prices. That is, each owner will have his own private objective function which he would like the firm to pursue, and the problem then is how to aggregate these into an overall objective function. (A similar aggregation problem arises if owners have the same tastes, but different subjective demand curves.)

In the imperfect competition literature, this aggregation-of-preferences problem has largely been ignored.[4] In some work (e.g. Fitzroy, 1974; Arrow and Hahn, 1971), more general objective functions than profit maximization, such as utility maximization, have been considered. In fact, Arrow and Hahn do not refer to the firm's objective function at all, but simply assume that the firm's reactions are continuous functions (or convex-valued correspondences) of the status quo position. This is enough to establish existence of equilibrium, but, of course, underlying this assumption must be a concavity condition similar to (A1) and (A9). It should also be pointed out that the precise assumptions made by Arrow and Hahn are overly strong and can be replaced by a weaker and more appealing set of assumptions, as shown by Silvestre (1977b).

Let me now turn to some comments about the overall Negishi approach. It is clear that the framework provided by Negishi is a very general one for looking at imperfect competition. This, however, is a weakness as well as a strength. The problem is that the very generality of the model gives it very little predictive power. *Given* particular subjective demand curves or conjectures, as embodied in (2.1) and (A7), the model will of course generate a small number of equilibria (possibly only one). However, the model does not tell us how these conjectures are formed. To an outside observer who is asked to predict the market outcome but who does not know what these conjectures are, almost anything could be an equilibrium; i.e., the set of allocations that are MCEs for *some* conjectures satisfying (2.1) and (A7) is very large.

To put it slightly differently, an economy with given demand conditions, sizes of firms, etc., could end up in a highly monopolistic state or a highly competitive state, depending on whether firms conjecture that they face low elasticities of demand or high ones. (The Arrow–Debreu model is a special case of the Negishi model in which firms' conjectured demand curves are perfectly elastic.) Negishi's theory does not tell us which is more likely. This does not seem very satisfactory. If, for example, agents are large relative to the economy, our feeling is that they will face low demand elasticities and so a highly monopolistic outcome is likely, whereas if agents are small relative to the economy, our feeling is that they will face high demand elasticities and so a highly competitive outcome is likely. In order to distinguish between these cases, however, we need to say something about what it means for conjectures to be *correct*; i.e., we must study *objective* rather than *subjective* demand. To this we now turn.

3 OBJECTIVE DEMAND (I)

In this and the next section we consider a number of general equilibrium models in which firms' actions are based on 'objective' rather than 'subjective' demand conditions. What distinguishes the objective demand approach from the subjective demand approach is the explicit modelling of a non-cooperative game that firms play.

Two classes of models have received most attention in the literature. One is based on the Cournot–Nash quantity setting approach and the other on price-setting behaviour. We consider the Cournot–Nash approach first. Two early contributions here are by Gabszewicz and Vial (1972) and Fitzroy (1974). The model presented below is similar in spirit to their models, but it differs in a number of respects.[5]

An important point that must be made at the outset is that, as soon as one moves from subjective to objective demand models, it is necessary, both for reasons of tractability and for reasons of economic sense, to become more specific. It is impossible to construct a completely general 'objective' model of imperfect competition. In narrowing the focus, therefore, let me begin by ruling out bilateral monopoly from our consideration. There is a sound economic reason for doing this. We have no satisfactory theory of bilateral monopoly even in partial equilibrium, and therefore we can hardly expect to develop one in general equilibrium. Among other things, cooperative behaviour may well be observed, and equilibrium may be characterized by price and quantity contracts rather than by a single uniform price. These considerations are outside the scope of the present paper.[6] For the same reasons, we will rule out all situations in which there are large agents on both sides of a market. The reader should understand that this assumption is being made in what follows, even though we will not always be explicit about it.

We begin with a fairly simple model. Consider the model of the last section. Assume that goods $L_1 = \{1, \ldots, l_1\}$ are non-produced goods. Let $L_2 = \{l_1 + 1, \ldots, l\}$ be produced goods and suppose that $L_1, L_2 \neq \phi$. Assume that consumers have positive endowments of non-produced goods:

$$\bar{x}_{ik} > 0 \text{ for all } i \text{ and } k \in L_1, \text{ and } \bar{x}_{ik} \geqslant 0 \text{ for all } i \text{ and } k \in L_2. \quad \text{(A10)}$$

Assume also that firms use non-produced goods to produce produced goods; i.e.,

$$y_{jk} \geqslant 0 \text{ for all } k \in L_2,\ y_{jk} \leqslant 0 \text{ for all } k \in L_1\ (j = 1, \ldots, n). \quad \text{(A11)}$$

Consumers consume both non-produced and produced goods. We replace (A4) by (A4′):

For each i: U_i is continuous, non-decreasing, strictly increasing in coordinates $k = 1, \ldots, l_1$, and quasi-concave. (A4′)

For each i, let $\Xi_i(p, w)$ be consumer i's demand correspondence when prices are p and i's wealth is w; i.e.,

$$\Xi_i(p, w) = \{x \mid x \in R^l_+ \text{ maximizes } U_i(x) \text{ subject to } p \cdot x \leqslant w\}. \quad (3.1)$$

We assume:

For each $k \in L_2$, there exists $\bar{p}_k < \infty$ such that:

if $p \in R^l_+$, $p_1 = 1$, $p_k \geqslant \bar{p}_k$, then for all i and $w > 0$,
$$x \in \Xi_i(p, w) \Rightarrow x_k = 0. \quad \text{(A12)}$$

(A12) says that there is a finite reservation price for each of the produced goods. Among other things, it rules out cases where an imperfectly competitive firm can increase its revenue indefinitely by reducing its output level and driving price to infinity. (Thus, (A12) rules out Cobb–Douglas utility functions.)

We have noted that there is in general no simple objective function for the firm under imperfect competition. In order to avoid this problem, we will assume that there is a class of individuals, called capitalists, who are the sole owners of firms and who consume only a single good (money?).[7] This single good is assumed to be one of the non-produced goods, say good 1. We also assume that each capitalist has an initial shareholding in only one firm. Under these conditions, the owners of each firm will all want their firm to maximize profit in terms of good 1, i.e. with good 1 as the numeraire. This is therefore the objective we assume that each firm pursues. Note that, if one capitalist has initial shareholdings in several firms, he will want the sum total of profits of all these firms to be maximized. This does not imply, however, that each firm should maximize profit, since as one firm's profit increases another's may fall.

The assumptions about ownership and the tastes of capitalists are clearly very strong. Our formal analysis below does not rely on these assumptions, but without them it is not clear why firms should maximize profit in terms of good 1 (or any other good). Later on we will discuss a way of relaxing these assumptions.

We will assume that all consumers are perfect competitors (this is reasonable if there is a large number of them) and that all firms are imperfect competitors. Each firm is assumed to choose its production plan to maximize profit, taking as given the production plans of all other firms. Given these production plans, we assume that prices of all goods adjust to clear markets. Thus the solution concept adopted is Cournot–Nash.

Suppose that the production plans $y_1, \ldots, y_n$ are selected. Relative to these production plans, we can define an exchange economy in which each consumer i has a modified initial endowment equal to

$$\bar{x}_i + \sum_{j=1}^{n} \bar{\theta}_{ij} y_j, \tag{3.2}$$

in which each consumer i faces the budget constraint

$$p \cdot x_i \leqslant p\left(\bar{x}_i + \sum_{j=1}^{n} \bar{\theta}_{ij} y_j\right) \tag{3.3}$$

as in (2.2); and where the market-clearing condition is

$$\sum_i x_i - \sum_i \left(\bar{x}_i + \sum_j \bar{\theta}_{ij} y_j\right) = 0 \tag{3.4}$$

as in (2.5). This exchange economy may have one equilibrium, several or none (the latter may be the case if some of the components of (3.2) are negative). Let

$$F = \{(y_1, \ldots, y_n) | \, y_j \in Y_j \text{ for all } j \text{ and there exist } p \in R^l_+ \text{ and } (x_1, \ldots, x_m) \text{ satisfying (2.2) and (2.5)}\} \tag{3.5}$$

be the set of vectors of production plans for which there is at least one exchange equilibrium. Given $y = (y_1, \ldots, y_n) \in F$, let

$$\pi(y) = \{p \mid p \geqslant 0, p_1 = 1, \text{ and there exists } (x_1, \ldots, x_m) \text{ satisfying (2.2) and (2.5)}\} \tag{3.6}$$

be the set of corresponding normalized equilibrium prices. Since we wish each firm to have a well defined pay-off as a function of its production plan, we assume that, in the case where $\pi(y)$ contains more than one element, an *exogenous* deterministic selection is made. Hence let $p: F \to R^l_+$ be a selection function satisfying

$$p(y) \in \pi(y) \text{ for all } y. \tag{3.7}$$

If $y \in F$ is chosen, $p(y)$ will then be the price vector that rules. Given y, we write $y_{-j} = (y_1, \ldots, y_{j-1}, y_{j+1}, \ldots, y_n)$ and $y = (y_{-j}, y_j)$.

Cournot-Nash equilibrium (CNE) A CNE relative to the selection function p is a $(m+n+1)$-tuple $[\hat{p}, (\hat{x}_i)_{i=1,\ldots,m}, (\hat{y}_j)_{j=1,\ldots,n}]$, where $\hat{p} \in R^l_+$, such that

$$x = \hat{x}_i \text{ maximizes } U_i(x) \text{ subject to } \hat{p} \cdot x \leqslant \hat{p} \cdot \bar{x}_i + \sum_{j=1}^{n} \bar{\theta}_{ij} \hat{p} \cdot \hat{y}_j \quad (i = 1, \ldots, m) \tag{3.8}$$

$$\sum_{i=1}^{m} \hat{x}_i - \sum_{j=1}^{n} \hat{y}_j - \sum_{i=1}^{m} \bar{x}_i = 0 \tag{3.9}$$

$$(\hat{y}) = \hat{p}, \text{ and } p(\hat{y}_{-j}, \hat{y}_j)\, \hat{y}_j \geqslant p(\hat{y}_{-j}, y_j)\, y_j \text{ for all } y_j \in Y_j, (\hat{y}_{-j}, y_j) \in F. \tag{3.10}$$

Note that we are allowing firms to choose only production plans that result in some exchange equilibrium (i.e. $(\hat{y}_{-j}, y_j) \in F$). Implicitly, we are making the somewhat unsatisfactory assumption that when equilibrium doesn't exist this has (unspecified) disastrous consequences for all firms.

In order to establish the existence of a CNE, we need further assumptions. Let $F_j = \{y_j \mid y_j \in Y_j$ and there exists y_{-j} such that $(y_{-j}, y_j) \in F\}$.

Proposition 3.1 Assume (A1), (A4′), (A10)–(A12). Assume also that (a) F is bounded; (b) $F = \Pi_{j=1}^{n} F_j$; (c) each F_j is homeomorphic to a convex set; (d) $\pi(y)$ is a singleton for all $y \in F$; and (e) the solution to the problem

$$\max_{\substack{y_j \in Y_j \\ (y_{-j}, y_j) \in F}} \quad p(y_{-j}, y_j)\, y_j$$

is unique for all $y_{-j} \in \Pi_{k \neq j} F_k$ $(j = 1, \ldots, n)$. Then a CNE exists.

The proof is along the lines of Gabszewicz and Vial (1972) and Fitzroy (1974), and we will only sketch it. First, it is easy to show that F is non-empty (since $0 \in F$) and closed and hence, by (b), so is F_j. For each $y \in \Pi F_j$, let $y' = (y_j')_{j=1,\ldots,n}$, where y_j' maximizes $p(y_{-j}, \tilde{y})\, \tilde{y}$ over $\tilde{y} \in F_j$. (d) implies that $p(y)$ is continuous in y, and therefore, by (e), the mapping $y \to y'$ is a continuous function from F to F. Therefore, by Brouwer's fixed-point theorem, the mapping has a fixed point. This fixed point is a CNE.

The assumptions of Proposition 3.1 are extraordinarily strong. (e) is similar to (A9) of the last section (note that (e) holds if $p(y_{-j}, y_j)y_j$ is strictly quasi-concave in y_j and Y_j is convex). The difference is that with subjective demand it is perhaps a matter of psychology whether perceived profit functions are quasi-concave, whereas, now, whether (e) (or (b)–(d)) are satisfied is an objective matter. In fact, there seems no reason at all to think that (b)–(e) will be satisfied in general. Roberts and Sonnenschein (1977) have given a number of examples where, even when the Y_j's are convex and (b)–(d) are satisfied, (e) is not satisfied and a CNE fails to exist. None of these examples seems at all pathological.[8] Furthermore, it is not even clear what assumptions on preferences and production possibilities are required to ensure (e).

One response to the non-existence problem is to allow firms to choose mixed strategies (this could also be considered in the subjective demand model of section 2). This will get over non-convexities arising from the non-satisfaction of (b), (c) and (e). However, if (d) is not satisfied, then $p(y)$ may be *discontinuous* at some y (see, e.g., K. Roberts (1980)), and, as a recent paper by Dierker and Grodal (1982) shows, even a mixed-strategy equilibrium may fail to exist.[9]

Note that none of the assumptions (b)–(e) is required to prove existence if $n = 1$, i.e. if there is a single firm (or, more generally, if there is a single imperfectly competitive firm, all other firms being price-takers). On this, see Cornwall (1977).[10]

I want now to put the existence question on one side and consider how easy it is to extend the Cournot–Nash framework itself. One simple extension is to allow for a competitive production sector. We already have competitive consumers, and competitive firms can be treated in the same way; if firms $1, \ldots, n'$ are price-takers, then their behaviour is represented by the supply functions (or correspondences) $\eta_j(p)$, where $\eta_j(p)$ maximizes $p \cdot y$ on Y_j. All this means is that the excess demand function (or correspondence) for the imperfectly competitive sector is now $\Sigma_i x_i(p) - \Sigma_i \bar{x}_i - \Sigma_{j=1}^{n'} \eta_j(p)$ rather than $\Sigma_i x_i(p) - \Sigma_i \bar{x}_i$ (see Fitzroy, 1974).[11]

A more complicated extension involves the introduction of intermediate goods. That is, suppose we wish to allow for the possibility that some imperfectly competitive firms B use inputs, widgets say, produced by other imperfectly competitive firms A. (There is no problem if competitive firms use inputs produced by imperfect competitors or vice versa.) Since we are ruling out bilateral monopoly, this must mean that either type A firms have monopoly power in the widget market and type B firms are perfect competitors in the widget market, or type B firms have monopsony power in the widget market and type A firms are perfect competitors. Consider the former case. For example, the situation might be one where each type B firm is large relative to its output market but small relative to the widget market, whereas type A firms are large relative to the widget market but are small relative to the market for their inputs, non-produced goods, say. The Cournot–Nash approach can be generalized formally to this case, but the problem is that it becomes extremely implausible. For suppose a type A firm increases its supply of widgets, thereby driving down their price. According to the Cournot–Nash assumption, type B firms will not change their production plans. But this seems absurd. Type B firms now find that an input with respect to which they are a price-taker has become cheaper. Surely type B firms will want to increase their demand for this input at the expense of other inputs. Also, type B firms will generally want to expand. This will certainly be the case if type B firms are competitive in all markets (something that we have already captured by using the supply functions $\eta_j(p)$ for competitive firms). It will also be the case if each type B firm is a monopolist in its product market, which maximizes $R(p_O) - C(p_I)$, where p_O is output price, p_I are input prices, R is revenue and C are costs. We would surely also expect it to be true when type B firms are oligopolists.[12]

The problem is that the Cournot–Nash assumption simply does not seem a 'rational' conjecture for the type A firms to make about the behaviour of the type B firms. Of course, one can argue that the Cournot–Nash assumption is never 'rational'. I will return to this in section 5. For the moment, let me just say that, while the Cournot–Nash assumption made by one oligopolist in an output market about how one of his competitors will react may not seem that plausible, it does not seem as implausible as in the above case.

But what is a rational (or plausible) conjecture? As we have noted, if type B firms are perfect competitors or monopolists in their product markets, we may be able to write down their objective functions and hence calculate explicitly their demand for type A firms' output in terms of price. A rational conjecture for type A firms might then be that type B firms respond according to this demand function. More generally, if type B firms are oligopolists in their output markets, we might assume that for each price of widgets there is a corresponding Cournot–Nash equilibrium in type B firms' output markets. This again can yield a well defined demand for type A firms' output as a function of price. Unfortunately, this way of looking at things quickly becomes very complicated, particularly if type B firms sell to type C firms, which sell to, . . . , type Z firms, which sell to consumers. Then one has to solve for a whole stack of Cournot–Nash equilibria in order to compute the demand function for type A firms' output. Problems also arise if there are multiple Cournot–Nash equilibria for a given price of widgets.

I know of no attempt to deal with this problem in any generality. Simple cases are studied in Phlips and Thisse (1981) and Hart (1982a).[13]

We see then that the Cournot–Nash approach to general equilibrium suffers from two sorts of limitations. First, one encounters considerable difficulties in establishing the existence of equilibrium. Second, once one departs from relatively simple cases, the formulation itself becomes unsatisfactory.

There is perhaps another reason for being unhappy about the Cournot–Nash approach. This is that each firm is expected to make a full general equilibrium calculation in order to determine its optimal production plan. It is stretching the imagination, to say the least, to believe that the local grocer, or any other small but imperfectly competitive agent, makes this sort of calculation. Perhaps for this reason a number of authors (see, e.g., Laffont and Laroque, 1976; Marschak and Selten, 1974; Silvestre, 1977) have considered models with the feature that agents take a fairly large number of variables as given when making their optimal production decisions. These are models with a strong partial equilibrium flavour. Such models also tend to have the feature that firms are price-setters rather than quantity-setters, although this is not crucial.[14] In the next section, we describe a model along these lines.

4 OBJECTIVE DEMAND (II)

In order to develop a general equilibrium model in which the influence of each agent is limited, we adapt the Cournot–Nash model introduced above. We now assume (as in section 2) that firms $j \in N^1 = \{1, \ldots, n'\}$ are perfect competitors, while firms $j \in N^2 = \{n'+1, \ldots, n\}$ are imperfect competitors. Firms use non-produced goods to make produced goods, and (A10)–(A12) are assumed still to hold. There is therefore no bilateral monopoly. We assume that firms in N^2 are price-setters which take other firms' prices as given, and we will suppose that each imperfectly competitive firm produces a different set of goods. This is to avoid discontinuous demand functions of the Bertrand variety (however, we allow perfectly competitive firms and imperfectly competitive firms to produce the same goods).

Given $j \in N^2$, let

$$M^j = \{k \in L_2 | y_k > 0 \text{ for some } y \in Y_j\} \tag{4.1}$$

be the set of outputs that firm j can produce. We assume

$$M^j \cap M^{j'} = \phi \text{ for all } j, j' \in N^2, j \neq j'. \tag{A13}$$

We also strengthen (A4′) and modify (A1) slightly:

For each i: U_i is continuous, strictly increasing when $x_{L_1} \gg 0$, and strictly quasi-concave. Furthermore, $U_i(x) > U_i(0) \Rightarrow x_{L_1} \gg 0$. (A4″)

For $j \in N^1$, Y_j is closed, $0 \in Y_j$ and Y_j is strictly convex, i.e. $y, y' \in Y_j, y \neq y', 0 < \lambda < 1 \Rightarrow \lambda y + (1-\lambda) y'$ is in the relative interior of Y_j. (A1′)

For all $j \in N^2$: Y_j is convex, closed, $0 \in Y_j$, and, for all $\bar{y}_{L_1} \in R_-^{L_1}$, $\{y \in Y_j | y_{L_1} \geqslant \bar{y}_{L_1}\}$ is bounded. (A1″)

The last part of (A1″) says that with a given bundle of inputs the outputs a firm can produce are bounded.

Above we made strong assumptions about ownership and the tastes of capitalists in order to ensure that imperfectly competitive firms had well defined objective functions. We will not make these assumptions in the present model, but will assume simply that firms maximize profit (in terms of non-produced goods). This is justified below.

Consider a situation in which prices are given by $p \in R_+^l$ and the profits of firms are $\Pi_1, \ldots, \Pi_n \geqslant 0$. Then consumer i's demand function is given by the solution of:

$$\max. \; U_i(x) \text{ s.t. } p \cdot x \leqslant p \cdot \bar{x}_i + \sum_{j=1}^{n} \bar{\theta}_{ij} \Pi_j = w_i. \tag{4.2}$$

This yields the demand function $\xi_i(p, w_i)$. Let $\mathbf{w} = (w_1, \ldots, w_m)$ and

$$\xi(p, \mathbf{w}) = \sum_{i=1}^{m} \xi_i(p, w_i). \tag{4.3}$$

The demand function facing imperfectly competitive firm j is then given by

$$\xi_{M^j}^j(p_{M^j}, p_{L \setminus M^j}, \mathbf{w}) = \xi_{M^j}(p, \mathbf{w}) - \sum_{k \in N^1} \eta_{kM^j}(p) \tag{4.4}$$

where $\eta_k(p)$ solves:

$$\max_{y \in Y_k} p \cdot y.$$

Each firm $j \in N^2$, facing this demand function, is assumed to choose the prices of its outputs, p_{M^j}, to maximize profit taking as given all other prices. We will assume that each firm j also takes $(\Pi_1, \ldots, \Pi_n)$ and hence $(w_1, \ldots, w_m)$ as given. At first sight, this assumption seems absurd. If firm j changes its prices, and other firms do not change their prices in response, then surely their profits will change. And surely firm j's profit, Π_j, will change, otherwise why is it making the move. Below, we justify the assumption that each firm takes the distribution of wealth as given. Of course, in equilibrium, the distribution of wealth is determined endogenously as a result of the production decisions of all firms.

We can now define an imperfectly competitive equilibrium (ICE).

Imperfectly Competitive Equilibrium (ICE) An ICE is a $(2m+n+1)$-tuple $[p, (x_i)_{i=1,\ldots,m}, (y_j)_{j=1,\ldots,n}, \mathbf{w}=(w_1,\ldots,w_m)]$, where $p \in R^l_{++}$, such that

$$x_i = \xi_i(p, w_i) \text{ for all } i \tag{4.5}$$

$$\text{for all } j \in N^1,\ y_j \text{ maximizes } p\cdot y \text{ subject to } y \in Y_j \tag{4.6}$$

$$\text{for all } j \in N^2,\ p^*_{M^j} = p_{M^j},\ y^*_j = y_j \text{ solve the problem:}$$

$$\text{choose } p^*_{M^j}, y^*_j \text{ to maximize } p^*_{M^j} y^*_{M^j} + p_{L\setminus M^j} y^*_{L\setminus M^j}$$

$$\text{subject to } y^*_{M^j} = \xi^j_{M^j}(p^*_{M^j}, p_{L\setminus M^j}, \mathbf{w}) \text{ and } y^* \in Y_j \tag{4.7}$$

$$w_i = p\cdot\bar{x}_i + \sum_{j=1}^{n} \bar{\theta}_{ij} p\cdot y_j \text{ for all } i \tag{4.8}$$

$$\sum_{i=1}^{m} x_i - \sum_{j=1}^{n} y_j - \sum_{i=1}^{m} \bar{x}_i = 0. \tag{4.9}$$

We are assuming in (4.7) that each monopolistically competitive firm must meet any demand ξ_{M^j} that is forthcoming at the prices it sets; i.e., rationing is impossible.[15]

The notion of equilibrium described above is similar to that used by Marschak and Selten (1974) in one of their models and by Silvestre (1978). (It is also related to the equilibrium of Laffont and Laroque, 1976.) These authors do not, however, justify the assumption that w is taken as given by monopolistic competitors.[16] We now provide such a justification, based on Hart (1982a).[17]

Imagine that, instead of there being one economy as described above, there are many such economies. These economies are identical and we will refer to them as different islands. Each island has n firms with production sets $Y_1, \ldots, Y_n$ (the first n' are perfectly competitive, the last $n-n'$ imperfectly competitive) and a competitive consumer sector with the same total endowment and demand behaviour as that of the m consumers in the economy above. Consumers and firms are deposited on a particular island and are assumed to be unable to move. We assume that consumers and firms only consume or produce on their island.

Consumers are assumed to have initial shareholdings in firms on several islands, however. Thus, there are profit flows between the islands. In view of this, we suppose that there is at least one commodity (money?) that can be transferred costlessly between islands and is desired on all islands.[18] To simplify matters, we assume that all non-produced goods play this role; i.e., all non-produced goods can be transported costlessly between different islands. Thus, arbitrage will ensure that prices of non-produced goods are the same on all islands. We assume, in contrast, that it is prohibitively expensive to transport produced goods. Thus, produced goods on different islands may have different prices.

An economic justification for the island framework is as follows. One can imagine that there are many different types or qualities of produced goods, rather than one (in contrast, non-produced goods are homogeneous). Consumers who are identical in other respects may have different preferences over quality. The consumers on a particular island, then, simply represent those consumers who like particular qualities of produced goods.

We now describe the consumers on each island in greater detail. Recall that on each island there is one firm of each type $j = 1, \ldots, n$. Number the islands $1, \ldots, T$. On each island we assume that there are K 'mini-consumers' of type i, where K is a large number. Each 'mini-consumer' of type i has an initial endowment $\bar{x}_i/K$ and a demand function $(1/K)[\xi_i(p, w_i)]$, where w_i/K is each mini-consumer's wealth. That is, on each island we imagine that there is a large number of small consumers with the same aggregate endowment and demand behaviour as one original consumer i. Each mini-consumer of type i is assumed to have, for each j, an initial shareholding $\bar{\theta}_{ij}/K$ in exactly one type j firm, i.e. in a type j firm on exactly one island. We will say that a particular mini-consumer has index $(t_1, t_2, \ldots, t_n)$ if the mini-consumer has an initial shareholding $\bar{\theta}_{i1}/K$ in the type 1 firm on island t_1, an initial shareholding $\bar{\theta}_{i2}/K$ in the type 2 firm on island t_2, ..., an initial shareholding $\bar{\theta}_{in}/K$ in the type n firm on island t_n. We assume that no consumer has shares in different firms on the same island; i.e., the t_i are distinct. The number of possible indices is then ${}^TP_n$ (P stands for permutation). We will assume

> For all $t = 1, \ldots, T$ and $i = 1, \ldots, m$: given any $t_1, \ldots, t_n = 1, \ldots, T$, where $j_1 \neq j_2 \Rightarrow t_{j1} \neq t_{j2}$, there are $(K/{}^TP_n)$ mini-consumers of type i with index $(t_1, \ldots, t_n)$ on island t. (4.10)

(4.10) says that there is a uniform distribution of consumers with different indices on each island (we do not worry about fractions of consumers). It implies that each island is a microscopic version of the whole economy, in the sense that each island has an identical population of consumers of different tastes and wealths. (4.10) also divorces the ownership of a firm's shares from the consumption of its goods, i.e. it ensures that a negligible fraction of a firm's shareholders are also customers of the firm.

Assumption (4.10) has three important implications. First, it implies that all islands have identical demands. In particular, given any distribution of profit $(\Pi_{jt})_{j=1,\ldots,n,\,t=1,\ldots,T}$, where Π_{jt} is the profit of the type j firm on island t, the distribution of wealth and hence consumer demand on each island will be the same. Second, if a particular firm (j, t) changes its profit from Π_{jt} to Π'_{jt}, this will have a negligible effect on consumer wealth on any island when T is large; for the wealth of only K/T mini-consumers of type i on the island (those who hold shares in firm (j, t)) will be affected, and the aggregate change in their wealth is

$$\left[\frac{\bar{\theta}_{ij}}{K}(\Pi'_{jt}-\Pi_{jt})\right]\frac{K}{T}=\frac{\bar{\theta}_{ij}}{T}(\Pi'_{jt}-\Pi_{jt})\to 0 \text{ as } T\to\infty.$$

This means that, when T is large, each firm is right to assume that it can have no influence on the wealth of its customers; i.e., it should take the distribution of wealth as given. Note also that each firm's actions will have only a negligible effect on the prices of non-produced goods, p_{L_1}, since these are traded in a large, centralized market; i.e., firms should take these prices as given too.

Finally, (4.10) justifies the assumption that imperfectly competitive firms maximize profits. For suppose firm (j, t) increases its profits by changing prices. We have seen that, when T is large, this will have a negligible effect on the economy of every island $t' \neq t$. Therefore prices and firms' profits will not change except on island t. Consider the initial shareholders of firm (j, t). By assumption, they do not own shares in other firms on island t. Therefore, the fact that firm (j, t)'s profits have risen (and the profits of firms on other islands have not changed) implies that they are wealthier. Furthermore, by (4.10), almost all of firm (j, t)'s initial shareholders live on islands $t' \neq t$ where prices have not changed; these consumers, being wealthier, are therefore better off. It follows that profit maximization is in the interest of all but a negligible fraction of initial shareholders (those living on island t), and is therefore a reasonable goal for imperfectly competitive, as well as perfectly competitive, firms to pursue.[19]

We see then that the island framework justifies the imperfectly competitive equilibrium defined in (4.5)–(4.9). (Of course, the island framework does not justify the Bertrand hypothesis that each imperfectly competitive firm takes the prices of other imperfectly competitive firms on the same island as given – this is simply an assumption.) In particular, conditions (4.5)–(4.9) describe a *symmetric* equilibrium in which prices, profits and hence the distribution of wealth are the same on every island.

Having justified the notion of equilibrium, we now establish its existence. We need a further assumption:

> For each $j \in N^2$ there exists a continuous function $\alpha_j(\mathbf{w})$ such that: for all $\mathbf{w} \geqslant 0$, $p_{L \setminus M^j} \gg 0$, the problem:
>
> choose $p_{M^j}, y_{L \setminus M^j}$ to max. $p_{M^j} \xi^j_{M^j}(p_{M^j}, p_{L \setminus M^j}, \mathbf{w})$ $+ p_{L \setminus M^j} y_{L \setminus M^j}$ s.t. $[y_{L \setminus M^j}, \xi^j_{M^j}(p_{M^j}, p_{L \setminus M^j}, \mathbf{w})] \in Y_j$
>
> has a unique solution $\overset{*}{p}_{M^j}, \overset{*}{y}_{L \setminus M^j}$ with $\|[\overset{*}{y}_{L \setminus M^j}, \xi^j_{M^j}(\overset{*}{p}_{M^j}, p_{L \setminus M^j}, \mathbf{w})]\| \leqslant \alpha_j(\mathbf{w})$. (A14)

(A14) says two things. First, each imperfect competitor's maximization problem has a unique solution. Second, whatever the input prices or the prices charged by other imperfect competitors are, there is an upper bound (depending on wealth) to the amount each imperfect competitor wants to supply.

Proposition 4.1 Assume (A1′), (A1″), (A3), (A4″) and (A10)–(A14). Then an ICE exists.

Proof: see Appendix.

Note that in the island framework proposition 4.1 establishes the existence of a symmetric equilibrium in which prices, profits, etc., are the same on every island. It is possible that a weaker set of assumptions would ensure the existence of a non-symmetric equilibrium.

Let me now make some comments about this notion of equilibrium. First, as we have noted, it has a strong partial equilibrium flavour. Each imperfect competitor faces a Marshallian demand function of the form $\xi_{M^j}(p_{M^j}, p_{L \setminus M^j}, \mathbf{w})$ and takes $\mathbf{w}$ and $p_{L \setminus M^j}$ as fixed. In equilibrium, of course, $\mathbf{w}$ is determined endogenously by the actions of all firms. In this sense the ICE is similar to the notion of equilibrium adopted by Marschak and Selten (1974) in one of their models and by Silvestre (1977b). It differs, however, from the equilibrium proposed by Marschak and Selten (1974) in a second model and by Nikaidô (1975). In particular, these authors consider models in which each imperfectly competitive firm's action may, through the effect on the firm's profits, influence the wealth of its customers and hence the firm's demand (the 'feedback' effect).

There seem to be two advantages of considering a model (e.g. the island model above) in which there is no feedback effect. First, the feedback effect is likely to cause the firm's demand function to be less well-behaved than the usual Marshallian demand function (as Nikaidô, 1975, points out, it may be upward-sloping, it is unlikely to satisfy gross substitutability, etc.). This means that an assumption like (A14) is perhaps less likely to be satisfied. Second, if there is a feedback effect arising, say, from the fact that owners of the firm also consume the firm's products, then, as we have noted, profit maximization is no longer a natural objective function for the firm, since the owners will be interested in low consumption-goods prices as well as high monetary profit.

The disadvantage of ruling out the feedback effect is, of course, that one is thereby being less general. Note however that, while it may be inappropriate to rule out the feedback effect in the case of very large imperfect competitors (e.g. General Motors), it may be quite realistic to do so in the case of small imperfect competitors (e.g. the local supermarket). Therefore, to the extent that our goal is to build models of monopolistic competition with a Chamberlinian flavour, where agents have 'local' monopoly power but no agent has 'global' monopoly power, it may be desirable on grounds of realism as well as tractability to rule out the feedback effect.[20]

Although the ICE notion of equilibrium yields a number of simplifications, it does not avoid the Roberts–Sonnenschein non-existence problem (owing to the nonconvexity of imperfect competitors' response correspondences). In particular, to prove the existence of equilibrium we had to make – without any micro-justification in terms of tastes or production possibilities – assumption (A14). Note, however, that a further problem that arises in the Cournot–Nash approach – the multi-valuedness of the equilibrium price correspondence $\pi(y)$ – does not occur when firms are price-setters. This is because, given the price decisions of imperfect competitors and prices for competitive goods, there is, for each exogenous distribution of wealth, a well defined demand for each good.[21] However, if firms were quantity-setters rather than price-setters, this problem would recur. This is because, given outputs $\mathbf{x}$ and wealth $\mathbf{w}$, the equation $\mathbf{x} = \xi(p, \mathbf{w})$ may not have a unique solution. Thus quantity-setting firms no longer have well defined payoff functions.

An attempt to weaken (A14) has been made by Silvestre (1978). He considers a weaker notion of equilibrium than ICE in which imperfectly competitive firms only satisfy their first-order conditions, but do not necessarily maximize profit; i.e., they set marginal revenue equal to marginal cost. Another way of looking at this is that they do maximize profit, but do not know the full demand curve ξ_{M^j} that they face; in particular, they know only the local slope $\partial \xi_{M^j}/\partial p_k$ and a single point $(p, \xi_{M^j}(p, \mathbf{w}))$ it passes through (the status quo position), and they conjecture that the remainder of the curve is linear. Suppose that $y_{M^j} = \xi_{M^j}(p, \mathbf{w})$ is invertible; i.e., we can write $p_{M^j} = \xi_{M^j}^{-1}(p_{L \setminus M^j}, \mathbf{w}, y_{M^j})$. If $(\partial \xi_{M^j}^{-1}/\partial y_k)_{k \in M^j}$ is a negative semi-definite matrix, and each firm's production set is convex, the firm's profit function will then be concave, and an equilibrium can be shown to exist. Negative semi-definiteness is of course a strong assumption. In the case of an imperfect competitor producing a single good, however, it says only that demand curves slope downwards. On the other hand, it does not seem that satisfactory to assume that firms only satisfy their first-order conditions. One might expect them at least to search for a local profit maximum, and of course 'marginal revenue equals marginal cost' doesn't guarantee that they are at one.

Finally, it should be noted that the ICE notion of equilibrium can be extended, at least in principle, to allow for intermediate goods (where we continue to rule out bilateral monopoly). The point is that, given the distribution of wealth and all prices, the demand for the outputs of imperfect competitors is determined, and this in turn determines demand for inputs (chosen to minimize costs). This means that each producer of intermediate goods faces a well defined demand for his output as a function of his prices, other prices and the distribution of wealth. Under the Bertrand assumption that all other prices are constant, he therefore has a well defined profit maximization problem. Note, however, that it may be unreasonable for the producer of an input to suppose that if he raises his price the prices of outputs will be unchanged. This is the same problem that arose in the Cournot–Nash approach, when we assumed that the producer of widgets conjectured that users of widgets would not expand or contract when the price of widgets changed. Note that the Bertrand assumption does allow for the possibility that users of widgets will demand fewer widgets relative to other inputs if the price of widgets rises.

5 RATIONAL OR REASONABLE CONJECTURES

We have considered two main approaches to modelling imperfect competition. In the subjective demand approach, agents' perceptions are correct in the sense that in equilibrium the prices that rule are those expected to rule; i.e., the equilibrium position lies on each agent's subjective demand curve. Agents may be quite wrong, however, about the consequences of choosing an action different from the equilibrium one, i.e. about the slope of their demand curve. In the objective demand approach, in contrast, agents are assumed to be able to calculate the consequences of a deviation from their equilibrium action, where this calculation is based on particular assumptions about how other imperfect competitors will react.

It is clear that the objective demand approach ties equilibrium down to a much greater extent than the subjective demand approach, *given* particular assumptions about reactions. However, as we vary the assumptions about reactions, the number of equilibria that the objective demand approach generates will be very large. In this respect, the objective demand approach is less 'objective' than it might seem.

For example, consider the ICE defined in the last section. There it was assumed that firms are price-setters. However, we could just as easily have defined a quantity-setting (Cournot–Nash) ICE, where each firm chooses its production plan y_j, taking as given the production plans of other firms and the distribution of wealth. (Now prices are determined by the equations $\mathbf{x} = \xi(p, \mathbf{w})$.) Moreover, we could define a large number of other 'conjectural variation' equilibria, according to the particular assumptions each firm makes about how other firms will react to a change in its production plan.

Which of these equilibria is the 'right' one? In one sense, both Cournot–Nash and Bertrand behaviour can be justified at the theoretical level. Suppose, for example, that each firm must make its production decision at date 1, but that goods are not marketed until date 2. Assume that each firm finds out the production decisions of other firms only at date 2. Under these conditions, a change in one firm's production plan *cannot* lead to changes in other firms' production plans since the other firms find out only when it's too late. Thus, in this case the Cournot–Nash hypothesis is correct. (This argument provides some justification for the Cournot–Nash model studied in section 3.) On the other hand, if firms have to set prices at date 1 (but can leave quantity decisions until date 2), and find out other firms' pricing decisions only at date 2, the Bertrand hypothesis is correct. Under this interpretation, the choice between Cournot and Bertrand is an empirical matter having to do with the relative flexibility of production plans and prices (one feels that the evidence is likely to favour Cournot).[22]

In many situations, the idea that firms' prices or quantity strategies cannot be observed by others, although theoretically useful, seems far fetched. If strategies can be observed, however, the issue of reactions and conjectures about them cannot be dodged. The question then becomes, what is a 'rational' conjecture? Early attempts to analyse 'rational' conjectures were made by Cyert and de Groot (1970) and Friedman (1968) in the context of dynamic games; for a recent treatment, see Maskin and Tirole (1982). In the last few years, a number of authors (see, in particular, Bresnahan, 1981; Hahn, 1977, 1978; Laitner, 1980; Marschak and Selten, 1978; Perry, 1982; and Ulph, 1981, 1984) have analysed the rationality of conjectures in a static context (although Laitner and Marschak–Selten also provide a dynamic treatment).

The basic idea behind this recent literature can be illustrated using the Negishi approach described in section 2. (The treatment that follows is based on Hart, 1982c. It differs in a number of respects from that found in the references above; the spirit is similar, however.) To simplify matters, we consider a partial equilibrium analysis of a single homogeneous good industry under oligopoly. Suppose the firms have cost functions $C_1(q_1)$, $C_2(q_2)$, $\ldots$, $C_n(q_n)$ and that the demand function for the industry is $Q = D(p)$. We assume:

D is a continuous function defined for all $p > 0$, with $D(p) = 0$ for $p \geqslant$ some $\bar{p} > 0$. Furthermore, D is strictly decreasing on $(0, \bar{p}]$. (5.1)

$C_i\colon R_+ \rightarrow R_+$ is strictly convex, increasing, twice continuously differentiable and satisfies $C_i(0) = 0$, $\bar{p} > C_i'(0) > 0$ $(i = 1, \ldots, n)$. (5.2)

(5.1) implies the existence of an inverse demand function, which we write $p = f(Q)$ (where $\bar{p} = f(0)$). (5.2) says that returns to scale are strictly decreasing. We assume (5.2) to simplify matters; all our results generalize to the case of constant returns.

We represent each firm's conjectures by an inverse demand function, as in Negishi's model. Specifically, the conjectures of firm i are given by the real-valued function

$$\alpha_i(q_i; \hat{p}, \hat{q}_i), \tag{5.3}$$

defined for all $q_i \geqslant 0$, $\hat{q}_i \geqslant 0$, $\hat{p} \geqslant 0$. The interpretation, as before, is that, given a status quo position where the price is $\hat{p}$ and firm i is supplying $\hat{q}_i$, firm i conjectures that if it changed its supply to q_i, the equilibrium price would change to $\alpha_i(q_i; \hat{p}, \hat{q}_i)$. Note that we do not now include the outputs $\hat{q}_j$, $j \neq i$, as part of the status quo. This is for simplicity, but a justification would be that firm i observes only its output and the market price, and not the outputs of other firms.

As in section 2, we make the consistency assumption

$$\alpha_i(q; p, q) = p \text{ for all } p, q \ (i = 1, \ldots, n). \tag{5.4}$$

We also assume that

$$\alpha_i \text{ is continuous } (i = 1, \ldots, n). \tag{5.5}$$

Definition A rational conjectural equilibrium is a $(2n+1)$-tuple $(\hat{p}, \hat{q}_1, \ldots, \hat{q}_n, \alpha_1, \ldots, \alpha_n)$, satisfying (5.4) and (5.5), such that

$$\hat{p} = f(\hat{q}_1 + \ldots + \hat{q}_n) \tag{5.6}$$

$$q = \hat{q}_i \text{ maximizes } \alpha_i(q; \hat{p}, \hat{q}_i)\, q - C_i(q) \ (i = 1, \ldots, n) \tag{5.7}$$

for all $i = 1, \ldots, n$ and $q_i \geqslant 0$, there exist $(q_j)_{j \neq i}$ such that $q_i + \Sigma_{j \neq i} q_j = D[\alpha_i(q_i; \hat{p}, \hat{q}_i)]$ and each q_j is a solution of:

$$\max \alpha_j[q; \alpha_i(q_i; \hat{p}, \hat{q}_i), q_j]\, q - C_j(q). \tag{5.8}$$

Here (5.6)–(5.7) are as in Negishi's model. Condition (5.7) says that each firm maximizes profit given its conjectures, and (5.6) says that demand equals supply. The new condition, having to do with the rationality of conjectures, is (5.8). This is interpreted as follows. Suppose firm i changes its output from $\hat{q}_i$ to q_i. According to its conjecture, the equilibrium price should change from $\hat{p}$ to $\alpha_i(q_i; \hat{p}, \hat{q}_i)$. This must mean that the new total output is $D[\alpha_i(q_i; \hat{p}, \hat{q}_i)]$; i.e., the output of other firms is $Q = D[\alpha_i(q_i; \hat{p}, \hat{q}_i)] - q_i$. But will firms $j \neq i$ want to supply this output in the new status quo situation $(\alpha_i(q_i; \hat{p}, \hat{q}_i), q_i)$; i.e., do there exist (q_j) such that $\Sigma_{j \neq i} q_j = Q$ and q_j maximizes profit subject to firm j's conjectures? Condition (5.8) says that there do. In other words, there is a new equilibrium for the economy in which firm i supplies q_i, firm j supplies q_j and the price is $\alpha_i(q_i; \hat{p}, \hat{q}_i)$. In this sense firm i's conjectures are correct.

Thus, in a rational conjectural equilibrium, each firm i's conjectures are correct given that other firms behave according to their conjectures.

Remark 1 In most of the literature on rational conjectures, conjectures are described somewhat differently. For example, in the case of duopoly, Ulph (1984) represents firm i's conjectures by a function $q_j = Q^i(q_i, \hat{q}_i, \hat{q}_j)$ which specifies the output that firm i thinks firm j would choose if, starting from the output levels $\hat{q}_i, \hat{q}_j$, firm i changed its output to q_i. Note that our way of representing conjectures is equivalent to this. For if the firms produce q_i, q_j, the price must be $f(q_i + q_j)$, which means that the conjecture Q^i corresponds to the Negishi demand curve $\alpha_i(q_i; \hat{p}, \hat{q}_i) = f\{q_i + Q^i[q_i, \hat{q}_i, D(\hat{p}) - \hat{q}_i]\}$.

The requirement that firms' conjectures are correct in the sense of (5.8) is less compelling than it might seem. Correctness is only considered relative to deviations from the equilibrium position $(\hat{p}, \hat{q}_1, \ldots, \hat{q}_n)$. In particular, consider some other status quo allocation $(p^*, q_1^*, \ldots, q_n^*)$ where $p^* = f(q_1^* + \ldots + q_n^*)$. According to (5.4), firm i conjectures that, if it does not deviate from q_i^*, the price will remain at p^*. But suppose q_j^* does not maximize $\alpha_j(q; p^*, q_j^*)\,q - C_j(q)$. Then firm j is not in equilibrium and so it will not stay at q_j^*. Thus p will change even if firm i stays at q_i^*. It follows that firm i's conjectures are incorrect in a rational conjectural equilibrium away from the equilibrium position.[23]

As an alternative to rational conjectures Hahn (1978) has proposed the weaker notion of reasonable conjectures. Hahn defines a reasonable conjectural equilibrium (RCE) as follows.

Definition A RCE is a $(2n+1)$-tuple $(\hat{p}, \hat{q}_1, \ldots, \hat{q}_n, \alpha_1, \ldots, \alpha_n)$ satisfying (5.4)–(5.7) and

for each $i = 1, \ldots, n$, there do not exist $p^*, q_1^*, \ldots, q_n^*$, where $p^* = f(q_1^* + \ldots + q_n^*)$ and q_j^* maximizes $\alpha_j(q; p^*, q_j^*)\,q - C_j(q)$ for all $j \neq i$, such that $p^* q_i^* - C_i(q_i^*) > \hat{p}\hat{q}_i - C_i(\hat{q}_i)$. (5.9)

In order to understand this definition, let us return to the notion of a Negishi equilibrium, as embodied in (5.6)–(5.7). The idea here is that $(\hat{p}, \hat{q}_1, \ldots, \hat{q}_n, \alpha_1, \ldots, \alpha_n)$ will be a resting point of the system since demand equals supply and each firm is maximizing profit given its conjectures. Suppose, however, that firms know each other's conjectures. Then if (5.9) is violated, firm i might reason as follows. Suppose I change my output to q_i^*. Then one possibility is that other firms will change their outputs to $(q_j^*)_{j \neq i}$ and the price will become p^*. Given their conjectures, all other firms will be in equilibrium at the new allocation $(p_1^* q_1^*, \ldots, q_n^*)$ (by (5.9)), while my profits will rise.

We see then that, if (5.9) is violated, firm i has an incentive to change its output. Of course, the change from $\hat{q}_i$ to q_i^* will not necessarily lead to the allocation $(p_1^*, q_1^*, \ldots, q_n^*)$, since there may be other allocations at which firms $j \neq i$ are in equilibrium relative to their conjectures. However, if firm i is sufficiently optimistic, it will be prepared to take this risk and will make the change from $\hat{q}_i$ to q_i^*, anyway. Thus the original Negishi allocation will be upset.

Under this interpretation, then, only an allocation satisfying (5.9) as well as (5.6) and (5.7) is a candidate for equilibrium.

Note that the thought experiment being made here concerns the consequences of one firm deviating from its conjectures. This suggests the following more formal interpretation of an RCE. Consider a game in which firms' strategies are conjectures (or models of the world). Suppose that, given particular conjectures, the outcome of this game is an allocation satisfying (5.6)–(5.7), i.e. a Negishi equilibrium relative to these conjectures. Suppose, moreover, that, if there are several Negishi equilibria relative to given conjectures, each firm assumes that the equilibrium most favourable to it will be chosen. Then an RCE is simply a Nash equilibrium of this game.

The notion of reasonable conjectures is in an important sense weaker than the notion of rational conjectures. For a firm's conjectures may be incorrect and yet it may still be maximizing profit given the conjectures, and hence behaviour, of other firms. That is, (5.9) does not imply (5.8) (while (5.8) essentially implies (5.9)). As long as (5.9) holds, however, one might argue that a firm has no incentive to change its conjectures even if they are incorrect, since it cannot profit by doing so.

How large is the set of reasonable conjectural equilibria? In order to answer this question, it is useful to focus on a subset of the RCE's, which we will call regular reasonable conjectural equilibria. For each $\tilde{p} \geqslant 0$, define the following supply correspondence:

$$S_i(\tilde{p}) = \{\tilde{q} \mid q = \tilde{q} \text{ maximizes } \alpha_i(q; \tilde{p}, \tilde{q})q - C_i(q)\}. \tag{5.10}$$

$S_i(\tilde{p})$ is the set of outputs $\tilde{q}$ for which firm i is in equilibrium given the price $\tilde{p}$; i.e., given the status quo $(\tilde{p}, \tilde{q})$, firm i has no incentive to move. Now $S_i(\tilde{p})$ may be empty for some $\tilde{p}$. We will say that an RCE is *regular* if $S_i(\tilde{p}) \neq \phi$ for all $\tilde{p} \geqslant 0$ and all i. In what follows we concentrate on regular reasonable conjectural equilibria (RRCE).

For a firm considering a deviation from its equilibrium conjecture α_i, what is relevant are the reactions of other firms, as embodied in the supply correspondences S_j. In Hart (1982c) it is shown that there is in fact a close relationship between an RRCE and a Nash equilibrium in these supply correspondences. For our present purpose, it is enough to note the obvious fact that (5.9) can be replaced by

For each $i = 1, \ldots, n$, there do not exist $p^*, q_1^*, \ldots, q_n^*$, where $p^* = f(q_1^* + \ldots + q_n^*)$ and $q_j^* \in S_j(p^*)$ for all $j \neq i$, such that $p^*q_i^* - C_i(q_i^*) > \hat{p}\hat{q}_i - C_i(\hat{q}_i)$. (5.11)

We now characterize the set of RRCE's. For each firm i, define h_i as follows:

$$h_i(p) = \begin{cases} q \text{ where } p = C_i(q)/q, \text{ if } p > C_i'(0) \text{ and the} \\ \quad \text{equation } p = C_i(q)/q \text{ has a solution} \\ \infty \text{ if } p > C_i'(0) \text{ and } p = C_i(q)/q \text{ has no solution} \\ 0 \text{ if } p \leqslant C_i'(0) \end{cases} \tag{5.12}$$

That is, h_i is firm i's average cost curve. Now, for each i and p, let

$$\phi_i(p) = pq - C_i(q) \text{ where } q = \max\left[0, D(p) - \sum_{j \neq i} h_j(p)\right]. \tag{5.13}$$

That is, $\phi_i(p)$ is firm i's profit at price p, given that all other firms are on their average cost curves and firm i supplies the residual. The function ϕ_i is continuous and $\phi_i(\bar{p}) = 0$. Let

$$\phi_i = \max_{p \geqslant 0} \phi_i(p). \tag{5.14}$$

Finally, define

$$\eta = \{(\hat{p}, \hat{q}_1, \ldots, \hat{q}_n) \mid \hat{p}\hat{q}_i - C_i(\hat{q}_i) \geqslant \phi_i \text{ for all } i;$$
$$\text{for all } i, \hat{p} \geqslant C_i'(\hat{q}_i) \text{ if } \hat{q}_i > 0; \text{ for all } i, \hat{p} \leqslant C_i'(\hat{q}_i) \text{ if } \hat{q}_i = 0;$$

$$\sum_{i=1}^{n} \hat{q}_i = D(\hat{p})\}. \tag{5.15}$$

To simplify matters, we assume in what follows that

For each i, $\max pD(p) - C_i[D(p)]$ has a unique solution, denoted p_i^M. (5.16)

(5.16) says that there is a unique profit-maximizing price for firm i if it acts as a monopolist. Note that (5.16) holds 'generically'.

We will say that $(\hat{p}, \hat{q}_1, \ldots, \hat{q}_n)$ is an RRCE allocation if there exist $\alpha_1, \ldots, \alpha_n$ such that $(\hat{p}, \hat{q}_1, \ldots, \hat{q}_n, \alpha_1, \ldots, \alpha_n)$ is an RRCE. The size of the set of RRCE allocations turns out to be sensitive to whether the following condition is satisfied.

For some i, $p_i^m \leqslant C_j'(0)$ for all $j = 1, \ldots, n, j \neq i$. ($\beta$)

The following is established in Hart (1982c).

Proposition 5.1 Assume (5.16). Then if (β) holds, there is a unique regular reasonable conjectural equilibrium allocation. On the other hand, if (β) does not hold, any element of η is a regular reasonable conjectural equilibrium allocation and furthermore η contains a continuum of elements.

We see then that, except in the case where (β) holds, i.e. where some firm can achieve monopoly profits at a price at which no other firm wishes to enter, there is a continuum of regular reasonable conjectural equilibria (and hence of reasonable conjectural equilibria).

A similar result has been established by a number of other authors (see Hahn, 1977; Laitner, 1980; and Ulph, 1984), although their analysis deals with the case of local rationality (or reasonableness – see below), while we have considered globally reasonable conjectures. The existence of a large number of reasonable conjectural equilibria is perhaps disappointing, given that one might have hoped that the requirement of reasonableness or rationality would have narrowed down the set of conjectural equilibria in the same way that the requirement of rationality of expectations does in other contexts. At the same time, it should be emphasized that the model does put some restrictions on the set of possible outcomes. To see this, it is helpful first to establish a link between reasonableness and local rationality.

Consider an RRCE. We have noted that (5.9) implies (5.11), where the S_j are defined in (5.10). Suppose that the supply correspondences $S_1, \ldots, S_n$ are in fact differentiable functions in a neighbourhood of the equilibrium price $\hat{p}$. Then (5.11) implies that, for each i,

$$p = \hat{p} \text{ maximizes } p[D(p) - \sum_{j \neq i} S_j(p)] - C_i[D(p) - \sum_{j \neq i} S_j(p)] \tag{5.17}$$

in a neighbourhood of $\hat{p}$. If D is differentiable and $\hat{q}_i > 0$, we therefore obtain the first-order condition

$$\hat{q}_i + \hat{p}\frac{de_i}{dp}(\hat{p}) - C_i'(\hat{q}_i)\frac{de_i}{dp}(\hat{p}) = 0 \tag{5.18}$$

where $e_i(p) = D(p) - \Sigma_{j \neq i} S_j(p)$. On the other hand, we know from (5.7) that

$$\hat{p} + \hat{q}_i \left.\frac{\partial \alpha_i}{\partial q}\right|_{q=\hat{q}_i} - C_i'(\hat{q}_i) = 0 \tag{5.19}$$

as long as α_i is differentiable. It follows that

$$\left.\frac{\partial \alpha_i}{\partial q}\right|_{q=\hat{q}} = \left[1 \Big/ \frac{de_i}{dp}(\hat{p})\right]. \tag{5.20}$$

That is, each firm's conjectured slope of its inverse demand curve must equal the actual slope. We see that under suitable differentiability and interiority assumptions, every RRCE is *locally rational.*

It follows directly from this that only in exceptional cases in a small economy will the Walrasian allocation, together with competitive (i.e. perfectly elastic) conjectures, be an RRCE. For this can only happen if $(de_i/dp)(\hat{p}) = -\infty$ for all i, which in turn implies $S_j'(p) = \infty$ for at least two j (assuming $D'(p) < \infty$). In the case of duopoly this in turn is possible only if both firms have identical constant marginal costs (on this see also Bresnahan, 1981; Ulph, 1984; and Perry, 1982). Note that, even in this case, there will, by proposition 5.1, be a continuum of other reasonable conjectural equilibria.

For the same reason, the Cournot–Nash allocation (assuming it exists), together with Cournot–Nash conjectures (i.e., $\alpha_i(q; \hat{p}, \hat{q}) = f\{q + [D(p) - \hat{q}]\}$, where f is the inverse demand curve), is an RRCE only in exceptional circumstances. This is simply a reflection of the fact that the conjectures $\alpha_i = f[q - \hat{q} + D(p)]$ yield a supply curve $S_i(p)$ for firm i which is not generally perfectly inelastic. Hence the conjecture of other firms, that firm i keeps its output constant when they change their outputs, is not locally rational.

The model therefore places severe restrictions on those combinations of allocations and conjectures that can be sustained as reasonable conjectural equilibria. However, it puts many fewer restrictions on the allocations that can be sustained as reasonable conjectural equilibria for *some* conjectures. For example, it will often be the case that both the Walrasian and Cournot–Nash allocations can be sustained as RRCE's with non-Walrasian and non-Cournot–Nash conjectures. In fact, we know from proposition 5.1 that this will be the case whenever the Walrasian and Cournot–Nash outcomes lie in η. It may also be the case even when the outcomes do not lie in η, since η is only a subset of the set of RRCE allocations.[24]

The conclusion must be then that, although rationality or reasonableness does put some restrictions on the outcomes that can arise in oligopoly, a considerable amount of indeterminateness remains. Thus rationality or reasonableness does not in any sense 'solve' the oligopoly problem.

6 WHAT IS PERFECT COMPETITION?

I want to consider now the relationship between the imperfectly competitive models that we have studied and the standard Walrasian or Arrow–Debreu model.

One interpretation of the Arrow–Debreu model is that it is simply the special case of Negishi's model in which firms conjecture that they face perfectly elastic demand curves. This view, although quite common, seems profoundly unsatisfactory. For, as we have argued in section 2, a very large class of allocations are equilibria for some conjectures. Unless we have some grounds for singling out perfectly elastic conjectures for attention, there seems no reason to focus on the Walrasian equilibrium.

Moreover, we have seen that, in general, perfectly elastic conjectures are not 'rational' (or reasonable). Only if each firm faces a perfectly elastic excess demand function, given that all other agents in the economy behave as price-takers, will they be so. In the partial equilibrium oligopoly model of section 5 this happens only when at least two firms have the same constant marginal cost. Even in this case, there exist many other reasonable conjectural equilibria.

A second interpretation of the Arrow–Debreu model is that it arises when firms are Bertrand price-setters. This idea has been formalized in a general equilibrium setting in a number of recent papers; see, e.g., Dubey (1982) and Simon (1982). (In order to overcome Edgeworth-type non-existence problems, the strategies of agents must be considerably more complicated than those envisaged by Bertrand.) We have argued in section 5 that Bertrand price-setting behaviour makes sense if each firm must make an irreversible decision about price before it learns the pricing decisions of other firms (in a one-shot game). While this assumption may be reasonable in some settings, it does not seem particularly realistic in general. This second interpretation, then, like the first, does not seem to provide very strong underpinnings for the Arrow–Debreu model.

A third interpretation of the Arrow–Debreu model is that it corresponds to the case where each agent is small relative to its market. This interpretation has been explored in a large number of recent papers; references include Gabszewicz and Vial (1972), Novshek (1980), Novshek and Sonnenschein (1978), Hart (1979, 1980), Roberts (1980), Roberts and Postlewaite (1976), Shubik (1973), Shapley and Shubik (1977), and Dubey *et al.* (1980). In much of this work it is assumed that firms are Cournot–Nash quantity-setters.[25] The basic idea, however, is much more general (see Dubey *et al.*, 1980). For an excellent introduction to this literature, see Mas-Colell (1980), and for a more formal survey see Mas-Colell (1982).

To understand the idea behind this third interpretation, consider the economy E described in section 4, where we assume now that all firms are imperfect competitors; i.e., $N^2 = N$. Now replicate this economy, so that there are r firms of type j, each with production set $Y_j (j = 1, \ldots, n)$, and r consumers of type i, each with endowment $\bar{x}_i$ and initial shareholding $(\bar{\theta}_{ij}/r)$ in each type j firm. Call this economy E_r. In the ICE of section 4, we assumed that firms are price-setters. I now want to modify the notion of equilibrium to allow for certain reactions by other agents.

We will assume that each type j firm (j, t) has conjectures of the form

$$S^j = S^j(p; \hat{p}, \hat{y}). \tag{6.1}$$

The interpretation is that, given an initial position where prices are $\hat{p}$ and average production of all firms other than (j, t) is $\hat{\bar{y}}$, $S^j(p;\hat{p}, \hat{\bar{y}})$ is (j, t)'s conjecture of the new average production of all firms other than (j, t) if prices change to p owing to the alteration in (j, t)'s production plan. Note that these supply curves S^j can be regarded as the obverse of a Negishi-type subjective demand curve. That is, given (6.1), the corresponding subjective demand curve in E_r is

$$r\xi_{L_2}(p, \mathbf{w}) - (nr-1)\, S^j_{L_2}(p;\hat{p}, \hat{\bar{y}}) \tag{6.2}$$

whose inverse is of the form (2.1). The S^j are also somewhat similar to the supply correspondences considered in the last section.

We assume

$$\begin{aligned}&S^j(p;\hat{p}, \hat{\bar{y}}) \text{ is a continuous function: } R^l_{++} \times R^l_{++} \times R^l \to R^l,\\ &\text{which satisfies } S^j(p;p, \hat{\bar{y}}) = \hat{\bar{y}}.\end{aligned} \tag{A15}$$

We also assume that these conjectures are independent of the replication r of the economy. This is not innocuous; for example, it rules out the case in which each firm expects other firms to imitate its choice of production plan. Note that the Cournot–Nash hypothesis is a special case of the above where $S^j(p;\hat{p}, \hat{\bar{y}}) = \hat{\bar{y}}$ for all p.

Definition A generalized price-setting ICE in E_r is a $(2m+nr+1)$-tuple

$$[\hat{p}, (\hat{x}_i)_{i=1,\ldots,m}, (\hat{y}_{jt})_{j=1,\ldots,n,\, t=1,\ldots,r}, \hat{\mathbf{w}} = (\hat{w}_1, \ldots, \hat{w}_m)],$$

where $\hat{p} \in R^l_{++}$, such that

$$\hat{x}_i = \xi(\hat{p}, \hat{w}_i) \text{ for all } i \tag{6.3}$$

$$\begin{aligned}&\text{For all } (j', t'),\ p_{L_2} = \hat{p}_{L_2} \text{ maximizes } p_{L_2} y_{L_2} + \hat{p}_{L_1} y_{L_1}\\ &\text{subject to } y \in Y_{j'} \text{ and } y_{L_2} = r\xi_{L_2}(p_{L_2}, \hat{p}_{L_1}, \hat{\mathbf{w}})\\ &- (nr-1)\, S^{j'}_{L_2}\left[(p_{L_2}, \hat{p}_{L_1}); \hat{p}, \frac{\left(\sum_{j=1}^{n}\sum_{t=1}^{r} \hat{y}_{jt}\right) - \hat{y}_{j't'}}{(nr-1)}\right]\end{aligned} \tag{6.4}$$

$$\hat{w}_i = \hat{p}\cdot\bar{x}_i + \sum_{j=1}^{n}\sum_{t=1}^{r} \frac{\bar{\theta}_{ij}}{r}\, \hat{p}\cdot\hat{y}_{jt} \text{ for all } i \tag{6.5}$$

$$\sum_{i=1}^{m} \hat{x}_i - \sum_{j=1}^{n}\sum_{t=1}^{r} \frac{\hat{y}_{jt}}{r} - \sum_{i=1}^{m} \bar{x}_i = 0. \tag{6.6}$$

Note that in (6.4) we imagine that each firm (j', t') sets the whole price vector p_{L_2}. However, we assume that these prices are then common to all firms, i.e. that they are market prices, and that (j', t') must choose its production plan to clear the market for goods in L_2 (so this is not a Bertrand model). As in section 4, each firm takes input prices and the distribution of wealth as given. We will not concern ourselves with the existence of a generalized ICE. Presumably, conditions similar to those in proposition 4.1 will ensure existence.

We consider now the behaviour of a generalized ICE when r is large. We make two further assumptions:

$$\sum_{i=1}^{m} \bar{x}_i \in R^l_{++} \tag{A16}$$

For all $j = 1, \ldots, n$, given $\hat{p} \in R^l_{++}$, $\hat{\mathbf{w}} \in R^m_+$, $\hat{\bar{y}} \in R^l$ satisfying $\xi_{L_2}(\hat{p}, \hat{\mathbf{w}}) - n\hat{\bar{y}}_{L_2} = 0$, there exists $\epsilon > 0$ such that the equation $\xi_{L_2}(p_{L_2}, \hat{p}'_{L_1}, \hat{\mathbf{w}}') - (n - \lambda)\, S^j_{L_2}(p_{L_2}, \hat{p}'_{L_1}; \hat{p}', \hat{\bar{y}}') = \mathbf{x}$ has a unique solution p_{L_2} for all

$$\|\hat{\mathbf{w}}' - \hat{\mathbf{w}}\| < \epsilon, \qquad 0 \leqslant \lambda < \epsilon, \ \|\hat{p}' - \hat{p}\| < \epsilon,$$

$$\|\hat{\bar{y}}' - \hat{\bar{y}}\| < \epsilon, \ \|\mathbf{x}\| < \epsilon. \tag{A17}$$

That is, we assume that there is a positive endowment of every good and that the excess demand function (6.2) has a well-defined inverse for large enough r (i.e. small enough λ).

Proposition 6.1 Assume (A4″), (A10)–(A11), (A15)–(A17) and that each Y_j is bounded, closed and contains zero. Let $[p^r, (x^r_i), (y^r_{jt}), (\mathbf{w}^r)]$ be a sequence of generalized ICE's in the economies E_r, where $\Sigma^l_{k=1} p^r_k = 1$. Define

$$y^r_j = \sum_{t=1}^{r} \frac{y^r_{jt}}{r}$$

for each j, r. Then the sequence $[p^r, (x^r_i), (y^r_j), \mathbf{w}^r]$ is bounded and every limit point $[\hat{p}, (\hat{x}_i), (\hat{y}_j), \hat{\mathbf{w}}]$ satisfies

$$\hat{x}_i = \xi_i(\hat{p}, \hat{w}_i) \text{ for all } i \tag{6.7}$$

For all j, $\hat{y}_j$ max $\hat{p} \cdot y$ on the convex hull of Y_j (6.8)

$$\hat{w}_i = \hat{p} \cdot \bar{x}_i + \sum_{j=1}^{n} \bar{\theta}_{ij} \hat{p} \cdot \hat{y}_j \tag{6.9}$$

$$\sum_{i=1}^{m} \hat{x}_i - \sum_{j=1}^{n} \hat{y}_j - \sum_{i=1}^{m} \bar{x}_i = 0. \tag{6.10}$$

Proof: see Appendix.

Proposition 6.1 tells us that a generalized ICE converges to a Walrasian equilibrium in per capita terms as $r \to \infty$ ((6.7)–(6.10) define a Walrasian equilibrium for the convexified, per capita economy). The intuition behind proposition 6.1 is straightforward. Suppose firm (j, t) produces y_j. Then from (6.2) prices p will satisfy

$$\xi_{L_2}(p, \mathbf{w}) - \left(n - \frac{1}{r}\right) S^j_{L_2}(p; \hat{p}, \hat{\hat{y}}) = \frac{y_{jL_2}}{r}. \tag{6.11}$$

When r is large, the right-hand side of (6.11) is approximately zero if Y_j is bounded. This means that the solution to (6.11) (unique by (A17)) is approximately independent of y_j. That is, when r is large, each firm is approximately a price-taker.

Note that, if Y_j is unbounded, y_{jL_2}/r may not tend to zero as $r \to \infty$ and so, even when r is large, a firm may be able to affect prices. In spite of this, proposition 6.1 can be shown to generalize to this case for Cournot–Nash conjectures (see Ushio, 1983a).[26]

Remark 1 As noted above, propositions similar to proposition 6.1 have been established by many authors, mainly for the case of Cournot–Nash behaviour. In this case, the proposition has been generalized to the case of entry (see Hart, 1980; Mas-Colell, 1982; Novshek, 1980; Novshek and Sonnenschein, 1978, on the case of free entry; and Guesnerie and Hart, 1982; Hart, 1979; Mas-Colell, 1983; and Novshek and Sonnenschein, 1983, on the case of barriers to entry).[27]

Assumption (A17) is important for the proposition. If, for example, uniqueness fails, a selection of the price vectors satisfying (6.11) must be made. This selection may have to be discontinuous at some points, and, as a result, proposition 6.1 may fail (see Roberts, 1980). (A16) (or some weaker version of it) is also important. It ensures that all markets are open. Without it, the economy may get stuck at a boundary where a number of goods that should be produced (and would be in the Walrasian equilibrium) are not. This can happen if the goods produced by different imperfectly competitive firms are so strongly complementary that it doesn't pay one firm to produce unless another does (see Hart, 1980; Makowski, 1980b).

Remark 2 Much recent work has also been done establishing the existence of equilibrium when r is large, again for the Cournot–Nash case (see, e.g., Novshek, 1980; Novshek and Sonnenschein, 1978, 1983; Roberts, 1980 and Mas-Colell, 1982, 1983). These papers also study the question of when a given Walrasian equilibrium is the limit of a sequence of Cournot–Nash equilibria. We cannot go into the existence argument in any detail. To get some idea of why existence is less of a problem in large economies, note that, as we have seen above, when r is large, firms are approximately price-takers if production sets are bounded. Thus, if there are decreasing returns to scale, the equation 'marginal revenue equals marginal cost' has a unique solution. This means that firms' response functions are single-valued; i.e., (A14) is automatically satisfied. (Various regularity conditions, which are satisfied generically, are required for this; see Roberts, 1980, Mas-Colell, 1982.)

Some of the above papers also establish existence when entry, subject to a fixed set-up cost, is allowed.[28] This complicates matters considerably, since the problem of an integral number of operating firms must be dealt with. In some cases, in order to overcome this problem, a small number of firms have to be allowed the use of mixed strategies (see Novshek and Sonnenschein, 1978; Mas-Colell, 1982). With free entry, Novshek and Sonnenschein (1978) have also shown that an additional assumption, which is a generalization of the idea that demand curves slope downwards, must be made to prove existence (for a discussion of this issue see Mas-Colell, 1982, 1983, and Novshek and Sonnenschein, 1978).

Remark 3 Proposition 6.1 shows that, in a large class of cases, if firms are small relative to their markets, an approximately competitive outcome will result. Note that proposition 6.1 does not require the assumption that conjectures are rational or reasonable: all it requires is that subjective demand curves are of the form (6.2). At first sight, this seems a weaker assumption. However, proposition 6.1 assumes that supply responses are continuous functions. In contrast, the supply responses associated with reasonable conjectures, i.e. the solutions of (5.10), may be correspondences. If these correspondences are convex-valued, it seems likely in view of proposition 6.1 that reasonable conjectural equilibrium allocations will (at least under some regularity assumptions) converge to the competitive outcome as $r \to \infty$. However, if the supply correspondences are not convex-valued, then a small change in price may lead to a discontinuous change in firms' outputs which suggests that problems of the sort discussed by Roberts (1980) may prevent convergence.

Subject to this last qualification, proposition 6.1 seems to provide a sound foundation for the third interpretation: that the Arrow–Debreu model corresponds to the case where each agent is small relative to his market.[29] I now want to make some further comments on how this view ties in with others that may be found in the literature.

In a series of papers Ostroy (1980) and Makowski (1980a, 1980b) have proposed the following test of perfect competition, called the no-surplus condition. Consider the Walrasian equilibrium of an economy. Suppose that there is some agent j for which the following is true: the agents other than j could not make themselves as well off as in the Walrasian equilibrium if they were forced to allocate only their own resources among themselves. Then j is contributing a positive surplus to the economy at the Walrasian equilibrium and the no-surplus condition fails. Ostroy and Makowski argue that the Walrasian equilibrium is not stable under these conditions since it will pay agent j to try to extract some of this surplus. Only if the no-surplus condition holds (for all agents), i.e. if no agent contributes a surplus, is the Walrasian equilibrium stable.

We can apply this test to the model of the last section. For simplicity consider the case of duopoly. It is clear that, if firms' marginal costs are strictly increasing, it is impossible for one firm by itself to offer other consumers the same quantities and prices and make the same profit, as when there are two firms. Thus each firm is contributing a positive surplus, and the Walrasian equilibrium is unstable. On the other hand, if both firms have the same constant marginal cost, then neither firm is essential to the allocation and the Walrasian equilibrium is stable; this is in spite of the fact that neither firm is small relative to its market.

As another example, where the no-surplus condition holds in a 'small' economy, suppose there are many identical potential suppliers of a good. Assume that each supplier faces initially strongly increasing returns to scale. Then the market may be only large enough to support a single operating firm. However, because of the large amount of potential competition from suppliers, we might expect the outcome to be highly competitive. In particular, the no-surplus condition is satisfied (assuming the Walrasian equilibrium exists). Note, however, that firms are not small relative to the market, and the Cournot–Nash outcome, for example, is far from competitive. The argument that a competitive outcome will prevail in this sort of situation has been made by Grossman (1981) in a recent paper. (Grossman makes a distinction between increasing returns arising from fixed costs and those arising from sunk costs; only in the former case will competition prevail, he argues; for in the latter case those firms that have sunk their costs will have some bargaining power relative to those firms that have not.) A somewhat similar argument may be found in Baumol, Panzar and Willig's (1982) analysis of contestable markets.

In both the above examples (duopoly when firms have constant, equal marginal costs, and the case of many identical suppliers), the Walrasian equilibrium is a reasonable conjectural equilibrium.[30] It is, however, not the only one in the duopoly case, and I would conjecture that it is also not the only one in the case of many identical suppliers. This suggests that the no-surplus condition should be regarded as a necessary, but not sufficient, condition for competition. In any case, the no-surplus condition will only rarely be satisfied in small economies, and thus this test does not support either the first or second interpretations of competition.

On the other hand, the no-surplus test is quite consistent with the third interpretation of perfect competition; for Ostroy (1980) has shown that in a large economy under quite general conditions each agent contributes an approximately zero surplus.

Finally, it should be noted that we have restricted our attention throughout to a static, one-period context. In repeated (especially infinitely repeated) situations, matters can look rather different. In particular, cooperative-like behaviour might be observed by firms, even though explicit collusion is impossible (see, e.g., Friedman, 1971; Green, 1980; Porter, 1983; Radner, 1980; and Brock and Scheinkman, 1981). For instance, in the oligopoly example of section 5, the following sort of trigger mechanism might be used to achieve the joint profit-maximizing outcome for firms: each firm chooses the joint profit-maximizing output in period t unless in period $(t-1)$ another firm has deviated from this; in this case, the firm chooses the Cournot–Nash output for ever more (or at least for a long time). If the discount rate is low enough, it can be shown that these strategies form a (perfect) Nash equilibrium for all firms (see Friedman, 1971; Radner, 1980; and Brock and Scheinkman, 1981).

If tacit collusion of this sort is possible, perfectly competitive behaviour is even less likely to occur than we have suggested. Even in an economy with a large number of small firms, trigger mechanisms of the above type may sometimes be used to achieve highly non-competitive outcomes. At the same time, under plausible assumptions, tacit collusion can be shown to be more difficult to sustain the larger is the number of firms. (On this, see Green, 1980; Porter, 1983; and Radner, 1980; as one example, Green and Porter show this will be the case if (a) firms cannot observe each other's outputs directly but can observe only a summary statistic, e.g. price; (b) price is a noisy signal because, say, demand is stochastic.)[31] Thus we are again led to the conclusion that the conditions for perfect competition are more likely to be satisfied when individual firms are small relative to their market.[32, 33]

7 CONCLUDING REMARKS

I have considered a number of approaches to modelling imperfect competition in a general equilibrium framework. The subjective demand approach developed by Negishi (1961, 1972), although both elegant and general, suffers from the weakness that the class of possible equilibria (given arbitrary conjectures) is very large. The objective demand approach ties equilibrium down to a much greater extent, at least given a particular solution concept such as Cournot–Nash (in prices or quantities), but at a cost in terms of simplicity. At the same time, we saw in section 4 that it is possible to develop a particular objective demand model in which a number of the more troublesome feedback effects are absent, and which has a strong partial equilibrium flavour. Such a model seems potentially tractable.

The objective demand approach becomes considerably less objective, however, once we allow for solution concepts other than Cournot–Nash, i.e. for different conjectures about reactions of other agents. This is even the case if we insist that agents' conjectures be rational (or reasonable). In fact, in section 5 we saw in a simple partial equilibrium model that there is a continuum of reasonable conjectural equilibria. This indeterminateness obviously carries over to a general equilibrium setting.

A major problem with all the models that we have considered is the difficulty of establishing the existence of equilibrium. In all cases, in order to prove existence we had to assume, without any justification in terms of tastes or production possibilities, that the responses of imperfect competitors are single-valued functions (or convex-valued correspondences). In the Cournot–Nash quantity-setting model, problems also arise if, given particular production plans by firms, there is more than one vector of prices that clears markets, i.e. if the inverse demand function is multi-valued. These existence problems would have been even more severe if, instead of assuming that there was a fixed number of firms, we had modelled the entry decisions of firms, in the presence of set-up costs, explicitly.

While the above existence problems are very serious, it should be pointed out that they are not really due to the general equilibrium nature of the problem. It would seem that exactly the same non-existence problems can occur in a partial equilibrium setting. In particular, there is no reason there either to expect imperfectly competitive agents' responses to be single-valued functions (or convex-valued correspondences). Also, given a situation where quantity-setting oligopolists produce several goods and face the demand function $D(P_1, \ldots, P_L)$, there is no reason why the equation $D(P_1, \ldots, P_L) = (q_1, \ldots, q_L)$ should have a unique solution.

It is true that, in the simplest partial equilibrium setting, where n identical oligopolists produce a homogeneous good and face non-increasing returns to scale, and where there is a single-valued inverse demand function, a Cournot–Nash equilibrium can be shown to exist (despite the non-convexity of response correspondences). This was established in two very interesting papers by McManus (1962, 1964) (and was proved independently by Roberts and Sonnenschein, 1976). However, these results do not extend to non-homogeneous goods, non-identical oligopolists and increasing returns to scale (d'Aspremont, Gabszewicz and Thisse, 1979; Novshek, 1980, and personal communication, 1983).

Finally, I have considered what light recent work throws on the old question of the meaning of perfect competition (the early literature on this includes Chamberlin, 1933; Robinson, 1933; and Kaldor, 1935). I argued that the views that perfectly competitive outcomes arise because agents happen to conjecture that they face perfectly elastic demand (or supply) curves, or because agents are Bertrand price-setters, do not provide a firm foundation for the Arrow–Debreu model. Only if individual agents are small relative to their markets (and sometimes not even then) does the Arrow–Debreu equilibrium have a strong claim on our attention.

APPENDIX

Proof of proposition 4.1

The set of feasible allocations is bounded. Hence there exists $K>0$ such that, if $(x_1, \ldots, x_m, y_1, \ldots, y_n)$ satisfies $x_i \in R^l_+$ for all i, $y_j \in Y_j$ for all j, $\Sigma_i x_i - \Sigma_j y_j - \Sigma_i \bar{x}_i \leqslant 0$, then $\|y_j\| \leqslant K$. For each j, let $\hat{Y}_j = \{y \in Y_j | \|y\| \leqslant K\}$ and let $S = \{p \in R^l_+ | \Sigma^l_{k=1} p_k = 1\}$. Given

$$(\hat{p}, \hat{y}_1, \ldots, \hat{y}_n) \in S \times \prod_{j=1}^{n} \hat{Y}_j,$$

let $\hat{\mathbf{w}}' = (\hat{w}'_1, \ldots, \hat{w}'_m)$ where

$$\hat{w}'_i = \hat{p}\bar{x}_i + \sum_{j=1}^{n} \bar{\theta}_{ij} \max(0, \hat{p}\hat{y}_j). \tag{1}$$

Clearly the $\hat{w}'_i$ are bounded; i.e., we can choose $\bar{w}$ such that

$$(\hat{p}, \hat{y}_1, \ldots, \hat{y}_n) \in S \times \prod_{j=1}^{n} \hat{Y}_j \Rightarrow \hat{w}'_i < \bar{w}$$

for all i. Let

$$\alpha_j = \max_{0 \leqslant w \leqslant \bar{w}} \alpha_j(w)$$

for each $j \in N^2$ (see assumption (A14)). Finally, for $j \in N^2$, define $\bar{Y}_j = \{y \in Y_j | \|y\| \leqslant \max(\alpha_j, K)\}$ and let $\Delta = \{p \in S | p_k \geqslant \delta$ for each $k\}$ where $1 > \delta > 0$.

Now consider a correspondence from

$$\Delta \times \prod_{j \in N^2} \bar{Y}_j \times \prod_{j \in N^1} \hat{Y}_j \times [0, \bar{w}]^m$$

into itself defined as follows:

$$(\hat{p}, \hat{y}_1, \ldots, \hat{y}_n, \hat{w}_1, \ldots, \hat{w}_m) \rightarrow (\hat{p}', \hat{y}'_1, \ldots, \hat{y}'_n, \hat{w}'_1, \ldots, \hat{w}'_m)$$

where

$$\hat{p}' \text{ maximizes } p\left[\xi(\hat{p}, \hat{\mathbf{w}}) - \sum_{j=1}^{n} \hat{y}_j - \sum_{i=1}^{m} \bar{x}_i\right] \text{ on } \Delta \tag{2}$$

For $j \in N^2$, $\hat{y}_j'$ maximizes $p_{M^j} y_{M^j} + \hat{p}_{L\setminus M^j}\, y_{L\setminus M^j}$ subject to $y_{M^j} = \xi^j_{M^j}(p_{M^j}, p_{L\setminus M^j}, \hat{\mathbf{w}})$ and $y \in Y_j$ (3)

For $j \in N^1$, $\hat{y}_j'$ maximizes $\hat{p}y_j$ on $\hat{Y}_j$ (4)

$$\hat{w}_i' = \hat{p}\bar{x}_i + \sum_{j=1}^{n} \bar{\theta}_{ij} \max(0, \hat{p}\hat{y}_j) \text{ for each } i. \tag{5}$$

By Kakutani's theorem, this correspondence has a fixed point $(p^*, y_1^*, \ldots, y_n^*, w_1^*, \ldots, w_m^*)$. From (3), (A12), (4) and the assumption $0 \in Y_j$, $p^*y_j^* \geqslant 0$ for all j. Let $z^* = \xi(p^*, \mathbf{w}^*) - \Sigma_j y_j^* - \Sigma_i \bar{x}_i$. It follows from Walras's Law and (2) (putting $p_k = [1-(m-1)\,\delta]$, $p_r = \delta, r \neq k$) that, for each k,

$$[1-(m-1)\,\delta]z_k^* + \delta \sum_{r\neq k} z_r^* \leqslant p^*z^* = 0. \tag{6}$$

Now let $\delta \to 0$. Suppose some coordinate of p^* tends to zero. Then by (A4″), $z_k^* \to \infty$ for some k. Since z_r^* is bounded below, (6) is contradicted. Hence without loss of generality $p^* \to \bar{p} \gg 0$, $z^* \to \bar{z}$, $y_j \to \bar{y}_j$, $w_i \to \bar{w}_i$.

It follows from (6) that $\bar{z} \leqslant 0$. Hence we can remove the bounds in the usual way to show that $(\bar{p}, \bar{y}_1, \ldots, \bar{y}_n, \bar{w}_1, \ldots, \bar{w}_m)$ is an ICE.

Proof of proposition 6.1

Boundedness of the sequence is obvious, as is (6.7), (6.9) and (6.10). Let $[\hat{p}, (\hat{x}_i), (\hat{y}_j), \mathbf{w}]$ be a limit point. Suppose (6.8) does not hold for some j. Then there must exist $y_j' \in Y_j$ such that $\hat{p}y_j' > \hat{p}\hat{y}_j$. Therefore there exists $\eta > 0$ such that, for large r, $\hat{p}y_j' > p^r y_{jt}^r + \eta$ for some t. Suppose firm (j, t) chose the prices $\bar{p}_{L_2}^r$ in E_r to solve

$$r\xi_{L_2}(\bar{p}_{L_2}^r, p_{L_1}^r, \mathbf{w}^r) - (nr-1)\, S_{L_2}^j \left[(\bar{p}_{L_2}^r, p_{L_1}^r); p^r, \frac{\left(\sum_{k=1}^{n}\sum_{s=1}^{r} y_{ks}^r - y_{jt}^r\right)}{(nr-1)} \right] = y_{jL_2}'. \tag{7}$$

By (A17), this equation has a unique solution for large r. Furthermore it is easy to see that $\lim_{r\to\infty}\bar{p}_{L_2}^r = \hat{p}_{L_2}$. Hence firm (j, t)'s profits $\bar{p}_{L_2}^r y_{jL_2}' + p_{L_1}^r y_{jL_1}'$ are approximately $\hat{p}y_j'$ under prices $\bar{p}_{L_2}^r$. This means that firm (j, t) could increase its profit by choosing $\bar{p}_{L_2}^r$, which contradicts the fact that it is in equilibrium. Q.E.D.

NOTES

I have benefited from the comments of a number of people. I would like to thank K. Arrow, J. Gabszewicz, M. King, L. Makowski, W. Novshek and H. Sonnenschein. I am particularly grateful for the suggestions of G. Bonanno and L. Corchon. The usual caveat applies.

1 That is $U_i(x') > U_i(x) \Rightarrow U_i[\lambda x' + (1-\lambda)x] > U_i(x)$ for all $0 < \lambda < 1$.
2 That is, given any $x \in R^l_+$, there exists x' such that $U_i(x') > U_i(x)$.
3 I am grateful to Mervyn King for referring me to Marshall.
4 This problem has, however, been the focus of the now sizeable literature on objectives for firms in stock market economies when there is uncertainty. For a recent summary of this literature, see Dreze (1982).
5 It should be mentioned that a third class of objective demand models, due to Shubik and a number of others, may also be found in the literature (see, e.g., Shubik, 1973, and Shapley and Shubik, 1977). In the Shubik approach, consumers as well as firms are treated as strategic agents and there is a commodity money in terms of which all agents make bids for goods. A paper that uses this approach to study general equilibrium in a production economy is Dubey and Shubik (1977).
6 Note that, if imperfectly competitive firms face a large, competitive consumer sector, and if there is a perfect resale market for their products, the only feasible contracts will be those involving a uniform price, since in all other cases arbitrage profits can be made. Some assumption like this underlies our analysis.
7 A similar assumption about capitalists is made in Mas-Colell (1982).
8 A small criticism of Roberts and Sonnenschein's non-existence examples can be made. In these examples, firms are assumed to maximize profit even though this is clearly not in the interest of their owners. Presumably, however, the examples could be modified to take account of this criticism.
9 Dasgupta and Maskin (1982) have given sufficient conditions for mixed strategy equilibria to exist in games where the strategy sets contain infinitely many elements. Unfortunately, these conditions are not satisfied in the present context. It is worth noting that the Dierker–Grodal non-existence example suffers from the same drawback as the Roberts–Sonnenschein examples: firms are assumed to maximize profit even though this is not in the interest of owners. Again, it is hard to believe that the example depends on this.
10 One reaction to the fact that existence does not obtain in general is to reject the model. Another is to restrict attention to a (possibly quite restrictive) class of preferences and production sets where existence (preferably in pure strategies) is guaranteed. For a discussion of the conclusions to be drawn from non-existence, see Roberts and Sonnenschein (1977).
11 The justification for assuming that firms $1, \ldots, n'$ are price takers might be that they are small relative to the economy.

12 In the extreme case where widgets are a pure intermediate good, an increase in supply by type A firms will, according to the Cournot–Nash assumption, lead to a situation of excess supply, and hence the price of widgets will fall to zero. On the other hand, an increase in widget demand by type B firms will lead to an infinite price. Clearly there can exist no Cournot–Nash equilibrium with positive widget production in this extreme case.

13 An alternative (and simpler) approach would be for type A firms to conjecture that type B firms keep their output constant but change their input mix (so as to minimize costs) when the price of widgets changes. I am grateful to Kenneth Arrow for suggesting this possibility.

14 Laffont and Laroque (1976), in fact, consider a model in which a mixture of prices and quantities is taken as given by a firm that is choosing its production plan.

15 A justification for this is the following. Suppose there is a perfect resale market for the firm's goods. Then if the firm tries to ration its customers, in order, say, to increase demand for one good at the expense of another, there will be an incentive for entrepreneurs to buy up the goods and resell them at a profit. This will defeat the purpose of the rationing.

16 Marschak and Selten assume that the profits of monopolistically competitive firms, but not the profits of all firms, are taken as given by each monopolistically competitive firm. For our purposes, the present formulation is more appropriate.

17 See also Guesnerie and Hart (1982).

18 This assumption was not made in Hart (1982a). It is, however, made in Guesnerie and Hart (1982).

19 In Hart (1982a), instead of (4.10), it was assumed that all type *i* consumers had the same initial shareholding in every type *j* firm. This assumption, like (4.10), implies that consumer demand is the same on all islands and that no firm can influence the distribution of wealth. It was claimed in Hart (1982a) that the assumption also implies that profit maximization will be in the interest of almost all the shareholders of any firm. This is unfortunately incorrect, and it appears that the more complicated formulation (4.10) is required to ensure this.

20 In one of the few attempts to develop a general equilibrium analysis of imperfect competition with differentiated products, Dixit and Stiglitz (1977) consider a model where each firm ignores the feedback effect. As in Marschak and Selten (1974) and Silvestre (1978), however, this assumption is not justified.

21 This suggests that the techniques of Dasgupta and Maskin (1982) might be used to establish the existence of an equilibrium in which firms choose mixed strategies, in the absence of (A14).

22 A recent paper which examines the role of the timing of decisions in generating Cournot–Nash or Bertrand outcomes is Kreps and Scheinkman (1983).

23 I am grateful to Hamid Sabourian for pointing this out to me.

24 The number of equilibria becomes much smaller, of course, if one is prepared to restrict the class of conjectures. For example, Ulph (1984) considers the

case of location-independent conjectures $\alpha_i(q;\, \hat{p}, \hat{q}) = f[D(\hat{p}) + \beta_i(q - \hat{q})]$ for some function β_i. In many cases equilibrium is then unique.

25 This is not so in the work of Shubik (1973), Shapley and Shubik (1977) and Roberts and Postlewaite (1976). Also, Shubik (1973) and Shapley and Shubik (1977) treat consumers and firms symmetrically rather than assuming, as in much of the literature, that consumers are price-takers while firms are imperfect competitors.

26 When production sets are unbounded, the convergence question is in general more delicate. In particular, under quite reasonable specifications convergence may not occur. For example, suppose that firms must decide whether to incur a fixed cost of entry at date 1, but choose how much to produce (given entry) only at date 2. Then, if firms are Bertrand price-setters at date 2 and marginal costs are constant, and the same for all firms, the (perfect) Nash equilibrium will involve a single firm entering at date 1 and choosing a monopoly price at date 2. Thus under these conditions even in a large economy competition will not prevail. Examples in this spirit have been studied by Shaked and Sutton (1982) in the context of product differentiation.

27 A number of recent papers have also considered the *rate* of convergence of Cournot–Nash equilibria to Walrasian equilibria. See Dasgupta and Ushio (1981), Fraysse and Moreaux (1980), Ushio (1982a), and Guesnerie and Hart (1982).

28 A paper that establishes existence in a simple model of entry, employing a quantity-setting version of the ICE notion of equilibrium of section 4, is Guesnerie and Hart (1982).

29 Further support for this interpretation may be found in the large literature establishing the equivalence of the core and the set of competitive equilibria in a large (continuum) economy. See, e.g., Hildenbrand (1974).

30 The relationship between the no-surplus condition and the requirement that agents face perfectly elastic demand functions (i.e. that perfectly elastic conjectures are rational) is discussed in Ostroy (1980) and Makowski (1980a, 1980b). In fact, Makowski in some of his work uses the rationality of perfectly elastic conjectures as the defining property of perfect competition.

31 A counter-example to this proposition may, however, be found in Brock and Scheinkman (1981).

32 We have assumed throughout that consumers have perfect information about the prices charged by firms. There is a large literature on the consequences of relaxing this assumption. One conclusion of this literature is that, even with a large number of small firms, competitive outcomes may not prevail. See, e.g., Diamond (1971).

33 Another interpretation of perfect competition should also be mentioned. This is the idea proposed by Arrow (1959), and taken up by Hahn (1978), that agents will be price-takers if the economy is in Walrasian equilibrium but will become price-setters if the economy moves away from this equilibrium (or is in disequilibrium). The trouble with this idea is that it is not

clear what primitive assumptions underlie it; that is, it is unclear what conditions on information, technology or tastes must be satisfied for an agent to recognize or exploit its monopoly power only when the economy is away from Walrasian equilibrium.

REFERENCES

Arrow, K. J. (1959), 'Towards a Theory of Price Adjustment', in A. Abramovitz (ed.), *The Allocation of Economic Resources*, Stanford University Press.

Arrow, K. J. and Hahn, F. H. (1971), *General Competitive Analysis*, Holden-Day, San Francisco.

d'Aspremont, C., Gabszewicz, J. and Thisse, J. (1979), 'On Hotelling's "Stability in Competition"', *Econometrica*, **47**, 1145–50.

Baumol, W. J.; Panzar, J. C. and Willig, R. D. (1982), *Contestable Markets and the Theory of Industrial Structure*, Harcourt, Brace, Jovanovich, New York.

Bresnahan, T. F. (1981), 'Duopoly Models with Consistent Conjectures', *American Economic Review*, **71**, 934–45.

Brock, W. A. and Scheinkman, J. A. (1981), 'Price-setting Supergames with Capacity Constraints', mimeo, University of Wisconsin.

Chamberlin, E. H. (1933), *The Theory of Monopolistic Competition*, Harvard University Press, Cambridge, Mass.

Cornwall, R. (1977), 'The Concept of General Equilibrium in a Market Economy with Imperfectly Competitive Producers', *Metroeconomica*, **29**, 57–72.

Cyert, R. and deGroot, M. (1970), 'Multiperiod Decision Models with Alternating Choice as a Solution to the Duopoly Problem', *Quarterly Journal of Economics*, **24**, 410–29.

Dasgupta, P. and Maskin, E. (1982), 'The Existence of Equilibrium in Discontinuous Economic Games. I: Theory', ICERD Discussion Paper no. 54, London School of Economics.

Dasgupta, P. and Ushio, Y. (1981). 'On the Rate of Convergence of Oligopoly Equilibria in Large Markets: An Example', *Economic Letters*, **8**, 13–17.

Debreu, G. (1959), *Theory of Value*, John Wiley, New York.

Diamond, P. A. (1971), 'A Model of Price Adjustment', *Journal of Economic Theory*, **3**, 156–68.

Dierker, H. and Grodal, B. (1982). 'Nonexistence of Cournot–Walras Equilibrium in a General Equilibrium Model with two Oligopolists', Discussion Paper no. 95, University of Bonn.

Dixit, A. K. and Stiglitz, J. E. (1977), 'Monopolistic Competition and Optimum Product Diversity', *American Economic Review*, **67**, 297–308.

Dreze, J. H. (1982), 'Decision Criteria for Business Firms', CORE Discussion Paper no. 8211.

Dubey, P. (1982). 'Price–Quantity Strategic Market Games', *Econometrica*, **50**, 111–26.

Dubey, P., Mas-Colell, A. and Shubik, M. (1980), 'Efficiency Properties of Strategic Market Games: An Axiomatic Approach', *Journal of Economic Theory*, **22**, 339–62.

Dubey, P. and Shubik, M. (1977), 'A Closed Economic System with Production and Exchange Modelled as a Game of Strategy', *Journal of Mathematical Economics*, **4**, 253–88.

Fitzroy, F. (1974), 'Monopolistic Equilibrium, Non-Convexity and Inverse Demand', *Journal of Economic Theory*, **7**, 1–16.

Fraysse, J. and Moreaux, M. (1980), 'Comportement limite des oligopoles de Cournot avec rendements croissants', Universite des Sciences Sociales de Toulouse.

Friedman, J. W. (1968), 'Reaction Functions and the Theory of Duopoly', *Review of Economic Studies*, **35**, 257–72.

Friedman, J. W. (1971), 'A Non-cooperative Equilibrium for Supergames', *Review of Economic Studies*, **38**, 1–13.

Gabszewicz, J. and Vial, J. P. (1972), 'Oligopoly "*à la* Cournot" in General Equilibrium Analysis', *Journal of Economic Theory*, **4**, 381–400.

Green, E. J. (1980), 'Non-cooperative Price Taking in Large Dynamic Markets', *Journal of Economic Theory*, **22**, 155–82.

Grossman, S. J. (1981), 'Nash Equilibrium and the Industrial Organisation of Markets with Large Fixed Costs', *Econometrica*, **49**, 1149–72.

Guesnerie, R. and Hart, O. D. (1982), 'Welfare Losses due to Imperfect Competition: Asymptotic Results for Cournot-Nash Equilibria with Free Entry', mimeo, London School of Economics.

Hahn, F. H. (1977), 'Exercises in Conjectural Equilibria', *Scandinavian Journal of Economics*, **79**, 210–24.

Hahn, F. H. (1978), 'On Non-Walrasian Equilibria', *Review of Economic Studies*, **45**, 1–17.

Hart, O. D. (1979), 'Monopolistic Competition in a Large Economy with Differentiated Commodities', *Review of Economic Studies*, **46**, 1–30.

Hart, O. D. (1980), 'Perfect Competition and Optimal Product Differentiation', *Journal of Economic Theory*, **22**, 279–312.

Hart, O. D. (1982a), 'A Model of Imperfect Competition with Keynesian Features', *Quarterly Journal of Economics*, **97**, 109–38.

Hart, O. D. (1982b), 'Monopolistic Competition in a Large Economy with Differentiated Commodities: A Correction', *Review of Economic Studies*, **49**, 313–14.

Hart, O. D. (1982c), 'Reasonable Conjectures', mimeo, London School of Economics.

Hildenbrand, W. (1974), *Core and Equilibria of a Large Economy*, Princeton University Press.

Kaldor, N. (1935), 'Market Imperfection and Excess Capacity', *Economica*, **2**, 33–50.

Kreps, D. M. and Scheinkman, J. A. (1983), 'Quantity Pre-commitment and Bertrand Competition Yield Cournot Outcomes', *Bell Journal of Economics*, Autumn, 326–37.

Laffont, J.-J. and Laroque, G. (1976), 'Existence d'un equilibre general de concurrence imparfaite: Une introduction', *Econometrica*, **44**, 283–94.

Laitner, J. (1980), '"Rational" Duopoly Equilibrium', *Quarterly Journal of Economics*, **95**, 641–62.

McManus, M. (1962), 'Numbers and Size in Cournot Oligopoly', *Yorkshire Bulletin*, **14**, 14–22.

McManus, M. (1964), 'Equilibrium, Numbers and Size in Cournot Oligopoly', *Yorkshire Bulletin*, **16**, 68–75.

Makowski, L. (1980a), 'A Characterisation of Perfectly Competitive Economies with Production', *Journal of Economic Theory*, **22**, 208–21.

Makowski, L. (1980b), 'Perfect Competition, the Profit Criterion and the Organisation of Economic Activity', *Journal of Economic Theory*, **22**, 222–41.

Marschak, T. and Selten, R. (1972), *General Equilibrium with Price-making Firms*, Lecture Notes in Economics and Mathematical Systems, Springer-Verlag, Berlin.

Marschak, T. and Selten, R. (1978), 'Restabilizing Responses, Inertia Supergames and Oligopolistic Equilibria', *Quarterly Journal of Economics*, **92**, 71–93.

Marshall, A. (1922), *Principles of Economics* (8th edn), Macmillan, London, 1922.

Mas-Colell, A. (1980), 'Non-cooperative Approaches to the Theory of Perfect Competition: Presentation', *Journal of Economic Theory*, **22**, 121–35.

Mas-Colell, A. (1982), 'The Cournotian Foundations of Walrasian Equilibrium Theory: An Exposition of Recent Theory', in W. Hildenbrand (ed.), *Advances in Economic Theory*, Cambridge University Press.

Mas-Colell, A. (1983), 'Walrasian Equilibria as Limits of Non-cooperative Equilibria. Part I: Mixed Strategies', *Journal of Economic Theory*, **30**, 153–70.

Maskin, E. and Tirole, J. (1982), 'A Theory of Dynamic Oligopoly, I: Overview and Quantity Competition with Large Fixed Costs', mimeo, Massachusetts Institute of Technology.

Negishi, T. (1961), 'Monopolistic Competition and General Equilibrium', *Review of Economic Studies*, **28**, 196–201.

Negishi, T. (1972), *General Equilibrium Theory and International Trade*, North-Holland, Amsterdam.

Nikaidô, H. (1975), *Monopolistic Competition and Effective Demand*, Princeton University Press.

Novshek, W. (1980), 'Cournot Equilibrium with Free Entry', *Review of Economic Studies*, **47**, 473–86.

Novshek, W. and Sonnenschein, H. (1978), 'Cournot and Walras Equilibrium', *Journal of Economic Theory*, **19**, 223–66.

Novshek, W. and Sonnenschein, H. (1983), 'Walrasian Equilibria as Limits of Non-cooperative Equilibria. Part II: Pure Strategies', *Journal of Economic Theory*, **30**, 171–87.

Ostroy, J. (1980), 'The No-surplus Condition as a Characterisation of Perfectly Competitive Equilibrium', *Journal of Economic Theory*, **22**, 183–208.

Perry, M. (1982), 'Oligopoly and Consistent Conjectural Variations', *Bell Journal of Economics*, **13**, 197–205.

Phlips, J. and Thisse, J. (1981), 'Pricing, Distribution and the Supply of Storage', *European Economic Review*, **15**, 225–43.

Porter, R. H. (1983), 'Optimal Cartel Trigger Price Strategies', *Journal of Economic Theory*, **29**, 313–38.

Radner, R. (1980), 'Collusive Behaviour in Non-cooperative Epsilon Equilibria of Oligopolies with Long but Finite Lives', *Journal of Economic Theory*, **22**, 136–54.

Roberts, D. J. and Postlewaite, A. (1976). 'The Incentives for Price-taking Behaviour in Large Exchange Economies', *Econometrica*, **44**, 115–28.

Roberts, D. J. and Sonnenschein, H. (1976), 'On the Existence of Cournot Equilibrium without Concave Profit Functions', *Journal of Economic Theory*, **8**, 112–17.

Roberts, D. J. and Sonnenschein, H. (1977), 'On the Foundations of the Theory of Monopolistic Competition', *Econometrica*, **45**, 101–14.

Roberts, K. (1980). 'The Limit Points of Monopolistic Competition', *Journal of Economic Theory*, **22**, 256–78.

Robinson, J. (1933), *The Economics of Imperfect Competition*, Macmillan, London.

Robinson, J. (1934), 'What is Perfect Competition?' *Quarterly Journal of Economics*, **49**, 104–20.

Shaked, A. and Sutton, J. (1982), 'Relaxing Price Competition through Product Differentiation', *Review of Economic Studies*, **49**, 3–14.

Shapley, L. and Shubik, M. (1977), 'Trade Using One Commodity as a Means of Payment', *Journal of Political Economy*, **85**, 937–68.

Shubik, M. (1973), 'Commodity Money, Oligopoly, Credit and Bankruptcy in a General Equilibrium Model', *Western Economic Journal*, **11**, 24–38.

Silvestre, J. (1977a), 'General Monopolistic Equilibrium under Non-convexities', *International Economic Review*, **18**, 425–34.

Silvestre, J. (1977b), 'A Model of General Equilibrium with Monopolistic Behaviour', *Journal of Economic Theory*, **16**, 425–42.

Silvestre, J. (1978), 'Increasing Returns in General Non-competitive Analysis', *Econometrica*, **46**, 397–402.

Simon, L. (1982), 'Bertrand, the Cournot Paradigm, and the Theory of Perfect Competition', mimeo, University of California, Berkeley.

Triffin, R. (1940), *Monopolistic Competition and General Equilibrium Theory*, Harvard University Press, Cambridge, Mass.

Ulph, D. (1981), 'On Market Size and Market Structure', mimeo, University College London.

Ulph, D. (1984), 'Rational Conjectures in the Theory of Oligopoly', *International Journal of Industrial Organisation*.

Ushio, Y. (1983a), 'Cournot Equilibrium with Free Entry: The Case of Decreasing Average Cost Functions', *Review of Economic Studies*, **50**, 347–54.

Ushio, Y. (1983b), 'On the Approximate Efficiency of Cournot–Nash Equilibria', mimeo, London School of Economics.

Comment

JEAN JASKOLD GABSZEWICZ

1 INTRODUCTION

Of all the dichotomies introduced in economics, none appears as asymmetric as the distinction between perfect and imperfect competition. While perfection is by now on a uniquely circumscribed concept (in economics!), markets may be imperfect in such a great variety of ways that a separate body of theory for each one of them should be appropriate. Furthermore, when you add to this mosaic of themes a methodological dichotomy based on the distinction between partial and general equilibrium analysis, you get a very sophisticated puzzle! Accordingly, when required to provide a survey of recent work on imperfect competition, the theorist cannot do otherwise than privilege a particular look to a particular niche of this wide spectrum. Professor Hart has chosen to examine closely the field of homogeneous oligopoly theory, as discovered from the viewpoint of general equilibrium theorists. Thus he decided to follow the suggestion made by Triffin (1962), according to which 'the new wine of monopolistic competition should not be poured into the old goatskins of particular equilibrium methodology' (p. 89).

Indeed, in the renewed outbreak of interest into the general equilibrium approach that had flowered in the 1950s, some hope was born of extending Walrasian theory to the imperfect competitive world. This hope was enhanced on the one hand under the impetus provided by the application of the core concept to the exchange model. The close scrutiny of the relationships between this concept and the concept of competitive equilibrium revealed that core theory could serve as a natural vehicle for developing a theory of imperfect competition into a general equilibrium framework.

In a pathbreaking paper, R. Aumann (1964) proved, indeed, that if the pure exchange economy consists of an 'atomless' set of traders, then the core of this exchange market must coincide with the set of its competitive allocations. Atomless economies could then serve as a reference point to contrast the outcomes in the core obtained in a 'mixed' exchange economy, involving *both* significant and negligible agents, with those outcomes that would obtain in a hypothetical economy in which the 'significant' agents had been replaced by an equivalent 'continuum' of small traders.

On the other hand, Professor Negishi (1961) proposed the first complete formal attempt to introduce oligopolies into a system of general competitive equilibrium. He suggested a notion of equilibrium based on the concept of 'subjective demand' functions, which express the expectation of the firm as to the relationship between the price it charges and the quantity of its output the market will buy. The property to be verified by the equilibrium is that the perceived demand curves should pass through the observed price and quantity points. The Negishi approach has recently received a considerable revival of interest.

Finally, in the last few years several papers have examined the possibility of extending the non-cooperative approach to the oligopoly problem, proposed by Cournot (1838), to a general equilibrium framework. The main objective of this extension was to provide groundwork for a non-cooperative theory of perfect competition, where 'the size of the market relative to individual agents would be a key explanatory variable for the tendency of non-cooperative behaviour to approximate perfect competition' (Mas-Colell, 1982: 2). Along this line of approach, no 'subjective' demand is assumed. Rather, firms are assumed to know the 'objective' demand function as in Cournot.

The major part of Hart's survey is organized around the two last directions defined above. (He has chosen to distinguish between them by using the terminology of 'subjective' and 'objective' demands.) Furthermore, his analysis focuses on (a) the existence problems raised by these theories, about the equilibrium concepts that are proposed (sections 2, 3 and 4), and (b) the relationships between the imperfectly competitive models he has studied and the Arrow–Debreu model (section 6). Section 5 forms something 'apart' from these main streams, reflecting personal recent research.

Professor Hart's survey is a brilliant piece of work, which succeeds in enclosing, in a relatively compact box, an intricate network of recent ideas and developments about imperfect competition. My comments appear as 'peripheral' with respect to his own overview, mainly because what had to be said along the lines of his project has indeed been said by him.

In tracing these lines, Professor Hart was obliged, for evident reasons of compactness, to drop out of his scope some major questions related to imperfect competition. The most important one, it seems to me, is the problem of product differentiation. As noted by Negishi,

> Although the imperfectness of markets . . . can also be attributed to the differentiation of the sellers (buyers) rather than the products, it is certainly true that the central theme of monopolistic competition is product differentiation. Which specific forms of products to produce is to be decided by firms, i.e. the stock of what commodities to exist should not be the *data* of the model. [Negishi, 1972: 104]

Even if some recent pieces of work about product differentiation are cast in general equilibrium terms, most contributions in this field are admittedly formulated into a kind of 'intermediate' model representing an industry (for instance, the spatial model proposed by Hotelling, 1929). Accordingly, Hart was perfectly right in letting them out of his focus. Being less constrained in my comments, however, I have taken the liberty of treading out of his footsteps, and evoke in my third section some recent work done under the heading of product differentiation. I have also related this work to the broader question of the level of generality at which imperfect competition should be modelled. My fourth section is devoted to some comments about the application of the core concept to the theory of imperfect competition (the first theme I was referring above). My fifth section consists of a short discussion on the problem raised by the often observed absence of equilibrium in models of imperfect competition. These comments echo those of Professor Hart about the same problem. But first, the following section is an attempt to provide a verbal guideline of the main streams covered by Hart's paper. It may be skipped without any damage by those who are accustomed to reading economics between mathematical symbols.

2 A VERBAL GUIDELINE TO HART'S PAPER

In sections 2, 3, 4 and 6, Professor Hart uses basically the same model. It consists of a set of goods, a set of firms and a set of consumers who own firms through their profit shares. Consumers are assumed to behave competitively under the constraint of their budget, defined as the value, at market prices, of their initial endowments plus their profit shares in the firms. Firms j are assumed to have a convex[1] production set Y_j, with irreversible production and $0 \in Y_j$. From one section to the other, however, the behaviour of firms varies according to the *actions* they are allowed to take, and according to the *objectives* they are assigned to pursue. In section 2 (subjective demand), the set of firms is partitioned into two subsets: first, the set of 'perfectly competitive' firms, which choose their production plans so as to maximize profits at given market prices; and, second, the set of 'monopolistically competitive' firms, which are assumed to choose their production plans in the following manner. Some 'initial position' of the economy being assumed to hold, characterized by a given price vector and a particular allocation, each monopolistically competitive firm is supposed to conjecture subjectively how varying its own production plan from this initial position will change the price vector operating in the economy, and thus its 'subjective' profits. Given a particular initial position, each monopolistically competitive firm is then assumed to alter its production plan in the direction that most increases these subjective profits. In section 3 (objective demand I), each firm is an imperfect competitor, and the choice of its production plan affects the initial endowments of the consumers who are the owners of the firm (in this model they receive a share of the output vector realized by the firm). Accordingly, to each set of production plans of the firms there corresponds an exchange economy, the initial endowments of which are conditional on the production plans chosen by the firms. Consequently, the equilibrium prices of this exchange economy are themselves conditional on these production plans; and, assuming that they are uniquely determined or selected, these prices may then serve to evaluate firms' profits realized at the corresponding production plans.

In section 4 (objective demand II) the set of firms is again partitioned into those that are 'pure competitors' and those that are 'imperfect competitors'. As usual, pure competitors choose their production plan so as to maximize profits at market prices. As for the imperfect competitors, each one of them is now assumed to produce a different set of goods, and to control the prices and quantities of these goods. (If pure competitors also produce some of these goods, they take the prices quoted by the imperfect competitor as given; total quantity is then the sum of the quantities resulting from both perfect and imperfect competitors' choice.) Consumers' individual demand functions depend on the decisions of imperfect competitive firms, both via the prices they quote and via the profit shares they distribute to the owners of the firms. Imperfect competitors are assumed to know this dependence partially only; i.e., each one of them knows how aggregate demand for its products is a function of the price vector he sets and other prices, but taking as given the distribution of wealth among the consumers. Then the monopolistically competitive firm is assumed to set the prices of the vector of products it controls, and to meet any demand that is forthcoming at these prices (no rationing).

The model of section 6 involves only monopolistically competitive firms of the sort described in section 4. However, starting from an 'initial position' of the economy, described by a price vector and the average production of the other firms, each producer is now supposed to conjecture how these other firms will change their average production as a result of a price change arising from the alteration of its own production plan.

To each of these various approaches to modelling imperfect competitive behaviour in a general equilibrium framework, there corresponds a particular equilibrium concept for the state of the economy. First, it is always assumed that, given the choices made by the agents, all the markets clear at equilibrium. Second, in the subjective approach of section 2, the equilibrium concept (MCE) requires that, considering the equilibrium itself as the starting position of the economy, each monopolistically competitive firm maximizes its 'subjective' profits obtained from the conjecture it forms about price changes, should it alter its production plan from the equilibrium.

Conscious rivalry among firms is excluded from the Negishi concept of equilibrium. By contrast, the concept used in sections 3 and 4 are non-cooperative equilibria (CNE is section 4, ICE in section 4): namely, a vector of strategies such that no individual imperfect competitor could increase its profits by unilateral deviation, if the other firms stick to their own strategies. In section 3 strategies are production plans, and prices are determined by market-clearing conditions. In section 4 strategies are prices, and quantities are determined directly from the aggregate demand function, since rationing is not allowed.

The equilibrium concept used in section 6 is of a Negishi type. Recall that each imperfect competitor is assumed to form conjectures about the change in the average production of the other firms, owing to its own move from a given initial position. An equilibrium, according to section 6, is a vector of prices and production plans, forming an initial position from which no imperfect competitor has advantage to move, taking into account the subjectively anticipated changes in the average supply of the others that such moves could entail.

The major question to be answered about these various conceptual approaches to imperfect competition is: for each of these equilibrium concepts, can we build a bundle of reasonable assumptions that would guarantee its existence? It turns out that in most cases existence can be obtained only at a very high price. The most 'unpleasant' assumption to be accepted is the quasi-concavity of profit functions ensuing from the fact that monopolistically competitive firms have convex-valued correspondences (see assumption (A9), assumption (e) in the statement of proposition 3.1, or assumption (A14). By contrast with competitive analysis, where this property follows directly from the microeconomic foundations of the model, here quasi-concavity must be assumed from the outset, without adequate justification in terms of tastes or technological possibilities (we shall come back to this problem in our section 5). Even if Professor Hart cannot dispense with this awkward assumption, he obtains existence results for very general formulations of the Negishi type and of the Cournot–Nash type of equilibrium (see propositions 2.1 and 3.1).

A second difficulty, present in most formulations of imperfect competition in general equilibrium analysis, is related to the so-called 'feedback effect', or 'Ford effect'. Henry Ford once explained that paying higher wages to his workers would lead them to buy a larger number of cars, increasing thereby the receipts of Ford Corporation, perhaps beyond the increase in costs entailed by wage increments! The point is that an imperfectly competitive firm may, through the effect of its own actions on profits, influence the wealth of its customers and hence the firm's demand. The feedback effect is also an awkward fact of imperfect competition in general equilibrium analysis. We should be grateful to Professor Hart for providing us, through his 'islands framework', with a model where the feedback effect tends to become negligible the larger the number of islands, justifying thereby the model proposed in section 4.

In the last section of the paper, Hart shows that, for a large class of models, if firms are small relative to their markets, a generalized imperfect competition equilibrium is an approximately competitive outcome (see proposition 6.1). He infers from this that 'the Arrow–Debreu model corresponds to the case where each agent is small relative to his market'. His formulation of this proposition is probably the most general statement that can be obtained from the idea of Cournot. The upsurge of interest in this celebrated idea that competition is restored when increasing the number of sellers acting non-cooperatively has recently generated a whole stream of interesting research. Section 6 of Professor Hart's paper gives wide account of this research effort (see also Mas-Colell, 1982).

3 MODELS OF PRODUCT DIFFERENTIATION

In his introduction, Hart asserts:

> A truly general theory of monopolistic competition or imperfect competition would incorporate not only non-negligible agents, but also product differentiation and imperfect information. ... In the present paper, however, I will retain the traditional assumptions of homogeneous products and perfect information and will depart from the Walrasian model only in allowing large, non-price-taking agents.

This choice raises, I think, two interrelated questions which I would like to discuss: Which are the interesting directions of deviation from the conditions of perfection? And at which level of generality should we model imperfect competition, given our present knowledge of its phenomena?

Roughly speaking, we may distinguish three increasing levels of generality: the market for a homogeneous product, the interrelated markets of products sold in a particular 'industry', and the system of markets in the general equilibrium framework. The first level is best illustrated by the example of Cournot (1838): a single type of homogeneous mineral water, the springs of which are owned by a few sellers supplying a large number of buyers. The 'intermediate' level is illustrated by the spatial analysis of Hotelling (1929): a homogeneous product sold by two or more sellers located at different places along the same road. The class of models proposed in the Hart's survey belongs to the third level of generality. The first level is sufficient to analyse the main effects on price formation of a small number of sellers selling the same homogeneous product, or the effects of collusion and entry in the corresponding market. It cannot suffice, however, for analysing the *combined* effects of both the small number and the product differences on price formation and entry. The intermediate level allows such an analysis, as illustrated by Hotelling's example of spatial competition, or the analysis of the Ready-to-Eat Cereals Industry by Richard Schmalensee (1978). It also allows the analysis of multi-product firms each choosing a line of products and their corresponding prices in the same industry. However, this intermediate level of generality does not allow the treatment of firms choosing their product lines across *different* industries, or linked to various industries via institutional set-ups (like conglomerates) or financial arrangements. Also it does not allow us to take full account of all implications of market power on the circular relationship between the decisions of monopolistic competitors and the consumers themselves. (The existence of such relationships is revealed for example by the 'feedback effect' discussed above.) The top level of generality should provide an adequate framework for treating such questions. Given the 'state of the arts' in imperfect competition analysis, however, I have the personal feeling that most of the questions that can be formulated at the intermediate level have not yet been solved. Professor Hart himself recognizes this fact when he convincingly argues (cf. Hart, 1983: 61) that the difficult problem of existence of an equilibrium is not really due to the general equilibrium approach he has chosen, but has still to be solved at the intermediate level of an industry where firms sell *different* products. Apart from the existence problem, many other questions remain open at the intermediate level, and look like promising territories for further research. Professor Hart has preferred to put them aside from the scope of his overview, and to concentrate on general equilibrium.[2] Let me, however, consider some of them briefly.

First, a definitional question arises: What precisely is meant by an 'industry'? Important progress in clarifying this concept, already appearing in the Chamberlinian notion of *group*, has been obtained recently, thanks to the 'characteristics' approach, pioneered by Lancaster (1979) and Baumol (1967). The notion of characteristic allows us to identify the subset of goods that share the same set of attributes, and are not shared by any goods outside the subset. Assuming that the utility function of consumers are separable between the 'group' characteristics and 'non-group' characteristics leads to a formal definition of a 'group' of potential products. A particular industry then consists of the set of firms producing one or more goods within a given group (on this point, see Archibald, Eaton and Lipsey, 1982, or Lancaster, 1979).

Second, the problem of product diversity in a given industry clearly calls for further study. In most models of value theory (like those considered in Hart's survey), the list of commodities constitutes a 'primitive' of the model. It turns out, however, that a basic decision of firms in an imperfect market concerns the choice of the product itself, or the line of products, the firm is willing to market. According to Chamberlin (1965), this is even the essence of monopolistic competition, as opposed to pure competition:

> under pure competition a producer may, of course, shift from one field of activity to another, but his volume of sales never depends, as under monopolistic competition, upon the product or the variety of products he chooses, for he is always a part of a market in which many others are producing the identical good. Where the possibility of differentiation exists, however, sales depend upon the skill with which the good is distinguished from others and made to appeal to a particular group of buyers. When both prices and 'products' may be varied, complete equilibrium must involve stability with respect to both [Chamberlin, 1965: 71, 72]

The existence of more or less close substitutes to each good plays a crucial role in defining the optimal choice of product variety by the firm. The usual definition of substitution between commodities, however, relies on price relationships, which makes it useless in analysing the choice of product variety by firms: prices cannot be pre-existent to the products themselves! To be operational in describing this choice, an alternative definition of 'proximity' between products is needed. If potential products appear as points in a space of characteristics, substitution between two goods in a given group can be measured in terms of the differences between the amounts of each attribute they embody. Recent progress has been made in the analysis of product variety, assuming a one-dimensional space of characteristics. Thus, Mussa and Rosen (1978) have fully described the optimal choice of a line of products by a monopolist in a given industry, out of a continuum of potential products of varying quality. More recent work, also assuming a one-dimensional space of characteristics, is in the process of extending the Mussa–Rosen approach to a situation of oligopolistic firms in a given industry, each choosing non-cooperatively its own line of products. Still, much remains to be done about this problem of product variety.

Third, the problem of entry in a differentiated industry is still, by and large, an open question. This entry problem has, however, been explored considerably in the case of an undifferentiated industry. A first path of exploration has been along the lines of limit pricing and entry prevention, a theme initiated by Bain (1956), Sylos-Labini (1957) and Modigliani (1958), and recently continued by Dixit (1980) and Spence (1977).[3] Another road has been the study of entry in a market where non-cooperative firms have fixed set-up costs (see Novshek, 1980; Novshek and Sonnenschein, 1978). On the other hand, in the case of a *differentiated* industry, characterized by a one-dimensional continuum of characteristics, it has been shown recently (see Gabszewicz and Thisse, 1980; Shaked and Sutton, 1983) that in many situations the industry cannot support more than a finite (possibly very small) number of products (and thus a finite number of firms) at a Nash equilibrium, even if there is a continuum of consumers with different tastes or incomes. This is *not* due to overhead costs, but rather to a property of demand. More precisely, this situation turns out to obtain especially when there is little diversity (in tastes or incomes) among the consumers. It is intuitively clear that, if tastes and incomes are very similar over the population, little consumer surplus is lost in offering the top-quality product only, at a price such that even the poorest consumer will buy it. By contrast, if incomes, say, are more widely dispersed, the surplus thereby enjoyed by richer consumers becomes larger – and so makes it more attractive to segment the market, opening room to more than a few firms at a Nash equilibrium. This result has an important implication. It shows that a lack of diversity in the consumers' population may lead to the existence of 'natural oligopolies' preventing entry of additional competitors, if entry is made by firms selling substitutes to the existing goods.

Let me conclude this section. Moving the course of economic analysis from perfect to imperfect competition implies that we are no longer considering only price and/or quantity decisions of firms. The analysis must extend to a wider class of strategies which, if they would not be considered, would deprive the field of imperfect competition from most of its substance, namely: Should the firm enter the industry or not? If yes, with which line of products? And then: with which prices and quantities? Of course, all these strategies are interrelated, since it is the *combined* choice of all of them that affects the level of profits. All these questions are clearly too complex to be taken up today at a level of a general equilibrium framework. Most probably, the 'address' models of value theory, inspired from Hotelling (1929) or Lancaster (1979), seem in the present state of the arts a more promising framework for capturing many interesting features of imperfect competition.

4 IMPERFECT COMPETITION AND THE CORE

Let me now turn to a second fundamental issue raised by Professor Hart's survey: the meaning of the term 'non-negligible agents'. Frequent uses of this terminology appear in Hart's analysis without further clarification about its conceptual content. It turns out, however, that a good deal of ambiguity surrounds this old term of our professional jargon. In particular, it is traditional in economic theory to identify the 'non-negligible agents' context with a market situation in which the number of sellers is 'not great enough to render negligible the influence of any one of them upon the market price' (Chamberlin, 1965: 31). But the number of sellers generally appears as a *primitive* element of the theory, the object of which is precisely to explore price formation! Thus it cannot be logically correct to let the result of the theory depend on premises, which use this result in their formulation!

I do not raise this point only because I pay a high price for logical consistency; my main reason is that I consider as a basic challenge to the theory of imperfect competition the need to explain how the number of *active* sellers in a market, as distinct from *potential* sellers, is determined, and how this determination interferes with the formation of price. What I have in mind in particular is the possibility, always open to the market participants, if they feel too numerous, of combining into a restricted number of decision centres so as to bias the collective decision mechanism. Von Neumann and Morgenstern had already perceived how such a collusive process could alter the competitive outcome:

> The classical definitions of free competition all involve further postulates besides the greatness of that number. E.g., it is clear that, if certain great group of participants – for any reason whatsoever – act together, then the great number of participants may not become effective; the decisive exchanges may take place directly between large 'coalitions' (such as trade-unions, consumers cooperatives, . . .), and not between individuals, many in number, acting independently. [von Neumann and Morgenstern, 1953: 15]

Samuelson is still more precise:

> if we think in oversimplified terms of social output as being produced by the few broad categories of homogeneous land, homogeneous labor, and the capital goods ultimately producible out of these primary factors, and if these primary factors are under the dispersed ownership of millions of different individuals, then contrived scarcity would seem out of the question. Each small factor owner faces a derived demand curve of virtually infinite elasticity; there is no discrepancy between marginal revenue and price to cause deadweight loss. But even here the competitive configuration is unstable. Unless we invoke a significant real cost to the formation of collusive communication, pushing the theory of games to its logical limits will lead to the following paradox. Let everyone in the system act like a pure competitor except the owners of one factor, say the owners of homogeneous land. Now let two small land-

> owners collude, acting tacitly or explicitly in common. Ending up still small relative to the whole, they will reap no advantage, but it is important to realize there will be no disadvantage in their colluding – and this can be said about the colluding of 100,000 landowners or 90 or even 100 per cent of all landowners. With respect to incipient collusion, then the *laissez-faire* system is under a kind of neutral equilibrium. But when millions of landowners act in concert, they do face a tilted demand curve and benefit by taking account of the discrepancy between marginal and average revenues. [Samuelson, 1968: 117]

This long quotation illustrates how price determination can depend on the possibility open to a set of initially negligible economic factors, of altering itself into a powerful group decision unit.

It turns out that a considerable amount of research work was devoted, in and around the 1970s, to theorizing about how such collusive processes could be fitted into the framework of a general equilibrium exchange model embodying a continuum of traders and *atoms*.[4] Since, in spite of its general equilibrium nature, no reference is made to this work in Professor Hart's survey, I would like to report briefly on this stream of research.

The starting point of this theory is the paper by Aumann (1964), which establishes the equivalence of the *core* and the set of competitive allocations for 'atomless' exchange economies. It is argued there that the most natural model for a market with perfect competition is one in which there is a continuum of traders without atoms. But Aumann notes:

> of course, to the extent that individual consumers or merchants are in fact *not* anonymous (think of General Motors), the continuous model is inappropriate. But in that case, perfect competition does not obtain either. In many real markets, the competition is indeed far from perfect; such markets are probably best represented by a mixed model, in which some of the traders are points in a continuum, and others are individually significant. [Aumann, 1964: 41][5]

Using such a mixed model, B. Shitovitz (1973) has shown that, even if the equivalence theorem proved by Aumann for atomless exchange economies does not necessarily hold when atoms are added to the continuum, it remains possible to characterize the core allocations of this mixed model with an appropriate price structure. More precisely, Shitovitz proved that to any allocation in the core there corresponds a price system such that no 'small' trader (in the atomless part) can, with the value of his initial bundle, buy a bundle that he prefers to his part of that allocation. (Nothing of that sort can be said about the 'large' traders (atoms).) Using this property, he proved also that, if all atoms consist of traders of the same type (identical initial endowment vectors and preferences), then the equivalence property is restored. Using independently a similar model, Gabszewicz and Mertens (1971) have shown that, if to each atom there corresponds an atomless set of traders similar to that atom and of sufficiently large measure, then again the equivalence theorem must hold.[6]

It is of interest here to recall a suggestive interpretation – in terms of 'syndicates' – of an atom in a measure space of traders, which gives some formal content to the above discussion about collusion of economic agents (see Gabszewicz and Drèze, 1971). To this end consider initially an atomless exchange economy consisting of n 'types' T_i, $i = 1, \ldots, n$; i.e., all traders in T_i have the same preferences and the same initial holdings. For simplicity let T_i be the right open interval $[i-1, i[$ and T_n the closed interval $[n-1, n]$. Let also T denote the class of Lebesgue measurable subsets of $T = \cup_{i=1}^{n} T_i$: T is the class of all 'coalitions'. *Syndicates* of traders are defined in the following manner. Let A_i be a subset of T_i for some i and imagine that all traders in A_i agree that no *proper* subset of them will form a coalition with traders outside A_i, so that only the group as a whole will enter into broader coalitions. Each A_i is a syndicate. The set of potential coalitions is now reduced to a subclass of the original σ-field T, namely the subclass $\tilde{\mathrm{T}}$ defined by

$$\tilde{\mathrm{T}} = \{S \in \mathrm{T} \mid \forall i \text{ either } S \cap A_i = A_i \text{ or } S \cap A_i = \phi\}.$$

It is readily seen that there is a complete formal analogy between the concept of a syndicate as we have just defined it and the concept of an atom. However, the formal concept of a syndicate can be directly interpreted as a group of agents delegating to a single decision unit the task of representing their parallel economic interests: the group acting in unison, any coalition of agents including a proper subset of the syndicate becomes impossible. In view of this complete analogy, all the above results established for an exchange economy with atoms are directly applicable to the collusive processes implicit in the definition of a syndicate. For instance, the result in Gabszewicz and Mertens (1971) shows that the process of syndicate formation must involve a sufficiently 'broad' class of traders before it can become effective at enlarging the core to allocations that hopefully improve the utilities of their members with respect to their competitive payoff.

I have devoted most of my comments in this section to discuss an explanation of economic power based on collusion. But, of course, this is only one of a number of possible causes of deviation from perfect competition. I have chosen this explanation mainly because it illustrates the fact that in many cases market power does not come as God's gift, but follows itself from the decisions of the agents. In other words, the fact that some agents are 'non-negligible' should not be considered as a primitive of the model, but rather should be explained in an endogenous manner.

5 EXISTENCE OF AN EQUILIBRIUM IN IMPERFECT COMPETITION

I would like to conclude my comments on Professor's Hart's survey with an informal discussion of the difficulty encountered in establishing the existence of an imperfect competition equilibrium. I have already pointed out above the awkwardness of the assumption of quasi-concavity of profit functions, used to get round the difficulty of proving existence. This assumption is particularly unpleasant since it cannot be derived from the microeconomic data of the model. Moreover, there are many non-pathological examples showing that the absence of equilibrium is far from being a 'curiosum' in the context of imperfect competition. Let me give a short catalogue of such situations.

First, there is the example provided by Roberts and Sonnenschein (1977) in the case of general equilibrium. However, as remarked by Hart, it is unnecessary to resort to a general equilibrium treatment for exhibiting non-existence; even in the most simple models of product differentiation it is easy to find counter-examples. To illustrate, consider the following model involving two firms. Firm I (resp. II) produces product 1 (resp. 2); and these products are substitutes. Let

$q_1(p_1, p_2)$ (resp. $q_2(p_1, p_2)$) denote the demand function for product 1 (resp. 2). Assuming zero costs, profit functions are, respectively, equal to $\pi_{\mathrm{I}}(p_1, p_2) = q_1(p_1, p_2)\cdot p_1$ and $\pi_{\mathrm{II}}(p_1, p_2) = q_2(p_1, p_2)\cdot p_2$. Clearly, this model seems to be the most natural extension of the Bertrand duopoly game where firms sell differentiated products. A particular case that fits into this model is the famous Hotelling's spatial model, for which

$$
\begin{aligned}
q_1(p_1, p_2) &= 0 && \text{if } p_2 < p_1 - c(l-a-b) \\
&= a + \tfrac{1}{2}(l-a-b) + \frac{1}{2c}(p_2 - p_1) && \\
& && \text{if } |p_2 - p_1| \leqslant c(l-a-b) \\
&= l && \text{if } p_1 < p_2 - c(l-a-b)
\end{aligned}
$$

and

$$
\begin{aligned}
q_2(p_1, p_2) &= 0 && \text{if } p_1 < p_2 - c(l-a-b) \\
&= b + \tfrac{1}{2}(l-a-b) + \frac{1}{2c}(p_1 - p_2) && \\
& && \text{if } |p_2 - p_1| \leqslant c(l-a-b) \\
&= l && \text{if } p_2 < p_1 - c(l-a-b)
\end{aligned}
$$

where a, b are the location parameters, c the unit transportation cost and l the total length of the road. No Nash equilibrium in pure strategies exists if either

$$\left(l + \frac{a-b}{3}\right)^2 \leqslant \frac{4l}{3}(a+2b),$$

or

$$\left(l + \frac{b-a}{3}\right)^2 \geqslant \frac{4l}{3}(b+2a).$$ [7]

Another example of a situation where no non-cooperative equilibrium exists is the well-known 'Edgeworth cycle', corresponding to the Cournot–Bertrand game with capacity constraints.[8]

One way of escaping the difficulty consists of allowing the use of mixed strategies. Dasgupta and Maskin (1982) have shown that an equilibrium in mixed strategies exists in many instances where no equilibrium in pure strategies is available. Even if some possible economic interpretations for the use of mixed strategies have been recently provided, I am not personally convinced by this *deus ex machina*.

Another attitude consists of recognizing that imperfect competition often generates economic contexts that are highly unstable, entailing thereby the absence of non-cooperative outcomes, and the need of coordination between the players. This point is well illustrated in the spatial competition model. It turns out that no equilibrium exists when the value of the location parameter a is close to the value of $l - b$, i.e. when the two merchants sell close substitutes. In that case, of course, a price war is highly credible, to the extent that a small undercut in price entails a large increase in market share. By contrast, if firms are far away from each other (products are less substitutes), such a price war is clearly less advantageous, since small price cuts no longer attract a large share of the market: then a non-cooperative equilibrium in prices may exist. Accordingly, it might be conjectured that the sellers will choose to locate far apart precisely in view of avoiding the damages of a price war. Otherwise, with less differentiation, coordination would be needed. The recognition of the intrinsic instability of certain economic contexts can be helpful in explaining the choices made by the economic agents; for the simple fact that they are aware that making some moves may well degenerate into an unstable situation can prevent them to make such decisions. Most probably, this type of reasoning could be formalized by embedding the various games under consideration in sequential games, where the use of 'destabilizing' strategies at a given stage would be prevented by the fear of unstable outcomes at later stages.

NOTES

1 An exception to this assumption is in section 6.

2 There are, however, some interesting pieces of work devoted to product differentiation in the framework of general equilibrium; Hart (1979) himself has an important contribution in this field. See also Drèze and Hagen (1978), Mas-Colell (1975), Negishi (1972), among others.

3 A good survey on this direction of research is provided in Encaoua, Geroski and Jacquemin (not yet published).

4 An *atom* in a measure space is any non-null measurable set E such that, for all sets E', $E' \subset E$, then either $\mu(E') = 0$, or $\mu(E') = \mu(E)$.

5 This model was not novel; it was already used in Milnor and Shapley (1961).

6 Other references include Aumann (1973), Champsaur and Laroque (1976) and Trockel (1976), among others.
7 In this example demand functions are discontinuous. However, the example can be adjusted to allow continuous demand functions; see d'Aspremont *et al.*, 1979: 1149, fn. 4.
8 MacLeod (1983) has recently shown that the absence of non-cooperative equilibrium is a general phenomenon in location models.

REFERENCES

Archibald, G. C., Eaton, B. C. and Lipsey, R. G. 'Address Models in Value Theory', in *Proceedings of an International Economic Association Conference on New Developments in Market Structure*, Ottawa (not yet published).

d'Aspremont, C., Gabszewicz, J. Jaskold and Thisse, J. F. (1979), 'On Hotelling's "Stability in Competition" ', *Econometrica*, **47**, 1145–50.

Aumann, R. J. (1964), 'Markets with a Continuum of Traders', *Econometrica*, **32**, 39–50.

Aumann, R. J. (1973), 'Disadvantageous Monopolies', *Journal of Economic Theory*, **6**, 1–11.

Bain, J. (1956), *Barriers to New Competition*, Harvard University Press, Cambridge, Mass.

Baumol, W. J. (1967), 'Calculation of Optimal Product and Retailed Characteristics: The Abstract Product Approach', *Journal of Political Economy*, **75**, 674–85.

Chamberlin, E. H. (1965), *The Theory of Monopolistic Competition* (8th edn), Harvard University Press, Cambridge, Mass.

Champsaur, P. and Laroque, G. (1976), 'A Note on the Core of Economies with Atoms or Syndicates', *Journal of Economic Theory*, **13**, 458–71.

Cournot, A. A. (1838), *Recherches sur les principes mathématiques de la théorie des richesses*, M. Rivière et Cie, Paris.

Dasgupta, P. and Maskin, E. (1982), 'The Existence of Equilibrium in Discontinuous Economic Games. 2, Applications', ICERD Discussion Paper no. 82/55.

Dixit, A. (1980), 'The Role of Investment in Entry Deterrence', *Economic Journal*, **90**, 95–106.

Drèze, J. H. and Hagen, K. P. (1978), 'Choice of Product Quality: Equilibrium and Efficiency', *Econometrica*, **46**, 493–515.

Edgeworth, F. Y. (1925), *Papers Relating to Political Economy*, vol. I, Macmillan, London.

Encaoua, D., Geroski, P. and Jacquemin, A. 'Strategic Competition and the Persistence of Dominant Firms: A Survey', in *Proceedings of an International Economic Association Conference on New Developments in Market Structure*, Ottawa (not yet published).

Gabszewicz, J. J. and Drèze, J. H. (1971), 'Syndicates of Traders in an Exchange Economy', in G. Szegö (ed.), *Differential Games and Related Topics*, North-Holland, Amsterdam, pp. 399–414.

Gabszewicz, J. J. and Mertens, J. F. (1971), 'An Equivalence Theorem for the Core of an Economy whose Atoms are not "too" Big', *Econometrica*, **39**, 713–21.

Gabszewicz, J. J. and Thisse, J. F. (1980), 'Entry (and Exit) in a Differentiated Industry', *Journal of Economic Theory*, **22**, 327–38.

Hart, O. (1979), 'Monopolistic Competition in a Large Economy with Differentiated Commodities', *Review of Economic Studies*, **46**, 1–30.

Hotelling, H. (1929), 'Stability in Competition', *Economic Journal*, **39**, 41–57.

Lancaster, K. (1979), *Variety, Equity and Efficiency*, Basil Blackwell, Oxford.

MacLeod, B. (1983), 'On the Non-existence of Equilibria in Differentiated Product Models', CORE DP 8338.

Marschak, T. and Selten, R. (1978), 'Restabilizing Responses, Inertia Supergames and Oligopolistic Equilibria', *Quarterly Journal of Economics*, **92**, 71–93.

Mas-Colell, A. (1975), 'A Model of Equilibrium with Differentiated Commodities', *Journal of Mathematical Economics*, **2**, 263–96.

Mas-Colell, A. (ed.) (1982), *Non-Cooperative Approaches to the Theory of Perfect Competition*, Academic Press, New York.

Milnor, J. W. and Shapley, L. S. (1961), 'Values of Large Games II: Oceanic Games', Rand Memo no. 2649.

Modigliani, F. (1958), 'New Developments on the Oligopoly Front', *Journal of Political Economy*, **66**, 215–32.

Mussa, M. and Rosen, S. (1978), 'Monopoly and Product Quality', *Journal of Economic Theory*, **18**, 301–17.

Negishi, T. (1961), 'Monopolistic Competition and General Equilibrium', *Review of Economic Studies*, **28**, 196–201

Negishi, T. (1972), *General Equilibrium Theory and International Trade*, North-Holland, Amsterdam.

Novshek, W. (1980), 'Cournot Equilibrium with Free Entry', *Review of Economic Studies*, **47**, 473–86.

Novshek, W. and Sonnenschein, H. (1978), 'Cournot and Walras Equilibrium', *Journal of Economic Theory*, **19**, 223–66.

Roberts, D. and Sonnenschein, H. (1977), 'On the Foundations of the Theory of Monopolistic Competition', *Econometrica*, **65**, 101–14.

Samuelson, P. A. (1968), 'The Monopolistic Competition Revolution', in R. E. Kuenne (ed.), *Monopolistic Competition Theories: Studies in Impact* (Essays in honor of E. H. Chamberlin), John Wiley, New York, pp. 105–44.

Schmalensee, R. (1978), 'Entry Deterrence in the Ready-to-eat Breakfast Cereal Industry', *Bell Journal of Economics*, **9**, 305–27.

Shaked, A. and Sutton, J. (1983), 'Natural Oligopolies', *Econometrica*, **51**, 1469–83.

Shitovitz, B. (1973), 'Oligopoly in Markets with a Continuum of Traders', *Econometrica*, **41**, 467–505.

Spence, M. (1977), 'Entry, Capacity, Investment and Oligopolistic Pricing', *Bell Journal of Economics*, **8**, 534–44.

Sylos-Labini, P. (1957), *Oligopolio e Progresso Technico*, Giuffrè, Milan.

Triffin, R. (1962), *Monopolistic Competition and General Equilibrium Theory*, Harvard University Press, Cambridge, Mass.

Trockel, W. (1976), 'A Limit Theorem on the Core', *Journal of Mathematical Economics*, **3**, 247–69.

von Neumann, J. and Morgenstern, O. (1953), *Theory of Games and Economic Behaviour*, Princeton University Press.

Comment

HUGO SONNENSCHEIN

Oliver Hart has given us an excellent survey of the state of monopolistically competitive general equilibrium theory. He has provided a good synthesis of the Negishi theory and the subsequent development of the objective demand approach. In addition, there is a most useful treatment of the imperfect competition foundations of perfect competition, where Hart's own work has been fundamental.

But Hart's contribution is more than a survey, and the word 'overview' in the title, although commendably modest, is not quite accurate. His is a paper that contains some important substantive contributions, and for the record they should be pointed out. Included in the presentation is an objective demand model in which general equilibrium feedback effects are absent. Firms are correct to assume that they cannot influence the wealth of their customers; in particular, under the assumptions of the model, profit maximization by firms is in the interest of (all but a negligible fraction of) shareholders. Since every general equilibrium model of imperfect competition must address the proper objective for firms, Hart's rationale for profit maximization is most welcome and should be relevant for future general equilibrium treatments.

Hart also goes beyond what can rightfully be considered survey material when he discusses the notions of rational and reasonable conjectures. These are interesting ideas. I have something to say about them and their role in monopolistically competitive theory, but before doing so I will begin by explaining the framework of my presentation.

First, rather than criticizing Hart's paper, I have tried to write an essay that complements it. I will *not* confine my attention to general equilibrium theory. To my mind, the problems with our understanding of monopolistic competitive processes lie less at the stage of tying things together to close the system than at the basic conceptualization of how a firm thinks about its strategic possibilities, and what actions (and reactions) it expects of its rivals. Second, I will not attempt to cover very much territory. My purpose is only to identify and to discuss two or three areas where there has been recent progress that looks to me especially promising for the development of monopolistically competitive theory. One of these is the theory of auctions (and some associated experimental economics) and the other concerns an idea that has been important in the theory of repeated games.

Let me now relate oligopoly theory to the theory of auctions. Consider a monopolistic market in which there are many consumers, each of whom has a reservation price for the single unit that he demands. This leads to a market demand function in the usual manner, and we assume that the monopolist cannot distinguish one consumer from another, although he knows the market demand function with certainty. We teach that in the case of a monopolist it does not matter whether price or quantity is the strategic variable. But this seems to me not as obvious as we make it out to be. I understand the game defined by 'the monopolist announces a price and each buyer decides whether or not to buy at that price.' However, I see no clear game associated with 'the monopolist announces a quantity.' What are the terms of exchange? Does everyone pay the same price? If so, why? Forget about uncertainty. From an 'auctions' point of view, one must specify the mechanism of exchange, for example sealed-bid discriminatory auction. I have a well-specified game when I say that the seller announces a quantity and buyers make bids for the good in a sealed-bid discriminatory auction. Finally, we must supplement this description with a solution concept; let us say, 'Nash equilibrium in undominated strategies.'

If, for example, there are two units placed on the market, and five buyers with reservation prices 5, 4, 3, 2 and 1, then all equilibria are something like:

Reservation price	Equilibrium bid
5	3
4	3
3	Uniform distribution over [2, 3]
2	1.5
1	1

In words, the buyers with reservation prices 5 and 4 both bid 3, the buyer with reservation price 3 bids no more than 3 with probability 1, and the buyers with reservation prices 2 and 1 each bid below their reservation price. Both units are sold for the lowest price at which two units are demanded, and of course, this is the competitive price associated with an output of two units (see Milgrom, 1984: 4). But the point is that it is a (non-trivial) *theorem* that has the conclusion that the price that obtains when supply is q^* is the demand price at q^*, and it is perhaps not so obvious that the assumptions of the theorem will necessarily be satisfied. The tentative conclusion is that, for a monopolist, quantity choice (with the institution of a discriminatory auction to make it into a game), and price choice are the same.[1] Well, not quite. For the price game the solution for the consumers is a dominant strategy, while for the quantity game it is a Nash equilibrium in undominated strategies. And of course, the form of the auction should matter. Might there be auction mechanisms that lead to a higher expected revenue for the seller? How would the seller do if he offered the units for sale sequentially?

Of course, this is but the 'tip of the iceberg.' Why should a monopolist not consider labeling his product with two or more different prices? Suppose that the monopolist places the object for sale 'on the shelf' with different prices stamped on each. If the agents come to the store in the right order (lowest reservation price first), then the monopolist can effectively discriminate. Of course, if they come in the order 'highest reservation price first,' he would suffer. It is a theorem (due to Vijay Krishna and Motty Perry, private communication, 1983) that, if the distribution of reservation prices is known and if all the orders in which the consumers might come to the store are equally likely, then the monopolist's best strategy is to charge a single price. As with the discriminatory auction, the law of one price is a result rather than an assumption, and the result fails if all orders are not equally likely.

I use these examples to make the point that price and quantity do not exhaust the institutional options, even with a single period of production and monopoly. A monopolist can choose from a variety of different forms of auction; he also may wish to place different prices on identical objects. I believe that a substantial reason for the nice results that have been achieved in auction theory is that the workers in that area appreciate the benefit that accrues to the precise specification of institutional detail. To put my case perhaps too strongly, I would suggest that monopolistically competitive theory will not go too far until we supply a similar degree of institutional detail. If we are lucky, then, as in the case of price-setting monopoly and quantity-setting monopoly with a discriminatory auction, the actual outcome will not depend critically on the institution that is specified. But we cannot expect always to be so fortunate, and this may be one of the important differences between the theories of perfect and imperfect competition.

Let me be more specific concerning the models that I have in mind. I find the following 'one-shot game' quite instructive. There are two firms; each has the same U-shaped average cost curve. There are many consumers; each consumer is defined by his reservation price. The strategy space for each firm is a quantity to produce and a minimum bid to accept. The strategy for each consumer is a price to bid and a firm to which the bid is to be directed. The game, which has some resemblance to a Shubik-type game of the variety considered by Pradeep Dubey (1982) and Leo Simon (1981), is of course 'murderously competitive.'

It is interesting to observe that the experimental approach to oligopoly theory now emphasizes models closer to the above game than to the Cournot or Bertrand framework. In much of this work there is the spirit of a 'double auction': sellers make offers and buyers make bids. Experimentalists have been led to this framework by an attempt to mimic the workings of actual markets. I believe that the experimental approach to oligopoly theory holds a great deal of promise (see Plott, 1982).

The aspect of the above research that appears to me most unsatisfactory is that it ignores the fact of repeated play. The latter is important in oligopolistic situations because it enables firms to enforce cooperative agreements. In examining the class of agreements that can be sustained, the rate of discount must play a major role. This is because I will depart from a cooperative agreement whenever the increment that I gain today exceeds the present value of the stream of negative increments that will accrue to me because of my defection. We are now, of course, in the world of oligopolistic supergames.

Now I relate these supergame ideas to Hart's presentation of the notion of 'rational and reasonable conjecture.' To be sure, I *might* be able to capture in some reduced-form matrix the long-term payoff that accrues when I defect and others react one period later with a new steady-state play (see Marschak and Selten, 1978). But what if the form of the reaction does not have any simple steady-state expression? For example, the 'threat' that might keep all oligopolists in line might be to retaliate against any deviation from a cartel agreement by playing, for just one period, a punishment play, and then returning to the agreement path. Any failure to implement this retaliation for deviation might be met with the one-period punishment play, and then a return to the agreement path, and so on.

In a major contribution to the theory of supergames, Dilip Abreu (1982) has recently developed a framework for analyzing the set of subgame perfect equilibria of repeated games with discounting. Applied to symmetric oligopoly with constant costs, his results show that the one-period punishments I have just alluded to are the most severe among the class of all subgame perfect symmetric punishments. In particular, they are more severe than the punishment, 'deviation from the cartel agreement will be met by the one-period Cournot–Nash play for all time forward.' Hence they support more collusive behavior than reversion to Cournot–Nash play does. The latter punishment is essentially the only one considered in the industrial organization literature.

For me, Abreu's results strongly suggest that the conjectural variations approach (rational conjecture, reasonable conjecture, etc.) may run the risk of obscuring the true possibilities for punishment and thus for collusive behavior. At the very least, I would suggest that we be sure to test the conjectural variations approach by examining the extent to which such games can be viewed as the reduced forms of infinitely repeated games and their equilibria shown to be payoff-equivalent to the equilibria of repeated games. The business of analyzing (in Hart's words) 'the rationality of conjectures in a static context' strikes me as hazardous business simply because it assumes implicitly that the retaliation available to an agent is a one-shot change in his single-period play.[2]

Let me emphasize that I do not wish to claim that supergame theory will of itself be equal to the task of putting monopolistic competition theory on track. The 'folk theorem' (see, for example, Rubinstein, 1979, and references) of supergame theory, despite losing some of its bite when discounting is introduced, tells us quite clearly that nothing like this can be true.[3] I can only claim that the perspective of repeated play helps to explain the possibility of outcomes that have a strongly cooperative feel to them. This appears to me fundamental for oligopoly theory.

Returning to my previous duopoly example, but now within the context of repeated games, I would recommend the theoretical and experimental analysis of the following market. Each duopolist has U-shaped average cost. He produces a quantity and decides on a minimum bid to accept. Each consumer makes a directed bid. The one-shot game is repeated, and there is discounting.

How collusive can the equilibria be?
How do the equilibria compare with the various set of equilibria of the corresponding one-shot reaction function game?
What happens when we add more sellers?
What happens when sellers are able to write contracts that guarantee buyers that they will pay the lowest price in the market?
What is the effect of similar variations in the institutional arrangements?
What if the commodity can be stored?
What if there is a variety of differentiated commodities?

CONCLUSION

I have argued that recent results in the theory of auctions, the experimental approach to economics and the theory of repeated games offer a variety of ideas that are useful for the theory of monopolistic competition. This is 'new blood' that I believe is much needed. My feeling is that the Negishi line, which builds on the Arrow–Debreu–McKenzie theory, has been pretty much played out. We should go past 'the market demand of a competitive sector' and model more completely the bid–offer process and the temporal structure of play. Neither price nor quantity is the proper strategic variable for oligopoly theory, and, as in the auction theory, the law of one price should be looked for as a result rather than taken as an assumption. My feeling is that, when modeled as a one-shot game, most of the processes we observe will be very competitive; that is, they will lead to perfect competition even with small numbers. Results in experimental economics support this view.

To my mind it is the fact that oligopolists get to see a piece of their competitors' play, can react, and can understand that their competitors can react to their reaction (as in repeated play), that leads to collusive agreements and fear of retaliation, and takes us away from perfect competition. Cooperation is more likely to break down when there are large numbers, when efficient scale is not small, or when information is incomplete (see Green and Porter, 1981). I would suggest that we put maximum effort into modeling repeated play explicitly; the analysis of 'rational conjectures in a static context' seems to me full of difficulty.

Finally, let me say that, while I regard matters of uncertainty and product differentiation as important and extremely interesting, I would hazard a guess that most of the central issues will be present under conditions of certainty (but incomplete information), and with a finite number of possible commodity types fixed in advance.

NOTES

My thinking on the subject of monopolistic competition has been very much influenced by recent Princeton graduate students. I mention in particular Dilip Abreu, Vijay Krishna, David Pearce, Motty Perry and Leo Simon. Comments by Abreu and Pearce helped to improve the presentation.

1 Actually, for the price game the monopolist would do better to choose $p = 4$ (or $p - 4 - \epsilon$); however, this is an artifact of the discontinuity of the demand function. With a large number of consumers the difference disappears.

2 A qualification is in order. In some situations it is quite natural to think of a game as being played in 'reaction function form.' Jones may tell his broker: 'buy if Smith buys.' The broker's task is to find a price that clears the market, given that some agents are conditioning on the action of others. In such a context conjectures about the reaction functions of competitors become conjectures about the plays of competitors. Presumably, this situation is not what we usually have in mind in oligopoly theory.

3 The preceding two sentences were prompted by a question from M. Kurz.

REFERENCES

Abreu, Dilip (1982), 'Repeated Games with Discounting: A General Theory and an Application to Oligopoly' (not yet published).

Dubey, Pradeep (1982), 'Price–Quantity Strategic Market Games', *Econometrica*, **50**, 111–26.

Green, Edward J. and Porter, Robert H. (1981), 'Noncooperative Collusion under Imperfect Price Information', Discussion Paper no. 81-142, Center for Economic Research, University of Minnesota.

Marschak, T. and Selten, R. (1978), 'Restabilizing Responses, Inertia Supergames, and Oligopolistic Equilibria', *Quarterly Journal of Economics*, **92**, 71–93.

Milgrom, Paul (1984), 'The Economics of Competitive Bidding: A Selective Survey', in *Social Goals and Social Organization. Volume in Memory of Elisha A. Pazner*, Cambridge University Press.

Plott, Charles R. (1982), 'Industrial Organization Theory and Experimental Economics', *Journal of Economic Literature*, **20**, 1485–1527.

Rubinstein, Ariel (1979), 'Equilibrium in Supergames with the Overtaking Criterion', *Journal of Economic Theory*, **21**, 1–9.

Simon, Leo K. (1981), 'Bertrand and Walras Equilibrium: A Theory of Perfect Competition for Finite Economies', PhD dissertation, Princeton University.

3

Differential Information, the Market and Incentive Compatibility

JERRY GREEN

1 INTRODUCTION

In this survey of the economics of incomplete information, I will try to compare and contrast some of the more prominent models in this area by re-expressing them in the form of games of incomplete information. The explosion of research in this area over the past ten years makes a complete survey impossible. My goal will be to show that the theory of games of incomplete information, which has also experienced a renaissance of late, is the natural theoretical structure within which to classify and analyze more particular, specialized, economic models.

On the whole, however, the recent literature on the economics of information stands as a remarkable achievement in economic theory. It has demonstrated that useful, empirically testable conclusions can be derived in complex situations previously beyond analytical tractability. It has raised new theoretical questions and has solved some of the more puzzling older ones. It has given us a framework within which welfare analysis can be carried out. Though its interaction with game theory proper is still in its infancy, there is already reason to be hopeful about the fruits of this union.

There are many recently studied economic models that fall within the scope of this survey. Examples include the theory of auctions, from both a descriptive and normative viewpoint; the theory of labor contracts between workers and their employers; bilateral contracts; nonlinear pricing by a monopolist; adverse selection models in insurance; labor market signalling and mechanisms for preference elicitation. And there are many more. The common characteristic in all these theories is the absence of complete information on the part of some agents and the difference between their knowledge and that of others.

This survey will highlight the differences between these models more than their similarities. It will attempt to classify the models along several lines. Each such dimension of classification will be set in terms of the characteristics of the game of incomplete information associated with this model.

The plan of this survey is as follows. In section 2 I review the basic models of games and generalized games with complete information. In section 3 the corresponding generalizations to the incomplete information case are given. Emphasis is placed on the nature and extent of communication possible within the game. Section 4 deals with the welfare analysis of the equilibria in these games.

Section 5 forms the body of the classificatory material in the survey. I show that many economic models with incomplete information can be represented as games of incomplete information with the addition of certain constraints on actions and utilities. These side-constraints represent the forces of competition present in the economic situation. The characteristics of these constraints, and of the associated game itself, are used as a classificatory device. Finally, in section 6 the welfare analysis of section 4 is applied to the models studied in section 5.

2 GAMES AND GENERALIZED GAMES

An economic model with complete information concerns the social choice over a set X of feasible outcomes. Each $x \in X$ is assumed to be a complete description of the social state resulting from the actions of all agents, in all its relevant details. Each agent has an evaluation over X in the form of a complete preorder.

The relationships among the players are formalized in one of two ways. In game-theoretic models one specifies a strategy space for each agent, S_i, and an outcome function

$$g: \times S_i \to X.$$

The interpretation of these strategies can be quite complex. They may involve actual or hypothetical actions of a player under various conditions arising in the actual 'play' of the game. The important point for present purposes is that each strategy n-tuple gives rise to a unique feasible outcome. All the players know the function g, and the evaluations of all the others. They also know that each of the others knows this, etc. In such a state of affairs the term 'common knowledge' has been used to describe the mutual awareness about the game and the other players.

Game-theoretic models are characterized by the idea that each player's strategy is chosen from a fixed set of possibilities and that the entire description of economic activity can be broken down into the actions of economic agents. This seems self-evident, as every action is the action of someone. However, it does not leave a role open for the economist's favorite construct – endogenous variables controlled by the 'invisible hand.' These variables may enter agents' objective functions, modify the constraints that they face, or alter the attainable set of allocations for the economy as a whole. If the endogenous variables are not set at their equilibrium values, the choices of individual agents will not be consistent.

Gerard Debreu (1952) was the first to take a model including endogenous variables and recast it in the form of a 'game.' His idea is elegant, simple and natural. One introduces a 'zeroth' (0th) player whose strategy is the selection of these endogenous variables. This agent's objective is to avoid infeasible collective actions, that is to insure that individual actions result in a social state $x \in X$.

To accomplish this at a formal level, it was necessary to extend the notion of a game in two ways. First, the space of outcomes was expanded to include those that could be contemplated and evaluated but which may not be feasible given actual economic resources. Second, instead of fixed strategy spaces, the strategy spaces of each player were allowed to depend on the strategy choices of others. In the competitive model of economic equilibrium, the price-setting actions of player zero affect each agent's choice set by changing the set of budgetarily feasible net trades available. The invisible hand was thus made visible. Games in this form are called *generalized games*; the 'generalization' at a formal level is in the mutual dependence of players' strategy spaces.

These two descriptions of economic models, as either games or generalized games, are quite condensed. They suppress all the detail about how the actual choices are made. These 'details' are of the essence in situations of incomplete information. Agents' decisions will be based partly on the information conveyed to them by other players, or by 'the market.' The nature of this information is endogenously determined in the equilibrium of the game or of the generalized game used to describe the economic model. In order to bring these considerations into the foreground, it is necessary to review the relationship between extensive and normal form games. This is the subject of the following section.

3 GAMES OF INCOMPLETE INFORMATION

Extensive and normal forms

The term 'games of incomplete information' is used to convey the idea that there may be some aspects of agents' environments about which they are uncertain, and that this uncertainty affects the conduct of their play. Games of incomplete information are games, in precisely the sense used in the last section: strategies collectively determine outcomes, and any strategy combinations are jointly feasible. The extensive form of games of incomplete information has been very important throughout the history of game theory. It is an attempt to describe the temporal structure of players' moves and of the evolution of their information. Precise mathematical formalizations are presented in several sources, of which Kuhn (1953) and Kreps and Wilson (1982) are perhaps the most readable.

The state of the game is associated with the nodes of a 'tree.' Associated with each non-terminal node is the name of a player whose turn it is to 'move.' To each terminal node one associates a social state, or a vector of payoffs to the players. Nature is also a player. When nature moves, the choice is made according to some given probabilities. Other players' moves can be random, but the choice of probabilities is at their own discretion.

When it is the turn of a player to move, he may not know the state of the game precisely. This is captured by partitioning the set of nodes at which a given player is to move into 'information sets.' The same choice, deterministic or stochastic, must be made throughout an information set. For this to make sense, the structure of the tree must be such that the same number of choices is available to a player throughout any given information set. At each terminal node of the tree the players have a payoff in von Neumann–Morgenstern utility.

In this very general situation, pure strategies are specifications of a choice of move at each information set. Mixed strategies allow for randomized choices. Each vector of mixed strategies determines a random path through the game tree and a distribution over the terminal nodes. The payoff to each player is just the mathematical expectation of his payoff at each of these nodes.

An *equilibrium* of a game is a situation in which each player's strategy is optimal given all the other players' strategies. For many purposes the equilibria of the game associated with the economic model characterize precisely the points of interest. If there are multiple equilibria, the theory does not predict which of them will 'actually' arise. The economic model does not provide a determinate theory, and economists have learned to live with this multiplicity of solutions.

In some other circumstances, however, there are equilibria of the associated game that seem not to describe a reasonable economic outcome. These cases arise quite frequently when the incompleteness of information is important. To eliminate these equilibria from consideration, much recent research has been devoted to imposing further restrictions on the equilibria. The essence of these restrictions is that players' strategies are required to be rational not only at the beginning of the game, but also at subsequent stages. This line of research has proven extremely valuable in narrowing the family of equilibria to usefully well-defined subsets that make economic sense. For most of this survey, however, we will see that the ordinary Nash equilibria of the games to be studied define the economic outcomes of interest. The refinements mentioned above will be of more importance in dynamic models with incomplete information, and this survey concerns primarily static situations.

The description of the extensive form of a game of incomplete information given above is incomplete if the economic model being studied involves endogenous variables that are not under the explicit control of any player. As mentioned in section 1, these cases correspond to generalized games, in which 'player 0' chooses the endogenous variables. To complete the description of the game we must provide player 0, somewhere during the course of play, with some of the information originally in the hands of the actual economic agents. To my knowledge, the only special case that has been examined is where player 0 is endowed with all of the information in the economy. It is then argued that, in an equilibrium of the generalized game, player 0's strategy will communicate all of this information to all of the participants.

This analysis of generalized games with incomplete information is incomplete in two respects. First, it does not give a realistic account of how player 0 comes to possess all this information. Second, the result about full dissemination is not robust to generalization with regard to the space in which the join of all private information lies. When this space is of higher dimensionality than the space of endogenous variables selected by player 0, serious problems concerning the existence of equilibria may arise. For these reasons, most of the rest of this survey will concentrate on games, rather than generalized games, of incomplete information.

Games with nature's move first

Any extensive game can be rearranged so that the moves of nature occur at the beginning. A move of nature occurring at a later stage can equally well be thought of as having been predetermined, but the information sets are such that its outcome is not yet known. Obviously, such rearrangements are strategically equivalent. We will adopt this format from this point onwards.

Many economic models have the feature that the only incompleteness of information suffered by the players concerns the choice made by nature. Although they may be differentially informed about nature's move, they have common and complete information about each other's moves. Typically, nature's move is interpreted as a parameter relevant to the preferences of all agents. One common specification of this idea is that agents' preferences are independently drawn from a fixed distribution, and that the preferences are purely individualistic in that they concern consumption of private goods without externalities. Another specification is that there is some common underlying parameter relevant to all their preferences and that nature's move consists of the choice of this parameter and the provision of an observation by each player that is statistically related to the parameter. In this model, the observations define 'conditional preferences.' As further information is exchanged during the course of play, the conditional preferences will evolve.

Other economic models allow for incompleteness of information by the players concerning each other's move, as well as about nature's move. Sometimes one of the players moves immediately after nature; his move is observable by others, and the remaining players then move simultaneously, in ignorance of each other's desires. These players can therefore condition their choices on the prior choices of the first player, as well as on any information they may have about nature's move.

A very important class of extensive-form games of incomplete information arises when all players must make a simultaneous choice, after nature's move is made. They are differentially informed about nature's move. Moreover, because the structure of the game is common knowledge, each can make inferences about what information is available to others. The equilibria of this type of extensive form are useful in analyzing the efficiency properties of outcomes. We consider this particular game in some detail in the next subsection.

The simultaneous-play extensive form

The simultaneous-play extensive form (SPE) is a family of games characterized by the facts that nature moves first and then players are informed of nature's move, although perhaps imperfectly. Then, simultaneously, the players make choices that, together with the true state, result in an outcome. There is no opportunity to revise actions or to communicate explicitly with the other players. SPE games differ according to the relationship between the space of possible choices by players and the space through which information about nature's move is conveyed to them.

In SPE games a strategy for player i is a mapping (possibly random) from the space of observations Y_i to the space of actions A_i. Let us denote these functions $a_i(y_i)$.

Following Harsanyi, we will say that $[a_i(y_i)]_{i=1,\ldots,n}$ constitute a Bayesian–Nash equilibrium if they are an equilibrium of the game of incomplete information. The adjective 'Bayesian' refers to the fact that the choice of $a = a_i(y_i)$ is optimal for agent i given his beliefs about the unknown state and about the $(a_j)_{j \neq i}$ as generated by the $(y_j)_{j \neq i}$ and the other players' strategies $[a_j(\cdot)]_{j \neq i}$. These beliefs are generated by his prior knowledge and the observation y_i. The Bayesian–Nash equilibria of the SPE have been amenable to analysis in some detail, and have provided a useful benchmark in welfare theory, as we will see in section 4.

Of considerable practical importance is the further special case in which A_i and Y_i coincide – that is, have the same cardinality or dimension – for each player. Let A_i and Y_i be described by the same set. In these games there is a natural interpretation of any strategy. It describes the announcement that the player makes to all the others concerning his private information. The 'identity function' then corresponds to the ever-truthful strategy. A player's willingness to provide a truthful response depends on his posterior beliefs about others' observations, on their strategies, and on the outcomes associated to various professed observations. Much attention has been focused on discovering which outcome functions induce the truth as a possible equilibrium of this SPE. This is not because the truth is an objective *per se*, but rather because the allocation rules thereby achievable are an important family of outcomes of the game. This is discussed further in section 4.

Economic games without the SPE assumption

There are some games in which the SPE assumption is not appropriate. Only a few have been analyzed, as they are generally much more complex. The players can draw inferences from the actions of others and use them to modify their behavior at a later stage of the game.

One extensive form of this type is where the players pass through a sequence of simultaneous plays. At each stage they learn all of the moves made previously, but not any of the current moves of the other players. Some of these stages may correspond to 'communication moves' (Farrell, 1983).

The increased complexity of these strategy spaces makes a given game at least potentially capable of achieving superior equilibria. This is especially true when the set of possible moves at each stage is small compared with the space of observations (as is true in Farrell's case).

An interesting game of this form is the ordinary ascending, or English, auction. The price of an item is increased stepwise. Any player's move at a given price is either to 'stay in' or to 'drop out.' When only one remains in, he wins the item and pays an amount equal to the step at which his nearest competitors were active. Each player can observe how many of the others remain active at each state. Because of a correlation in valuations across individuals, each regards the number of active competitors he has as a relevant predictor of the value the item will have to him. An equilibrium of this game provides each player with a 'dropout function $k(p)$,' telling him to drop out at a price p if his own information is y and there are $k(p)$ or fewer other active bidders. This model has been used by Milgrom and Weber (1982b) to analyze how the seller's expected revenue responds to changes in the quality of information available and to the extent to which it is shared.

All of these games share the common feature that information about nature's move is not revised in the course of play, except in so far as it may be revealed by the strategies of other players. Whatever private information is available is given to the players at the beginning. It conditions their beliefs about the information, and hence the conduct of play, by the others. It is this aspect of the extensive form that makes these games much more tractable than the vast complexity that characterizes games of incomplete information in general.

4 WELFARE ANALYSIS, MECHANISMS AND GAMES OF INCOMPLETE INFORMATION

Welfare analysis has both positive and normative aspects. We may want to evaluate the outcome of a game against a standard of potentially achievable outcomes. Alternatively, we may examine the role of a social planner who must design a means of collective decision-making in order to achieve, in equilibrium, certain pre-specified objectives. In this section I will show how the theory of games of incomplete information is useful for both types of welfare analyses.

Following the notation of section 3, let $Y = Y_1 \times, \ldots, \times Y_N$ be the information revealed by nature to all of the participants, taken collectively. Because we assume that the revelation of nature's move is made exclusively at the first step in the game, before any actions of the players are taken, we can, without loss of generality, suppose that the set of feasible social outcomes depends on $y \in Y$. Thus, if X is the space of all conceivable social outcomes, the correspondence

$$\phi: Y \to X$$

describes the states that could actually be attained for some set of players' actions, given nature's move.

Each player i has preferences that depend on the pair $(y, x) \in Y \times X$. In any game or economic model, the *result* can be described as a probability distribution over $Y \times X$ having support on $\{(y, x) | x \in \phi(y)\}$. Let μ be a distribution over this set. Player i's evaluation of (y, x) is assumed to be expressed in the von Neumann–Morgenstern utility function

$$u_i: Y \times X \to R.$$

The *ex ante* expected utility of i is

$$u_i(\mu) = \int u_i(y, x) \, \mathrm{d}\mu.$$

After i learns his private information about nature's move he might evaluate the outcome μ somewhat differently. Letting $\mu(y_{-i}, x | y_i)$ be the conditional distribution of other players' private information y_{-i} and the outcome x given his information y_i, we can define, following Holmstrom and Myerson (1983), i's *interim* utility of μ given y_i as

$$U_i(y_i, \mu) = \int u_i(y_i, y_{-i}, x) \, d\mu(y_{-i}, x \,|\, y_i).$$

Similarly, the *ex post* utility of the result μ, when nature's move has been y, is the expected utility integrating over the conditional distribution of x given y:

$$U_i(y, \mu) = \int u_i(y, x) \, d\mu(x \,|\, y).$$

In alternative applications, each of the evaluations $U_i(\mu)$, $U_i(y_i, \mu)$ and $U_i(y, \mu)$ will be useful.

Let us use this formal structure to evaluate the performance of an economic system: the positive welfare analysis described at the beginning of this section.

Expressing the economic model as a game, each player has a strategy space, S_i, describing his play as it depends on his private information and on all his subsequent observations of other players' moves. The game is a mapping from the set of all possible strategies to the space of results. Let

$$g: \times S_i \to \Delta$$

where Δ is the set of all probability measures concentrated on $\{(y, x) | y \in \phi(x)\}$. Players choose their strategies $s_i \in S_i$ to maximize

$$U_i[y_i, g(s_i, s_{-i})].$$

An *equilibrium* $s^* = (s_1^*, \ldots, s_N^*)$ is a set of strategies such that each is optimal given the others.

The domain of positive welfare analysis is to discuss the efficiency of the equilibria of g relative to other strategy N-tuples in $\times S_i$. Note however that, although the game is played by each player maximizing his *interim* utility, it is possible to evaluate the results of the game according to the vector of *ex ante* utilities of the N players, or according to the vector of *ex post* utilities of the N players given $y \in Y$, as well as according to the interim utilities themselves.

Generally speaking, a game will not have efficient equilibria. The competitive equilibria of a neoclassical general equilibrium model are a notable exception. Extending this result to the case of incomplete information in general equilibrium theory has proved difficult – see Laffont (1983). Section 6 will be devoted to a summary of positive welfare results, recast in the general setting presented above.

Normative welfare analysis using this structure is also possible. Indeed, most of the results of the theory of incentive compatibility are of this type. There are two forms that this type of theory can take, according to whether or not there is an active mediator who can serve as a conduit for the information revealed to him.

In normative welfare analysis without a mediator, the strategy spaces S_i and the game g are considered variable. A planner or designer can choose $S = \times S_i$ and $g: S \to \Delta$ arbitrarily, subject to the restriction that $g(s)$ has support on $\{(y, x) | x \in \phi(y)\}$. We will refer to the planner's choice as a *design*. Once the design $(g, S_1, \ldots, S_N)$ is in place, its equilibria represent the results attained. The only active players in the design are the actual economic agents. The planner's only role is to set up the game.

One design can be compared with another on any of the three temporal bases described above. For example, an *ex ante* efficient design is one with an equilibrium result μ such that it is not possible to find another design having an equilibrium μ' and $U_i(\mu') \geqslant U_i(\mu)$ for all i, with strict inequality for some i.

A special form of design has been studied by Farrell (1983). These are called 'games of communication.' The strategies describe a two-stage process. In the first, the players make moves that are payoff-irrelevant in the sense that they have no binding force on their moves in the second part of the game, where strategic interaction actually determines the outcome. The purpose of the first part of the game is to make communication possible. The study of optimal designs is just beginning, but it clearly represents one of the important new ideas in welfare economics with incomplete information.

Normative welfare analysis with a mediator is a much more extensively explored research area. To model the set of attainable results when a mediator is present, we insert an active role for the mediator in the play of the game. The players' strategies are described in three stages. First, they are given a set of messages M_i that they can send to the mediator. Then the mediator sends a message $\hat{m}_i \in \hat{M}_i$ to the players, and finally the players choose their strategies in the payoff-relevant strategy space $\hat{S}_i$ as a function of their private information and the information revealed to them through the mediator's message.

Such a process is called a *mechanism*. It is described diagrammatically in figure 3.1. The mechanism is specified by the spaces $M_1, \ldots, M_N$, $\hat{M}_1, \ldots, \hat{M}_N$, $\hat{S}_1, \ldots, \hat{S}_N$ and the functions

$$h_i^1 : M_1 \times, \ldots, \times M_N \rightarrow \hat{M}_i$$

$$h_i^2 : \hat{S}_1 \times, \ldots, \times \hat{S}_N \rightarrow X.$$

The players' strategies f_i^1, f_i^2 are defined coordinate-wise:

$$f_i^1 : Y_i \rightarrow M_i$$

$$f_i^2 : Y_i \times \hat{M}_i \rightarrow \hat{S}_i.$$

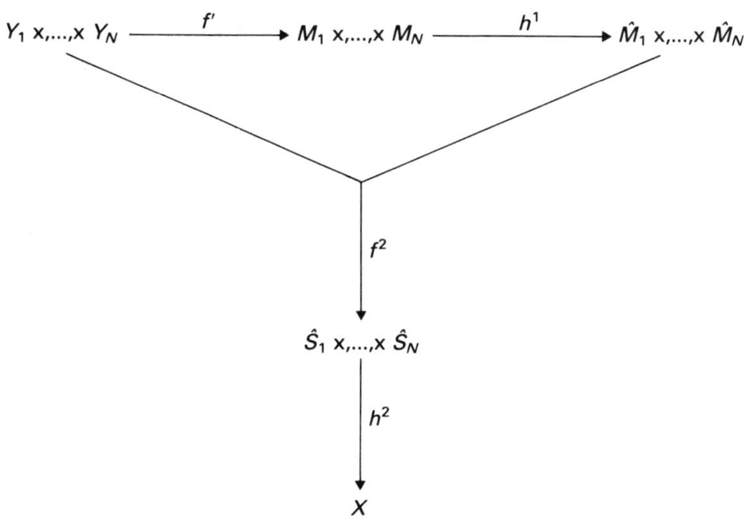

Figure 3.1

Mechanisms are more powerful than designs because the mediator can effect communication patterns via the choice of h^1 that could not be attained by decentralized agents. For example, player 1 could be informed of player 2's observation $y_2 \in Y_2$ only if his own observation were some particular $\bar{y}_1 \in Y_1$, and this observation could be hidden from him otherwise. Without a mediator this might not be possible – and in some cases it has been observed that it is socially desirable.

The structure of mechanisms presented above may seem to be very general and very complex. However, the basic results in the theory of incentive compatibility show that the mechanism design problem can be greatly simplified without loss of generality. A mechanism is said to *implement* a result μ if it has an equilibrium such that the induced joint distribution of (y, x) is μ. The *revelation principle* states that, if μ is implementable, we can find another mechanism in which $M_i = Y_i$ and $\hat{M}_i = \hat{S}_i$ for each i, and an equilibrium of this mechanism such that f_i^1 is the identity function for each i, and such that μ is also implemented by this mechanism. This reduces the mechanism design problem to the choice of $(\hat{S}_i, h_i^1, h_i^2)$. The objective, again, may be to optimize μ according to any of the criteria given above. Myerson (1983) has shown that this is a linear programming problem and has given a constructive method for its solution.

Notice that, if μ is implementable by a truth-inducing mechanism as described above, the game being played is actually of the SPE form discussed in section 3. Thus there is no loss of generality in restricting designs to the SPE form when a mediator is present. Without a mediator, the issue is more complex and remains unresolved at present. In particular, it is an open question as to whether the two-stage designs studied by Farrell can implement all the feasible results without a mediator, or whether some multi-stage strategy spaces, perhaps without simultaneous play, might be superior in some cases.

5 ECONOMIC MODELS WITH DIFFERENTIAL INFORMATION

I will now turn to a selective survey of models of economic behavior under conditions of differential information. The goal is to classify these models according to the special features embodied in each when formulated as a game of incomplete information. All of the systems studied are of the form described in section 3. Nature's move is differentially revealed to the participants at the beginning of play. The subsequent course of play, the stochastic structure of nature's move, and its revelation are the features that separate one system from another.

To describe the main lines along which I will make this classification, some preliminary remarks are necessary. Most of the models in the economics of differential information are partial equilibrium in nature. Something other than the agents' characteristics is held fixed, and is treated parametrically by the participants. There are two main types of 'partial equilibrium constraints.' First, there are conditions determining the voluntary participation or non-participation in the system. Alternative forms of these constraints are described and illustrated in the following subsection. Second, there are those auxiliary conditions related to endogenous variables determined in the system, other than the utility levels produced. Examples might be the prices faced by these agents or aspects of their market opportunities such as the competitive conditions in their industries. These obviously are an ingredient in determining their welfare, but they do not do so completely. The impact of these constraints is somewhat different in nature than explicit utility constraints. These models are discussed in the second subsection.

A third line of classification relates to the comparison of the strategy spaces of each agent with that agent's information set. In the SPE, discussed above in section 3, these sets were identified. Although this is of substantial normative significance, it turns out that in many actual games the strategy space is smaller than the space of observables. This feature leads to some problems in these models, as well as to some of their more interesting properties. It is covered in the third subsection.

Finally, we describe how the welfare properties of these models are influenced by their attributes in these regards.

One should note that the lines along which I distinguish these models do not form an exhaustive classificatory scheme. Some specific models have specific attributes mentioned in more than one of these subsections, and their properties are determined by the combined presence of these features rather than by any one of them alone. Some 'boxes' are 'empty.' Nevertheless, I hope that a discussion along these lines is useful.

Participation constraints

Consider an equilibrium of a game of incomplete information where $h: Y \to X$ is implemented. This produces the utility allocation $U: Y \to R$ defined by $y \nrightarrow u_i[h(y)|y]$ for each i. Let Φ be the set of all implementable utility allocations. Usually there will be many allocations in Φ, and often the planner, or mechanism designer, has a preference ordering over them. For example, X may include the possibility of making monetary transfers to the planner, for which the planner's utility is increasing. In such cases, the planner's problem of implementing that u which is best according to his criterion must be solved subject to some constraints. In the example above, the absence of constraints would permit the planner to increase uniformly the transfers to be paid by every y without inducing any distortions in the self-selection problem. Such large transfers are unreasonable.

The most natural type of constraints in these problems is 'participation constraints.' They express the ideas of voluntary participation in the process. Formally, there is an action available to each agent called *non-participation*. Any agent who chooses this action obtains a payoff $u_0(y)$.

The form of the participation constraints depends on the timing of the actions, the information-gathering and the commitment process inherent in the model. The natural points at which one can 'quit' are: *ex ante*, before learning y_i; interim, after learning y_i but before the interaction among the players produces a result; and *ex post*, after y is revealed and $u[y, h(y)]$ results. These lead to the three types of constraints:

$$\mathop{E}_{y} u_i[h(y), y] \geqslant \mathop{E}_{y} u_0(y)$$

$$\mathop{E}_{y_{-i}|y_i} u_i[h(y), y\,|y_i] \geqslant \mathop{E}_{y_{-i}|y_i} u_0(y)$$

$$u_i[h(y), y] \geqslant u_0(y).$$

Each of these forms of the participation constraint is appropriate for certain applications.

In procedures to select a public project, one should be able to obtain the *ex ante* consent of those involved that the process is beneficial. This is discussed extensively in Green and Laffont (1979). Given tastes, some people may have to pay more than the project is worth to them. But that is not a sufficient reason to reject the procedure.

On the other hand, when scarce private goods are involved, it is often more reasonable to allow the agents to select out of the procedures after they learn their valuation. Thus, auctions typically cannot collect revenues from those who concede all their chances of winning (see Milgrom and Weber, 1982a).

The difference between *ex post* and interim participation is of some interest when the private information does not precisely define the value of the object being auctioned. *Ex post* participation would allow the individual to withdraw his bid after learning its true value. This is not often reasonable, since the uncertainty about its value is one of the primary reasons for using the auction mode of allocation. Interim participation seems better in this case. *Ex post* participation is most relevant when one can voluntarily quit the organization – as in the case of local public goods in a small community.

Auction theory has usually used the interim constraint in a special way. The private information, Y_i, of each agent has been modeled as a real number, or an observation from an ordered set, with respect to which the utility function is monotonic. A lowest possible value of Y_i called $\underline{y}_i$ exists. Furthermore, it is assumed that the utility of withdrawal from the auction is independent of the true value of the item being sold. This is reasonable for items that are not subsequently resold to the same group of participants, but it may not hold in general. These two hypotheses imply that, if all agents are to be induced to participate, then it suffices to make the agent with $y_i = \underline{y}_i$ participate. The fact that the interim participation constraint can be expressed so simply provides auction models with a good deal of their tractability. The general nature of participation constraints in models with a one-parameter family of agents' preferences is explored in detail by Cooper (1982).

Auxiliary equilibrium conditions

By auxiliary equilibrium conditions I mean those constraints on the outcome of the model that are expressed as relations among endogenous variables other than the utilities or expected utilities produced in the equilibrium. Auxiliary equilibrium conditions are therefore intrinsically of a partial equilibrium nature. They have been most commonly used in economic models in which the uncertainty concerns individuals' unobservable characteristics and in which the statistical distribution of these characteristics in the population is effectively known because of the large numbers of individuals. This situation is not necessary for the presence and operation of auxiliary equilibrium conditions, but it makes their treatment much simpler.

Models of signalling (see Spence, 1973) are a clear example of the application of auxiliary economic conditions in a situation of incomplete information. Consider the prototypical example of unknown productivity signalled by educational attainment. The equilibrium is characterized by a function associating a wage to each level of education. This induces a joint distribution of productivity and education. In equilibrium it is also required that, for each level of education, the wage rate equals the average productivity conditional on that education. Thus the system is constrained not by any agent's utility, but rather by the form of the equilibrium relations.

It may be possible to convert the signalling model's constraint into a participation constraint of the type discussed earlier by treating the employers explicitly. They hire labor, paying the indicated wage, and in order to make them participate their profits (utility) must be non-negative.

I do not know whether it is always possible to integrate the utility constraints and auxiliary equilibrium conditions. It is possible above because of the large-numbers assumptions, making profits non-stochastic and identifying 'profits' with the 'utilities' of particular agents. In more general circumstances this may not be possible. In any case, making a distinction between these types of constraints seems analytically useful.

Dimensionality of observables and unobservables

Many of the features discussed in the last two subsections have special properties because of the equality of the dimensionality of the space of unobservables with the strategy spaces, and observable choices, of the economic agents. Indeed, all the models used to date have the property that the observables are one-dimensional and the unobservables are either one-dimensional or else consist of a discrete set of points – that is, a special type of zero-dimensional set. The advantage of this formulation is that the self-selection constraints, in the presence of a monotonicity condition (see Riley, 1979), can be expressed as a differential equation (in the former case) or as a system of inequalities with some very special properties (in the latter).

The more general problem of higher-dimensional spaces of unobservables remains almost totally unexplored. For a decision rule to be implementable, it is necessary both that it respect the incentive compatibility constraints and that, viewed as a function from the unobservables to the individual's outcome, it be of a rank not greater than the dimensionality of the pre-specified strategy space. J. Green and Laffont (1982) and E. Green (1982) have shown that this conjunction of these two conditions is extremely restrictive. One cannot specify a mapping from the unobservables to the strategies arbitrarily and then append a mapping from strategies to outcomes so as to make the indicated strategies of the game of incomplete information form an equilibrium. In general, there will be no game form, other than trivial cases where the social state is unresponsive, that induces the specified pattern of equilibrium strategies. The equivalence classes of unobserved parameters that can be induced by some game form are a predetermined family, related to the functional form of agents' objectives.

One case in which it is natural to construct a game with a smaller strategy space than the space of observables arises when the information is verifiable. The observer has, in his possession, some reproducible evidence that could be divulged to others. Moreover, the others know that, if he has in fact made certain observations, he will have the evidence to back them up. His choice therefore is to disclose the information or not. But he may not lie and say that he has seen some other observation, for he will not have the evidence to make it credible, public knowledge. Such a model is explored in Green and Laffont (1983).

6 WELFARE ANALYSIS OF ECONOMIC MODELS WITH DIFFERENTIAL INFORMATION

One advantage of having recast economic models with differential information as games of incomplete information is that we can perform a welfare analysis of their equilibria on a sound footing. To make a meaningful comparison of the equilibria of an economic model with those of a hypothetical alternative, it is essential to preserve both the information structure of the economic model and the individual's incentives. The comparison concerns the equilibria of the game of incomplete information induced by the economic model and the equilibria of a game designed by the economic analyst. This new game must use the same initial structure of information as the economic game. It must provide nature, or the artificial 'player 0,' with only such information as might properly be thought to comprise prior information. In particular, we cannot *give* this central player any information specific to economic agents – although the game may be structured to elicit this voluntarily from them.

Quite surprisingly, many of the economic systems discussed in section 5 are efficient in this sense. As this is certainly not true of games of incomplete information in general, we inquire in this section as to the reasons why efficiency arises in these cases.

The economic systems studied in section 5 can be divided into those that are actually mechanisms, or games among the economic agents, and those that require the equilibrating variables to be determined by a market manager who is not among these agents. The issue of efficiency is much simpler for the mechanisms. Here, interim efficiency is often established in the usual economic environments, with outcomes and private information individual-specific and without externalities, and with the aggregate feasible set non-stochastic. The reason is simply that interim and *ex post* efficiency coincide in these environments, and *ex post* efficiency is ensured because of the anonymity of the mechanisms considered and the monotonicity of *ex post* utility evaluations in the underlying parameters.

An example of these mechanisms is auctions in which all economic agents are on one side of the market and where their information is an estimate of the value of the good to them having the monotone likelihood ratio property. The highest evaluator will always win the auction. Note, however, that there are some situations where interim efficiency does not obtain. These are models in which there is random variation in the evaluations on both sides of the market, as in Weitzman's (1974) study of price versus quantity trading rules, Green and Honkapohja's (1983) more general model of long-term contracting, or Wilson's (1982) model of a one-shot sealed-bid double-auction (both sides bidding, and market-clearing taking place at a price determined by these bids).

These models are *ex post* inefficient because some initially beneficial trades are not undertaken in equilibrium. It follows, therefore, that they are interim and *ex ante* inefficient. Note that in Green and Honkapohja (1983) the incentive-compatibility-constrained efficient set is characterized subject to a dominant strategy equilibrium being achieved among the agents. The game they describe is implicitly not the SPE, where the solution concept is that Bayesian–Nash is played by each agent after he learns the true value of his parameter. Wilson uses the Bayesian–Nash solution concept. His analysis demonstrates that the double-auction is not an efficient mechanism, and that, when uncertainty affects both buyers and sellers, the efficient mechanism is likely to depend on the statistical distribution of the willingness to pay. This is to be contrasted with the one-sided auction models. There, the attainable utility frontiers for each valuation depend upon this distribution, but any one of several mechanisms (in the risk-neutral case) can always achieve a point on this frontier.

Finally, we come to the economic models that are not mechanisms and are not modeled as games in the SPE form. I will discuss two varieties: the learning-from-prices models of Green (1973) and Grossman (1981), and the signalling models of Spence (1973) and Riley (1979). The former do not result in interim-efficient allocations, whereas the latter have one interim-efficient equilibrium and many other inefficient equilibria.

Let the agent's observations in the learning-from-prices model be y_i and let prices be formed by the market-maker according to the function $p(y_1, \ldots, y_n)$. Agent i's indirect utility, *ex post*, can be written as $v_i(y_1, \ldots, y_n, p)$, which, for each fixed price vector, would represent the maximized value of his utility given all the information. Integrating out y_{-i} we obtain the indirect interim utility $v_i(y_i, p)$. Because p is still a random variable given y_i, the agent is at risk for the fluctuations in p induced by other agents' information. An interim-efficient mechanism would insure the agent against these risks. The learning-from-prices models permit some of the risks to be mitigated; but only when all information is effectively conveyed by prices, as in Grossman (1977) or Radner (1979), is full insurance possible. When prices do not form a sufficient statistic, as in Bray (1981), an alternative mechanism based on such a statistic would be able to interim-dominate the learning-from-prices equilibrium.

Signalling models do not have this difficulty. The price vector is non-stochastic because there is no aggregate uncertainty in the model. The incentive-compatibility constraints are effectively built into the signalling equilibrium wage structure. Therefore they do not allow any ability group to benefit without a corresponding decrease in utility for a higher ability group, or else a violation of the implementability requirement.

REFERENCES

Bray, M. (1981), 'Future Trading, Rational Expectations and the Efficient Market Hypothesis,' *Econometrica*, **49**, 575–96.

Cooper, R. (1982), 'Towards a Solution to the General Problem of Self-Selection,' Cowles Foundation, Yale University (mimeograph).

Debreu, G. (1952), 'A Social Equilibrium Existence Theorem,' *Proceedings of the National Academy of Sciences of the USA*, **38**, 886–93.

Farrell, J. (1983), 'Communication in Games I: Mechanism Design without a Mediator,' Massachusetts Institute of Technology (mimeographed).

Green, E. (1982), 'Decentralizability of Truthful Revelation and Other Decision Rules,' California Institute of Technology Discussion Paper no. 419.

Green, J. (1973), 'Information, Efficiency and Equilibrium,' Harvard Institute of Economic Research Discussion Paper no. 284.

Green, J. and Honkapohja, S. (1983), 'Bilateral Contracts,' *Journal of Mathematical Economics*, **11**, 171–87.

Green, J. and Laffont, J-J. (1979), *Incentives in Public Decision-Making*, North-Holland Publishing Company, Amsterdam.

Green, J. and Laffont, J-J. (1982), 'Limited Communication and Incentive Compatibility,' Harvard Institute of Economic Research Discussion Paper no. 919.

Green, J. and Laffont, J-J. (1983), 'Partially Verifiable Information and Mechanism Design,' Harvard Institute of Economic Research Discussion Paper no. 995.

Grossman, S. (1977), 'The Existence of Futures Markets, Noisy Rational Expectations and Informational Externalities,' *Review of Economic Studies*, **64**, 431–49.

Grossman, S. (1981), 'An Introduction to the Theory of Rational Expectations under Asymmetric Information,' *Review of Economic Studies*, **48**, 541–60.

Holmström, B. and Myerson, R. (1983), 'Efficient and Durable Decision Rules with Incomplete Information,' *Econometrica*, **51**, 1799–1819.

Kreps, D. and Wilson, R. (1982), 'Sequential Equilibria,' *Econometrica*, **50**, 863–94.

Kuhn, H. (1953), 'Extensive Games and the Problem of Information,' *Annals of Mathematic Studies*, **28**, 193–216.

Laffont, J-J. (1983), 'On the Welfare Analysis of Price-revealing Equilibria,' Walras–Bowley Lecture presented to the Econometric Society, 22 June 1983.

Milgrom, P. and Weber, R. (1982a), 'A Theory of Auctions and Competitive Bidding,' *Econometrica*, **50**, 1089–122.

Milgrom, P. and Weber, R. (1982b), 'The Value of Information in a Sealed-bid Auction,' *Journal of Mathematical Economics*, **10**, 105–14.

Myerson, R. (1983), 'Bayesian Equilibrium and Incentive Compatibility: An Introduction,' Northwestern University Graduate School of Management Discussion Paper no. 548.

Radner, R. (1979). 'Rational Expectations Equilibrium: Generic Existence and Information Revealed by Price,' *Econometrica*, **47**, 655–78.

Riley, J. (1979), 'Informational Equilibrium,' *Econometrica*, **47**, 331–60.

Spence, A. M. (1973), *Market Signalling: Information Transfer in Hiring and Related Processes*, Harvard University Press, Cambridge, Mass.

Weitzman, M. (1974), 'Prices versus Quantities,' *Review of Economic Studies*, **41**, 477–92.

Wilson, R. (1982), 'Double Auctions,' Stanford University Technical Report no. 391.

Comment

BENGT HOLMSTRÖM

I

Models that explore the economic ramifications of asymmetric information are at the center of present-day developments in economic theory. The recognition that efficient economic organization has to respect informational constraints in addition to standard resource constraints has opened up new broad fields of inquiry in which much of traditional economic wisdom can be and needs to be re-examined. With the innovation of a tractable apparatus for analyzing strategic behavior under asymmetric information, this research program is now well on its way.

Jerry Green's lecture probes the theoretical underpinnings of this new methodology. His objective is to show that most of the models can be studied in a unified way within the framework of games of incomplete information, sometimes called Bayesian games. In this view, any economic organization, by specifying the actions to be undertaken, the information to be communicated and the rewards to be paid, induces a Bayesian game. The task of efficient economic organization is to design the rules of the game optimally, which means structuring the game so that the socially most preferred equilibrium obtains. This exercise is commonly referred to as 'mechanism design.'

The mechanism design approach to economic organization is an elegant and effective theoretical tool. It derives its analytical power from the fact that the optimal design problem, thanks to the revelation principle, can be formulated as a simple (actually linear) programming problem, where standard resource constraints are augmented by the incentive constraints implied by privately held information and discretionary actions. Its economic contribution comes with the novel organizational implications that the incentive constraints yield in specific contexts, as I will illustrate shortly.

Green's focus on the mechanism design approach and its game-theoretic background is appropriate in view of its unifying role in the field. It represents the culmination of years of experimentation with more specialized, example-like models of incentive problems. In passing I mention that Green's model is not as general as it could be. It accounts for private information about the state of nature, but leaves out unobservable actions. In the language of incentive theory it therefore covers problems of self-selection but not those of moral hazard. This is a relatively inessential omission and I mention it only because I will refer to both types of incentive problems later on.[1]

A more substantial omission is the lack of illustrative applications that would suggest the economic relevance of Green's general framework. In my comment I will try to cover this aspect with some examples. My discussion has a broad focus, reflecting on the central economic issues, the significance of the formal analysis and the limitations and challenges that this line of research faces.[2]

II

Why should one study asymmetric information models? What prodded research in this direction? Evidently, the answers are to be found in limitations of received micro-theory. The competitive model does not perform well in some economic dimensions. I list three of them here.

First, it cannot accommodate any form of non-market organization and is silent on the question why some transactions take place across markets while others are conducted outside the price system, most notably within firms. This leaves the suspicion that explanations of non-market organizations will have a bearing on allocations determined across markets as well. A good example of the legitimacy of such suspicions against overly aggregate modelling can be found in recent work on implicit contract theory, which as I see it undermines the efforts of fixed-price models.[3]

Another shortcoming of the competitive model is its inability to provide a satisfactory model of price formation. The artificial construct of an auctioneer gives few indications of how real-world markets actually operate and how they perform the task of aggregating widely dispersed information. This point has been best articulated in Hayek's harsh critique of the competitive model (not to be confused with his admiration of the competitive system), which came in response to a stalemate in the socialist controversy. In Hayek's view, the true challenge for economic theory is to analyze and explain how different economic systems utilize the private knowledge of its citizens.

A third weakness of received micro-theory is its failure to support realistic welfare judgments. The second welfare theorem, stating that all Pareto optima can be supported by price equilibria after suitable reallocations of endowments, makes no contribution toward an understanding of the inevitable trade-off between equity and efficiency that one faces when choosing between different economic systems. It suggests, unrealistically, that the two issues can be separated.

With due respect for the accomplishments of the competitive model, I note that these are substantial limitations. To the extent that models of incomplete information can help in patching some of these gaps, it is clear that important advances have been made. Let me now turn to that assessment.

III

I begin with the positive implications of mechanism design. These stem from the Coasian view that, in a competitive world, markets and hierarchies (to use Williamson's language) will form in ways that exhaust cooperative gains. Under asymmetric information, and with a small number of traders, the price system will not perform well and will consequently be replaced by more complex modes of transaction. These forms can be derived by solving for the optimal transaction mechanism in Green's program.

As a simple illustration, consider defense procurement. There is only one seller and one buyer and considerable uncertainty about the ultimate cost of the system. If the trade were made on a fixed-fee basis, all the risk-bearing would eventually fall on the seller, and the cost of that risk-bearing might even prevent the trade from taking place. On the other hand, if the fee were to be fully indexed to actual cost, the seller would have no incentive to engage in expensive cost-reducing activities in so far as these activities cannot be monitored and the costs reimbursed. A prototypical moral hazard situation obtains. The solution – the optimal design – is a cost-plus contract in which the buyer carries part of the risk, but the seller retains some incentive for cost reductions. By Coase's argument, this also becomes a positive prediction. It is different from what one would get under complete information, and clearly more consistent with empirical evidence.

Cost-plus contracts may not be the most interesting objects of study economically, but similar forces are at work in other contexts as well. Perhaps the most analyzed and important is the employment relationship. Opportunism here relates both to the difficulties with which one can observe sincere labor supply and to the informational advantages enjoyed by employees in the form of job expertise, private knowledge of preferences, talent, etc. The resulting incentive problems mitigate a simple exchange of wage for labor and more complex forms of contracting emerge. Agency theory, by studying what optimal transaction modes the mechanism design program predicts, has obtained significant insights into the idiosyncratic features of the employment relationship. Formal models can now explain bonus payments, monitoring practices, budgeting procedures, management by objectives, the incidence of authority, the relationship between responsibility and reward, organizational slack and relative performance evaluation, to name a few.[4]

Space considerations prevent me from going into the details of any of these results. Instead, let me point out one significant ingredient in many of the models (specifically, those of self-selection), namely the *ex post* inefficiency of optimal contracts. In order to elicit truthful information from a more informed person, it is usually necessary to force him to prove himself by having him accept a trade that is distorted relative to the full information optimum. A good example has been given recently in the labor contracting literature (see the *Quarterly Journal of Economics* symposium). If an optimal contract calls for lower wages in low-productivity states (for risk-sharing purposes), but the firm alone observes productivity, incentive efficiency will dictate that reduced wages have to be 'purchased' by distorting the employment level from its *ex post* optimum. This may explain unemployment. Analogously, one can explain the incidence of strikes. They can be viewed as a means by which labor unions force firms to be honest about productivity (Hayes, 1983). More generally, bargaining impasses, which never could occur between fully informed rational agents, may well take place in models of incomplete information (Ordover and Rubinstein, 1983).

These naturally occurring inefficiencies, it should be emphasized, reflect nothing more than legitimate costs of information transfer. They may also be viewed as stemming from rents that accrue to parties that hold an informational monopoly.[5] With either interpretation it is evident that the possibility of reconciling *ex post* inefficiencies with rational behavior holds the key, potentially, to explanations of a vast number of institutional phenomena that are beyond reach for received micro-theory.

Indeed, there is no shortage of work on the 'new institutional economics.' In fact, the situation is rather the reverse: institutions can be explained in too many ways nowadays. The incomplete information paradigm has opened up a huge new parameter space with which to play, and econometric work is lagging far behind in discriminating between competing theories. This is a serious problem, particularly since so often the normative conclusions are quite sensitive to the specific informational asymmetries involved, while the positive predictions are not.[6] As an example, take the discussion about government regulation of warranties; warranties could be explained either via moral hazard or via self-selection arguments, but with rather different conclusions concerning regulatory action.[7] Part of the problem is that in information economics we are not blessed with suitable assumptions on the information technology that would impose the kind of discipline with which we are familiar in classical economics, in which convexity does a wonderful job.[8] Even so, one would like authors to search more extensively for discriminating predications – after all, the legitimacy of this kind of explicit and detailed transaction cost economics rests partly with the ability to generate predictions beyond the phenomena that one wants to explain.

Understanding firms and other forms of non-market organization is of interest in its own right, of course. But as I mentioned before, the central question is whether this refined microeconomics leads to any aggregate implications of overall economic significance. Compared with the number of studies that deal with purely organizational features, there has been rather little work that extends to aggregate issues.[9] It may be time to focus some more attention on this fact.

As an illustration, I find the following question well worth pursuing: Does it really matter (in the aggregate) that real-world decisions are made by managers rather than by an amorphous ownership syndicate? To some extent this question has been explored. For instance, models by Jensen and Meckling (1976), Ross (1977) and Grossman and Hart (1982) have shown how managerial incentives may dictate a unique capital structure for the firm. This will obviously imply a different price and distribution of capital than conventional value maximization would suggest. Laurence Weiss and I have recently looked at another managerial model, in which we show that capital will be underemployed in less productive states to prevent managers from misrepresenting rates of return for their advantage. In the aggregate this reduced capital spending will result in larger capital and output fluctuations than a Walrasian model would predict. Such amplifications could also be generated from portfolio considerations. Managers will tend to choose investments that are more highly correlated with the aggregate, because such choices will aid relative performance evaluation and consequently reduce incentive costs. The social outcome is a riskier market portfolio and too little experimentation.

These results suggest that there is promise in attempting to operationalize a managerial theory of the firm. In particular, a study of managerial competition, induced by explicit and implicit relative performance measurement, should yield valuable insights into capital spending, risk-taking and even some macroeconomic phenomena. I also think the ultimate resolution to the longstanding controversies concerning the objective function of the firm will be found along these lines.

My call for more empirical concern as well as aggregate implications should obviously not be interpreted as saying that we already have some explanation of all characteristics of non-market organization. For instance, we are a long way still from formulating models that come even close to explaining richer corporate structures with hierarchies and layers of decentralized decision-making. We are even further away from Coase's dream of an endogenous explanation of the division of transactions between markets and hierarchies. In fact, I believe there are some serious difficulties in generating models that explain hierarchies, which relate to formalizing information-processing costs.

All models that have been discussed so far (and all that fit Green's general framework) turn on information costs of a particular kind. They deal with costs of inducing proper incentives for transmitting information truthfully or of not abusing informational advantages. One could call them strategic information costs. These costs should be carefully distinguished from those that deal with a limited ability to process information, incentive issues notwithstanding. While there have been attempts to incorporate such costs into formal models – most notably through the indirect approach of team theory (Marschak and Radner, 1972) – these have been much less successful, because of the difficulties with which one can quantify information. Nevertheless, since information-processing costs are bound to play a significant role in a fuller understanding of non-market organization (hierarchies in particular), one would hope that future research would not one-sidedly focus on strategic information costs.

IV

Next I turn to some comments on the normative implications of mechanism design. Hurwicz (1972) was the first to formulate the choice of an optimal economic system as a problem of mechanism design. His formulation was not Bayesian even though it recognized asymmetric information explicitly. As subsequent work has shown (Hurwicz and Schmeidler, 1978), incentive constraints will have no bite in that case; mechanisms can be designed that reach the Walrasian outcome.[10] The Bayesian formulation, which imputes market power to informed agents, is for this reason clearly the preferred one (witness the positive implications discussed above).

Hurwicz's objective was partly to shed light on the socialist controversy. One might ask if the modern game design approach contributes at all to our understanding of this big debate. The answer is an emphatic 'No!' The program that is being solved in computing an optimal mechanism assumes that all private information is passed to the central authority which makes the final decision. There is no sense in which information-processing is decentralized the way we envision it to be in market economies. Explicit models of price formation seem necessary if we are to understand how markets really operate. Work by R. Wilson (1977, 1983), Milgrom (1981b) and

Myerson and Satterthwaite (1983) is a promising start in this direction.[11] They have shown, in a more genuine sense than traditional welfare theorems, how simple markets (auctions) have the ability to aggregate dispersed information efficiently. Yet, these markets are still centrally administered. If one is to reach Hayek's desired conclusion, that markets outperform central planning, I am afraid one has to come to grips with information-processing costs. I already expressed some pessimism on that endeavor.[12]

I conclude that the mechanism design approach is not about to deliver an answer to the ultimate question of what an optimal economic system ought to look like. But it can claim success on more limited normative issues. With its help we have clarified our understanding of the free-rider problems surrounding public goods, and we have received guidance on taxation policy. Both subjects have been extensively explored in recent years through models that fit Green's general paradigm.[13] For reasons of space I will not make further comments on them here. Instead, I would like to close with a few general remarks on welfare measurement under incomplete information.

Under incomplete information, and with utilities independent of each other, it is a straightforward matter to define the concept of Pareto optimality. An allocation is Pareto-optimal if one cannot find another feasible allocation that is better for at least one individual and no worse for all the others. With incomplete information this seemingly simple definition becomes ambiguous on (at least) three grounds. What do we mean by feasibility? On what information should we base our evaluation of whether an allocation is better for an individual or not? And what information should we assume the person has who is picking the optimal allocation (or contemplating reallocations)?

The proposed definition, also discussed in Green's paper, is that of incentive efficiency. In this notion a feasible allocation is one that may depend on private information but only in an incentive-compatible way. Agents must have an incentive to reveal their information truthfully so that the allocation can actually be implemented. Also, we should not assume that the social planner, who is responsible for the final choice, has more information than is common knowledge in society (i.e. that is known by all). Consequently, a reallocation must never hurt any agent in any of his potential information states. Thus an allocation is incentive-efficient if and only if it is not common knowledge that there is a better incentive-compatible allocation available.

This definition has some peculiar features. Compared with the classical definition, it no longer separates the question of attaining efficiency from that of being in an efficient state. The two are one and the same. Also, what is to be considered efficient depends on the information structure in society, not merely on endowments and production technology. Third, the definition involves a paradoxical element of non-cooperative game theory through the use of incentive compatibility. All of these features may seem objectionable in view of the objective and cooperative nature an efficiency concept should have. Yet, they seem inevitable consequences of the private information paradigm.

Incentive efficiency, in respecting the private information each agent has by making sure he does not suffer in any of his information states, becomes a very weak efficiency concept for normative purposes. It is difficult to propose changes in allocations such that everybody is better off no matter what his type is. My conclusion is that welfare judgments, for most practical purposes, have to involve distributional considerations – i.e. interpersonal comparisons of utility. The separation between production efficiency and distribution of wealth, embodied in the classical welfare theorems, is not a feasible proposition.

This may not be a profoundly novel insight. It is well recognized (among welfare practitioners at least; see Okun, 1975) that there is an inevitable tension in striving for efficiency and equity at the same time. Nor do I think work on incentive efficiency, yet at least, suggests very practical ways in which this trade-off can be computed, because of the role played by the information structure. Nevertheless, we have now a formal model in which the trade-off is clearly visible and in which the costs of inducing information revelation – in the form of distortions from first-best – are made explicit. This in its own right is a powerful welfare declaration and a firm base from which to proceed.

The constrained nature of incentive inefficiency brings up a methodological point as well. We are well accustomed to the idea that in judging market outcomes one should not assume that the planner has more instruments available than the market participants.

Such limitations have most often included access to insurance, that is, contingent claims of various forms. To this should now be added informational constraints. In incomplete information models it is sometimes possible to spot improvements that can be made, because providers of substitutes for missing insurance markets do not account for all the social benefits and costs in the individual optimization programs.[14] However, these inefficiencies are often seen with the eye of the modeler, who has more information than is common knowledge in the economy. In such cases suggested policy measures may end up depending on other information than is common knowledge (in particular, on preference information). This is a violation of the principles behind incentive efficiency, if no attention is paid to the mechanism by which the needed information can be truthfully elicited. Thus, incentive efficiency prods us toward a 'new welfare economics' in which the actual implementation of welfare plans (in the form of functional mechanisms) becomes an integral part of the welfare analysis.

NOTES

1 For models that incorporate both types of informational asymmetries, see Holmström (1977) and Myerson (1982).

2 Needless to say, my thoughts are gathered from a wide set of sources, much wider, unfortunately, than the reference list can credit. Here I would like to mention especially Arrow (1974), Coase (1937), Hayek (1945), Hurwicz (1972), Knight (1965) and Williamson (1975), whose writings had substantial influence on my thoughts. I have interpreted and borrowed freely from these sources.

3 Implicit contract theory can explain sticky (real) prices. However, the accompanying optimal quantity rules do not accord with the (*ad hoc*) rules postulated in fixed-price theory.

4 For some formal models of agency see Jensen and Meckling (1976), Stiglitz (1975), Mirrlees (1976), Harris and Raviv (1979), Holmström (1979, 1982a), Shavell (1979), Lazear and Rosen (1981), Grossman and Hart (1983), Antle and Eppen (1983).

5 In this context it is of some interest to note that Knight, who, in his influential contribution to the theory of profit, made a sharp distinction between uncertainty and risk, argued that only uncertainty could account for rents. With the later development of subjective probability theory, this distinction was judged a mistake. However, if we reinterpret his uncertainty as asymmetric information – and that is not unjustified by his writings – we find that Knight's distinction is not that misplaced after all.

6 These problems are familiar from the earliest days of studying signalling phenomena (Spence, 1974).

7 I discuss this matter to some extent in Holmström (1982b).

8 Work on useful restrictions on information technology should have high priority. An example of the big payoff that such work can have is Milgrom's (1981a) discovery of the monotone likelihood ratio property. The value of the rational expectations framework should be judged in this same light.

9 One reason for this may be the well-known problems of non-existence of equilibrium that often arise in adverse selection models (Rothschild and Stiglitz, 1976; C. A. Wilson, 1977).

10 Wilson (1983) makes this point clearly.

11 Shubik's early work on explicit market mechanisms deserves also to be mentioned, though informational asymmetries are not considered.

12 However, see Milgrom and Weber (1983) for a comparison of prices vs. quantities that relates to information-processing costs.

13 See Green and Laffont (1979) for an analysis of public goods and Mirrlees's (1971) seminal article on taxation.

14 See for instance Newbery and Stiglitz (1982).

REFERENCES

Antle, R. and Eppen, G. (1983), 'Resource Rationing, Organizational Slack and Project Auditing,' GSB, University of Chicago (mimeographed).

Arrow, K. (1974), *The Limits of Organization*, W. W. Norton & Co., New York.

Coase, R. (1937), 'The Nature of the Firm,' *Economica*, **4**, 386–405; reprinted in G. Stigler and K. Boulding (eds), *Readings in Price Theory*, R. D. Irwin, Homewood, Illinois, 1952.

Green, J. and Laffont, J.-J. (1979), *Incentives in Public Decision Making*, North-Holland, Amsterdam.

Grossman, S. and Hart, O. (1982), 'Corporate Financial Structure and Managerial Incentives,' in J. McCall (ed.), *Economics of Information and Uncertainty*, University of Chicago Press.

Grossman, S. and Hart, O. (1983), 'An Analysis of the Principal–Agent Problem,' *Econometrica*, **51**, 7–45.

Harris, M. and Raviv, A. (1979), 'Optimal Incentive Contracts with Imperfect Information,' *Journal of Economic Theory*, **20**, 231–59.

Hayek, F. (1945), 'The Use of Knowledge in Society,' *American Economic Review*, **35**, 519–30.

Hayes, B. (1983), 'Unions and Strikes with Asymmetric Information,' CMSEMS Discussion Paper no. 547, Northwestern University.

Holmström, B. (1977), 'On Incentives and Control in Organizations,' unpublished dissertation, Graduate School of Business, Stanford University.

Holmström, B. (1979). 'Moral Hazard and Observability,' *Bell Journal of Economics*, **10**, 74–91.

Holmström, B. (1982a), 'Moral Hazard in Teams,' *Bell Journal of Economics*, **13**, 324–40.

Holmström, B. (1982b), 'The Provision of Services in a Market Economy,' paper presented at the ARA/Wharton Conference on the Future of the Service Economy, Universtiy of Pennsylvania, November 1982.

Holmström, B. and Weiss, L. (1982), 'Managerial Incentives, Risk-taking and Aggregate Implications,' *Review of Economic Studies* (forthcoming).

Hurwicz, L. (1972), 'On Informationally Decentralized Systems,' in C. B. McGuire and R. Radner (eds), *Decision and Organization*, North-Holland, Amsterdam.

Hurwicz, L. and Schmeidler, D. (1978), 'Construction of Outcome Functions Guaranteeing Existence and Pareto Optimality of Nash Equilibria,' *Econometrica*, **46**, 1447–74.

Jensen, M. and Meckling, H. (1976), 'Theory of the Firm: Managerial Behavior, Agency Costs and Ownership Structure,' *Journal of Financial Economics*, **3**, 305–60.

Knight, F. (1965), *Risk, Uncertainty and Profit*, Harper and Row, New York.

Lazear, E. and Rosen, S. (1981), 'Rank-order Tournaments as Optimum Labor Contracts,' *Journal of Political Economy*, **89**, 841–64.

Marschak, J. and Radner, R. (1972), *Economic Theory of Teams*, Yale University Press, New Haven, Conn., and London, chapter 2.

Milgrom, P. (1981a), 'Good News and Bad News: Representation Theorems and Applications,' *Bell Journal of Economics*, **12**, 380–91.

Milgrom, P. (1981b), 'Rational Expectations, Information Acquisition, and Competitive Bidding,' *Econometrica*, **49**, 921–43.

Milgrom, P. and Weber, R. (1983), 'Organizing Production in a Large Economy with Costly Communication,' Cowles Foundation Discussion Paper no. 672, Yale University.

Mirrlees, J. (1971), 'An Exploration in the Theory of Optimum Income Taxation,' *Review of Economic Studies*, **38**, 172–208.

Mirrlees, J. (1976), 'The Optimal Structure of Incentives and Authority Within an Organization,' *Bell Journal of Economics and Management Science*, **7**, 105–31.

Myerson, R. (1982), 'Optimal Coordination Mechanisms in Principal–Agent Problems,' *Journal of Mathematical Economics*, **10**, 67–81.

Myerson, R. and Satterthwaite, M. (1983), 'Efficient Mechanisms for Bilateral Trading,' *Journal of Economic Theory*, **29**, 265–81.

Newbery, D. and Stiglitz, J. (1982), 'The Choice of Techniques and the Optimality of Market Equilibrium with Rational Expectations,' *Journal of Political Economy*, **90**, 223–46.

Okun, A. (1975), *Equality and Efficiency*, The Brookings Institution, Washington, DC.

Ordover, J. and Rubinstein, A. (1983), 'On Bargaining, Settling and Litigating: A Problem in Multistage Games with Imperfect Information,' TR 83-07, New York University.

Ross, S. (1977), 'The Determination of Financial Structure: The Incentive Signalling Approach,' *Bell Journal of Economics*, **8**, 23–40.

Rothschild, M. and Stiglitz, J. (1976), 'Equilibrium in Competitive Insurance Markets: An Essay on the Economics of Imperfect Information,' *Quarterly Journal of Economics*, **90**, 629–49.

Shavell, S. (1979), 'Risk-sharing and Incentives in the Principal–Agent Relationship,' *Bell Journal of Economics and Management Science*, **10**, 55–73.

Shubik, M. (1976), 'A Trading Model to Avoid Tatonnement Metaphysics,' in Y. Amihud (ed.), *Studies in Game Theory and Mathematical Economics*, New York, pp. 129–42.

Spence, A. M. (1974), *Market Signalling*, Harvard University Press, Cambridge, Mass.

Stiglitz, J. (1975), 'Incentives, Risk and Information: Notes Towards a Theory of Hierarchy,' *Bell Journal of Economics*, **6**, 552–79.

Stiglitz, J. and Weiss, A. (1981), 'Credit Rationing in Markets with Imperfect Information,' *American Economic Review*, **71**, 393–410.

Symposium on Labor Contracting (1983), *Quarterly Journal of Economics*, Supplement.

Williamson, O. (1975), *Markets and Hierarchies: Analysis and Antitrust Implications*, Free Press, New York.

Wilson, C. A. (1977), 'A Model of Insurance Markets with Incomplete Information,' *Journal of Economic Theory*, **16**, 167–207.

Wilson, R. (1977), 'A Bidding Model of Perfect Competition,' *Review of Economic Studies*, **44**, 511–18.

Wilson, R. (1983), 'Double Auctions,' Stanford University (mimeographed).

Comment

JOHN G. RILEY

Over the last decade, research on equilibrium and efficiency with differential information has exhibited 'boom-town' characteristics, with rapid higgledy-piggledy growth in many different directions. Therefore Green's successful attempt to lay bare the common foundation stones for this research is most welcome.

However, in choosing to approach the subject at this level, he has not provided the outsider with much of an idea as to the practical insights we have to show for all the research effort. Thus, a primary goal this Comment is to provide some more concrete examples.

One simple classification scheme that I find helpful is to distinguish between models in which one party to a contract has an exogenously determined informational advantage and models in which the cost of monitoring results in informational differences arising after contracting has taken place. To take the traditional insurance example, in the former case the problem is one of *adverse selection*, since any insurance contract will, *ceteris paribus*, be more valuable and hence more likely to be purchased by an individual with a higher probability of loss. In the latter case the problem is one of providing an incentive to take care, since the higher is the insurance coverage, the lower is the reward for avoiding a loss. This is known, rather quaintly, as the *moral hazard* problem. As the illustration suggests, moral hazard and adverse selection are likely to appear together in practice. However, applied theory has, thus far, wisely focused on one or the other.

Since I have worked almost exclusively on problems of adverse selection, I plan to focus on recent results in this sub-field. In so doing I hope to present a convincing case that this new research has indeed led to a new appreciation of our diverse market institutions.

1 COMPETITIVE SELF-SELECTION MECHANISMS

The literature on adverse selection is naturally subdivided once more. In one subclass of models a single individual on one side of the market negotiates with one or more individuals on the other side of the market. In some of these models the focus is on a 'principal' negotiating a performance contract with an 'agent' who will then act on the principal's behalf. However, this 'principal–agent problem' is really just one of many applications of the theory of monopoly with differential information.

The second subclass of models, to which I shall turn now, is that in which there are many individuals on both sides of the market. To take a very simple case, suppose workers differ in their productivity only in industry X and that productivity levels are distributed continuously on [0, 1]. Then we can describe a worker with productivity θ as being of type θ. All workers have productivity k in industry Y. Product y has a relative price of p.

As emphasized by Spence (1973) and Rothschild and Stiglitz (1976), any activity with a lower marginal cost for an individual with a higher productivity can operate as a potential signal. To simplify our illustration still further, suppose each worker begins with an endowment $\bar{x}$ of commodity x and that the cost in units of x for type θ to signal at level s is $c(s, \theta)$. Then the indirect utility of an individual of type θ, if accepting a job with wage w and signal requirement s, is

$$u(s, w; \theta, p) = V[p, w - c(s, \theta) + \bar{x}]. \qquad (1)$$

Then the assumption of lower marginal signalling costs for higher levels of θ implies that, for any signal–wage pair $\langle s, w\rangle$, the steepness of a worker's indifference curve through this point,

$$\left.\frac{dw}{ds}\right|_u = \frac{-(\partial u/\partial s)}{\partial u/\partial w} = \frac{\partial c}{\partial s} \qquad (2)$$

is decreasing in θ.

Employers, unable to observe θ, form expectations about the productivity of individuals signalling at different levels. Taking a game-theoretic approach, if employers are modeled as wage-setters it is intuitively clear that, in equilibrium, wages cannot exceed expected marginal products. Then, if the signalling level s is a strictly increasing function of θ, we require, in equilibrium,

$$w[s(\theta)] = \theta. \tag{3}$$

On the other side of the market, each worker takes the wage schedule $w(s)$ as given and chooses $\langle s, w(s) \rangle$ to maximize his own payoff.

All this is depicted in figure 1. Those individuals for whom $\theta < pk$ enter industry Y while the remainder choose to signal and are hired in industry X. As the relative price, p, rises, the supply of y relative to x rises. Hence there is some p and implied $w(s)$ at which all markets clear.[1]

The argument thus far is very much in the spirit of Walrasian equilibrium models. With constant returns to scale, wages are equal to value products of labor and all agents are price-takers. Hence it is natural to refer to $w(s)$ as a Walrasian equilibrium wage schedule.

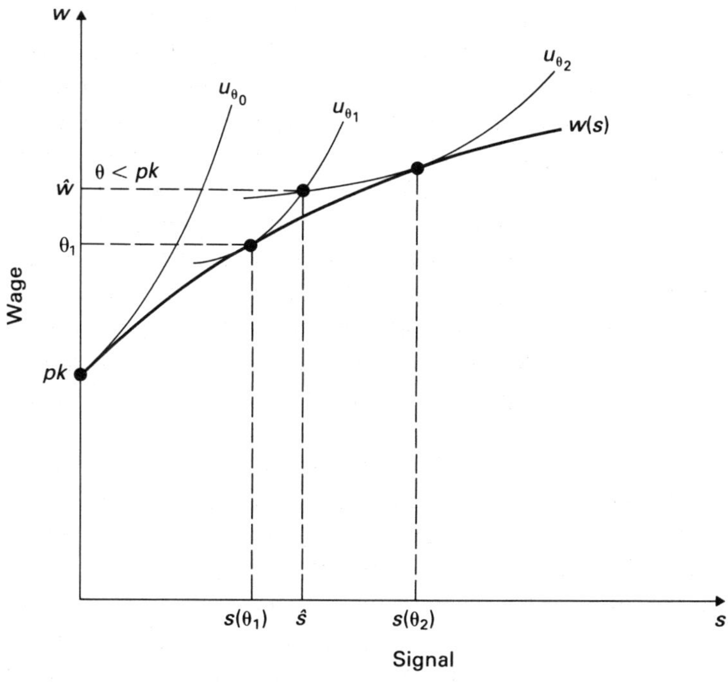

FIGURE 1 Wage competition

However, the price-taking assumption makes sense only if price competition is not in the interest of any agent.

In terms of our simple model, we must ask whether it is in the interest of any firm to offer a higher wage for some level of the signal. From the figure it should be clear that a higher wage for no signal will result in losses as long as industry Y is sufficiently large; for such an offer is attractive to all workers in this industry, and each has a productivity less than pk. The remaining question then is whether an offer such as $\langle \hat{s}, \hat{w} \rangle$ can be profitable.

Note that all those types between θ_1 and θ_2 find the offer attractive and that $\theta_2 > \hat{w} > \theta_1$. Then, as long as the distribution of types has a density function that declines sufficiently rapidly, it is intuitively reasonable that the offer will result in losses. Conversely, if the density function increases sufficiently rapidly, the offer will be profitable (Riley, 1979). Thus, in general there is no Cournot–Nash equilibrium.

Following Wilson (1977), there have been several attempts to resolve the dilemma of non-existence by introducing the idea that agents will take into account the responses of others when considering new actions (Miyazaki, 1977; Riley, 1979). The least demanding of these alternative equilibrium concepts, with respect to informational requirements, is the 'reactive equilibrium.' Loosely, a set of strategies $s_1^*, \ldots, s_n^*$ for n competing agents is a reactive equilibrium if two conditions are satisfied. First, for any agent i and any alternative strategy s_i that raises i's payoff, there is another agent j who can benefit at the expense of agent i. Second, there is no further reaction by a further agent that can make agent j's reactions unprofitable. The idea, then, is that agent i will recognize agent j's clear incentive to react and therefore will be deterred from choosing s_i rather than s_i^*. It is not difficult to confirm that the Walrasian equilibrium wage schedule depicted in figure 1 is a reactive equilibrium – in fact, the unique reactive equilibrium.

Just how satisfactory is this equilibrium concept or the related concepts of Wilson and Miyazaki? As a primary promoter I would not pretend to offer a disinterested judgment. Instead, I will note that there is an alternative partial resolution of the dilemma.

Intuitively, the extent of the gains to signalling depends upon the rate at which the cost of signalling declines with the unobservable quality parameter θ, or, more precisely, the elasticity of the marginal cost of signalling with respect to θ. Taking a simple version of the above model with $c(s, \theta) = A(s)/B(\theta)$, I have been able to establish that the profitability of wage competition is also closely related to the elasticity of signalling costs (Riley, 1983). Indeed, as long as this elasticity is sufficiently great for all θ, and does not decline too rapidly with θ, all wage competition is unprofitable. Thus the problem of non-existence tends to arise in those situations in which the potential gains to signalling are relatively small.

Having summarized the state of the theory, I shall conclude this section by indicating some of its applications. While the empirical investigation into the importance of educational signalling has been inconclusive, largely because of data limitations, the model has been used successfully to explain a range of economic institutions, and to suggest the implications of government intervention to 'correct' apparent inequities. For example, in insurance markets individuals are offered lower premiums per dollar of coverage if they are willing to accept a higher deductible or insurance rate. This can be interpreted as a method of sorting out the low-risk types from the high-risk types, just as illustrated in figure 1 (see Dahlby, 1983). A second natural application of the theory is in explaining bank practice of offering lower interest rates to individuals willing to provide greater collateral. Willingness to share risk is interpreted as a signal of a more favorable project. Yet another application is in explaining the development of state security regulations enabling promoters of new stock offerings a way of committing themselves to holding shares for a specified time period. A larger commitment of this type implies a greater exposure to risk and thus can be used as a signal of a more favorable project (Knadler-Morris, 1983; Leland and Pyle, 1977).

2 MONOPOLY SELF-SELECTION MECHANISMS

In the competitive model of the previous section, individuals on one side of the market announce offers, and individuals on the other side, because of systematically varying preferences, accept offers, that differ systematically. The model is closed by requiring that there are no alternative more profitable offers.

With only one individual announcing offers, the self-selection constraints are not changed in any essential way. If the 'individual' announcing offers is really the central authority, the model is closed by characterizing information-constrained Pareto-efficient offers. Alternatively, if the individual is a private monopolist, it is natural to seek out those offers that maximize his own gain.

The classic paper on efficient government contracting is the discussion of optimal income taxation by Mirrlees (1971). This paper can fairly be described as the foundation stone of almost all the recent research on monopoly with differential information. The new results have emerged via the judicious use of additional structural restrictions.

One simple and striking result due to d'Aspremont and Gerard-Varet (1979) follows from the assumption that the returns to different agents can be expressed in terms of money. Any Pareto-efficient allocation then involves lump-sum redistribution of the sum of the individual returns. d'Aspremont and Gerard-Varet consider a case in which there are externalities and each agent has some private information. For simplicity, suppose there are just two agents and that the payoff to agent i, $\pi_i(a, \theta_i)$, is a function of the actions (a_1, a_2) taken by the two agents and the private information θ_i. The goal then is to construct some incentive scheme to maximize

$$\pi_1(a, \theta_1) + \pi_2(a, \theta_2). \tag{4}$$

Let $a^*(\theta_1, \theta_2)$ be the full-information solution to this optimization problem. As long as θ_i is known to be a random draw from some distribution $F_i(\cdot)$, it is in fact possible to achieve the full-information solution despite the fact that the central authority has no private information. The key idea is that, if agent 2 is required to pay agent 1 an amount equal to agent 2's expected gain conditional upon agent 2 telling the truth about his value of θ_2, then agent 1 will have an incentive to do so also. Arguing symmetrically for agent 2, if agent 1 tells the truth, the incentive scheme gives agent 2 an incentive to tell the truth, as postulated. Then truth-telling is an equilibrium.

To be more precise, agent 2 is required to pay agent 1

$$T_{21}(\hat{\theta}_1) = \operatorname*{E}_{\theta_2} \pi_2[a^*(\hat{\theta}_1, \theta_2), \theta_2]$$

if agent 1 announces that his private information is $\hat{\theta}_1$. Similarly, agent 1 is required to pay agent 2

$$T_{12}(\hat{\theta}_2) = \operatorname*{E}_{\theta_1} \pi_1[a^*(\theta_1, \hat{\theta}_2), \theta_1].$$

With agent 2 telling the truth, agent 1's expected profit, if he announces $\hat{\theta}_1$, is

$$\underset{\theta_2}{\mathrm{E}}\, \pi_1[a^*(\hat{\theta}_1, \theta_2), \theta_1] + T_{21}(\hat{\theta}_1) - \underset{\theta_2}{\mathrm{E}}\, T_{12}(\theta_2)$$
$$= \underset{\theta_2}{\mathrm{E}}\, \{\pi_1[a^*(\hat{\theta}_1, \theta_2), \theta_1] + \pi_2[a^*(\hat{\theta}_1, \theta_2), \theta_2]\}$$
$$- \underset{\theta_2}{\mathrm{E}}\, T_{12}(\theta_2). \tag{5}$$

By definition, $a^*(\theta_1, \theta_2)$ maximizes (4). Then $\hat{\theta}_1 = \theta_1$ maximizes (5).

Turning now to the private monopoly problem, consider an individual wishing to sell a unique object to one of two risk-neutral buyers each of whom has a valuation, θ_i, which is an independent draw from the distribution $F(\cdot)$. In any selling scheme, the payoff to buyer i is just his valuation times the probability of winning, W, less the expected payment R; that is,

$$u_i(W, R; \theta_i) = \theta_i W - R. \tag{6}$$

Then, as depicted in figure 2, indifference curves in $\langle W, R\rangle$ space are everywhere less steep for an individual with a higher valuation, θ. To simplify matters we shall consider only those selling schemes in which the object is assigned to that buyer valuing at the most from among those participating. Consider the offer curve $R = \phi(W)$. A buyer with valuation θ chooses $W(\theta)$ to maximize (6); that is, $W(\theta)$ satisfies

$$\phi'(W) = \frac{\partial u/\partial W}{\partial u/\partial R} \equiv \theta. \tag{7}$$

Also, for this object to be purchased by the participant valuing it the most we require

$$W(\theta) > 0$$
$$\rightarrow W(\theta_i) = \text{Prob}\,\{\text{all other valuations less than } \theta_i\} = F^{n-1}(\theta_i). \tag{8}$$

As long as F is strictly increasing, $F^{n-1}(\cdot)$ is invertible. Then (7) and (8) define an ordinary first-order differential equation. All this is depicted in figure 2. Note that for any selling procedure there will be some critical valuation θ_0 such that, for $\theta < \theta_0$, the indifference curve through the origin does not touch the set of offers; that is, those for whom $\theta < \theta_0$ choose not to participate.

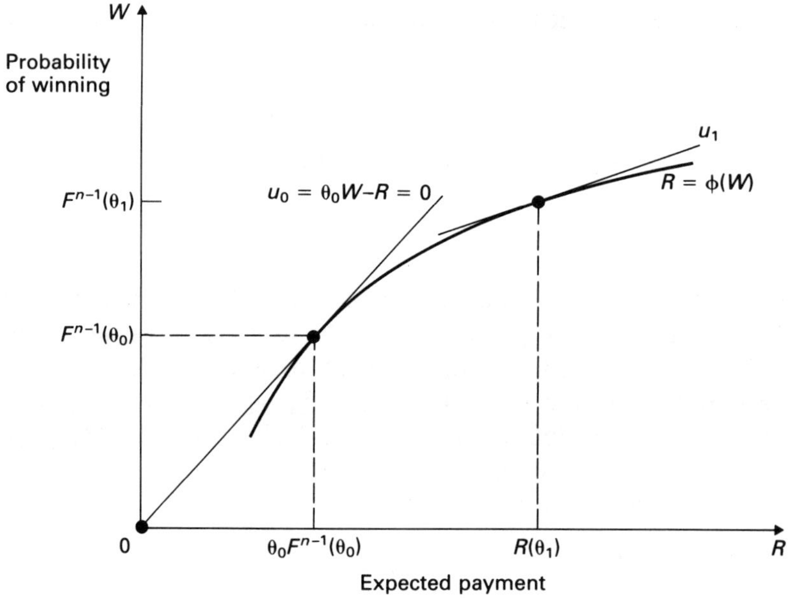

FIGURE 2 Self-selection

From all this we may conclude that the only substantive choice of the seller is the choice of the 'entry value' (see Myerson, 1981; Riley and Samuelson, 1981). It follows almost immediately that the two common auctions – sealed-high-bid and ascending-bid – must generate the same expected revenue; for in either auction, by setting a minimum price θ_0, the seller gives all these with valuations greater than θ_0 an incentive to bid. Furthermore, in each auction it is readily confirmed that the unique symmetric equilibrium bidding strategy is a strictly increasing function of a buyer's valuation. Thus, the bidder with the highest valuation is the winner. As we have just seen, these two conditions completely determine the expected revenue function $R = \phi(W)$ and hence the expected revenue received from each buyer type, $\phi[F^{n-1}(\theta)]$, $\theta \geqslant \theta_0$.

This *revenue equivalence theorem* has been the starting point for much recent research on the implications of weakening the three basic assumptions of (1) risk neutrality, (2) independent valuations and (3) symmetry of beliefs. The results to date are summarized in figure 3.

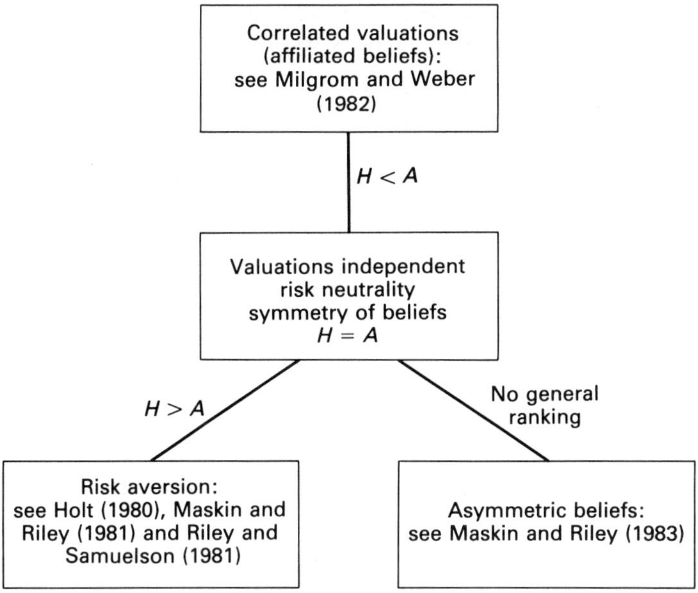

FIGURE 3 Comparison of expected revenue from scaled high-bid auctions (H) and open ascending-bid auctions (A)

In many practical applications it seems likely that none of the three assumptions will be satisfied exactly. Thus there is a need for some careful numerical analysis to determine the likely magnitude of the different effects. Despite the fact that there is no completely general ranking of the two auctions with asymmetric beliefs, it is my conjecture that this is likely to be the dominating effect. Suppose, for example, that there are two buyers. Buyer 1 has a valuation that is a random draw from a uniform distribution on $[0, 1]$. Buyer 2 has a valuation that is a random draw from a uniform distribution on $[0, k]$. For all $k \neq 1$ the unique equilibrium of the high-bid auction generates greater expected revenue than the ascending-bid auction. Moreover, as table 1 indicates, even if k is not drastically different from unity, the percentage increase in revenue is far from insignificant.

Asymmetry of beliefs seems especially likely in contract bidding. Each potential contractor has essentially the same information about the nature of the project but a different opportunity cost of completing the project, proximity to the job, etc. With some of the latter

TABLE 1 Comparison of the sealed-high-bid and open-ascending-bid auctions with asymmetric beliefs

Valuations uniformly distributed on [0, 1] and [0, k]

k	*Percentage gain*
1	0
1.67	6
2	10
3	21
⋮	⋮
∞	100

information being common knowledge, beliefs are thus independent and asymmetric.

Thus far in this section I have attempted to steer clear of game theory's Scylla and Charybdis – existence and uniqueness.[2] With independent valuations and symmetry of beliefs it can be shown that there is a unique equilibrium of the high-bid auction (see Maskin and Riley, 1982). Moreover, in the ascending-bid auction each individuals' dominant strategy is to bid his own valuation. However, under weaker assumptions there is no longer clear sailing. I shall conclude with a striking example of the problems that can arise.[3]

Suppose that there are two potential buyers for an oil field whose value, θ, is known. The probability of 'success' in any sample drilling is proportional to θ. To simplify the exposition I take the constant of proportionality to be unity. At the time of the auction both buyers know that s_0 out of n_0 sample wells were 'successes.' Buyer i also has private information about the number of successes s_i in n_i further sample drillings. Each buyer knows how many holes the other has drilled but not the number of successes.

The seller announces that the oil field will be sold to the highest bidder in a sealed 'second bid' auction, that is, at the second-highest bid.[4] Suppose buyer 2 adopts the bidding strategy

$$b_2 = B_2(s_2)$$

where $B(\cdot)$ is a strictly increasing function. Then we can define the inverse bid function for buyer 2 as

$$s_2 = S_2(b_2).$$

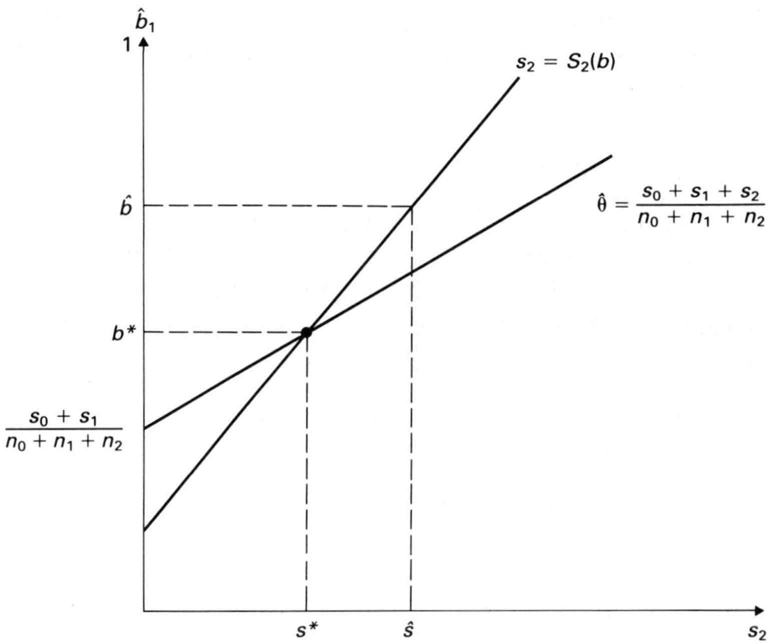

FIGURE 4 Equilibrium bidding with affiliated beliefs

This is depicted in figure 4 along with buyer 1's valuation

$$\hat{\theta} = \frac{s_0 + s_1 + s_2}{n_0 + n_1 + n_2}$$

for each possible value of the unknown s_2. If buyer 1 bids $\hat{b}$ he wins if $s_2 \leqslant \hat{s}$, while if he bids b^* he wins if $s_2 < s^*$. But if $s_2 \in (s^*, \hat{s})$ buyer 1 wins and pays buyer 2's bid, which is strictly greater than the expected value of the oil field. Then buyer 1 is strictly better off bidding b^*. Since an almost identical argument establishes that buyer 1 is also worse off bidding less than b^*, we have confirmed that

$$b_1 = b^* = \frac{s_0 + s_1 + s^*}{n_0 + n_1 + n_2}, \quad \text{where } s^* = S_2(b^*). \tag{9}$$

Combining these results, and noting that (9) must hold for all s_1, we obtain

$$b = \frac{s_0 + S_1(b) + S_2(b)}{n_0 + n_1 + n_2}. \tag{10}$$

Initially we suppose that $n_1 = n_2 = \bar{n}$. With symmetric informational differences it is natural to seek a symmetric equilibrium. From (10), with $S_1(b) = S_2(b)$, we obtain

$$b_i = \frac{s_0 + 2s_i}{n_0 + 2\bar{n}}, \quad i = 1, 2. \tag{11}$$

Thus the symmetric equilibrium bidding strategy is for each buyer to behave as if the other has the same private information. This is a simple illustration of the equilibrium bidding strategies characterized so elegantly by Milgrom and Weber. However, more generally, it is readily confirmed that the inverse bid functions

$$\left.\begin{aligned} S_1(b) &= \beta[(n_0 + n_1 + n_2)\, b - s_0] \\ S_2(b) &= (1-\beta)\,[(n_0 + n_1 + n_2)\, b - s_0] \end{aligned}\right\} \quad 0 < \beta < 1 \tag{12}$$

satisfy (10). Inverting (12), we obtain

$$\begin{aligned} b_1 = B_1(s_1) &= \frac{s_0 + \frac{1}{\beta} s_1}{n_0 + n_1 + n_2} \\ b_2 = B_2(s_2) &= \frac{s_0 + \frac{1}{1-\beta} s_2}{n_0 + n_1 + n_2}. \end{aligned} \tag{13}$$

It is also readily confirmed that, for $0 < \beta < 1$, $B_2(s_2)$ intersects $\hat{\theta} = (s_0 + s_1 + s_2)/(n_0 + n_1 + n_2)$ from below as depicted in figure 4. Then for all $\beta \in (0, 1)$ the pair of bid functions given by (13) are equilibrium bid functions. As argued above, it is not unreasonable to set $\beta = \frac{1}{2}$ when $n_1 = n_2$. However, with $n_1 = n_2$ I see no way to eliminate the continuum of equilibria.

To conclude on a highly speculative note, this example suggests that, even in relatively simple and highly specified models, we may be asking too much in the search for non-cooperative game equilibria in order to explain observed behavior. Perhaps the best we can hope for in some cases is to identify a set of logically consistent strategies.

NOTES

1 As this example makes clear, there is no conceptual difficulty in converting the usual partial equilibrium formulation of the signalling model into a

general equilibrium model. The alternative approach, suggested by Green, is simply to impose the zero profit condition as an auxiliary constraint. However, as I shall now argue, this makes economic sense only if it is coupled with a stability condition.

2 Like the youthful Scylla, existence was once glorified for her beauty!

3 I am indebted to Edward Leamer for suggesting this example. See also Leamer (1983).

4 With two buyers this is equivalent to an open-ascending-bid auction even with affiliated beliefs (see Milgrom and Weber, 1982).

REFERENCES

Dahlby, B. G. (1983), 'Adverse Selection and Statistical Discrimination: An Analysis of Canadian Automobile Insurance,' *Journal of Public Economics*, **20**, 121–30.

d'Aspremont, C. and Gerard-Varet, L. A. (1979), 'Incentives and Incomplete Information,' *Journal of Public Economics*, **16**, 25–45.

Holt, C. (1980), 'Competitive Bidding for Contracts under Alternative Auction Procedures,' *Journal of Political Economy*, **88**, 433–45.

Knadler-Morris, C. (1983), 'Asymmetry of Information, Signaling and the States' Security Regulations,' UCLA (mimeographed).

Leamer, E. E. (1985), 'Bid Ask Spreads for Subjective Probabilities,' *Studies in Bayesian Econometrics and Statistics*, in honor of B. de Finetti, P. K. Goel (ed.), North-Holland, forthcoming.

Leland, H. E. and Pyle, D. H. (1977), 'Informational Asymmetries, Financial Structure, and Financial Intermediation,' *Journal of Finance*, **32**, 371–87.

Maskin, E. S. and Riley, J. G. (1982), 'Uniqueness of Equilibrium in Open and Sealed Bid Auctions' (mimeographed).

Maskin, E. S. and Riley, J. G. (1983), 'Auctions with Asymmetric Beliefs,' UCLA Working Paper no. 254.

Maskin, E. S. and Riley, J. G. (1984), 'Optimal Auctions with Risk-averse Buyers,' *Econometrica*, **52**, 1473–518.

Milgrom, P. and Weber, R. J. (1982), 'A Theory of Auctions and Competitive Bidding,' *Econometrica*, **56**, 1089–122.

Mirrlees, J. (1971), 'An Exploration in the Theory of Optimum Income Taxation,' *Review of Economic Studies*, **38**, 175–208.

Miyazaki, H. (1977), 'The Rat Race and Internal Labor Markets,' *Bell Journal of Economics*, **8**, 394–418.

Myerson, R. (1981), 'Optimal Auction Design,' *Mathematics of Operations Research*, **6**, 58–73.

Riley, J. G. (1979), 'Informational Equilibrium,' *Econometrica*, **47**, 331–60.

Riley, J. G. (1985), 'Competitive Signalling Reconsidered,' *Journal of Political Economy*, forthcoming.

Riley, J. G. and Samuelson, W. F. (1981), 'Optimal Auctions,' *American Economic Review*, **71**, 381–92.

Rothschild, M. and Stiglitz, J. E. (1976), 'Equilibrium in Competitive Insurance Markets: An Essay on the Economics of Imperfect Information,' *Quarterly Journal of Economics*, **90**, 629–49.

Spence, A. M. (1973), *Market Signalling: Information Transfer in Hiring and Related Processes*, Harvard University Press, Cambridge, Mass.

Wilson, C. A. (1977), 'A Model of Insurance Markets with Incomplete Information,' *Journal of Economic Theory*, **16**, 167–207.

4

The Economics of Saving A Survey of Recent Contributions

MERVYN KING

1 INTRODUCTION

The determinants of saving, whether individual or collective, have a major influence on the future welfare of households. There is a substantial literature both on the positive and the normative theories of intertemporal allocation of resources. Enquiries into the nature and causes of the wealth of nations go back a long way.

It is perhaps surprising that, given this tradition, there remain still some fundamental disagreements about the determinants of household savings and over the circumstances in which government intervention is desirable. An impression frequently conveyed in the literature, for example, is that the empirical status of the life-cycle model of savings behaviour is in doubt. Many studies have claimed to reject the model, and a typical summary of the literature is that 'for all its elegance and rationality, the life-cycle model has not tested out very well. . . . Nor have efforts to test the life-cycle model with cross-section micro-data worked out very well' (Courant *et al.*, 1982). If there is doubt about the relevance of the life-cycle model, then there is equally sharp disagreement about the appropriate policy response to private savings decisions. Few empirical magnitudes can have attracted so much attention and controversy as the impact of social security on the level of private savings and the interest elasticity of savings. Furthermore, the choice of the tax base has returned to the forefront of policy discussion, and this issue centres critically around the optimal tax treatment of savings and its relationship to the current tax system.

There are, therefore, a number of important policy problems for which an understanding of individual savings behaviour is crucial. I shall not attempt to survey the policy debate but will focus instead on the underlying determinants of household consumption and savings decisions. Recent discussions of savings and taxation (both optimal and actual) include Atkinson and Sandmo (1980), Auerbach and Kotlikoff (1981), King (1980), King and Fullerton (1984), Kotlikoff (1973), Sandmo (1984) and Summers (1982). The relationship between pensions and savings is analysed in Aaron (1982), Blinder (1982) and Dicks-Mireaux and King (1984).

I shall argue below that the major failing of existing empirical studies is that, by and large, they have failed to pose the correct questions. There are two reasons for this. First, there is a tendency to regard the life-cycle model as an all-or-nothing model, which must explain the behaviour of the entire population or of none of it. It seems that in fact there is evidence that the life-cycle model, taken in its broadest sense, is consistent with the observed behaviour of a majority of households, but that there exists a minority of households for which the model appears to be inadequate.

The important question is, then, what are the characteristics of those households that appear to deviate from the life-cycle pattern? The second reason is that empirical studies test a *joint* hypothesis of the life-cycle model and a particular parameterization of preferences. If the model fails, then the correct inference is that the joint hypothesis can be rejected. One cannot infer from this that the life-cycle model is inappropriate. This raises a deeper question of exactly what it is about the life-cycle model that is distinctive and that separates it from alternative explanations of savings behaviour. It is immediately clear that one of the problems in testing the life-cycle model is the absence of a coherent alternative model with which it can be compared. An alternative rigorous model is required from which to develop empirical predictions in order that we may be able to distinguish one model from the other. I shall assume below that the distinctive characteristics of the life-cycle model are that individual behaviour is 'forward-looking', that individuals optimize over their expected remaining lifetime, and that the cost of acquiring information about the future is not so prohibitive that only current observations are used to determine current consumption.

The empirical questions that I shall ask will be (1) Can the observed data be better explained by a model of 'myopic' or 'irrational' behaviour than by the life-cycle model? (2) Is there any evidence that individual behaviour is influenced more by constraints (over and above the lifetime budget constraint) than by preferences? This is a crucial matter for policy purposes, because the main implication of the life-cycle model is that individuals can separate their consumption profile from their income profile. Hence government policies directed at individual welfare, which is normally assumed to be defined over consumption, can be aimed at influencing lifetime income. This gives great flexibility about the particular stage in the life cycle at which help can be directed. If, in contrast, individuals face constraints such that the separation of consumption from income can no longer be maintained, then the precise timing of support for individuals becomes important. These issues clearly lie at the heart of the debate over unemployment insurance and social security.

The plan of the paper is as follows. In section 2 I discuss the life-cycle model in both deterministic and stochastic settings. I shall try to derive the empirical predictions implied by the model. Section 3 considers alternative models, and examines constraints in both labour and capital markets. Section 4 discusses the evidence from aggregate time-series data and micro-data for individual households. Bequests are the subject of section 5, and the conclusions of the survey are summarized in section 6.

2 THE THEORY OF HOUSEHOLD SAVINGS BEHAVIOUR

The 'life-cycle model' of household savings behaviour is normally associated with the names of Modigliani (Modigliani and Brumberg, 1954; Modigliani and Ando, 1957) and Friedman (1957). But the analysis of the intertemporal allocation of consumption by utility-maximizing consumers was stated clearly by Fisher (1907), Ramsey (1928) and Hicks (1939). The contribution of Modigliani and Friedman was to translate the abstract notion of an optimal consumption profile into a model that could be estimated econometrically. In so doing, they demonstrated the empirical relevance of the principal implication of the life-cycle model, namely the separation of the consumption and income profiles. Current consumption was not determined primarily by current income; hence Friedman's concept of 'permanent income' and Modigliani's stress on the role of wealth in the consumption function.

Duesenberry (1948, 1949) also demonstrated the weakness of the link between consumption and current income by noting that, in the Depression, cross-section data from the 1935–6 Study of Consumer Purchases showed that a large number of families reported expenditure in excess of income for the year. By contrast, in the 1941 survey there were far fewer deficiencies. In other words, the consumption function varied over the trade cycle. Duesenberry attributed this to a relative income effect, by which consumption was positively related not only to current income but also to the ratio of current income to its highest past level. At face value this seems less convincing than the life-cycle or permanent income hypothesis. Professional footballers who base their consumption plans on their highest income ever attained are seen in the bankruptcy courts from time to time, but most of their playing colleagues are evidently more careful. In fact, Duesenberry argued for a distributed lag of past incomes (but with a ratchet effect) in the consumption function. The main difference between this formulation and the life-cycle model is that the latter is based on a forward-looking view of behaviour, whereas the former stresses the backward-looking aspect of behaviour.

These models represented a departure from the Keynesian consumption function and the empirical work that it spawned. To this day, however, the majority of econometric studies of aggregate consumption have taken income as the main exogenous variable. Yet the theoretical basis for this assumption is weak. In part, it rests on:

> The fundamental psychological law, upon which we are entitled to depend with great confidence both *a priori* from our knowledge of human nature and from the detailed facts of experience, is that men are disposed, as a rule and on the average, to increase their consumption as their income increases but not by as much as the increase in their income. [Keynes, 1936: 96]

It may be argued that the assumption that the marginal propensity to consume out of current income is greater than zero and less than unity is not strong, and in defending his proposition Keynes wrote subsequently: 'it does seem to me that I have said one of the simplest and most indisputable things imaginable' (letter to Mrs E. Gilboy, 1 February 1939: Keynes, 1973: 276). Yet the stability of the relationship between consumption and current income is the cornerstone of the 'Keynesian' consumption function, although Keynes himself viewed it as a short-run relationship which, because it was denominated in wage units, shifted with the real wage. Its determinants are usually assumed to be exogenous, and in econometric models of aggregate consumption are represented by fixed coefficients. But as Muth (1960) showed, the propensity to consume out of current income depends, in a life-cycle setting, on the stochastic process generating incomes. For any given dynamic model of incomes, a life-cycle theory leads to a particular Keynesian consumption function. One must be careful, therefore, when using aggregate data, to discriminate among alternative models of the motives for savings. Schumpeter foresaw the difficulty when, in dismissing Keynes's use of the phrase 'fundamental psychological law' as an abuse of language, he wrote:

> Keynes's well-known psychological law about the propensity to consume ... avers that both individuals and societies will, if they experience an increase in income, normally increase their expenditure or consumption but by less than the increase in income. Whether this is so or not, it is a statement of statistically observable fact which Keynes raised to the rank of an assumption. Nothing is gained, except a spurious dignity, by calling it a psychological law. [Schumpeter, 1954; 1059–60 fn]

We shall return to the dynamic structure of the aggregate consumption function in section 4. In this section we concentrate on developing the microeconomic implications of the life-cycle model which may be tested using data for individual households. A non-stochastic model of life-cycle behaviour is explored first, and then we analyse the consequences of introducing uncertainty into the model. The role of constraints (borrowing or liquidity constraints, for example) will be an important issue in later discussion.

A non-stochastic life-cycle model

To illustrate the main issues, we consider first a simple non-stochastic model of an individual making an optimal consumption plan over the life cycle. No attempt will be made to provide a complete survey of all of the literature on life-cycle models (a recent bibliography of the literature may be found in Mann, 1981).

The individual will be assumed to have a well-defined preference ordering over consumption and labour supply in each period and over the value of gifts and bequests made. We denote this by

$$U = U(\mathbf{C}_1 \ldots \mathbf{C}_T, L_1 \ldots L_T, B) \tag{2.1}$$

where $\mathbf{C}_t$ is the vector of consumption of different goods in period t
L_t is labour supply in period t (the length of the period is normalized to unity)
B is the present value at the beginning of period 1 of lifetime expenditure on gifts and bequests
T is the non-stochastic length of life

Two points may be noted about (2.1). First, concern about succeeding generations is represented solely in terms of the appearance of bequests in the utility function. There are several ways of modelling bequests, and these will be discussed below in section 5. At this stage we assume only that bequests are set equal to their optimal value, denoted by B^*, and then the allocation of consumption over the life cycle is determined conditional on this value. Whatever bequests are at the optimum, consumption will still be allocated optimally across ages. Second, changes in household composition over the life cycle mean that in practice the model is usually applied to data for households rather than individuals. This raises a number of questions, such as the nature of decision-making within the household and the variation of 'needs' over the life cycle, which we shall discuss only where they are germane to specific aspects of savings behaviour under consideration.[1] In general, however, we shall use 'individual' and 'household' interchangeably, although of course this ignores a number of interesting questions concerning household formation.

The essence of the life-cycle model is that individuals face only a single constraint, namely the lifetime budget constraint, which we may write as.

$$\sum_{t=1}^{T} \frac{\mathbf{p}_t{}'\mathbf{C}_t}{d_t} + \sum_{t=1}^{T} \frac{w_t(1-L_t)}{d_t} + B \leqslant \sum_{t=1}^{T} \frac{w_t}{d_t} + I \tag{2.2}$$

where $\mathbf{p}_t$ is a vector of current prices of the different consumption goods in period t
w_t is the wage rate in period t
d_t is the discount factor in period t and equals $\Pi_{j=1}^{t}(1+r_j)$
r_t is the nonstochastic interest rate in period t

I is the present value at the beginning of period one of inheritances and gifts received.

We shall assume that transactions take place at the end of each period. All prices are net of tax.

Equation (2.2) states that the present value of lifetime expenditure on consumption, on leisure and on bequests must equal (at most) the present value of an individual's endowment (or 'full wealth') of potential earnings and inheritances. The first-order conditions for a maximum of (2.1) subject to the constraint (2.2) are given by

$$\mathbf{U}_{ct} - \frac{\lambda \mathbf{p}_t}{d_t} = 0 \qquad t = 1, \ldots, T \tag{2.3}$$

$$U_{Lt} + \frac{\lambda w_t}{d_t} = 0 \qquad t = 1, \ldots, T \tag{2.4}$$

$$B = B^* \tag{2.5}$$

where λ is the multiplier associated with the lifetime budget constraint, and $\{\mathbf{U}_{ct}, U_{Lt}\}$ is the vector of partial derivatives of U with respect to $\mathbf{C}_t$ and L_t respectively. There are two ways in which we may use these first-order conditions for empirical work. The first is to invert the system of equations (2.3)–(2.5) and solve for the optimal consumption and labour supply vector in terms of the exogenous prices and endowments:

$$\mathbf{C}_t = \mathbf{c}^t(w_1 \ldots w_T, \mathbf{p}_1 \ldots \mathbf{p}_T, r_1 \ldots r_T, I) \tag{2.6}$$

$$L_t = l^t(w_1 \ldots w_T, \mathbf{p}_1 \ldots \mathbf{p}_T, r_1 \ldots r_T, I). \tag{2.7}$$

The functions $\mathbf{C}$ and l have period superscripts which reminds us that the period here represents not clock time but age. Note also that there will in general be differences in age-specific wage rates among cohorts reflecting productivity growth. The difficulty in estimating equations of the form (2.6) and (2.7) is evident. We require information on prices and endowments in each period of the life cycle, and even with large panel data sets we do not have sufficient observations. Typically, panel data sets contain fewer than ten observations on each individual. This problem can be overcome to some extent by restricting the form in which preferences are specified. A common restriction is to assume that preferences are additively separable over time, which implies that (2.1) becomes

$$U = \sum_{t=1}^{T} u_t(\mathbf{C}_t, L_t). \tag{2.8}$$

It is easy to see that this specification means that the system of first-order conditions for current consumption and labour supply may be inverted to yield a demand system which, conditional upon the value of the multiplier λ, depends only upon current prices and interest rates. In other words, the influence of exogenous variables for periods other than the current period comes entirely through their effect on the multiplier λ, the value of which is independent of age. If the form of u_t is independent of age but individuals have a non-zero rate of time preference, we have

$$u_t = \frac{u(\mathbf{C}_t, L_t)}{s_t} \tag{2.9}$$

$$s_t = \prod_{j=1}^{t} (1 + \rho_t) \tag{2.10}$$

where ρ_t is the rate of time preference in period t.

In this special case the functional form of the demand system is independent of age, and the age profiles of consumption and labour supply depend upon the age profiles of real wages, interest rates and rates of time preference. If we treat consumption as a single composite good (which assumption we shall maintain for the sake of convenience), then consumption and labour supply at age t may be written as

$$\mathbf{C}_t = f(\lambda\tilde{p}_t, \lambda\tilde{w}_t) \tag{2.11}$$

$$L_t = g(\lambda\tilde{p}_t, \lambda\tilde{w}_t) \tag{2.12}$$

where

$\tilde{p}_t = \mathbf{p}_t \left(\frac{s_t}{d_t}\right)$, the effective price of consumption

$\tilde{w}_t = w_t \left(\frac{s_t}{d_t}\right)$, the effective wage rate.

In this two-commodity framework, with consumption and leisure as substitutes, both consumption and labour supply will be higher in periods with higher 'effective' real wages. Normalizing the price of consumption to unity, we may interpret w as the real wage and r as the real interest rate.[2] In the particular case where not only are preferences additively separable over time but also the intratemporal preference ordering u is weakly separable between consumption and leisure, the age profile of consumption depends only upon the 'effective' price of consumption. When the real interest rate equals the rate of time preference, this effective price is constant and the age profile of consumption is flat. In general, however, consumption depends upon the profile of wage rates.

It is important to bear this in mind when evaluating evidence relevant to the life-cycle model. Using US data, Thurow (1969) found that both income and consumption rose with age, peaking in the age range 45–54. This might suggest a much higher correlation between consumption and current income than would be implied by a life-cycle model. But, as Heckman (1974) pointed out, the correlation could be explained by the age profile of wage rates. This can be seen from equations (2.11) and (2.12). Consider the special case in which the interest rate equals the rate of time preference. Normalizing the price of consumption to unity, we have

$$\mathbf{C}_t = f(\lambda, \lambda w_t) \tag{2.13}$$

$$L_t = g(\lambda, \lambda w_t). \tag{2.14}$$

Conditional upon the value of λ, these equations may be regarded as compensated demand functions, where compensation is defined as maintaining constant the value of λ. The partial derivatives of (2.13) and (2.14) with respect to the price of consumption and the wage rate may be thought of as substitution effects. Differentiating (2.3) and (2.4) with respect to own prices, it can be seen that, because the direct utility function is quasi-concave in consumption and leisure, the compensated (in terms of λ) own substitution effects are negative. This means that the partial derivatives of (2.13) and (2.14) with respect to the real wage (the only price in the two-commodity case) are positive.

Since λ is independent of age, it is clear that both consumption and labour supply reach a maximum at the age at which the wage rate reaches its maximum. Consumption, earnings and the wage rate will all be positively correlated, and will reach a peak at the same age. Typical profiles of wage rates reach a maximum at an age of about

50, and so this model can provide an explanation of the empirical findings of Thurow.

In the more general case, in which the interest rate is not equal to the rate of time preference, consumption, earnings and the wage rate peak at different ages. Their time paths may be explored by differentiating the 'constant marginal utility of lifetime wealth' demand functions (2.11) and (2.12). An empirical analysis of labour supply in this framework may be found in MaCurdy (1981). We shall return to the general case later when we shall use empirical evidence on age–earnings profiles and labour supply functions to generate profiles for asset holdings over the life cycle. We shall argue that, under most plausible assumptions, savings will generally be low early in working life, will rise as earnings increase with age, and then will flatten out, becoming negative in retirement. This pattern implies a 'hump-shaped' profile for asset holdings over the life cycle. Although unsurprising, it suggests that failure to observe a hump-shaped age profile for assets might constitute direct evidence against life-cycle savings behaviour. We assess such evidence in section 3. Given the difficulty of estimating the life-cycle model directly, either in general form (equations 2.6 and 2.7) because of lack of data on prices over the life cycle or in the special case of additive separability (equations 2.11 and 2.12) because of the endogeneity of λ, a simple direct test using data on wealth holdings has considerable appeal.

The difficulty of estimating the life-cycle model is illustrated by the specifications employed in the early studies by Friedman and Modigliani. Friedman (1957) assumed that (a) consumption can be regarded as a composite good, (b) labour supply in each period is exogenous, and (c) preferences defined over consumption at different ages and bequests are homothetic. With these assumptions, the first-order conditions (2.3) imply that we may write consumption as

$$C_t = k_t \cdot W \tag{2.15}$$

where W is lifetime wealth (the present value of labour earnings and inheritances), and k_t depends upon the interest rate and household characteristics but is otherwise independent of economic variables. If we define 'permanent income' as the annuity value of lifetime wealth, then consumption is proportional to permanent income. The problem is that permanent income is generally unobservable. Friedman used a distributed lag function of current and past incomes with geometrically declining weights. But there is no reason to suppose that this will measure the annuity value of W, and, in particular, given an age profile for earnings, the appropriate weights will be a function of age. More fundamentally, however, the life-cycle model is essentially forward-looking, and the use of distributed lags of past incomes, however general a lag structure we permit, is backward-looking. To incorporate this basic insight into an empirical specification requires an alternative approach. This leads us to the second way in which we may use the first-order conditions (2.3)–(2.5).

If we continue to regard consumption as a single composite good and normalize its price to unity, then by taking the ratio of the first-order conditions at successive ages we have

$$\frac{U_{c,t}}{U_{c,t-1}} = \frac{1}{1+r_t} \qquad t = 2, \ldots, T \tag{2.16}$$

The interest rate here is that paid on assets held at the beginning of period t when consumption and savings decisions in period $t-1$ have been made. Equation (2.16) is a simple yet rather powerful result. The marginal (lifetime) utility of consumption declines with age at the rate of interest. In other words, for a given interest rate the marginal rate of substitution between consumption in any two neighbouring periods is the same; for a particular representation of preference (2.16) can be solved to generate an age profile for consumption and hence savings. Since many of the unobservable characteristics of an individual, such as future earnings, affect current consumption through the shadow price of lifetime wealth, elimination of the multiplier λ produces a more tractable specification. In terms of econometric terminology, λ represents a 'fixed effect' for the individual, and by taking first differences (or ratios) its influence on the specification may be removed. Since the unobservable fixed effect is usually correlated with the observable independent variables, estimation of equations that include fixed effects ('permanent income', for example) are likely to yield biased parameter estimates.[3]

To illustrate this approach, consider the intertemporal linear expenditure system with lifetime utility given by

$$U = \prod_{t=1}^{T} (C_t - \bar{c})^{\alpha_t} (\bar{1} - L_t)^{\beta_t}. \tag{2.17}$$

Substituting (2.17) into (2.16) yields

$$C_t - \bar{c} = \frac{\alpha_t}{\alpha_{t-1}} \cdot (1+r_t)(C_{t-1} - \bar{c}). \tag{2.18}$$

If we further assume that the α_t coefficients decline at a constant rate with age, then we obtain the following linear regression model for individual consumption:

$$C_t = \bar{c} + a_1(1+r_t) + a_2(1+r_t)\,C_{t-1}. \tag{2.19}$$

The parameters a_1 and a_2 are independent of age, and hence the model could be estimated on aggregate data as well as panel data for individual households. In fact, the longer span of most time series for aggregate consumption means that the use of aggregate data might have some advantages because it would enable the variation of real interest rates over time to be exploited.[4]

In the light of the attention paid to the problem of unobservable variables in the early literature on estimation of the life-cycle consumption function, it is perhaps surprising that the approach based on (2.16) was not pursued by such authors. Treatment of the multiplier λ as a fixed effect has been used by Heckman and MaCurdy (1980) and MaCurdy (1981) to analyse labour supply and labour force participation. But it was not until the analysis of *stochastic* models of life-cycle behaviour (Hall, 1978; Sargent, 1978), which we discuss in the following subsection, that use of a condition equivalent to (2.16) appeared. This was unfortunate, because the use of (2.16) has nothing as such to do with a stochastic model, and the understandable focus in recent work on the incorporation of rational expectations into the life-cycle model has observed two points that are crucial if the results of estimating the model are to be interpreted as a test of the life-cycle model. The first is that, although (2.16) is a general result, empirical tests employing this framework have been embedded in models that assume that preferences are additively separable over time. Without this assumption it may be difficult to solve (2.16) to find the implied difference equation for consumption, and in general the coefficients of the difference equation would be age-dependent. The resulting nonlinear model would not be easy to estimate, and, if the model were fitted to aggregate time-series data, there would be insufficient degrees of freedom to identify the model.

The second point is that, even if we assume intertemporal separability, there is no reason to impose the further assumption that preferences for consumption and leisure within a given period are separable.[5] If intratemporal separability is assumed, then (2.9) and (2.16) lead to a simple first-order difference equation for the level (or some transformation of the level) of consumption, and this is illustrated in the example given above of the linear expenditure system (see equations 2.17–2.19). Even here, however, the coefficients will not be time-invariant if the real interest rate changes over time. With a more general representation of preferences, the time series process describing the behaviour of consumption will depend upon the processes governing the evolution of wage and interest rates. The reduced form for consumption will not be a simple first-order difference equation.

The main conclusion from this discussion is that empirical tests of the life-cycle model based on (2.16), although attractive in principle because of the elimination of the unobservable multiplier or fixed effect, are unlikely to be conclusive because they are tests of the joint hypothesis that (a) individuals are life-cycle savers, and (b) preferences may be parameterized in a particular way. In a regression of consumption on its own lagged value, evidence that additional lagged values of either consumption or other variables are statistically significant does not in itself constitute evidence against the life-cycle model. It may equally be interpreted as a rejection of the assumption that preferences are both inter- and intratemporally separable. Since I am aware of no strong independent evidence for the two separability assumptions, and there is evidence against separability of consumption and leisure (Deaton and Muellbauer, 1980, chapter 5), it is probably more appropriate to regard (2.16) as a vehicle for research within the life-cycle framework, and not a test of the framework as such.

To test the life-cycle hypothesis itself we shall examine evidence on the amounts of wealth owned by individuals at different ages. We shall compare the observed levels of wealth with the levels that would be predicted by a life-cycle model. Although there is little evidence on the response of savings to wage and interest rates, there have been many studies of the response of labour supply. Using the 'stylized facts' about labour supply behaviour, we shall construct an indirect utility function describing preferences between consumption and leisure, and compute the implied age profile for wealth. To do this we shall ignore some of the factors that lead to diversity in observed wealth–age profiles, such as timing of marriage, birth of children, and expenses of child-rearing. The labour supply function we shall use is given by

$$L_t = a - b\exp(-\gamma w_t) - cy_t \tag{2.20}$$

where the price of consumption has been normalized to unity, and y_t denotes 'full' expenditure in period t on consumption and leisure (in a static model this is equivalent to Becker's 'full income'). This form implicitly assumes intertemporal, though not intratemporal, separability:

$$y_t = C_t + w_t(1 - L_t). \tag{2.21}$$

The choice of the nonlinear labour supply function (2.20) was motivated by the desire to produce a model consistent with the available empirical evidence on life-cycle profiles of hours of work and wage rates, and capable of generating endogenous retirement behaviour. The specification of (2.20) allows this, as shown below. The indirect utility function corresponding to (2.20) may be derived as follows. Using the implicit function theorem and Roy's identity for the demand for leisure, we have (omitting age subscripts)[6]

$$\frac{dy}{dw} = 1 - L = (1-a) + be^{-\gamma w} + cy. \tag{2.22}$$

Integrating, we obtain

$$ye^{-cw} = -\left(\frac{1-a}{c}\right)e^{-cw} - \frac{b}{c+\gamma}e^{-(c+\gamma)w} + k \tag{2.23}$$

where k is the constant of integration, which we shall take as the level of indirect utility v. Hence

$$v(w, y) = e^{-cw}\left(y + \frac{1-a}{c} + \frac{b}{c+\gamma}e^{-\gamma w}\right). \tag{2.24}$$

This indirect utility function is continuous, increasing in income and decreasing in the wage rate (providing $L \leqslant 1$, i.e. $a - cy \leqslant 1$).[7] It defines instantaneous utility, and with intertemporal separability lifetime utility is defined by[8]

$$U = \sum_{t=1}^{T} \frac{\ln v(w_t, y_t)}{s_t}. \tag{2.25}$$

The individual maximizes U subject to the lifetime budget constraint

$$\sum_{t=1}^{T} \frac{y_t}{d_t} = W \tag{2.26}$$

where W is 'full wealth'. We shall ignore bequests and inheritances. If the shadow price of full wealth is λ, then the evolution of total expenditure (on goods and leisure) over time is determined by the condition

$$\frac{1}{v}\frac{\partial v}{\partial y} = \lambda\left(\frac{s_t}{d_t}\right). \qquad \forall t \tag{2.27}$$

This gives

$$y_t = \frac{1}{\lambda}\left(\frac{d_t}{s_t}\right) - \left(\frac{1-a}{c}\right) - \frac{be^{-\gamma w_t}}{c+\gamma}. \tag{2.28}$$

The value of the multiplier λ may be obtained by substituting (2.28) into (2.26).

To justify the specification of (2.20) and (2.25), and also to parameterize the model, we examine evidence on the age profile of wages, earnings and hours of work. The main exogenous influence on the optimal life-cycle plan is the age profile of wage rates. Maintaining the assumption of perfect certainty, we assume that adult life begins at age 15 and ends at 75. From entry into the labour market at age 15 until age 60, wage rates are assumed to be given by

$$\ln w_t = \alpha_0 + \alpha_1(t-15) + \alpha_2(t-15)^2 \qquad 15 \leqslant t \leqslant 60. \tag{2.29}$$

The starting wage is normalized to unity ($\alpha_0 = 0$). Wage rates typically rise, reach a maximum in middle age, and then decline. Using data for males from the 1966 Survey of Economic Opportunity, Heckman (1974) found that the maximum wage was reached in the age bracket of 48–50, and a similar result was found by Hurd (1971) using the same data. We assume that the maximum is at age 48 and that the ratio of peak wage rates to the initial wage rate is, in real terms, 1.5. These assumptions define values for α_1 and α_2. After the age of 60, the potential wage rate (net of tax) is assumed to decline rapidly (at a rate μ) toward some minimum level, w_m, according to

$$w_t = w_m + (w_{60} - w_m)\, e^{-\mu(t-60)} \qquad t > 60. \tag{2.30}$$

This produces a pattern of wage rates that, together with the labour supply function (2.20), imply a sharply decreasing labour supply after the age of 60 which is equivalent to endogenous 'retirement', where retirement is defined as a marked reduction in hours worked rather than a constraint that hours worked must be zero. The parameters of the labour supply function are chosen to accord with the following stylized facts. First, hours worked do not vary significantly over the life cycle in the pre-retirement phase even though wages do vary. Second, hours worked peak before the age at which wage rates attain a maximum. This implies that the rate of time preference is less than the rate of interest. For the simulation we take the real interest rate to be 2 per cent per annum, and the rate of time preference to be 1 per cent. Using SEO data for males, Heckman (1974) found that hours of work reached a maximum in the age range 39–44, compared with a maximum for wage rates in the age bracket 48–50. In the simulation reported below the wage rate is assumed to reach a maximum at age 48, and the model predicts a peak for labour supply at age 40, with a maximum in earnings at age 45. Empirical studies of earnings have found age profiles for male earnings that peak in the age range 45–50 (Mincer, 1976; Psacharopoulos and Layard, 1979; Thurow, 1969; King and Dicks-Mireaux, 1982). Not all of these studies adjusted for the cohort effect on earnings–age profiles, and so their findings are not strictly comparable. Panel data show less evidence of a peak in earnings prior to retirement (USA, 1976).

The third stylized fact is that, after some conventional 'retirement' age, taken to be 60 in our simulation, both potential earnings and hours of work decline quite rapidly. We do not impose the constraint that after some given age labour supply and hence earnings are zero: instead, the model generates endogenous withdrawal from full-time employment as the wage rate falls and allows for the aged to supply a small number of hours worked after the normal retirement age. This is perhaps more realistic than the assumption that hours of work fall to zero, although I make no attempt to justify the wage equation (2.30) on the basis of statistical evidence. The value of the minimum wage rate in retirement was assumed in the simulation to be 0.1, which may be compared with the maximum pre-retirement wage of 1.5, and μ was taken to be 0.5. In addition to any earnings, the individual is assumed to receive social security or a private pension after the age of 60 equal to 50 per cent of the net-of-tax wage at age 60. The pension remains constant in real terms until death.

To produce a model capable of simulating life-cycle behaviour described by these three stylized facts, we choose the following values for the parameters of the indirect utility function:[9]

$$a = 1.0$$
$$b = 0.9$$
$$c = 0.1$$
$$\gamma = 0.65$$

The life-cycle pattern of labour supply generated by the model is shown in figure 4.1. To calibrate the number of hours worked per week I have assumed that 10 hours per day are devoted to sleep and other necessary activities, leaving 98 hours a week available to allocate between work and leisure. Hours worked rise early in life as the wage rate increases, remain roughly constant for the bulk of working life (reaching a maximum at age 40), decline slowly as 'retirement' approaches, and, finally, fall sharply after the age of 60. It should be emphasized that this pattern is not imposed but is the optimal response to the assumed age profile of wage rates.

The pattern of asset accumulation over the life cycle is given by the equation

$$A_t = (1+r_t)\,A_{t-1} + w_tL_t + x_t - C_t \qquad t = 1, \ldots, T \quad (2.31)$$

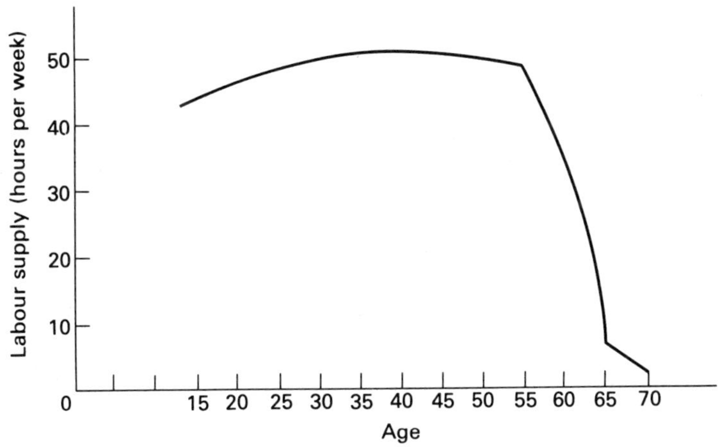

FIGURE 4.1 Labour supply over the life cycle

where A_t is the level of assets excluding pension wealth held at the end of period t (note the distinction between assets, A_t, and full wealth, W), and x_t is receipts of social security and pensions in period t. If, as before, we ignore inheritances, the initial condition is $A_0 = 0$. The age profile of asset holdings is shown by the solid line in figure 4.2. It measures the ratio of assets to permanent income where the latter measures the constant annual annuity value of full wealth. It shows the 'hump-shaped' pattern of the life-cycle model. Holdings of assets rise during working life and are consumed in retirement. Asset holdings reach a maximum before retirement, and in figure 4.2 this occurs at age 51.

The simulated age profile shown in figure 4.2 may be compared with actual age profiles estimated from household data. To do this we require a survey of asset-holdings of a random sample of the population drawn from all ages. Unfortunately, many of the available surveys (such as the National Longitudinal Survey of Mature Men used by Diamond, 1977, and Diamond and Hausman, 1982, and the Retirement History Survey used by Blinder *et al.*, 1980) cover only part of the life cycle, such as the period immediately prior to and after retirement. But the 1977 Survey of Consumer Finances in

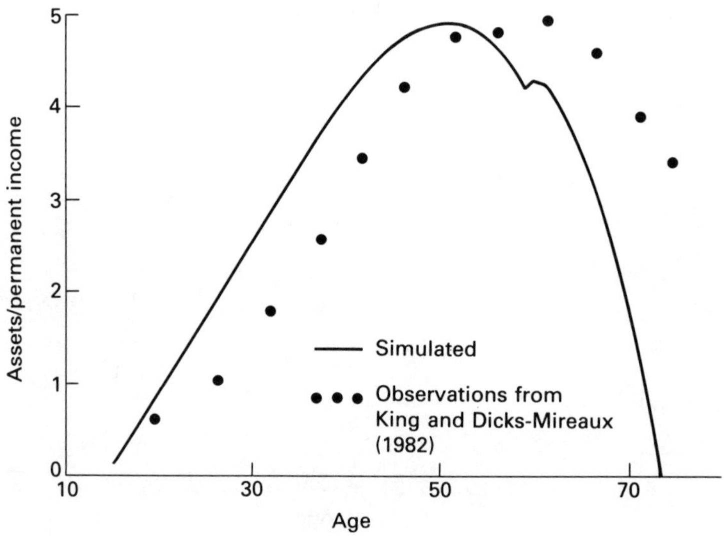

FIGURE 4.2 Assets over the life cycle

Canada collected data on assets and debts for a sample of 12,734 families of all ages. An analysis of these data in relation to the life-cycle model may be found in King and Dicks-Mireaux (1982). These authors constructed an estimate of 'permanent income' for each household in the sample, and the average values of the ratio of asset-holdings (excluding pension wealth) to permanent income for each five-year age group are plotted on figure 4.2.

The 'hump-shaped' pattern is clearly evident for the actual and simulated age profiles of asset holdings. At first glance, therefore, the data are consistent with the hypothesis that, on average, household behaviour can be explained by the life-cycle model. The major respect in which the actual deviates from the simulated profile is the low rate at which wealth is run down after retirement. These observed low rates of decumulation are inconsistent with a life-cycle model in which the date of death is known with certainty. This is hardly surprising. Benjamin Franklin's well-known observation that 'in this world nothing can be said to be certain, except death and taxes' omits some crucial considerations of timing. If we assume that (a) the only uncertainty is that about date of death and (b) preferences are intertemporally separable with instantaneous utility given by (2.9), then we may follow Yaari (1965) and Tobin (1967) and write expected utility over remaining lifespan as

$$U = \sum_{t=\tau}^{M} p(t,\tau)\frac{u(C_t, L_t)}{s_t} \tag{2.32}$$

where τ is current age
M is maximum possible age
$p(t, \tau)$ is probability of survival until age t given that one has survived to age τ

The first-order conditions for the optimal consumption and labour supply plan may be written (eliminating the multiplier on the budget constraint) as:

$$\frac{u_{c,t}}{u_{c,t-1}} = \frac{1}{\Pi_t}\left(\frac{1+\rho_t}{1+r_t}\right) \tag{2.33}$$

where Π_t is the probability of surviving from age $(t-1)$ to age t (unity minus the mortality rate). Hence we may regard uncertainty about date of death as equivalent to an age-specific increase in the rate of time preference. The impact of this on consumption and asset holdings is ambiguous. On the one hand, greater uncertainty about length of life leads to a desire for certain consumption in the present, and on the other hand it results in a desire to save for a potentially longer future life. The outcome will depend upon the household's aversion to risk, and its rate of time preference. For very high rates of risk aversion the wish to avoid the risk of a low level of utility can clearly produce an optimal savings plan characterized by low rates of decumulation of wealth after retirement. In the limiting case in which the household maximizes the minimum value of (discounted) instantaneous utility, 'full expenditure' in each period, y_t $(t = \tau, \ldots, M)$, will be equal to the annuity value of full wealth over the maximum lifespan. Hence, even though survival to great age may be highly improbable, the household will retain sufficient wealth to enable it to maintain its standard of living up to the maximum possible age.

It is immediately apparent that the need for such savings is greatly diminished by the existence of insurance against date of death. Purchases of annuities, especially indexed annuities, would enable households to decumulate wealth more rapidly. The absence or small size of markets in such annuities has been used to explain low rates of decumulation. Davies (1981) used data on life expectancy at different ages to simulate a life-cycle model with exogenous labour supply assuming constant relative risk aversion. For degrees of risk aversion in excess of three, the predicted rates of decumulation were low, and comparable with the actual rates shown in figure 4.2. (See King and Dicks-Mireaux, 1982, for further discussion of this point.)

The problem with this explanation is that the results are sensitive to the existence of pensions and social security. Pensions provide an alternative to annuities and, indeed, one of the arguments for publicly provided pensions is that they compensate for the market's failure to provide indexed annuities (Diamond, 1977). With indexed pensions or social security, the need to maintain asset holdings against the eventuality of longevity is much reduced. This suggests a way of testing the hypothesis that the life-cycle model can explain observed low rates of decumulation. For a given level of assets, the rate of decumulation in the later stages of life should be positively correlated with the ratio of the pension to permanent income. The level of assets itself would normally be negatively correlated with pension and social security wealth. These two aspects of the impacts of pensions on asset-holdings, the 'insurance' effect and the 'wealth' effect respectively, must be disentangled if the hypothesis that observed low rates of decumulation can be explained by the life-cycle model is to be tested empirically. Unfortunately, existing studies do not separate these two effects (for example, neither Diamond and Hausman, 1982, nor King and Dicks-Mireaux, 1982, test the hypothesis). For the moment, therefore, the question remains open.

Another natural question is how sensitive the hump-shaped pattern for asset holdings is to changes in the assumptions made to generate the simulated profile. We shall comment briefly on four assumptions. First, bequests were omitted from the model. Detailed discussion of this topic is deferred until section 5, but if target bequests are equal to some fraction of permanent income and there are no *inter vivos* gifts, then terminal wealth tends to this value rather than to zero. This does not, however, explain low rates of decumulation. The main effect is to raise the peak value of asset holdings and shift the profile upwards. The second assumption is the rate at which real wages grow over the life cycle. In the simulation the ratio of peak wages to starting wages was taken to be 1.5. With a value of 3.0 the maximum value of asset holdings is little changed, and the main consequence is that households go into debt in the early years of the life cycle. Third, a higher pension (with unchanged taxes in working life) lowers the level of household saving. If the pension is 75 per cent instead of 50 per cent of final earnings, then the ratio of assets to permanent income reaches a maximum of 2.9 at age 45 rather than 4.9 at age 51.

The fourth assumption made was that the rate of time preference is less than the real interest rate. Some households may, however, exhibit much higher rates of time preference. It seems implausible to suppose that this could be true of a majority of households, because it would then be difficult to account for the sustained growth rate in aggregate per capita consumption in the absence of a very high rate of technical progress. But it may not be unrelated to the findings of both Diamond and Hausman (1982) and King and Dicks-Mireaux (1982) that around 20 per cent of the households in their samples had very low or negative levels of assets. I discuss this point below, but it is worth pointing out that, in the simulation reported above, merely setting the rate of time preference to 2 per cent (holding all other parameters constant) is sufficient to ensure that the optimal plan leaves the household in debt in every period of life except for the initial and terminal values (this result depends on the pension to final earnings ratio). With this rate of time preference (equal to the assumed real interest rate), consumption, labour supply, the wage rate and earnings all reach a peak at the same age (see the discussion following (2.14)). Consumption is approximately constant over the life cycle and households borrow against future earnings to finance this level of consumption in the early part of life, running down the level of debt as they become older but paying off the last instalment of debt only in the final period. In practice, it may be difficult to borrow against future labour earnings, in which case households may consume all of their income, at least in the first half of their working life.

From this example it is clear that observed values for asset holdings that are either low or negative may be perfectly consistent with life-cycle behaviour. But for this to be the case, households with small or negative values for asset holdings should exhibit different patterns of labour supply behaviour from those of households with low rates of time preference. Labour supply should peak at a later age for households with lower ratios of assets to permanent income. If this correlation is not present, then the ability of the life-cycle model to explain low asset-holdings is much diminished. To my knowledge this test has not been carried out, and the demands on data are substantial. One would require panel data covering both labour supply and asset holdings.

The preceding discussion has ignored the complications that result from variations in the timing of household formation, entry into the labour force, imperfections in the capital market, marriage and the birth of offspring, all of which will influence the age profile of asset holdings. In any empirical study these factors must be modelled explicitly or left to increase the magnitude of the residual variance. Their omission here is not intended as a reflection on their quantitative significance: rather, the aim has been to focus on the empirical implications of forward-looking life-cycle behaviour.

Two main conclusions emerge from the above. The first concerns the nature of the empirical tests, which could be regarded as constituting evidence against the life-cycle model. There are many policy issues for which we need to know whether households are forward-rather than backward-looking, or whether they are likely to face constraints additional to the lifetime budget constraint. In other words, is the life-cycle model, in its broadest sense, a good description of household behaviour? As with static demand analysis, tests of the model are in fact tests of the joint hypothesis of life-cycle behaviour on the one hand and a particular parameterization of preferences on the other. Most empirical findings that claim to reject the life-cycle model could, often more plausibly, be said to reject the assumptions made about preferences. In particular, even if we are prepared to accept the assumption of intertemporal separability (which is crucial to empirical tests of a stochastic life-cycle model, as we shall see below), the assumption of intratemporal separability is very strong and requires verification.

The two major respects in which observed savings behaviour might appear to deviate from the life-cycle model are (1) low rates of decumulation among the aged, and (2) low or negative asset holdings for a sizeable minority of the population. But, as explained above, there are circumstances in which these phenomena are consistent with life-cycle behaviour, and we proposed two empirical tests that would throw light on the issue. The first was to estimate the insurance and the wealth effects of pensions separately; the second was to compare the labour supply behaviour of small (or negative) assetholders with that of wealthier individuals. To carry out these tests, detailed and high-quality microdata on individual households will be required. Aggregate data are inadequate for the task. As in the case of static demand analysis, almost any set of aggregate observations can be consistent with an underlying life-cycle model.

The second conclusion relates to the treatment of unobservable variables in the consumption function, a problem of longstanding concern. We have seen that one way to avoid this problem is to take the ratio of successive first-order conditions as in equations (2.16) and (2.33). In econometric terminology, taking first differences eliminates the fixed effect associated with each observation. The idea behind this is that, instead of solving for the complete consumption profile as a function of all of the exogenous variables, we simply exploit the Euler equation for the household's optimal control problem. In other words, we abandon the econometric specifications of Friedman and Modigliani and revert to Frank Ramsey. This approach has played a central role in recent work on consumption decisions under uncertainty, in which the first-order conditions are expressed in terms of the stochastic Euler equation. We now turn, therefore, to an analysis of the life-cycle model under uncertainty.

A stochastic life-cycle model

We have already discussed the impact of uncertainty over the length of life on the optimal savings plan. There is a conflict between the desire to save more for a possibly longer future life and the desire to enjoy current consumption that is certain (Yaari, 1965; Champernowne, 1969; Levhari and Mirman, 1977; and Davies, 1981). More important perhaps is the uncertainty surrounding future earnings and rates of return (as well as future changes in household consumption). Among those who have investigated the former are Hall (1978), Sargent (1978) and Eden and Pakes (1981); Sandmo (1970) and Levhari and Mirman (1977) analyse uncertainty about interest rates.

It is clear that, once we admit uncertainty into the picture, the market structure that is assumed is of critical importance. With a complete (but finite) set of Arrow–Debreu contingent commodity markets, the optimal savings plan can be analysed in the framework of the certainty model of the preceding subsection expanded to include all relevant contingent commodities. In practice, not all, or even many, of these markets operate, and we might consider the opposite extreme case in which, in any period, only spot markets exist. The absence of futures markets means that, although the current real wage is non-stochastic, future wage rates and asset returns are uncertain. The economy follows a sequence of temporary equilibria, and each period individuals receive new information which in general leads them to revise their savings plans. In such a model expectations are obviously crucial, and an assumption about how expectations are formed and modified over time is required to close the model. This assumption replaces that of a complete set of Arrow–Debreu markets.

Consider an individual who has reached age t. For simplicity we maintain the assumption of a composite consumption good, and for the moment we assume a fixed length of life. If we adopt the axioms required for expected utility maximization, then the individual's objective function is

$$U_t = E_t U(\bar{C}_1, \ldots, \bar{C}_{t-1}, C_t, \ldots, C_T; \bar{L}_1, \ldots, \bar{L}_{t-1}, L_t, \ldots, L_T; B) \tag{2.34}$$

where the expectations operator E_t uses all available information at age t.

This replaces the non-stochastic objective function (2.1), and reflects the fact that past levels of consumption and labour supply are given. The budget constraint is still given by (2.2), but (a) past levels of consumption and earnings may be replaced by the scalar value of current assets, which captures all that is relevant about previous periods; and (b) the constraint is defined over stochastic future wage and interest rates.

In the absence of futures markets the only decision variables are current consumption and labour supply. The first-order conditions are

$$E_t U_{ct} = \lambda_t p_t \tag{2.35}$$

$$E_t U_{Lt} = \lambda_t w_t \tag{2.36}$$

where λ_t is the multiplier associated with the budget constraint defined over the remaining lifespan and is the shadow price of current assets. Even though the current real wage is non-stochastic, it is not possible in general to express labour supply conditional on current 'full expenditure' as a deterministic function of parameters and observable variables. Expectations, as represented by the joint distribution of future wage and interest rates, will influence labour supply not only through a wealth effect on current full expenditure, but also through their impact on marginal rates of substitution.

As before, we may eliminate the multiplier by writing down the stochastic Euler equations (normalizing the price of consumption to unity):

$$E_t U_{ct} = E_t\{U_{c,\,t+j} d_j\} \qquad j = 1, \ldots, T-t \tag{2.37}$$

$$E_t U_{Lt} = E_t\left(U_{L,\,t+j} \frac{w_t}{w_{t+j}} d_j\right) \qquad j = 1, \ldots, T-t \tag{2.38}$$

where the real stochastic discount factor is

$$d_j = \prod_{k=1}^{j} (1 + r_{t+k}).$$

These equations may be derived from a straightforward variational argument (note that this ignores the possibility of corner solutions). The expected utility lost by giving up one unit of consumption now must be equal to the expected utility gained by consuming the proceeds of the extra saving at any future date. Equally, the expected utility gained by taking an extra unit of leisure now, holding consumption at each date constant, must be equal to the expected utility lost at any future date from the sacrifice in leisure required to make up the forgone earnings. In addition to (2.37) and (2.38) there is a third equation, describing the rate at which current consumption will be substituted for current leisure, which is derived from the ratio of (2.35) to (2.36).

As with the non-stochastic Euler equation (2.16), the first-order conditions are of limited use unless the utility function is restricted. In general, it is impossible to solve for the explicit stochastic time-path of consumption and asset holdings, but it is clear that the past (lagged values of consumption and labour supply) can affect current decisions. An obvious restriction to examine is intertemporal separability, where U is given by equation (2.9). In this case the left-hand sides of equations (2.37) and (2.38) are non-stochastic, enabling the conditions to be written as

$$E_t\left(\frac{u_{c,t+j}\cdot d_j}{u_{ct}\cdot s_j}-1\right)=0 \qquad j=1,\ldots,T-t \tag{2.39}$$

$$E_t\left[\frac{u_{L,t+j}}{u_{Lt}}\frac{w_t}{w_{t+j}}\left(\frac{d_j}{s_j}-1\right)\right]=0 \qquad j=1,\ldots,T-t \tag{2.40}$$

where s_j, the time preference factor, is defined analogously to d_j.

These conditions must hold for all individuals, and since the expectation equals zero it is clearly independent of the information set available to the individual. Hence, as pointed out by Grossman and Shiller (1981), any specification based on (2.39) is robust with respect to any asymmetries in access to information. For additive separability over time, (2.35) and (2.36) may be written in the conventional non-stochastic form:

$$\frac{u_{ct}}{u_{Lt}}=\frac{1}{w_t}. \tag{2.41}$$

In special cases it may be possible to derive explicitly the decision rule that relates consumption and labour supply to the stochastic processes generating wage and interest rates (Hansen and Sargent,

1980, 1981). But for more general assumptions about preferences this is not possible, and empirical work must be based on the estimation of the stochastic Euler equations (2.39) and (2.40). These equations state that the expectation of a given nonlinear function, conditional on information available at time t, is zero. The information set at time t includes current and past values of variables such as wage rates, and, whatever values these variables may take, the expectation of the nonlinear function is zero. Hence the value of the function is orthogonal to any variable that appears in the information set.

This suggests that the appropriate method for estimating the stochastic Euler equations is a nonlinear instrumental variables procedure, and this was proposed by Hansen and Singleton (1982). The method minimizes the deviations of the sample values of the orthogonality conditions from zero, and the metric in which these deviations are measured is chosen to produce the smallest asymptotic covariance matrix. The resulting estimates for the parameters of the direct or indirect utility function are consistent and, under relatively weak conditions on the underlying stochastic processes, are also asymptotically normal (Hansen and Singleton, 1982). Since it is possible to imagine a large number of variables entering the information set at time t, there are likely to be more orthogonality conditions than parameters to be estimated. In this sense the model is over-identified. The over-identifying restrictions can be tested using the distance of the sample values of the orthogonality conditions from zero as a test statistic.

An alternative explanation of the estimation procedure is as follows. We may rewrite the equations as

$$E_t f^c\left(C_t, L_t, C_{t+j}, L_{t+j}, \frac{d_j}{s_j}\right) = 0 \tag{2.41}$$

$$E_t f^L\left(C_t, L_t, C_{t+j}, L_{t+j}, w_t, w_{t+j}, \frac{d_j}{s_j}\right) = 0. \tag{2.42}$$

The actual values of f^c and f^L may deviate from zero because new information accrues after time t. If individuals have expectations such that their revisions are uncorrelated with their original plans (for which rational expectations is a sufficient condition), then we may express (2.41) and (2.42) in terms of the following regression model with C_{t+j} and L_{t+j} as the dependent variables:

$$f^c\left(C_t, L_t, C_{t+j}, L_{t+j}, \frac{d_j}{s_j}\right) = \epsilon^c_{j,t+1} \tag{2.43}$$

$$f^L\left(C_t, L_t, C_{t+j}, L_{t+j}, w_t, w_{t+j}, \frac{d_j}{s_j}\right) = \epsilon^L_{j,t+1}. \tag{2.44}$$

The error terms have zero mean but the covariance matrix is a function of the underlying stochastic processes generating wage and interest rates. This implies cross-equation restrictions and suggests that the distribution of the error terms should be consistent with the observed joint distribution of wage and interest rates. But if we regard the elements of the covariance matrix as free parameters, the model to be estimated consists of a pair of nonlinear simultaneous equations for each value of j. The inclusion of future wage and interest rates in the model necessitates the use of instrumental variables for consistent estimates.

This model provides a framework for the investigation of the role of intertemporal substitution in consumption and labour supply. Recently, much attention has been devoted to the question of whether such substitution can explain aggregate fluctuations in employment and consumption. The magnitude of the substitution effects is relevant to major policy issues such as the nature of unemployment, the design of the tax system (income vs. expenditure as the tax base) and the effects of public borrowing. It is important to note, therefore, that existing empirical studies have examined only very special cases of the model given by equations (2.43) and (2.44). First, only estimates for the case $j = 1$ have been reported. For forecasting purposes higher values of j would be relevant to a comparison of alternative models. Second, except for the study by Mankiw, Rotemberg and Summers (1982), it has been assumed that preferences are weakly separable between consumption and leisure. This implies that the model for consumption is

$$f^c\left(C_{t+1}, C_t, \frac{1+r_{t+1}}{1+p_{t+1}}\right) = \epsilon_{t+1}. \tag{2.45}$$

In other words, either the level of consumption or some transform of the level of consumption follows a first-order difference equation, and if real interest rates (and the rate of time preference) are constant the parameters of this equation are time-invariant. This is the 'Hall consumption function' (Hall, 1978). From (2.39) we may write this as

$$u_{c,t+1} = \frac{1+\rho}{1+r} u_{ct} + \eta_{t+1} \tag{2.46}$$

where $E(\eta_t) = 0$, but if the error term is introduced as in (2.39) then there is no reason to suppose that it is homoscedastic. If the stochastic shocks are small, then we can take a linear approximation to the marginal utility of consumption, and consumption is related only to its own previous value. In fact, consumption follows a random walk with drift. Given the assumption of weak separability between consumption and leisure and the validity of the linear approximation, no lagged variables other than last period's consumption itself will contain any explanatory power in a regression equation for consumption. This is the analogue to the orthogonality condition discussed above. Unfortunately, it has been widely stated in the literature that a test of the life-cycle model is the significance or otherwise of additional lagged variables in a regression model for consumption. This is false. If any relevant explanatory variables are omitted from the model, then additional lagged values of consumption or income may appear to be significant.

Two examples are important. First, consider the case when interest rates vary over time. If interest rates are omitted from the estimation of (2.46), as in Hall's original paper, the reduced form for consumption will not follow a random walk with drift. Suppose that the real interest rate itself follows a simple autoregressive process. Then consumption would follow a higher-order autoregressive process, and the significance of additional lagged values of consumption would indicate nothing about the consistency of observed behaviour with a life-cycle model.

More interesting, perhaps, is the fact that most of the studies of consumption assume that preferences for consumption and leisure are separable. To analyse the case when preferences are not separable, it is helpful to use the indirect rather than the direct utility function. In the stochastic case the objective function (2.25) becomes

$$U_t = E_t \sum_{j=t}^{T} \frac{\ln v(w_j, y_j)}{s_j}. \tag{2.47}$$

A simple variational argument leads to the following Euler equation for full expenditure y_t:[10]

$$E_t\left(\frac{1}{v_{t+1}}\frac{\partial v_{t+1}}{\partial y_{t+1}}\frac{1+r_{t+1}}{1+\rho_{t+1}}-\frac{1}{v_t}\frac{\partial v_t}{\partial y_t}\right)=0 \tag{2.48}$$

which may be written as

$$E_t f^y\left(y_{t+1}, y_t, w_{t+1}, w_t, \frac{1+r_{t+1}}{1+\rho_{t+1}}\right)=0. \tag{2.49}$$

Within each period, labour supply is given by a non-stochastic application of Roy's identity and consumption then follows from the within-period budget constraint (2.21). The attraction of this dual approach is that it exploits the two-stage budgeting structure implied by the assumption that preferences are intertemporally separable. At the first stage full expenditure is given by the stochastic process implied by (2.48). Then in any period, given the level of full expenditure, consumption and labour supply are determined exactly as in the non-stochastic model. Commodity demands, conditional on the level of full expenditure, are given by a conventional static model, and the behaviour of full expenditure is governed by the single stochastic Euler equation. Given a functional form for the indirect utility function (for example (2.24) above), this system can be estimated by instrumental variables procedures, and may well be easier to implement than instrumental variables estimation of the equations derived from the direct utility function.[11]

For the preferences described by (2.24) used in the simulation of the previous subsection, full expenditure follows the path

$$y_{t+1}=\frac{1-a}{c}\left(\frac{r_{t+1}-\rho_{t+1}}{1+\rho_{t+1}}\right)+\left(\frac{1+r_{t+1}}{1+\rho_{t+1}}\right)y_t + \frac{b}{c+\gamma}\left(\frac{1+r_{t+1}}{1+\rho_{t+1}}e^{-\gamma w_t}-e^{-\gamma w_{t+1}}\right)+\eta^y_{t+1}. \tag{2.50}$$

The time-path of consumption is given by

$$C_{t+1}=\frac{1-a}{c}\left(\frac{r_{t+1}-\rho_{t+1}}{1+\rho_{t+1}}\right)+\left(\frac{1+r_{t+1}}{1+\rho_{t+1}}\frac{1-cw_{t+1}}{1-cw_t}\right)C_t + h(w_{t+1}, w_t)+\hat{\eta}_{t+1} \tag{2.51}$$

where the function h is given by

$$h(w_{t+1}, w_t) = -w_{t+1}\left((1-a)\,\frac{1+r_{t+1}}{1+\rho_{t+1}} + be^{-\gamma w_{t+1}}\right)$$

$$+\frac{b}{c+\gamma}(1-cw_{t+1})\left(\frac{1+r_{t+1}}{1+\rho_{t+1}}\,e^{-\gamma w_t} - e^{-\gamma w_{t+1}}\right)$$

$$+\frac{1+r_{t+1}}{1+\rho_{t+1}}\,\frac{1-cw_{t+1}}{1-cw_t}\,(1-a+be^{-\gamma w_t})\,w_t. \qquad (2.52)$$

It is clear that consumption does not follow a simple random walk with drift. If we compare (2.51) with the Hall consumption function (Hall, 1978),

$$C_{t+1} = a_0 + a_1 C_t + \mu_{t+1}, \qquad (2.53)$$

we may observe two obvious differences. The first is that in (2.51) the coefficient on lagged consumption is not time-invariant and will depend on changes in real wage and interest rates. The second is that the linear specification (2.53) omits the h function defined over current and lagged wage rates. Suppose that the specification (2.51) were correct. Estimates of the Hall consumption function would then produce evidence of (a) parameter instability in the coefficient of lagged consumption, (b) the existence of additional variables with significant explanatory power in the regression, and (c) serially correlated residuals generated by a stochastic process, the order of which would depend upon the process-generating wage and interest rates. The extra variables would be correlated with the h function, and hence obvious candidates would be current and lagged labour earnings.

Alternatively, by substituting out from the process-generating wage and interest rates, we could obtain a reduced form for consumption in terms of its own lagged values which would involve a nontrivial higher-order lag distribution.

All of this raises the issue of the objectives of an econometric investigation into savings and consumption behaviour. If the aim is simply to obtain the best forecasting equation for purposes of projecting developments in the economy, then there is no compelling theoretical reason to restrict the specifications over which we search to models such as (2.53). A time-series analysis using unrestricted lags would be the appropriate search procedure. But if we are interested in predicting the response of consumption to changes in policy variables (for example, changes in the taxation of capital income, or the introduction of permanent or temporary taxes on expenditure), then the use of the reduced-form equation for consumption is unhelpful (for reasons known as the Lucas critique). Even if we can model the effect of the policy changes on the parameters of the Euler equation (as in (2.51) for example), the resulting model simply tells us the rate at which consumption changes once we are in the new regime: it does not tell us how consumption will change as we move from one regime to another. To examine this we need to solve for the optimum decision rule, which relates consumption and labour supply to the joint distribution of wage and interest rates. As mentioned above, only in special cases will it be possible to find an explicit form for the decision rule, and the comparative statics of stochastic models of this kind is an area requiring further research.

Finally, we might wish to examine the hypothesis that consumers are forward-looking rational planners unconstrained in current markets. The main insight in the Hall model is that in such a world consumers' plans would change only upon the receipt of new information about the future, and that new information would by definition be unpredictable: hence changes in lifetime wealth would follow a random walk. It is easy to show that the basic result behind this intuition is that the marginal utility of lifetime wealth follows a random walk. The assumption required is that preferences are additively separable over time. With this assumption, then from the objective function (2.47) and the budget constraint defined over remaining lifetime, at any time t

$$\frac{1}{v_t}\frac{\partial v_t}{\partial y_t} = \lambda_t \tag{2.54}$$

where λ_t is the multiplier associated with the budget constraint and is the marginal utility of wealth. Substituting into the Euler equation (2.48) yields

$$E_t\left[\left(\frac{1+r_{t+1}}{1+\rho_{t+1}}\right)\lambda_{t+1} - \lambda_t\right] = 0. \tag{2.55}$$

The marginal utility of wealth follows a random walk with drift where the drift parameter depends upon the real interest rate and the rate of time preference. From (2.35) it immediately follows that the marginal utility of consumption follows a random walk with the same drift parameters. But unless preferences between consumption and leisure are separable, it does not follow that consumption itself follows a random walk (even as a linear approximation). No amount of sophisticated econometric analysis of the time-series behaviour of consumption will throw light on the relevance of the stochastic life-cycle model. We need either to examine the cross-equation restrictions implied by the model for the joint behaviour of consumption and labour supply (an investigation for which the data requirements are prodigious), or to examine the predictions of alternative models. In the following section we ask, therefore, What are the implications of a model that allows for the possibility that individuals may be constrained in either the capital or the labour market?

To conclude the discussion of stochastic life-cycle models, we may note the following three points. First, uncertainty about length of life may be analysed, as noted above, by allowing an age-specific rate of time preference. This means that age will enter into models of consumption using micro-data (whether cross-section or panel data), and that demographic variables will be relevant to the aggregate consumption function.

Second, in this section we have concentrated on drawing out the implications of the first-order conditions for individual optimization. The results are equations for optimal individual or aggregate consumption and labour supply conditional upon the joint distribution of wage and interest rates. But this is only part of the story. As in static demand analysis, we may aggregate equations (2.39) and (2.40) across individuals and invert the system to obtain a model for equilibrium asset prices. Work along these lines has been carried out by Lucas (1978), Shiller (1981) and Grossman and Shiller (1981). The endogenous distribution of prices is related to the exogenous distribution of shocks to output (originating with technological or other changes). Hence, just as income in a Keynesian consumption function may be jointly determined with consumption, so the distribution of wage and interest rates in a stochastic life-cycle model may be jointly determined with aggregate consumption and labour supply. Much more study of these issues is required if we are to construct models of tax incidence, for example, in a stochastic setting.

Third, it is apparent that the extension of the life-cycle model to a stochastic world alters less the specification of the equations to be estimated than the methods of estimation. Given the assumption of intertemporal separability, the dynamic specifications for consumption and labour supply that follow from the result that the marginal utility of wealth follows a random walk are the stochastic analogue of the 'constant marginal utility of wealth' demand functions discussed in the preceding subsection. The stochastic Euler equations for consumption and labour supply can be estimated by a generalized instrumental variables procedure. Tests of the significance of variables other than lagged consumption in a regression equation for consumption tell us more about the appropriate parameterization of preferences than about the relevance of the life-cycle model. In particular, if the intratemporal preference ordering is not separable, then consumption does not follow a random walk with drift. A much wider range of models needs to be tested before we can be confident of robust results in this area. It is also important not to confuse the reduced form with the underlying structural model. The omission of relevant variables can lead to a complicated distributed lag model for consumption. This is uninformative about the underlying behavioural model, and the lag structure may exhibit parameter instability (a common feature of aggregate time-series studies of consumption).

3 ALTERNATIVE MODELS

In this section we examine the empirical predictions of models that might be regarded as alternatives to the life-cycle model. To some extent this is semantic. Our definition of the life-cycle model is that individuals are assumed to be 'forward-looking' and to face a single lifetime budget constraint. In contrast, Kurz (1981) has argued that the essence of the life-cycle model is that individuals plan only over their own lifespan because the inclusion of bequests in a satisfactory manner leads inexorably to a concept of intergenerational equilibrium that cannot be represented as the outcome of an individual optimization problem of the kind discussed above. In other words, 'optimal bequests' are not appropriately analysed in a model of individual family optimization.

We discuss first the consequence of quantity constraints in either the labour or the capital market. The most obvious example of such a constraint is involuntary unemployment. In the absence of constraints, labour supply and consumption are given by Roy's identity and the within period budget constraint. Suppose, however, that some individuals are constrained at zero labour supply.[12] Then we may define a virtual wage, w_t^*, and virtual full expenditure y_t^*, such that, at the virtual budget constraint, the individual would choose to work zero hours and consume the observed consumption level C_t. The virtual wage and full expenditure are determined by

$$1 = -\frac{-\partial v(w_t^*, y_t^*)}{\partial w_t^*} \bigg/ \frac{\partial v(w^*, y_t^*)}{\partial y_t^*} \tag{3.1}$$

$$y_t - y_t^* = w_t - w_t^*. \tag{3.2}$$

The Euler equation in the constrained case is more complicated. Assuming that there are no constraints in the capital market (or, more accurately, that there is at least one asset market in which individuals are unconstrained), the variational argument for the optimal allocation of full expenditure over time yields the following modified version of (2.48):

$$E_t \left\{ \frac{1+r_{t+1}}{1+\rho_{t+1}} \frac{1}{v_{t+1}} \left[\left(\frac{\partial v_{t+1}}{\partial w_{t+1}^*} \frac{dw_{t+1}^*}{dy_{t+1}} \right) + \left(\frac{\partial v_{t+1}}{\partial y_{t+1}^*} \frac{dy_{t+1}^*}{dy_{t+1}} \right) \right] - \frac{1}{v_t} \left[\left(\frac{\partial v_t}{\partial w_t^*} \frac{dw_t^*}{dy_t} \right) + \left(\frac{\partial v_t}{\partial y_t^*} \frac{dy_t^*}{dy_t} \right) \right] \right\} = 0. \tag{3.3}$$

When there are no constraints, (w^*, y^*) is equal to (w, y) and (3.3) reduces to (2.48). Note, however, that if we substitute the constrained version of (2.54) into (3.3) we obtain (2.55). Even in the presence of labour market constraints, the marginal utility of wealth, and hence the marginal utility of consumption, follows a random walk. If preferences between consumption and leisure are separable, then consumption itself will (approximately) follow a random walk, and unemployment, or any other quantity constraints, will have no place in the consumption function. In general, however, with non-separable preferences equation (3.3) has some interesting implications for the time-series analysis of consumption.

In order to illustrate the way in which constraints affect the specification of the aggregate consumption function, we shall consider a simple model in which it is assumed that individuals know in period t whether or not they will be constrained in period $(t+1)$.

There are four cases to examine:

Case 1: individual unconstrained in both periods t and $(t+1)$
Case 2: individual constrained in period t but not $(t+1)$
Case 3: individual constrained in period $(t+1)$ but not t
Case 4: individual constrained in both periods t and $(t+1)$

Consider the simple case in which the real rate of interest is non-stochastic and equal to the rate of time preference. Assume also that the real wage is expected to remain constant. Then with these assumptions (of unchanged relative prices), both full expenditure and consumption will follow a random walk when individuals are unconstrained (case 1). But relative virtual prices will also be constant, and so if individuals are constrained in both periods, consumption will follow a random walk in case 4 also.[13] Consumption does not, however, follow a random walk when individuals are constrained in one period but not in the other. In cases 2 and 3, consumption follows a nonlinear stochastic process in which lagged earnings and wage rates appear in addition to lagged consumption. This suggests that it is changes in the unemployment rate, not the level of unemployment itself, that should enter the consumption function when the relevant constraints are those in the labour market.

To illustrate the empirical specifications that constraints may produce, we consider the nonlinear labour supply function used above (equation (2.20)). Rather than solve explicitly for the virtual prices, we adopt a rather different view of unemployment in which the individual faces not a constraint on the number of hours worked but a very low wage rate. Redundancy leads to a contraction in market opportunities and the potential wage rate falls sharply. The new wage rate depends upon alternative employment opportunities. How much, for example, could a redundant professor of economics earn by cleaning his neighbour's car or windows? I shall assume that the answer is zero. At a zero wage optimal labour supply is very small (see figure 4.1). In a formal sense, the resulting unemployment is 'voluntary', although the individual is not receiving the same wage offer as otherwise identical workers and in this sense it is 'involuntary'. For this preference ordering the stochastic time-path of consumption is given by equation (2.51). When $r_t = \rho_t$ and $w_{t+1} = w_t$, the h function has the property that

$$h(w, w) = 0. \tag{3.4}$$

This is true for any level of the wage rate. Hence in both the 'no unemployment' case *and* the 'continuing unemployment' (zero wage in both periods) case, consumption follows a pure random walk:

$$C_{t+1} = C_t + \eta_{t+1}. \tag{3.5}$$

In cases 2 and 3 consumption is given by

$$C_{t+1} = \left(\frac{1-cw_{t+1}}{1-cw_t}\right) C_t + h(w_{t+1}, w_t) + \eta_{t+1} \tag{3.6}$$

where (w_{t+1}, w_t) is equal to $(w, 0)$ in case 2 and $(0, w)$ in case 3. From (2.52),

$$h(w, 0) = -(1-cw)\, h(0, w). \tag{3.7}$$

This implies that the changes in consumption ΔC in the two cases, conditional on the same level of current consumption, are inversely related according to

$$(\Delta C)_2 = -(1-cw)\,(\Delta C)_3. \tag{3.8}$$

It might be interesting to test this model on panel data for four distinct groups in the population: (1) those in continuing employment, (2) those in continuing unemployment, (3) those entering unemployment and (4) those becoming re-employed. The model implies strong cross-equation restrictions on the consumption functions for the four groups (equations (3.5) and (3.8)).

Suppose that a fraction α of consumption in period t is by people who are becoming re-employed and a fraction β is by people entering the state of unemployment. Suppose also that the average wage of those losing jobs is equal to the average wage of those finding jobs. Then the aggregate per capita consumption function is of the form

$$C_{t+1} = \left[1 + cw\left(\frac{\beta}{1-cw} - \alpha\right)\right] C_t + h(w, 0)\left(\alpha - \frac{\beta}{1-cw}\right) + \eta_{t+1}. \tag{3.9}$$

If labour supply is income-inelastic ($c = 0$), then[14]

$$C_{t+1} = C_t + (\alpha - \beta)\, h(w, 0) + \eta_{t+1}. \tag{3.10}$$

The random walk path of consumption is shifted up or down by a factor proportional to the *change* in the unemployment rate (measured by $\alpha - \beta$).

Implicit in the above discussion was the assumption that individuals knew into which of the four transition states they belonged. More generally, we could allow for uncertainty about the state in which an individual might expect to find himself next period. Expectations about future levels of unemployment would enter the model yielding an optimal level of 'precautionary savings' to act as a cushion against future unemployment. The path for consumption will be given by equation (3.3), modified to allow for the possibility that in period $(t+1)$ the individual may experience either a virtual budget constraint (w^*_{t+1}, y^*_{t+1}) or an actual budget constraint (w_t, y_t), depending on whether or not he will be unemployed next period.

Another set of constraints that render the basic life-cycle model inapplicable is capital market constraints. Because of the difficulty of borrowing against future labour earnings, individuals who wish to consume more than their current income, and have run down their (liquid) assets to zero, may face a borrowing constraint.[15] The significance of such constraints is that the optimal intertemporal allocation of resources is no longer described by a stochastic Euler equation. Moreover, it is plausible to suppose that the incidence of borrowing constraints is highly correlated with constraints in the labour market, that is with unemployment. Formally, we could define the virtual non-stochastic interest rate and virtual lifetime wealth to be those values at which the individual would exactly choose the levels of full expenditure to which he or she were constrained. With a binding constraint on borrowing, full expenditure y_t is constrained to the value of the current endowment w_t. In a stochastic setting this approach does not lead to tractable specifications because only in very special cases is it possible to obtain an explicit solution for the optimal time-path of full expenditure that is required in order to solve for the virtual interest rate and virtual wealth.

But we may illustrate the likely impact of capital market constraints on the behaviour of consumption. In period t there are two groups: those who face binding constraints on borrowing and those who do not. The consumption path of the unconstrained group is given by the appropriate stochastic Euler equation – equation (2.48) if they are free to choose their labour supply or equation (3.3) if they are rationed in the labour market. For the constrained group there are two possibilities. First, they may expect to be constrained again in period $(t+1)$, in which case the expectation at time t of their consumption in period $(t+1)$ is the expected value of labour earnings in period $(t+1)$ conditional on earnings in period t. Second, they may anticipate being unconstrained next period, in which case consumption would be expected to return to a 'normal' level reflecting lifetime opportunities. The value of this expectation can be determined only by solving the stochastic control problem facing the individual. But if he is very similar to a group of currently unconstrained consumers, then we can use observations on their current consumption to form an expectation of his consumption next period.

A formal analysis of borrowing constraints is complicated by two factors. First, the timing of such constraints is endogenous to individuals' own savings plans, and hence the identification of the 'constrained group' is by no means obvious. Second, the optimal loan contract may contain a mixture of individual-specific interest rates and repayment periods, as well as upper limits on borrowing. Asymmetry in information about the risk of future unemployment will affect the outcome. In order to illustrate the nature of the consumption function when we allow for constraints in both capital and labour markets, we consider a very simple example. Individuals who do not experience unemployment are assumed never to be constrained in the capital market. For individuals who do experience unemployment we make the following assumptions. In period t it becomes known (both to the individual concerned and to lenders) that an individual will be unemployed in period $(t+1)$. Borrowing constraints are imposed only upon the current and prospective unemployed. If the person is already unemployed we assume that he has run down his assets by the end of period t and hence that his consumption in period $(t+1)$ will be constrained to his receipt of unemployment benefit. If the person is employed, we assume that he does not have such large debts that upon receipt of the 'bad news' he is unable to reduce current consumption and save an optimal amount to provide a cushion against the future unemployment (a precautionary motive for savings). In other words, after the receipt of the bad news, the optimal level of asset holdings is positive and the individual is not constrained in the capital market in period t.

We assume also that unemployment strikes randomly among the population. For the example analysed above, in the context of labour market constraints, we have that expected per capita income in period $(t+1)$, conditional on information available in period t, in the four transition states is as follows.

1 *Group 1* (employed in both periods):

$$E_t(C_{t+1}) = C_t. \tag{3.11}$$

2 *Group 2* (unemployed in t but with a job in $(t+1)$: as someone who is currently unemployed, we assume that an individual in this group is unable to borrow (even though he is about to return to work).[16] The Euler equation, in the form of an equality, does not apply. As an approximation we regard this individual in period $(t+1)$, once he is back at work, as a random drawing from the population. For this individual also, therefore,

$$E_t(C_{t+1}) = C_t \tag{3.12}$$

where the C_t is an observation of the consumption of the currently employed. If the average earnings of those liable to unemployment were smaller than for the population as a whole, then C_t would be replaced by, say, λC_t. Although (3.11) and (3.12) appear identical, this is only because we have assumed for simplicity that λ equals unity.

3 *Group 3* (employed in t but facing unemployment in $(t+1)$): given our assumptions, the Euler equation applies to this group and is given by equation (3.6):

$$E_t(C_{t+1}) = \frac{1}{1-cw} C_t + h(0, w). \tag{3.13}$$

4 *Group 4* (unemployed in both periods): we assume that the average replacement ratio (ratio of unemployment benefit to current real earnings) is r:

$$E_t(C_{t+1}) = rE_t(w_{t+1} L_{t+1}) = rwL. \tag{3.14}$$

Let the unemployment rate be u_t, and assume that a fraction θ_t of the employed lose their jobs and a fraction δ_t of the unemployed find jobs in period t. This implies that

$$\theta_t(1-u_t) + (1-\delta_t)\, u_t = u_{t+1}. \tag{3.15}$$

Aggregate per capita consumption is given by

$$E_t(C_{t+1}) = \left[1-(1-\delta_t)\,u_t + \frac{\theta_t cw(1-u_t)}{1-cw}\right] C_t$$

$$+ [\theta_t(1-u_t)\,h(0,w) + rwu_t(1-\delta_t)\,L]. \qquad (3.16)$$

A regression model for consumption based on (3.16) would include not only lagged consumption, but also lagged earnings, the unemployment rate and the change in the unemployment rate. There are some interesting special cases ($\theta = 0$, moving out of recession; $\delta = 1$, boom; $r = 1$, replacement ratio of unity), but these are left to the reader.

One of the implications of borrowing constraints is that, for individuals whose consumption is constrained to current receipts, the marginal propensity to consume out of current receipts is unity. For unconstrained individuals the marginal propensity to consume out of current income is less than unity, although its actual size depends on the stochastic process generating current incomes. This feature has been the focus of previous work on capital market constraints (such as Flemming, 1973; Appelbaum and Harris, 1978; Dolde, 1978; and Koskela, 1978). Of more interest in equation (3.16) is the fact that, except in special cases, the aggregate consumption function depends upon the distribution of individuals among the four transition states. The distribution of expectations about future unemployment will influence the level of aggregate consumption conditional upon the value of past consumption.

The existence of constraints means that it is not possible to ignore aggregation problems when modelling the level of aggregate consumption. In his study of the effects of income distribution on the aggregate consumption function, Blinder (1975) found surprisingly little evidence of the effect of conventional measures of distribution on the level of aggregate consumption. This may well be because aggregation becomes important only when constraints are relevant. A simple example of this is the contrast between the linear Hall consumption function and equation (3.16). The Hall function holds even if there is a distribution of wages among individuals. Anticipated changes in income distribution (resulting from, perhaps, changes in the degree of progression in the tax system) would be reflected in individuals' current consumption plans. Conditional on the value of lagged consumption, no additional information is contained in a statistic measuring the income distribution. But of course it does not follow from this that changes in the degree of progression in the tax system have no effect on the level of consumption. In general, they will have significant effects, but to model these in a stochastic setting is by no means straightforward, given, as remarked above, the lack of explicit solutions to the decision rule relating consumption decisions to the current observed state of the economy.

In the analysis of constraints it was clear that virtual prices entered the consumption function, and since these are a function of quantities (constraints), there is clearly a basis for a Keynesian consumption function in which quantities are relevant explanatory variables. But there are other non-Walrasian features that might usefully be incorporated into the model. We did not analyse the role of futures markets, and more particularly the consequences of explicit or implicit contracts which may last for many periods. Such contracts have been the subject of much discussion in the literature on the labour market (see Hart, 1983), and lead also to virtual prices which differ from observed prices. There is scope for future work on the impact of contracts on the behaviour of consumption. It is clear that one of the major empirical trends in the postwar period has been the rapid growth of 'contractual saving', and a large proportion of average savings bears a predetermined relationship to the level of labour income. Where there are other opportunities for adjusting savings at the margin, this fixed relationship may be of little consequence. But these alternative opportunities may receive less favourable tax treatment (and in general do), and if the allocation of savings among alternative assets is relevant, contracts will play a role.

There are several deeper objections that can be made to the life-cycle model. First, as mentioned above, Kurz (1981) has pointed out that, if bequests are modelled, then a concept of intergenerational equilibrium rather than individual optimization subject to exogenous constraints may be a more appropriate way of viewing the problem. Second, some individuals may either be rather poor at, or have no interest in, stochastic control theory. We return to this below. Third, individuals may not act as 'rational planners'. This objection is not helpful unless it leads to an alternative view of consumer behaviour. One possibility is to regard consumers as 'myopic'. But if this means little more than the possibility that some consumers have high rates of time preference, then such behaviour can be analysed within the framework set out above. It is clear from the discussion in earlier sections that a combination of a high rate of time preference and borrowing constraints will lead to an outcome in which myopic individuals are generally constrained by current resources.

Another view is that the problem of decision-making under uncertainty is so great that the normal 'as if' justification for analysing optimal behaviour does not apply. Psychologists such as Tversky and Kahneman (1982) have argued that when constructing subjective probabilities people use a limited number of heuristic principles which can sometimes lead their subjective probabilities to violate Bayes's theorem. They provide empirical evidence to support this claim, and in part the evidence derives from an inability of individuals to comprehend more than a certain part of the problem at any one time. Behaviour of this kind could lead to irrational expectations such that the current subjective probabilities used by individuals were unduly dominated by the most recent observed outcome. The omission of relevant prior information was, in fact, one of the empirical phenomena observed by Tversky and Kahneman (1982). Alternatively, the costs of decision-making under uncertainty may be so great that individuals devise rules of thumb for their consumption and saving behaviour.

Other approaches would see individuals behaving stochastically. In other words, instead of choosing a single action from a choice set based on an assessment of the likely outcomes, individuals' choices in identical circumstances can be inconsistent. Barbera and Pattanaik (1981) have analysed the conditions under which stochastic choices can be represented as a lottery among a large number of different preference orderings. In a somewhat different vein, Thaler and Shefrin (1981) and Shefrin and Thaler (1982) analyse the savings decision as the outcome of a conflict between a split personality in which a 'higher' self, concerned with the long-run consequences of current decisions, attempts to gain control over the 'lower' self, which is concerned only with immediate pleasure. They formulate the problem as a principal–agent model. This does not seem appropriate. In their model it is possible for the higher self to ensure that the lower self always follows an optimal life-cycle savings plan. There is no asymmetry of information, and the essence of a principal–agent problem is lacking. More relevant would be a formulation in terms of a bargaining model in which the two opposing sets of values tussled for dominance in the individual's mind.

For any of these alternative models to be helpful, it must be possible to derive empirical predictions that differ from the predictions of a life-cycle model. As we have seen, very many types of behaviour can be rationalized by a life-cycle model. Nevertheless, for certain kinds of behaviour (such as low or negative wealth-holding) to be explicable in a life-cycle framework, there are cross-equation restrictions for the behaviour of consumption, labour supply and asset holdings over the life cycle. It may be possible to test these restrictions in order to shed light on the extent to which the observed data are the result of forward-looking rational planning or represent the outcome of a family failing to cope with its own financial affairs. These different explanations for observed savings behaviour are not simply a matter of intellectual curiosity, but have a bearing on a wide range of policy issues such as the pensions system, redistribution over the life cycle, and income maintenance schemes. So-called 'paternalistic' intervention by government may be an appropriate second-best response to the high costs of obtaining information.

There is one final point to be made about the assumption of rational expectations in a life-cycle model. This assumption is most useful when it is reasonable to suppose that individuals have a sufficiently large number of observations of events for them to learn about the stochastic process generating the observations. Subjective probabilities can be related to observable frequencies. For this to be possible, the stochastic processes must be stationary. But when planning over a life cycle many of the relevant events will be observed only once. Most people expect to retire: when it comes to planning for retirement, learning by doing is somewhat difficult.

4 EMPIRICAL STUDIES OF SAVINGS BEHAVIOUR

In this section we shall survey some of the recent empirical work on consumption and savings behaviour. The focus will be on the light that these studies shed on the relevance of the models discussed above rather than on their respective merits as forecasting equations of consumption.

At the outset three problems inherent in the empirical studies of consumption should be mentioned. All of the studies mentioned below are deficient with respect to at least one of these, and this should be borne in mind when interpreting the results. First, although we have ignored the influence of household composition on the optimal consumption profile, it is clear that changes in the composition of families will in general lead to changes in the optimal pattern of consumption. The difficulties in identifying the effects of household composition on consumption patterns in cross-section data are well known, and existing results are far from robust. In studies using aggregate data, changes in demographic structure should appear in a fully specified model.

Second, there are difficulties in defining the consumption variable used for empirical work. The models used above implicitly assume that the consumption good yields a flow of consumption services. The most natural variable to use in empirical work, therefore, is the value of consumption of non-durables and services plus the imputed service flow from durable goods. But most studies exclude durables. This is partly because there are assumed to be costs of adjustment to durables although these are not explicitly modelled. An assumption about separability of preferences between consumption of non-durables and the consumption of durables is made in order to justify a specification of consumption-excluding durables. This strengthens the general conclusion that the models estimated are tests of the joint hypothesis of forward-looking behaviour and a particular parameterization of preferences.

Third, in models using time-series data (whether aggregate or panel data) a choice must be made about the length of the period. Often this is dictated by the availability of data. But if the length of period used by consumers for planning purposes differs from that used in the estimation, time aggregation biases will be present.

Studies using aggregate data

Any study based on aggregate data is obviously open to the charge that the existence of aggregation bias means that almost any set of aggregate data could be consistent with underlying rational individual behaviour. Clearly, one of the attractions of the simple linear Hall consumption function is that (leaving aside demographic changes) the model aggregates perfectly. A more interesting question is the use of such models to test the life-cycle hypothesis. This refers back to a point made in the introduction. The use of such tests (such as the significance of additional lagged variables in the consumption function) has been to accept or reject the life-cycle model. An alternative inference, with rather different implications for policy, is that part of the population behaves according to the life-cycle model while another part does not. We shall argue below that this is not an unreasonable conclusion to draw from the data, and its investigation requires the use of micro-data for individual households.

Before summarizing the results of tests using aggregate data, it may be helpful to point to two stylized facts about aggregate postwar data that are in large part responsible for the results described below. The first is that shocks to the economy tend to result in positively correlated movements in consumption and labour supply. In other words, consumption and hours worked are procyclical. If we rule out the possibility that leisure is an inferior good, then this observation will be consistent with rational individual behaviour only if the real wage moved procyclically by enough to justify the changes in hours worked. But the aggregate real wage has not moved in this fashion. It might be argued that this reflects the fact that the aggregate real wage used in these studies is an average of the wage for those in employment. But whether we regard some households as unemployed in the sense that they face a constraint on hours worked or unemployed in the sense used above, that their market wage is close to zero, the analysis above predicts that aggregate models will fail unless they deal explicitly with unemployment and constraints in the labour market.

The second stylized fact concerns the lessons we might hope to draw about the intertemporal elasticity of substitution of consumption. This is relevant to those models that allow the interest rate to be time-dependent. Any model that uses factual observations on rates of return to compute predicted expected real rates of return (whether explicitly or as instrumental variables) will observe that there has been a fall during the postwar period in the expected rate of return, whereas the growth rate of consumption has changed rather little. Hence it will be difficult to conclude from aggregate data that the response of consumption to changes in interest rates is anything other than rather small.

It is not surprising, therefore, to find that tests of the stochastic life-cycle model have been rather disappointing. The study nearest to the theoretical model set out above is that of Mankiw, Rotemberg and Summers (1982). They estimated the stochastic Euler equations for consumption and labour supply using aggregate quarterly data for the United States in the period 1947–80. To do so they used the instrumental variables technique discussed in section 2. The two major findings were that the orthogonality restrictions implied by the first-order conditions were rejected, and that the implied utility function often was not concave. Some of their estimates allow for a non-separable preference ordering, and in this respect their study is unique. The preference ordering that they assume is of the following rather special form:

$$U = \frac{1}{1-\gamma}\left\{\frac{C_t^{1-\alpha}-1}{1-\alpha} + d\left[\frac{(1-L_t)^{1-\beta}-1}{1-\beta}\right]\right\}^{1-\gamma}. \tag{4.1}$$

When $\gamma = 0$ then preferences are separable. Given the difficulties with aggregate data mentioned above, it may well be that no other preference ordering would improve matters, but there is something to be said for experimenting with a functional form consistent with the existing results on labour supply as suggested in section 2 above. Perhaps the main conclusion to be drawn from this study, however, is that it is important to incorporate constraints in the labour and capital markets into an empirical specification. This is closely related to the proposition that over the business cycle changes in hours worked are not spread evenly among the working population, but tend to fall disproportionately on a minority. The nonlinear labour supply function of section 2 has the property that, for any given change in the aggregate real wage of the population as a whole, a change in hours worked is much smaller if the change in wages is equal for all than if the change in wages takes the form of a small proportion receiving a zero wage offer.

Hansen and Singleton (1982) also estimate the Euler equations and report a rejection of the restrictions implied by the model using postwar US data. Although Hall (1981) does not estimate the Euler equations as such, he makes assumptions about the stochastic processes underlying the model such that he is able to derive an explicit form for the time-path of consumption. He assumes that both the interest rate factor and the marginal utility of consumption are log-normally distributed, and so the reduced form is a bivariate regression for consumption and the real interest rate. This is because the product of two lognormally distributed random variables is itself lognormally distributed, and so (2.39) reduces to a regression model. Preferences between consumption and leisure are assumed to be separable. The nature of the stochastic processes for wage and interest rates required for the distribution of marginal utility to be lognormal is unclear. The model was estimated using postwar annual data for the United States and the coefficient on the expected interest rate was small.

The remaining studies do not estimate the stochastic Euler equations derived from an explicit model of optimizing behaviour, but specify a regression model. A formal justification of the specification employed requires the assumption of a non-stochastic interest rate. In fact, all but two studies assume a constant interest rate. Wickens and Molana (1982) and Muellbauer (1983) both deal with time-dependent interest rates, but their specifications hold only under the assumption of point expectations. All studies except the two last mentioned use seasonally adjusted data (as do Mankiw *et al.*) despite the autocorrelation of residuals that this practice may induce. All of the papers assume separable preferences between consumption and leisure. Hayashi (1982) is the only study to use both data for consumption on non-durables and also the imputed flows from durable goods. Hayashi also uses annual rather than quarterly data for the United States from 1948 to 1978 and concludes that disposable income has some explanatory power in addition to its role in the determination of permanent income. Hayashi interprets his point estimates as implying that 17.1 per cent of the population is liquidity-constrained. In contrast, Hall (1978) used quarterly data for the United States to estimate the linear model discussed above and concluded that lagged values of disposable income were insignificant. He did find, however, that the lagged value of the stock market index had some explanatory power. The papers by Sargent (1978), Flavin (1981) and Muellbauer (1983) all use the additional information that, if labour income follows an autoregressive process, there must be cross-equation restrictions between the innovations in consumption and the stochastic process of income. Flavin corrects Sargent's error in including capital income in his definition of the relevant stochastic process, and concludes that consumption is more sensitive to current income innovations than is implied by the observed autoregressive process for income. This conclusion is conditional on the belief that real interest rates are constant.

As Bernanke (1982) and Wickens and Molana (1982) have pointed out, much of this excess sensitivity of consumption to current income may well be due to the omission of changes in real interest rates. Using data for the UK, Wickens and Molana (1982) found that the Hall model, adjusted for time-varying interest rates, fitted well and provided a good explanation of aggregate consumption. Muellbauer (1983), however, found that, although the basic Hall model fitted quarterly UK data for the period 1955–79 surprisingly well, the model was clearly rejected when it was tested over two subperiods within the postwar period. In a study of the joint behaviour of expenditure on non-durables and durables, Bernanke (1982) found that the life-cycle model could be rejected using quarterly data for the United States. Given the assumptions of quadratic utility and a non-stochastic interest rate, Bernanke found explicit solutions for the behaviour of consumption in terms of lagged consumption and past stocks of durable goods.

Finally, there is the voluminous literature on econometric studies of the Keynesian consumption function, which relates consumption to current and distributed lags of disposable income. Much of this work in recent years has been directed towards exploring the role of inflation in the consumption function; see, for example, Hendry and von Ungern-Sternberg (1980), Davidson *et al.* (1978), Davidson and Hendry (1981), and Pesaran and Evans (1982). These studies confirm that the best forecasting equation for consumption is one that includes variables additional to lagged consumption.

The conclusions we might draw from the studies are as follows. First, if one's main aim is to obtain the best forecast of future consumption, then a rather eclectic view of the appropriate consumption function seems appropriate. Any lagged variable that improves the predictive power could be included, although it is likely that the equation will exhibit parameter instability if the stochastic processes determining the exogenous variables relevant to consumption decisions are changing. But most forecasters are in the habit of re-estimating their equations on a regular basis. Such an approach does not tell us very much about the underlying model of behaviour. For this we need to contrast empirical predictions of competing models. Our analysis of the stochastic life-cycle model with constraints in capital and labour markets suggests that it is unlikely that aggregate data will enable us to distinguish between competing explanations of observed behaviour. The results to be obtained from aggregate models are largely dictated by the two stylized facts mentioned at the beginning of this section. Moreover, very few of the above studies estimated a model based on explicit optimizing behaviour under uncertainty. Nevertheless, it is clear that tests using aggregate data generally support the view that consumption is too sensitive to current income for us to accept the life-cycle model without some modification, such as the introduction of borrowing constraints for at least part of the population.

Studies using household data

In principle, the use of individual micro-data gives us many more observations with which to test the implications of the life-cycle model. It allows us to estimate the proportion of the population for which this model appears relevant. But it draws attention also to two problems that are often overlooked at the aggregate level. First, there is the question of the quality of the data. With the development of econometric techniques it has become increasingly common (if not even fashionable) to use panel data for which we have observations on the same household for several periods. Such data do allow us to test the stochastic life-cycle model using the formulations derived above. This is an advantage over cross-section survey data. But panel data incur problems of attrition as households drop out of the survey, and often the data for later years in the panel are obtained in a less reliable fashion, such as by interviews on the telephone. Some of the cross-section surveys, in contrast, are based on detailed interviews where the respondents are asked to provide documentary evidence of their replies. In assessing the quality of data it is helpful to understand how the data were collected and to adopt an appropriate estimation procedure.

The second problem, sometimes used to justify the use of aggregate data, is that once individual data are used it is difficult to deny the existence of heterogeneous preferences. Where these preference parameters are correlated with observable variables, it may be very hard to identify the model. This problem, however, provides no justification for the use of aggregate data. If preferences are indeed correlated with observable variables, then any aggregate model will exhibit chronic parameter instability. This suggests that models should be formulated in such a way that it is not unreasonable that the preference parameters are assumed to be uncorrelated with the explanatory variables.

Given the wealth of information obtained in micro-data sets, it is often helpful to use this in two ways. The first is to test explicit models such as the stochastic life-cycle model, and the second is to display the correlations between recorded variables in the survey. We shall discuss examples of both. The stochastic life-cycle model relates to the rate of change of consumption. None of the studies using individual household data had access to sufficiently long time-series of changes in consumption of individual households to enable the model to be tested as it has been on aggregate data. But the change in consumption can be related to the innovations in the stochastic process generating incomes; and by estimating these processes one can test the cross-equation restrictions on the innovations in consumption and income implied by the life-cycle model. This was attempted by Hall and Mishkin (1982), who examined data for 2309 families from the University of Michigan's panel study of income dynamics. The measure of consumption was annual expenditure on food used at home and expenditure in restaurants. Data on the rates of change of consumption for five years were available. Hall and Mishkin assumed that labour income consisted of three components: (1) a deterministic component, which was age-dependent; (2) a first stochastic component, which measured changes in lifetime prospects and was assumed to follow a random walk; and (3) a second stochastic component measuring transitory fluctuations and assumed to be described by a moving-average time-series process. They assumed also that the utility function in consumption (but not defined over labour supply) was quadratic and a non-stochastic interest rate equal to the rate of time preference. With these assumptions, the change in consumption is given by the following equation:

$$\Delta C = \epsilon_t + \beta_t \eta_t \tag{4.2}$$

where ϵ_t is the innovation in the first stochastic component and η_t is the innovation in the transitory stochastic component. Because the first stochastic component is assumed to follow a random walk, its innovations will be expected to be permanent and the marginal propensity to consume out of this component will be equal to the marginal propensity to consume out of permanent income. Innovations in the transitory stochastic component will have a much smaller impact on current consumption, and the value of β_t is the annuity value of an innovation in the transitory component. Because this is assumed to follow a moving-average time-series process, the value of β_t depends upon interest rates, expected lifetime and also the parameters of the moving-average process. But it will clearly be less than unity. The variance of changes in consumption will be a function of the variances of the stochastic processes generating income. The ratio of the marginal propensity to consume out of transitory income relative to the marginal propensity to consume out of lifetime income was estimated to be 0.29. Given the estimated moving-average process for income, this estimate would be consistent with life-cycle behaviour only at real interest rates of around 30 per cent. Hence the model appears to be rejected. By augmenting the model to allow for the possibility that a certain fraction of consumption is constrained to be equal to current income, Hall and Mishkin find that about 80 per cent of consumption can be explained by the life-cycle model and 20 per cent appears to be determined by current income. They do not, however, test the more interesting model in which a certain fraction of individuals follow the life-cycle model and the remaining fraction are constrained: instead, the same model is imposed for all individuals. The mixture model proposed above has yet to be tested.

Using the same model for the stochastic processes generating income, Bernanke (1981) found that, for data on expenditures on motor cars of 1434 households, the life-cycle model could be accepted and the test that consumption was constrained by current income was rejected. When integrating the demand for durables with that for non-durables, however, Bernanke (1982) rejected the life-cycle model (although this test used aggregate data).

The studies cited above examined the behaviour of consumption. An alternative approach is to examine the pattern of wealth holdings and their relationship with age in a cross-section of households. An ambitious attempt to estimate the age profile of asset holdings was attempted by Blinder *et al.* (1980) who, assuming perfect certainty and a specific functional form for the additively separable utility function of consumption, estimated the deterministic path for wealth holdings given the individual household's earnings profile. This was obtained using data for 4133 white males from the Longitudinal

Retirement History Survey. The optimizing model implies a very specific nonlinear function of asset holdings over the life cycle, and because of the tight parameterization the model proved hard to estimate with imprecisely determined parameters.

One obvious difficulty with such a model is that there is no reason to believe that optimal behaviour under uncertainty can be proxied by adding a stochastic error term to a model of optimal behaviour under certainty. An example of this is the low rate of decumulation of wealth one would expect to find after retirement in the presence of uncertainty about date of death and an absence of sufficient real annuity markets. Nevertheless, one would expect to find a hump-shaped pattern of wealth holding for a majority of the population if the life-cycle model were an adequate description of their behaviour. The existence of such a pattern has proved hard to find. Lydall (1955), using data from the 1953 Oxford Institute of Statistics Survey, found no tendency for wealth to decline with age, and a similar result was found by Mirer (1979) in the United States for a sample of 2713 couples. But this finding was obtained using a simple regression of wealth on age.

In these studies no attempt was made to control the wealth–age relationship for the effect of differences in permanent income, the amount of wealth held in the form of pension rights, and the fact that the life-cycle model implies a highly nonlinear relationship between the ratio of wealth to permanent income and age. Using data for 12,734 Canadian families in 1977, King and Dicks-Mireaux (1982) found that a hump-shaped profile for asset holdings over the life cycle could be detected even for assets excluding rights to pensions and social security payments. The estimated profile was plotted in figure 4.2 above. There was evidence of decumulation after retirement, although the rate of decumulation is much less than would be predicted by a life-cycle model.

We have commented in section 2 on the possibility that low rates of decumulation can be explained by uncertainty about date of death. We suggested an empirical test to allow for this possibility by estimating separately the wealth and insurance effects of pensions. Slightly higher rates of decumulation, of up to 5 per cent per annum, were found by Diamond and Hausman (1982) in a study based on data from the National Longitudinal Survey of Mature Men.

An interesting observation, common to both the Diamond–Hausman and King–Dicks-Mireaux studies, is the fact that a substantial proportion of the sample reported extremely low levels of asset holdings. Diamond and Hausman (1982) found that 19.7 per cent of the sample reported a net worth below $1000 in 1966, and King and Dicks-Mireaux (1982) found that 23.4 per cent of their sample had a net worth in 1977 of less than C$2500 (a comparable figure, allowing for inflation and the exchange rate). It is conceivable that such low levels of asset holdings are consistent with the life-cycle model if individuals have somewhat higher-than-average rates of time preference and expect to receive pensions comparable to their earnings before retirement. But King and Dicks-Mireaux found no correlation between the incidence of low wealth holdings and the ratio of pensions to permanent income.

Although further study is required, there does seem to be evidence that the population consists of groups with different types of savings behaviour. One question that follows naturally, therefore, is: What are the characteristics that determine whether households behave according to the life-cycle model or according to some other model? King and Dicks-Mireaux found that there was a distinct difference between households who reported a negative net worth and those who reported a positive but low net worth. Those with negative net worth were significantly younger than the rest of the population, and this finding is consistent with the view that young households incur debts, which are recorded in the survey, to purchase relatively expensive durable goods, which are often excluded from such surveys. But households with positive though very low asset holdings were not significantly younger than the rest of the population, although they shared certain characteristics. The households with small amounts of assets were much more likely to have unemployed members or members receiving extremely low levels of current earnings. This is consistent with the view of constraints in labour and capital markets discussed in section 3. Another finding was that, even controlling for the level of permanent income and earnings, education had additional explanatory power in determining whether a household held 'adequate' assets. Households in which the head had received a high level of education were more likely to hold larger amounts of assets. It would probably be unwise to speculate, but there may be something in the view that the ability to manage one's own financial affairs and make provision for retirement is correlated with the level of education.

Low ratios of wealth to permanent income were found also in a study of Japanese data by Shimono and Tachibanaki (1982), who found that for workers with 'lifetime' contracts the ratio of wealth to income at age 55 (the normal age of retirement from the main job in Japan) was on average about 4, whereas for workers employed without such contracts the ratios were significantly lower. Again, there are educational differences between the two groups, and it would be interesting also to model the expected differences in wealth holdings resulting from the different types of labour contracts under which the two operate.

We have contrasted studies that examine either the change in consumption over time or the level of asset holdings over the life cycle. It is also possible to examine the cross-section variations in consumption and its relationship with age. Using data for over 1900 married couples from the Retirement History Survey, Kotlikoff, Spivak and Summers (1982) computed the constant consumption stream between the current age and anticipated age at death that could be financed from current assets and expected future returns. They computed also a constant consumption stream for the entire lifetime of each couple that could be financed from lifetime earnings and pension receipts (using matching records on earnings from the Social Security Earnings File). A comparison of the two consumption streams indicates the ability of households to maintain in retirement a consumption level close to that which could have been financed throughout the entire working life. A substantial proportion of households have ratios of potential constant consumption over remaining lifetime to constant consumption over entire lifetime that are greater than unity. This is adduced as evidence that, given the present social security system in the United States, there is little evidence of inadequate savings for retirement by the aged. Hamermesh (1982) has argued, however, that it may be more appropriate to compare potential consumption during retirement with consumption immediately after retirement. Using this standard, rather than consumption over entire lifetime, he found that many individuals in the Retirement History Survey experienced declines in consumption during retirement. To the extent that it is optimal for consumption to decline in retirement, either because of greater leisure or ill health, this pattern may not be disturbing. It is also the case that the elderly consume the services of durables to a greater extent than those of young households. But further study of the consumption patterns of the retired would throw some light on the issue.

The main conclusion of this section must be that support for the life-cycle model is mixed. The phenomenon worthy of further investigation is the identification of the characteristics that determine whether households are more likely to follow the life-cycle model or an alternative model of savings behaviour. This approach has not as yet been formally modelled, but it appears to be fruitful, and to test it one would like data on individual families for two or three years with emphasis on the quality of the data on incomes, consumption and assets. It would not be inappropriate to sacrifice the length of the panel to improve the quality of the survey responses.

5 BEQUESTS

The introduction of bequests raises a number of important questions which we shall do no more than mention, such as the way in which the bequest motive enters the donor's utility function, the division of legacies among recipients, the timing of gifts and the allocation of expenditures on children's education. But whatever the optimal level of bequests that emerges from these considerations, a potential donor will still allocate consumption over his or her life cycle using the same criteria as analysed in preceding sections. The existence of bequests does not, therefore, alter the first-order conditions determining the rate of change of consumption over the life cycle. It does, however, introduce some new dimensions into the discussion of savings.

If the utility of an individual is defined over the utility level of his heirs, then he belongs to an infinite chain of families. This means that there can be no intergenerational externalities and the existence and size of government debt and social security, whether funded or pay-as-you-go, has no real effect (Barro, 1974, 1978). This is because individuals can alter their bequests so as exactly to offset the intergenerational redistribution implied by policy and to attain the original optimum (although taxes may lead to additional efficiency losses). In this way, private transfers will offset the public transfers implied by debt or social security policy. The result depends, however, on the ability of individuals to reach an interior optimum. If the private transfers required to offset the effects of policy lead to a corner solution (for example, negative bequests may not be feasible), then the neutrality result no longer obtains.

To test the validity of the view that individuals care about the welfare of their descendants, we could examine the empirical significance of the neutrality proposition. There are, however, two problems with this test. First, social security wealth is unobservable, and empirical proxies are subject to the errors-in-variables bias, which will lead to estimated coefficients on social security wealth that may be below their true value. The insignificance of social security wealth in a regression may be the result of errors in measurement rather than the optimal behaviour of an infinitely lived family. Second, the infinitely lived family may behave in exactly the same way as a completely myopic family. The introduction of an unfunded pension scheme would lead pure life-cycle savers to reduce their current saving, and hence social security would depress their capital accumulation. But infinitely lived families would continue to accumulate assets so that future generations would be able to meet the cost of social security schemes. Equally, myopic families would ignore the future entitlements to social security and its introduction would leave savings patterns unaffected. This observational equivalence can be settled only by *a priori* reasoning or alternative empirical tests.

There is a deeper question about whether the decision to give or leave bequests should be regarded as the outcome of an individual optimization or whether we should take into account also the response of the recipient. Kurz (1982) has argued that gifts and bequests should be seen as the outcome of an intergenerational game in which the interdependence in utilities is explicitly recognized and embodied in the appropriate equilibrium concept. One example of such an equilibrium would be a Nash equilibrium in which the bequests of each generation were optimal given the bequests made by all other generations. There are two problems with this view. First, as pointed out by Kurz, the notion of an equilibrium of a game in which most of the players are absent is unclear. Second, there are some difficulties in defining equilibrium for an economy in which bequests play a key role when some families have no heirs (Bewley, 1981).

Viewing bequests as the outcome of an intergenerational game is only one of a number of ways of modelling the phenomenon. For example, we could assume that parents care about their children's opportunities rather than their utility as such, and define parental utility over own consumption and the budget sets of heirs. There is no game-theoretic aspect here, and bequests enter the utility function in a way that depends upon children's talents and endowments. Alternatively, we could view bequests as constituting an inducement for children to spend time with their parents. This approach has been modelled by Bernheim, Shleifer and Summers (1983).

Within a life-cycle framework, the timing of gifts and bequests clearly influences the age profile of asset holdings (Atkinson, 1971). We have no good theory concerning the timing of gifts. Bequests also have implications for the composition of household portfolios. With uncertainty over date of death, savings for post-retirement consumption will be in the form of annuities (if indexed annuities are available), and the riskiness of legacies can be reduced by the purchase of life insurance. Differential mortality rates and the valuation of life insurance are a major problem in interpreting cross-section evidence on wealth-age profiles (Shorrocks, 1975).

In two studies based on data collected for the US President's Commission on pension policy, Kurz (1981, 1982) derived specifications for asset holdings within a life-cycle model and for transfers (whether gifts made or received) in a model of intergenerational equilibrium. Optimal transfers were assumed to be a linear function of current assets, the wage rate, net social security wealth, public transfers and a vector of socioeconomic characteristics. The parameters of the model are shown to be generation-dependent. This causes a problem for empirical work, because in the formal model each generation lives for only two periods, and hence there is no confusion between the age of an individual and his generation. It would appear from the model that the relevant explanatory variables in Kurz's equation should be those for a generation, and hence should be lifetime-equivalent values of assets and the wage rate rather than the values at any particular age.

In principle, we need to distinguish between generational differences in the explanatory variables and differences that result simply because we are observing individuals at different stages of their life cycle. This distinction was not made in the empirical work. Leaving this to one side, Kurz proposes three tests of the model. First, the effect of social security wealth on transfers should be such that any increment to the net social security wealth of a generation will result in an equal increment to transfers to the next generation. Changes in public policy cannot affect the intergenerational equilibrium, as in the Barro model. Second, the structural equation determining transfers should hold at all stages of life and hence should be relevant for both recipients and donors. Third, the effect of social security wealth on private savings should be such that private savings will be unaffected by changes in social security wealth, again leaving the intergenerational equilibrium undisturbed. The results of the first test were inconclusive. The second test led to a rejection of the model of intergenerational equilibrium. The third test, on an equation for asset holdings, led to support for the model. One problem with these results is that they could all be affected by errors in variables if the social security wealth variable is measured with error. This would lead to an unnecessary rejection of the model in the first test and acceptance in the third test.

Despite the difficulties in modelling bequests empirically, it is clear that the subject merits further work at both the theoretical and the empirical level. For some households, although probably a minority, bequests are likely to represent one of the main motives for accumulation of wealth.

6 CONCLUSIONS

We may briefly summarize the findings of the Survey as follows. The literature has drawn a number of false inferences about the relevance of the life-cycle model from empirical studies. We have tried to sort out those empirical tests that would throw light on the issue from those that merely reflect assumptions about the parameterization of preferences. The proposed tests rely on the cross-equation constraints imposed by the life-cycle model (for example, those between consumption and labour supply profiles) and on the way in which constraints should enter the model.

There is an unfortunate tendency for studies based on aggregate data to regard the life-cycle model as one that applies to everyone or no one. In fact, there is a remarkable conformity in the findings using cross-section data, panel data and aggregate time-series data, namely that about 20 or 25 per cent of the population behaves in a way that may well be inconsistent with the life-cycle model, whereas for the rest of the population observed savings behaviour is not inconsistent with the model. The findings of Diamond and Hausman and King and Dicks-Mireaux with cross-section data, the panel study of Hall and Mishkin, and the numerous aggregate time-series studies all produce coefficient estimates that point towards this conclusion. The problem with aggregate data is that we know that the stylized facts are inconsistent with the view that aggregate behaviour can be explained as if it were generated by a representative individual following a life-cycle model (see section 4 above). Hence, studies based on aggregate data are bound to find significant coefficients on some variables which appear to violate the predictions of a pure life-cycle model. But the interesting question is whether these violations are common to all households, or reflect the fact that changes over the business cycle fall disproportionately on a minority of the population. My conjecture is that it will prove fruitful to explore the latter point of view, and the issue is important for policy purposes.

The life-cycle model allows individuals to separate their consumption in any year from their current income. In this framework the stage of the life cycle at which taxes or transfers are levied is a matter of indifference. If individuals are forward-looking but are constrained in any period, then their lifetime welfare cannot be measured by the present value of lifetime endowment. There is a role for policy in either relaxing the constraints or using transfers to compensate for the reduction in the utility that results from the existence of binding constraints. Obviously, unemployment insurance is an example of this type of policy. For individuals who are backward-looking or 'myopic', or whose behaviour is described by an alternative model, there may be scope for paternalistic intervention.

It is important for future empirical work to try to identify the characteristics of individuals who do not follow a life-cycle pattern of behaviour. In theoretical terms, the difficulty is that we need a coherent alternative model to analyse such behaviour. Such a model would need to take into account the following considerations. First, in a life-cycle context there is little possibility of learning by doing (or at least by personal experience). Decisions about retirement and savings for the future cannot be compared with decisions about purchases of breakfast cereal or soap powder. Convergence to rational expectations is a process that depends upon observations of past errors and their incorporation into revised beliefs about the underlying process generating observed data. Over the life cycle it is unlikely that the underlying processes are stationary. Given that those currently retired have experienced at least one major war and can now purchase products that could not have been conceived in their youth, decisions about retirement raise again the old issue of risk versus uncertainty.

A second consideration is that the cost of thinking about the future may well exceed the expected benefit from devoting more time to planning retirement portfolios. This is either because of the complications of decision-making under uncertainty (which may lead to bounded rationality) or because thoughts of the future may imply contemplating unpleasant outcomes such as ill health. The implications of such behaviour for policy are unclear. Paternalistic intervention to help individuals who behave in this way runs the risk that other individuals will, by anticipating the policy response, be able to benefit substantially. Moral hazards of this sort might justify some element of compulsory saving for all individuals, and the analysis of optimal public policy in an economy with different types of savings behaviour appears to be a fruitful topic. Empirical work can make a contribution here by quantifying the relative importance of different models. Just as Friedman's (1957) study of the consumption function evolved out of empirical work on family budgets by Dorothy Brady and Margaret Reid, it is the interplay between empirical findings and theoretical models that is likely to take us a step forward. From this point of view, the aim of empirical work should be less to estimate parameters or obtain the best predictions for the future than to fulfil the hopes of Keynes (1973; 296), in a letter to Roy Harrod, that 'the object of statistical study is not so much to fill in missing variables with a view to prediction as to test the relevance and validity of the model.'

NOTES

I am indebted to numerous colleagues for helpful discussions, but in particular I must thank Tony Atkinson and Nick Stern, my collaborators on the SSRC Research Programme 'Taxation, Incentives and the Distribution of Income', as well as Peter Diamond, John Flemming, Roger Gordon, Mordecai Kurz, Jim Poterba, Agnar Sandmo, Bob Shiller and Larry Summers. The research reported here is part of the NBER's research programme in Taxation and Financial Markets and Monetary Economics and its project in Macroeconomics. Any opinions expressed are those of the author and not those of the National Bureau of Economic Research.

1 For further discussion see Becker (1981) and Deaton and Muellbauer (1980, chapter 8). Tobin (1967) presents simulations based on an explicit life-cycle pattern of family composition.
2 We are abstracting from changes in tax rates. Such changes would mean that the normalization would be appropriate only if the relevant tax rates were introduced explicitly into the model.
3 The fixed effect is the multiplier λ and so must be a function of the parameters of the individual's optimization problem.
4 This is true only if we can assume that all individuals face the same real interest rate. Conversely, if interest rates vary across individuals (because of different marginal tax rates, for example) then the equation could be estimated using micro-data.
5 This assumption is made in all of the recent work on consumption and also in the labour supply study of Heckman and MaCurdy (1980).
6 For a further discussion of the derivation of the indirect utility function from estimated labour supply functions see Hausman (1981a).
7 For the Slutsky condition to hold, the expenditure function corresponding to (2.24) must be concave in the wage rate. This implies that $c(1-L) - b\gamma \exp(-\gamma w) \leqslant 0$. This condition is always satisfied in our simulations, and would be violated only at very high wage rates.
8 Although U is defined only up to a positive monotonic transformation, the cardinalization of v does matter because it determines the intertemporal allocation of total expenditure. The cardinalization assumed in (2.24) and (2.25) was chosen to yield age profiles for labour supply consistent with the empirical evidence cited in the text (see figure 4.1).
9 Although the parameter values have been chosen to replicate observed life-cycle profiles of labour supply and earnings, it is interesting to note that the labour supply function is consistent also with results from cross-section studies. If we take a first-order expansion of the exponential term in equation (2.20), we obtain the linear model of labour supply estimated by Hausman (1981a, b). The coefficient values are remarkably similar. For example, the coefficient on the hourly wage estimated by Hausman was 495.1 compared with 585.0 implied by our parameters. Both the intercept term and the 'income' coefficient are similar, although in our specification 'income' is replaced by the current period's 'full expenditure' on consumption and leisure. This is endogenous to the optimal life-cycle plan. If we include an extra second-order term in the exponential expansion, we obtain the restricted quadratic specification proposed by Stern (1983), in which labour supply is quadratic in the wage but linear in other variables.
10 Stochastic Euler equations in the case of additive separability over time have been derived by LeRoy (1973), Lucas (1978) and Hall (1978), among others.

11 This is because in the dual form there is only a single stochastic Euler equation to be estimated regardless of the number of commodities over which preferences are defined.

12 Constraints at positive quantities of labour supply can be handled in a straightforward manner.

13 The variance of first differences of consumption will, however, differ in the constrained case. Explicit examples can be obtained by using the preference ordering used for the simulation in section 2 for which the virtual wage may be obtained in implicit form. It is easy to confirm that when $r = \rho$ and $w_t = w_{t-1}$, both y_t and C_t follow a random walk in both cases 1 and 4.

14 In the simulations in section 2 we found that a value for c of 0.1 fitted the stylized facts and a similar coefficient was found by Hausman (1981a) for the linear approximation of our nonlinear labour supply function.

15 Of course, many individuals do borrow against future earnings to purchase durable goods such as owner-occupied houses because the durables may be used as collateral. But it is more difficult to borrow for the purpose of consumption of non-durables, and this is another reason for believing that borrowing constraints are likely to be more relevant to those who have suffered substantial falls in earnings, such as the unemployed.

16 Perhaps because it is easier for lenders to monitor announcements or rumours about redundancies (which tend to affect many easily identified individuals) than anticipated returns to work.

REFERENCES

Aaron, H. J. (1982), *Economic Effects of Social Security*, Brookings Institution, Washington DC.

Appelbaum, E. and Harris, R. (1978), 'Imperfect Capital Markets and Life-Cycle Savings', *Canadian Journal of Economics*, **11**, 319–24.

Atkinson, A. B. (1971), 'The Distinction of Wealth and the Individual Life-Cycle', *Oxford Economic Papers*, **23**, 239–54.

Atkinson, A. B. and Sandmo, A. (1980). 'Welfare Implications of the Taxation of Savings', *Economic Journal*, **90**, 529–49.

Auerbach, A. J. and Kotlikoff, L. J. (1981), 'National Savings, Economic Welfare and the Structure of Taxation', National Bureau of Economic Research Working Paper no. 729.

Barbera, S. and Pattanaik, P. K. (1981), 'Rationalizability of Stochastic Choices in Terms of Random Orderings', University of Birmingham (mimeograph).

Barro, R. J. (1974), 'Are Government Bonds Net Wealth?' *Journal of Political Economy*, **82**, 1095–117.

Barro, R. J. (1978), 'The Impact of Social Security on Private Saving: Evidence from the US Time Series', American Enterprise Institute, Washington DC.

Becker, G. S. (1981), *A Treatise on the Family*, Harvard University Press, Cambridge, Mass.

Bernanke, B. (1981), 'Permanent Income, Liquidity, and Expenditure on Automobiles: Evidence from Panel Data', National Bureau of Economic Research Working Paper no. 756 (mimeograph).

Bernanke, B. (1982), 'Adjustment Costs, Durables and Aggregate Consumption', National Bureau of Economic Research Working Paper no. 1038.

Bernheim, B. D., Shleifer, A. and Summers, L. H. (1983), 'The Manipulative Bequest Motive' (mimeograph).

Bewley, T. (1981), 'The Indeterminacy of Interest Rates', Northwestern University Discussion Paper no. 491 (mimeograph).

Blinder, A. S. (1975), 'Distribution Effects and the Aggregate Consumption Function', *Journal of Political Economy*, **83**, 447–75.

Blinder, A. S. (1982), 'Private Pensions and Public Pensions: Theory and Fact', National Bureau of Economic Research Working Paper no. 902.

Blinder, A. S., Gordon, R. H. and Wise, D. E. (1980), 'Life-cycle Savings and Bequests: Cross-sectional Estimates of the Life-cycle Model', National Bureau of Economic Research Working Paper no. 619.

Champernowne, D. G. (1969), *Uncertainty and Estimation in Economics*, vol. 3, Holden-Day, San Francisco.

Courant, P., Gramlich, E. and Laitner, J. (1982), 'A Dynamic Micro-estimate of the Life-cycle Model', presented to the Brookings Institution Conference on Retirement and Aging, Washington, DC (mimeograph).

Davidson, J. E. H. and Hendry, D. F. (1981), 'Interpreting Econometric Evidence: The Behaviour of Consumers' Expenditure in the UK', *European Economic Review*, **15**, 177–92.

Davidson, J. E. H., Hendry, D. F., Srba, F. and Yeo, S. (1978), 'Econometric Modelling of the Aggregate Time-series Relationship Between Consumers' Expenditure and Income in the United Kingdom', *Economic Journal*, **88**, 661–92.

Davies, J. B. (1981), 'Uncertain Lifetime, Consumption and Dissaving in Retirement', *Journal of Political Economy*, **89**, 561–77.

Deaton, A. S. and Muellbauer, J. (1980), *Economics and Consumer Behaviour*, Cambridge University Press.

Diamond, P. A. (1977), 'A Framework for Social Security Analysis', *Journal of Public Economics*, **8**, 275–98.

Diamond, P. A. and Hausman, J. A. (1982), 'Individual Retirement and Savings Behaviour', presented to the NBER/SSRC Conference on Microdata and Public Economics, Oxford.

Dicks-Mireaux, L. and King, M. A. (1984), 'Pension Wealth and Household Savings: Tests of Robustness', *Journal of Public Economics*, **23**, 115–39.

Dolde, W. (1978), 'Capital Markets and the Short-run Behavior of Life-cycle Savers', *Journal of Finance*, **33**, 413–28.

Duesenberry, J. S. (1948), 'Income–Consumption Relations and their Implications', in *Income, Employment and Public Policy, Essays in Honor of Alvin H. Hansen*, W. W. Norton, New York.

Duesenberry, J. S. (1949), *Income, Saving and the Theory of Consumer Behavior*, Harvard University Press, Cambridge, Mass.

Eden, B. and Pakes, A. (1981), 'On Measuring the Variance–Age Profile of Lifetime Earnings', *Review of Economic Studies*, **48**, 385–94.

Fisher, I. (1907), *The Rate of Interest: Its Nature, Determination and Relation to Economic Phenomena*, Macmillan, New York.

Flavin, M. A. (1981), 'The Adjustment of Consumption to Changing Expectations about Future Income', *Journal of Political Economy*, **89**, 974–1009.

Flemming, J. S. (1973), 'The Consumption Function when Capital Markets are Imperfect: The Permanent Income Hypothesis Reconsidered', *Oxford Economic Papers*, **25**, 160–72.

Friedman, M. (1957), *A Theory of the Consumption Function*, Princeton University Press.

Grossman, S. J. and Shiller, R. J. (1981), 'The Determinants of the Variability of Stock Market Prices', *American Economic Review*, **71**, Papers and Proceedings, 222–7.

Hall, R. E. (1978), 'Stochastic Implications of the Life-cycle–Permanent Income Hypothesis: Theory and Evidence', *Journal of Political Economy*, **86**, 971–87.

Hall, R. E. (1981), 'Intertemporal Substitution in Consumption', National Bureau of Economic Research Working Paper no. 720.

Hall, R. E. and Mishkin, F. S. (1982), 'The Sensitivity of Consumption to Transitory Income: Estimates from Panel Data on Households', *Econometrica*, **50**, 461–81.

Hamermesh, D. S. (1982), 'Consumption during Retirement: The Missing Link in the Life Cycle', University of Michigan (mimeograph).

Hansen, L. P. and Sargent, T. J. (1980), 'Formulating and Estimating Dynamic Linear Rational Expectations Models', *Journal of Economic Dynamics and Control*, 2, 7–46.

Hansen, L. P. and Sargent, T. J. (1981), 'Linear Rational Expectations Models for Dynamically Interrelated Variables', Chapter 8 in R. E. Lucas and T. J. Sargent (eds), *Rational Expectations and Econometric Practice*, Allen and Unwin, London.

Hansen, L. P. and Singleton, K. J. (1982), 'Generalized Instrumental Variables Estimation of Nonlinear Rational Expectations Models', *Econometrica*, **50**, 1269–86.

Hart, O. D. (1983), 'Optimal Labour Contracts under Asymmetric Information: An Introduction', *Review of Economic Studies*, **50**, 3–35.

Hausman, J. A. (1981a), 'Exact Consumer's Surplus and Deadweight Loss', *American Economic Review*, **71**, 662–76.

Hausman, J. A. (1981b), 'Labour Supply', in H. J. Aaron and J. A. Pechman (eds), *How Taxes Affect Economic Behaviour*, Brookings Institution, Washington, DC.

Hayashi, F. (1982), 'The Permanent Income Hypothesis: Estimation and Testing by Instrumental Variables', *Journal of Political Economy*, **90**, 895–918.

Heckman, J. J. (1974), 'Life-cycle Consumption and Labour Supply: An Explanation of the Relationship Between Income and Consumption over the Life Cycle', *American Economic Review*, **64**, 188–94.

Heckman, J. J. and MaCurdy, T. E. (1980), 'A Life-cycle Model of Female Labor Supply', *Review of Economic Studies*, **47**, 47–74.

Hendry, D. F. and von Ungern-Sternberg, T. (1980), 'Liquidity and Inflation Effects on Consumers' Expenditure', in A. S. Deaton (ed.), *Essays in the Theory and Measurement of Consumers' Behaviour*, Cambridge University Press.

Hicks, J. R. (1939), *Value and Capital*, Oxford University Press.

Hurd, M. (1971), 'Changes in Wage Rates Between 1959 and 1967', *Review of Economics and Statistics*, **53**, 189–99.

Keynes, J. M. (1936), *The General Theory of Employment, Interest and Money* (page references to *The Collected Writings of John Maynard Keynes*, vol. VII, Macmillan, London).

Keynes, J. M. (1973), *The Collected Writings of John Maynard Keynes*, vol. XIV. *The General Theory and After Part II Defence and Development*, Macmillan, London.

King, M. A. (1980), 'Savings and Taxation', in G. A. Hughes and G. M. Heal (eds), *Public Policy and the Tax System*, Allen and Unwin, London.

King, M. A. and Dicks-Mireaux, L. (1982), 'Asset Holdings and the Life Cycle', *Economic Journal*, **92**, 247–67.

King, M. A. and Fullerton, D. (eds) (1984), *The Taxation of Income from Capital: A Comparative Study of the US, UK, Sweden and West Germany*, Chicago University Press.

Koskela, E. (1978), 'On the Theory of Consumption Function with Borrowing Constraints', *Schweizerische Zeitschrift für Volkswirtschaft und Statistik*, **114**, 739–52.

Kotlikoff, L. J. (1973), 'Taxation and Savings' (mimeograph).

Kotlikoff, L. J., Spivak, A. and Summers, L. H. (1982), 'The Adequacy of Savings', *American Economic Review*, **72**, 1056–69.

Kurz, M. (1981), 'The Life-cycle Hypothesis and the Effects of Social Security and Private Pensions on Family Savings', Stanford University Institute for Mathematical Studies in the Social Sciences, Technical Report no. 335 (revised) (mimeograph).

Kurz, M. (1982), 'Capital Accumulation and the Characteristics of Private Intergenerational Transfers', Stanford University Institute for Mathematical Studies in the Social Sciences, Technical Report no. 364 (mimeograph).

LeRoy, S. F. (1973), 'Risk Aversion and the Martingale Property of Stock Prices', *International Economic Review*, **14**, 436–46.

Levhari, D. and Mirman, L. J. (1977), 'Savings and Consumption with an Uncertain Horizon', *Journal of Political Economy*, **85**, 265–81.

Lucas, R. E. (1978), 'Asset Prices in an Exchange Economy', *Econometrica*, **46**, 1429–45.

Lydall, H. (1955), 'The Life Cycle in Income, Saving and Asset Ownership', *Econometrica*, **23**, 131–50.

MaCurdy, T. E. (1981), 'An Empirical Model of Labor Supply in a Life-cycle Setting', *Journal of Political Economy*, **89**, 1059–85.

Mankiw, N. G., Rotemberg, J. J. and Summers, L. H. (1982), 'Intertemporal Substitution in Macroeconomics', National Bureau of Economic Research Working Paper no. 898.

Mann, N. E. W. (1981), 'A Bibliography of Life-cycle and Related Studies', QSEP Research Report no. 9, McMaster University, Hamilton (mimeograph).

Mincer, J. (1976), 'Progress in Human Capital Analysis of the Distribution of Earnings', in A. B. Atkinson (ed.), *The Personal Distribution of Incomes*, Allen and Unwin, London.

Mirer, T. W. (1979), 'The Wealth–Age Relationship Among the Aged', *American Economic Review*, **69**, 435–43.

Modigliani, F. and Ando, A. (1957), 'Tests of the Life-cycle Hypothesis of Savings', *Bulletin of the Oxford University Institute of Economics and Statistics*, **19**, 99–124.

Modigliani, F. and Brumberg, R. (1954), 'Utility Analysis and the Consumption Function: An Interpretation of Cross-section Data', in K. Kurihara (ed.), *Post-Keynesian Economics*, Rutgers University Press, New Brunswick, NJ.

Muellbauer, J. (1983), 'Surprises in the Consumption Function', *Economic Journal*, Supplement of conference papers.

Muth, J. F. (1960), 'Optimal Properties of Exponentially Weighted Forecasts', *Journal of the American Statistical Association*, **55**, 299–306.

Pesaran, M. H. and Evans, R. A. (1982), 'An Inflation-adjusted Life-cycle Explanation of UK Personal Savings: 1953–80', University of Cambridge (mimeograph).

Psacharopoulos, G. and Layard, R. (1979), 'Human Capital and Earnings: British Evidence and a Critique', *Review of Economic Studies*, **46**, 485–503.

Ramsey, F. P. (1928), 'A Mathematical Theory of Saving', *Economic Journal*, **38**, 543–59.

Sandmo, A. (1970), 'The Effects of Uncertainty on Saving Decisions', *Review of Economic Studies*, **37**, 353–60.

Sandmo, A. (1984), 'The Effects of Taxation on Savings and Risk-taking', in A. J. Auerbach and M. S. Feldstein (eds), *Handbook of Public Economics*, North-Holland, Amsterdam.

Sargent, T. J. (1978), 'Rational Expectations, Econometric Exogeneity and Consumption', *Journal of Political Economy*, **86**, 673–700.

Schumpeter, J. A. (1954), *History of Economic Analysis*, Allen and Unwin, London.

Shefrin, H. M. and Thaler, R. H. (1982), 'A Self-control-based Theory of Personal Saving', Cornell University Working Paper no. 82-12 (mimeograph).

Shiller, R. J. (1981), 'Do Stock Prices Move Too Much to be Justified by Subsequent Changes in Dividends?' *American Economic Review*, **71**, 421–36.

Shimono, K. and Tachibanaki, T. (1982), 'Savings and Life Cycle: A Cohort Analysis', Kyoto University (mimeograph).

Shorrocks, A. F. (1975), 'The Age–Wealth Relationship: A Cross-section and Cohort Analysis', *Review of Economics and Statistics*, **57**, 155–63.

Stern, N. H. (1981), 'Hours of Work in the UK in the 1970s', SSRC Programme on Taxation, Incentives and the Distribution of Income, Discussion Paper no. 15 (mimeograph).

Stern, N. H. (1983), 'On the Specification of Labour Supply Functions', SSRC Programme on Taxation, Incentives and the Distribution of Income, Discussion Paper (mimeograph).

Summers, L. H. (1982), 'Tax Policy, the Rate of Return and Savings', National Bureau of Economic Research Working Paper no. 995.

Thaler, R. H. and Shefrin, H. M. (1981) 'An Economic Theory of Self-control', *Journal of Political Economy*, **89**, 392–406.

Thurow, L. (1969), 'The Optimum Lifetime Distribution of Consumption Expenditure', *American Economic Review*, **59**, 324–30.

Tobin, J. (1967), 'Life-cycle Saving and Balanced Growth', in W. Fellner *et al.*, *Ten Economic Studies in the Tradition of Irving Fisher*, John Wiley, London.

Tversky, A. and Kahneman, D. (1982), 'Judgement under Uncertainty: Heuristics and Biases', chapter 1 in D. Kahneman, P. Slovic and A. Tversky (eds), *Judgement under Uncertainty: Heuristics and Biases*, Cambridge University Press.

USA (1976), *Report of the Consultant Panel on Social Security*, US Government Printing Office, Washington DC.

Wickens, M. R. and Molana, H. (1982), 'Stochastic Life-cycle Theory with Varying Interest Rates and Prices', University of Southampton Discussion Paper, no. 8224 (mimeograph).

Yaari, M. E. (1965), 'Uncertain Lifetime, Life Insurance and the Theory of the Consumer', *Review of Economic Studies*, **32**, 137–50.

Comment

PETER DIAMOND

1 INTRODUCTION

In his survey, Mervyn King has given us three distinct discussions. One is an overview of basic issues in and current approaches to estimating savings behavior. The second is a new simulation of life-cycle accumulation which is compared to Canadian data. The third is a brief peek at existing empirical work.

King's discussion of basic issues is the type of careful, thoughtful, insightful discussion I have come to expect from him. I found nothing there I would disagree with. Naturally, I would have shaped the discussion somewhat differently, putting the stress in different places. I want to begin, then, by recasting the discussion of basic issues in a different shape. King's discussion is built around finding the appropriate maximization problem to describe savings behavior of a large fraction of households, with particular attention to the difficulties of estimation. I want to start with a description of my own savings problems, ignoring the problems that other people might have in estimating the parameters of my utility function. I will then shift to a discussion of the basic empirical questions.

2 OVERVIEW OF BASIC ISSUES

While I have a position with relatively little job uncertainty, I still feel that the uncertainties I face are a major part of my decision process. Among these are the evolution of academic salaries (in general, at MIT, and for me personally to run through the factors I would use to estimate), the development of consulting opportunities, the changes in mandatory retirement, the length of time I will really feel like continuing work (including the risk of disability), the development of my wife's career, the value of the MIT pension plan around the time I retire, the value of the house I own when I next consider moving. All these risks seem important. My 'preferences' also seem highly uncertain. Perhaps uncovered medical expenses and education for my children are the largest single uncertainties.

Now, it is certainly possible that I act as if I maximized a lifetime utility function subject to a known lifetime budget constraint. However, this seems to me implausible – the uncertainties seem too large. While any estimatable model is a simplification, this simplification seems to leave out elements that are too important to have much faith in the predictions of the resulting estimated model, given the usual quality of empirical fit. (That is, no one expects the precision one finds with simple experiments, which could be used to counter the argument of important omitted elements.) Focusing on the certainty model misses my desire for insurance and may get wrong my response to parameter changes. Also implausible is the thought that the preferences for the uncertainty problem that I perceive (or for some certainty approximation) show intertemporal separability. I seem to myself too much a creature of habit. King is far more cautious on this issue, merely claiming to be unaware of any strong independent evidence for separability. One further implausibility is that of an age-invariant static utility function (even in terms of aggregates, not to mention commodity groups). From these differences between my perceived choices and the simple certainty problem, it seems to me unlikely that one can use the certainty model for a good test of the extent to which I am forward looking in my savings behavior, or for a reliable basis for estimating my response to a changed economic environment.

This sojourn into introspection leads me to two conclusions. One is that insuring random income and expenditure streams may be an important part of the workings of the market and an important place for public intervention to achieve an improved allocation. One aspect of improved insurance ought to be a greater ability to borrow against future (random) income, and thus marginal rates of substitution that are more uniform in the economy. The second conclusion is that microeconometric analyses of wealth or savings data seem far more likely to be useful as descriptive statistics of patterns of individual behavior and individual differences than as a successful estimation of a precise maximization problem being solved. That is, the underlying picture of the true maximization problem is more useful as a guide to relevant variables than as a source of a satisfactory explicit simple equation. It seems likely to be better in this case to have an approximate description of the true maximization problem than to have a precise description of the wrong one. Descriptive data can be very important for understanding the economy and forming public policy, so I do not denigrate such empirical efforts by reaching this *a priori* conclusion (which also seems strongly supported by the limited success of empirical studies to date).

I want to continue with the introspection which is natural for a theorist confronted with empirical work. While, as a good economist, I am trying very hard to maximize expected lifetime utility, it is certainly possible that I am doing a poor job. In particular, I may be doing a rotten job of forecasting important future economic variables. The psychological literature that King cites suggests that this is likely and, importantly, may involve systematic biases that are common to many of my fellow would-be optimizers. Perfect foresight (of future social security legislation, for example) is clearly unsatisfactory as part of the estimating framework. Probably, rational expectations is also unsatisfactory. But that must await further work on forecasting and decision-making. Without waiting for the psychological literature to reach its conclusions, one can plausibly look at consumption–age profiles to check the likelihood of an improved allocation from compulsory savings (in addition to the gains from social security from providing insurance against poor life-cycle earnings outcomes). Ideally, one would want pre-social insurance data for a good test, but the question of adequacy of savings seems interesting to explore with recent data.

King discusses another possibility which often seems true of my behavior: that my attempt to do lifetime maximization is complicated by my tendency to spend (and consume) at some times at a rate that is much higher than I wish I had followed when later (or earlier) times are at hand. As modeled by Hellwig (1973), this converts my behavior into a game rather than a maximization problem. I find this plausible, especially when near an ice cream store.

King didn't discuss a third possibility – that I don't maximize and don't optimize in my game with myself but simply follow (perhaps complicated) rules-of-thumb that I have acquired over time. (One could get more sophisticated about the interaction of attempted optimization and rules-of-thumb as in Nelson and Winter, 1982.) I don't think one would do badly by assuming that I let my home equity and pension plan grow and otherwise spend everything I receive. Thus, institutional arrangements may play a large part in determining my savings rate. This still leaves the problem of describing when I switch houses and what I switch to, as well as my labor supply decisions. There may be some empirical validity in the old idea that savings rates are different out of wages and returns to capital (of the same lifetime significance). I don't know of attempts to address this directly. In some circumstances this would contradict behavior describable by maximization subject to a conventional budget constraint. The different relative price and informational implications of changes in wages and capital incomes in an uncertain environment and the probably different preferences of those with capital rather than labor incomes makes this more difficult to test than one might guess at first glance. There may also be some empirical validity in the idea that Marglin (1975) has explored – that spending simply adjusts to income with a lag. At the aggregate level, this leads to the types of equations normally estimated from a Friedman or Modigliani perspective. The idea has not been explored with micro-data which could distinguish these hypotheses.

It is also true that, from time to time, I think about my sons' lifetime prospects. It strikes me as likely that people with different wealths and incomes think about this to differing degrees. Menchik and David (1980) claim to have found very different behavior relative to planned bequests for individuals with different permanent income levels.

I am left with the same conclusions that King reached: first, that direct empirical examination of consumption and leisure is more appropriately regarded 'as a vehicle for research within the life-cycle framework, and not as a test of the framework as such'; second, that it is likely that some noticeable fraction of the population is behaving in ways very different from the standard life-cycle framework – whether this be non-maximizing behavior or substantial concern with bequests. And I am left with the feeling that we are severely limited in the amount we can learn from existing data sources.

Having examined my own savings propensities, I want to turn now to the questions that one might ask of existing data sets. For policy recommendations, one should draw on the most accurate picture one has of the workings of the economy. In chapter 1 above, Aumann has argued that a different prescription is appropriate for theoretical work. It is clear that a different prescription is followed also by most empirical analyses of savings, in that highly inaccurate assumptions are regularly employed as part of estimation. Rather than attempt to fully explain savings, it may be useful to attempt to answer specific questions about savings. In any case, I want to pose a sequence of specific questions as another way of organizing a view of the savings literature.

1 Does the future matter in the determination of current savings? If people come to believe that future social security benefits, interest rates or wages will be different, do they change current savings? It seems implausible that the answer is no.

2 Does the future matter in exactly the same way that the present matters (apart from discounting)? More concretely, do forecasted future wages and pension benefits (or *ex post* realized wages and pension benefits) enter current savings decisions in the same way that current wages do? It seems implausible that the answer is yes, for the reasons I indicated in my introspective musings.

3 Do the differences in impact between present and future variables arise only from uncertainty and the difficulty of borrowing against future income sources? If the expected answer is yes, the research program is to push the conventional optimizing model in the direction of a more detailed description of the economic environment. Even if the expected answer is no, this may still be the best first step in continued research, although it leads naturally to the next question.

4 In what ways do we think the savings decision differs from optimizing choice? For hypotheses to explore, it is natural to look at both the psychological literature and analyses of other economic variables where similar government interventions have been considered, such as product safety. Some pension plans have opt-out provisions. For others, workers must opt in. It is possible that these differently structured questions about savings lead to different levels of pension take-up and different savings levels. (Of course, estimation is difficult unless workers are randomly allocated between these schemes.) It would be good to have particular hypotheses explored as well as simply asking whether individual savings levels 'look' optimal.

Let me define the far future as beginning after the death of the saver. Then we can ask similar questions about the far future.

5 Does the far future matter in the determination of current savings? If people come to believe that taxes will be higher in the far future, do they change current savings? It seems likely that the answer is different for different people and for different future economic variables, depending, perhaps, on the salience and proximity of their impact. It is possible that future variables are not very important for savings and yet that people give a positive weight to bequests rather than a zero weight.

6 Does the far future matter in exactly the same way as the future (except for discounting)? Alternatively, can we think of savings as optimization subject to a single infinite horizon budget constraint? For most people I think the answer is clearly no, with intergenerational transactions depending upon the complications of interpersonal interactions. Given specific models of this single optimization, one can test some implications. With some formulations, adult children and older parents should have the same *ex post* marginal rates of substitution between consumption levels in different years. Yet, I suspect it is common for children to have rising consumption levels while parents have falling ones. This would contradict the model with certain additional hypotheses.

7 How do we think bequest levels are determined, and how do these interact with savings decisions? The diversity of gift and bequest behavior is underlined by Kurz in his discussion to follow. I agree with him that we have barely begun to think seriously about these questions.

In considering savings behavior, it is worth remembering that different policy questions will direct attention to different empirical questions. Simultaneously, bequest attitudes may be important for understanding aggregate wealth accumulation and unimportant for evaluating the need for compulsory savings.

3 SIMULATING SAVINGS

I turn next to King's simulation study. He assumes a particular stationary within-period indirect utility function, intertemporal additivity, a wage profile and a pension system, and simulates the wealth–age profile. He concludes that the simulation is at least crudely similar to the age profile of average asset holdings in Canada that he and Dicks-Mireaux have analyzed. The major deviation is the lower rate of wealth decumulation after retirement in the actual data. He proposes to adjust for this problem by introducing stochastic death. This will correct the 'problem' provided there is sufficient risk aversion. (I feel particular concern about the implausibility of intertemporal separability when considering the relevant magnitude of risk aversion.) Of course, this correction depends on the absence of suitable annuities, suggesting a test of the importance of this mechanism by examining decumulation rates for individuals with different levels of indexed pensions relative to lifetime income. The problem with this approach is that the large differences in indexed annuities, at least in the United States, are related to length of government employment, which is unlikely to be independent of other taste differences.[1]

King does not explore the alternative of reconciling the simulation with the data by assuming that individuals are, at least somewhat, aware of their own life tables.[2] Those with longer life expectancy would dissave more slowly and are a greater fraction of the sample at later ages. With longitudinal data one could examine the importance of this phenomenon.

This comparison of simulation and data averages does not reveal the great variety in dissaving behavior. Using the National Longitudinal Survey, Jerry Hausman and I (Diamond and Hausman, 1984) found that 58 per cent of those retired in both 1966 and 1969 (and with real wealth above $1000 in 1966) decumulated real assets between these two dates. This ignores unindexed pensions, which are a reason for accumulation, and indexed pensions, which should be (approximately) irrelevant. From 1969 to 1971, 51 per cent of retirees had a decrease. From 1971 to 1976, 74 per cent had a decrease. In contrast, for those not retired in both years, the fractions showing decreases were 51, 45 and 70 per cent. While retirees have a somewhat greater propensity to dissave, a more interesting aspect of these numbers is the great spread in behavior[3] and the large differences over different time periods, encompassing different economic conditions. This makes simple summary statistics, such as a single regression coefficient, of limited value for many purposes. In addition to highlighting diversity, use of longitudinal data rather than cross-section data appears to give a different answer to the sign of wealth changes with time for retirees. Hausman and I consistently found a negative coefficient on time since retirement in the different formulations of our wealth accumulation model (Diamond and Hausman, 1980, 1984). This stands in contrast to the cross-section studies cited by Kurz (except for that of Shorrocks, 1975). It is natural to think of the sample selection bias, especially in estate data, as playing a central role in this difference. Part of the difference with estate data is also likely to come from the different populations, since estate data come only from the wealthy, who are likely to behave differently, on average, from the rest of the population.

The theme of diversity in savings behavior is central to King's survey. It is also central to my thinking about savings issues. Recognizing the limitations in survey data, it is still interesting to contemplate the diversity in individual behavior shown in the data. For this purpose, I have reproduced one table from my 1980 study with Hausman relating wealth accumulation from 1966 to 1969 to the wealth level in 1966 (and excluding those with wealth below $1000 in 1966). The data come from the National Longitudinal Survey and are based on a national sample of 45–59-year-olds with over-sampling of blacks. Both accumulation and decumulation are well represented at all wealth levels. (For example, over half those with more than $58,000 in 1966 reported less wealth in 1969.) The same overall diversity appears for alternative pairs of years and division of the population into deciles by permanent income rather than wealth. (Nearly 40 per cent of those with permanent income above $10,400 had less reported wealth in 1969 than in 1966.)

As an example of the importance of recognizing diversity, consider the analysis by Kotlikoff and Summers (1981) of the division of consumption into life-cycle and inheritance-bequest components.[4] They consider a single representative consumer in a steady state. Then, the effect of an inheritance on consumption is strongly affected by the need to leave a bequest that preserves the steady state. For example, there is no effect of inheritance-bequests on consumption if the rate of interest equals the rate of growth. With a diverse population, this strong conclusion disappears. That is, recognizing the realistic growth of new fortunes and the dissipation of old ones, one can have a steady-state distribution of bequests, equality of interest and growth rates and a sizeable impact of inheritances on

TABLE 1 Total wealth 1966, relative to ratio of total wealth 1969 to total wealth 1966 ($ thousands, 1966)

Total wealth 1966		*Ratio of total wealth 1969 to total wealth 1966*											
Frequency *Row %* *Col. %*		*<0.0*	*0.0–0.5*	*0.5–0.75*	*0.75–1.0*	*1.0–1.25*	*1.25–1.50*	*1.50–1.75*	*1.75–2.0*	*2.0–2.50*	*2.50–3.0*	*>3.0*	*Total (%)*
1.0	296	75	77	42	60	35	67	40	53	69	31	156	705
—	.	10.64	10.92	5.96	8.51	4.96	9.50	5.67	7.52	9.79	4.40	22.13	(12.72)
4.0	.	43.35	15.16	7.28	5.67	3.21	8.78	9.35	20.46	25.56	24.80	53.61	
4.0	207	38	64	65	95	109	116	55	44	53	26	48	713
—	.	5.33	8.98	9.12	13.32	15.29	16.27	7.71	6.17	7.43	3.65	6.73	(12.86)
7.3	.	21.97	12.60	11.27	8.98	9.99	15.20	12.85	16.99	19.63	20.80	16.49	
7.3	244	29	57	84	111	161	110	70	32	29	15	23	721
—	.	4.02	7.91	11.65	15.40	22.33	15.26	9.71	4.44	4.02	2.08	3.19	(13.01)
10.9	.	16.76	11.22	14.56	10.49	14.76	14.42	16.36	12.36	10.74	12.00	7.90	
10.9	242	12	68	71	142	152	113	64	27	44	17	9	719
—	.	1.67	9.46	9.87	19.75	21.14	15.72	8.90	3.76	6.12	2.36	1.25	(12.97)
15.0	.	6.94	13.39	12.31	13.42	13.93	14.81	14.95	10.42	16.30	13.60	3.09	
15.0	258	6	62	57	142	146	123	81	27	24	3	16	687
—	.	0.87	9.02	8.30	20.67	21.25	17.90	11.79	3.93	3.49	0.44	2.33	(12.39)
21.3	.	3.47	12.20	9.88	13.42	13.38	16.12	18.93	10.42	8.89	2.40	5.50	
21.3	275	0	44	90	152	169	111	46	32	24	6	6	680
—	.	0.00	6.47	13.24	22.35	24.85	16.32	6.76	4.71	3.53	0.88	0.88	(12.27)
31.2	.	0.00	8.66	15.60	14.37	15.49	14.55	10.75	12.36	8.89	4.80	2.06	
31.2	277	7	51	72	190	174	77	27	26	24	12	18	678
—	.	1.03	7.52	10.62	28.02	25.66	11.36	3.98	3.83	3.54	1.77	2.65	(12.23)
58.0	.	4.05	10.04	12.48	17.96	15.95	10.09	6.31	10.04	8.89	9.60	6.19	
	313	6	85	96	166	145	46	45	18	3	15	15	640
>58.0	.	0.94	13.28	15.00	25.94	22.66	7.19	7.03	2.81	0.47	2.34	2.34	(11.55)
	.	3.47	16.73	16.64	15.69	13.29	6.03	10.51	6.95	1.11	12.00	5.15	
Total (%)	.	173	508	577	1058	1091	763	428	259	270	125	291	5543
	.	(3.12)	(9.16)	(10.41)	(19.09)	(19.68)	(13.77)	(7.72)	(4.87)	(4.87)	(2.26)	(5.25)	(100.00)

consumption. Such a model could be built with either planned or unintended bequests.[5]

This rejection of the interpretation by Kotlikoff and Summers of the particular numbers they calculated does not lead me to reject the idea that the very wealthy are important in aggregate wealth accumulation and that they are likely to be concerned with future uses of their wealth. (One could apply a life-cycle model even here, once one recognizes that the marginal utility of consumption can reach zero and that work and accumulation can have positive utility for their own sakes. Thus, even the people leaving very large estates are not necessarily forward-looking beyond their own lifetimes, although a standard life-cycle model will not fit their behavior.)

4 EMPIRICAL STUDIES

I come, third, to existing empirical studies, and here I am disappointed with King's survey. In cautious terms King cites the results claimed by different authors without telling us the extent to which he believes in them. I wish he had been more forthcoming. In section 4, King mentions 14 studies using aggregate data and ten studies using household data. It would be a tall order to have a detailed critique of all these different papers to help us conclude what to believe; it would be nice to have some details, however, For example, referring to Hall and Mishkin (1982), King says that the model appears to be rejected and that 20 per cent of consumption appears to be determined by current income. On the other hand, he tells us that, using the same model for automobiles instead of food, Bernanke (1981) found that the life-cycle model would be accepted and the test that consumption was constrained by current income was rejected. Is this just the difference between food and cars? Or are there other differences? I wish King had told us what he thinks.

King tells us that Kotlikoff, Spivack and Summers (1982) find an ability of households to maintain in retirement a consumption level close to that which could have been financed throughout their entire working life and conclude that there is little evidence of inadequate savings for retirement by the aged with current social security levels. Hamermesh (1982b) prefers to compare potential retirement consumption with actual consumption immediately after retirement and finds that many people cannot sustain their consumption level. Moreover, in the follow-up survey he finds many with declining consumption. Are these just two satisfactory answers to two different questions, or should one have doubts about one or both findings? Again, King doesn't tell us what he thinks. More generally, I wish we had more neutral evaluations of empirical results to complement existing debates in the literature.

Despite my disappointment here, I find this paper an admirable survey and recognize the immensity of the work involved in producing the survey I would like to see. King brings out very nicely the need to reshape the questions being asked and points to several ways of addressing them. Also, I agree with his central conclusion: that the world is complicated and diverse and that empirical studies should reflect this. I am grateful for the opportunity of reading his paper.

NOTES

1 The current lack of private indexed annuities in the United States can be interpreted as a lack of demand, and so support for the importance of bequest motives. Given the difficulties of marketing, ease of imitation, difficulties of intertemporal pooling, and career risk aversion of insurance executives, I do not find the non-existence of an indexed annuity market to be necessarily supportive of a lack of demand. A simple test of the alternative hypothesis of supply difficulties will be the developments after the appearance of federal indexed debt, should that ever happen. I would expect to see a sizeable growth, in time, of indexed annuities.

2 This possibility has been explored by Hamermesh (1982a).

3 Those reporting a doubling of real wealth were 11, 9 and 6 per cent of retirees for the three time periods and 10, 10 and 6 per cent for non-retirees.

4 For a detailed critique of the quantitative findings of Kotlikoff and Summers see Modigliani (1983).

5 For example, if bequests are unintended and inheritances are completely consumed in the ritual marking death, there is no effect of inheritances on savings. More strongly, consumption could rise in anticipation of inheritances, implying that the capital stock would be larger if the government confiscated and instantly spent all estates.

REFERENCES

Bernanke, B. (1981), 'Permanent Income, Liquidity, and Expenditure on Automobiles: Evidence from Panel Data,' National Bureau of Economic Research, Working Paper no. 756.

Darby, M. (1979), 'Effects of Social Security on Income and the Capital Stock,' American Enterprise Institute, Washington.

Diamond, P. and Hausman, J. (1980), 'Individual Savings Behavior,' Report to the National Commission on Social Security.

Diamond, P. and Hausman, J. (1984), 'Individual Retirement and Savings Behavior,' *Journal of Public Economics*, **23**, 81–114.

Hall, R. and Mishkin, F. (1982), 'The Sensitivity of Consumption to Transitory Income: Estimates from Panel Data on Households,' *Econometrica*, **50**, 461–81.

Hamermesh, D. (1982a), 'Expectations, Life Expectancy, and Economic Behavior,' National Bureau of Economic Research, Working Paper no. 835.

Hamermesh, D. (1982b), 'Consumption During Retirement: The Missing Link in the Life Cycle,' University of Michigan (mimeograph).

Hellwig, M. (1973), 'Sequential Models in Economic Dynamics,' PhD dissertation, Massachusetts Institute of Technology.

Kotlikoff, L., Spivack, A. and Summers, L. (1982), 'The Adequacy of Savings,' *American Economic Review*, **72**, 1056–69.

Kotlikoff, L. and Summers, L. (1981), 'The Role of Intergenerational Transfers in Aggregate Capital Accumulation,' *Journal of Political Economy*, **89**, 706–32.

Marglin, S. (1975), 'What Do Bosses Do, II,' *Review of Radical Political Economics*, **7**, 20–7.

Menchik, P. and David, M. (1980), 'The Effect of Income Distribution and Redistribution on Lifetime Savings and Bequests,' NBER Conference Paper no. 58.

Modigliani, F. (1983), 'The Life-cycle Hypothesis and National Wealth – A Rehabilitation' (unpublished paper).

Nelson, R. R. and Winter, S. G. (1982), *An Evolutionary Theory of Economic Change*, Harvard University Press, Cambridge, Mass., and London.

Shorrocks, A. F. (1975), 'The Age–Wealth Relationship: A Cross-section and Cohort Analysis,' *Review of Economics and Statistics*, **57**, 155–63.

Heterogeneity In Savings Behavior A Comment

MORDECAI KURZ

The life-cycle and permanent income hypotheses were developed by Modigliani and Brumberg (1954), Ando and Modigliani (1963) and Friedman (1957) in response to the Keynesian consumption function. In the initial debate it was argued that the Keynesian consuming household is far too responsive to current income while ignoring the possibility of establishing its optimal long-term consumption pattern based on its wealth. In his comprehensive review, Professor King continues to draw the line by proposing that the distinctive characteristic of the life-cycle model is that individual behavior is what he calls 'forward-looking,' as distinct from the Keynesian household, which is myopic. Unfortunately, the concept of 'forward-looking' is so imprecise that the paper contains a confusion with regard to the relationship between the life-cycle hypothesis and the bequest motive. In my view the clarification of this issue is essential to the understanding of the modern debate about savings behavior. I will therefore present some basic concepts to enable a rigorous discussion of the issue.

1 THE LIFE-CYCLE AND THE INTERGENERATIONAL HYPOTHESES

To define a model analogous to King's equations (2.1)–(2.2), I assume that generations are born at time $t = jT$ where j are integers. A member of generation t lives for T periods, at the end of which an offspring arrives who is a member of generation $(t + T)$, which is the date at which he starts economic activity. I now introduce the following notation:

C_τ^t = consumption of a member of generation t at time τ

$\mathbf{C}_t = (C_t^t, C_{t+1}^t, \ldots, C_{t+T-1}^t)$

L_τ^t = labor input of a member of generation t at time τ
$\mathbf{L}_t$ = $(L_t^t, L_{t+1}^t, \ldots, L_{t+T-1}^t)$
$\mathbf{Z}_t$ = $(\mathbf{C}_t, \mathbf{L}_t)$
T = length of life of each generation
A_t = initial wealth of a member of generation t
B_{t+T} = bequest of a member of generation t at time $(t+T)$
W_t = the wage rate at time t
r_t = the interest rate at time t
R_τ^t = $\prod_{x=\tau}^{t+T} (1+r_x), t \leqslant \tau \leqslant t+T$

The life-cycle hypothesis as presented by King amounts to specifying the utility function of generation t as

$$U_t(\mathbf{C}_t, \mathbf{L}_t, B_{t+T}) \tag{1a}$$

and the behavioral assumption that individuals select $(\mathbf{C}_t, \mathbf{L}_t, B_{t+T})$ so as to maximize (1a) subject to the budget constraint as

$$B_{t+T} = A_t R_t^t + \sum_{\tau=t}^{t+T-1} (W_\tau L_\tau^t - C_\tau) R_\tau^t. \tag{1b}$$

The *intergenerational hypothesis*, to which I turn next, rejects the myopic view of the life-cycle hypothesis. The intergenerational hypothesis starts from the proposition that the welfare of the children influences the utility level of the parents. To understand the well-known difficulties caused by this interdependence, note that one may express it in the following recursive form:

$$u_t = U_t(\mathbf{C}_t, \mathbf{L}_t, U_{t+T}, U_{t+2T}, \ldots, U_{t+kT}). \tag{2}$$

It is common to interpret the primitive function $U_t(\cdot)$ as the utility 'function' of generation t. However, one can iterate relation (2) such that, for each sequence of functions $U_t(\cdot)$, there exists a sequence of functionals $\hat{U}_t$ defined over the infinite dimensional vectors

$$(C^t, L^t) = [(\mathbf{C}_t, \mathbf{L}_t), (\mathbf{C}_{t+T}, \mathbf{L}_{t+T}), \ldots]$$

such that, for each (C^t, L^t), the functions u_t satisfy the equality

$$u_t = \hat{U}_t(C^t, L^t). \tag{3}$$

Since $\mathbf{Z}_t = (\mathbf{C}_t, \mathbf{L}_t)$, we write $(C^t, L^t) = (\mathbf{Z}_t, \mathbf{Z}_{t+T}, \ldots)$; and in the separable example of

$$U_t(\mathbf{Z}_t, u_{t+T}) = v_t(\mathbf{Z}_t) + \left(\frac{1}{1+\rho}\right)^T u_{t+T} \tag{4a}$$

it is clear that (2) implies

$$\hat{U}_t = \sum_{j=0}^{\infty} \left(\frac{1}{1+\rho}\right)^{jT} v_{t+jT}(\mathbf{Z}_{t+jT}). \tag{4b}$$

One may think of the sequence of generations as playing a game where each generation selects a strategy pair $(\mathbf{Z}_t, B_t)$ subject to the budget constraint (1b). The outcome is a sequence of vectors (C^t, L^t) and payoffs $\hat{U}_t(C^t, L^t)$. What is peculiar to this game is not the fact that there are an infinite number of players but rather that, under the conditions $\mathbf{Z}_t \geqslant 0$, $B_t \geqslant 0$, the *strategy* of each generation determines the *strategy set* of the next generation. This makes it inconvenient to work with the complex payoff function $\hat{U}_t(C^t, L^t)$, and for this reason I introduce the indirect utility function $V_t(A_t)$. This function is defined as the maximal utility attained by t given that he starts with assets A_t and given that generation $t + jT$ attains maximal utility starting from A_{t+jT} where the relationship between A_{t+jT} and $A_{t+(j+1)T}$ is defined by

$$A_{t+(j+1)T} = A_{t+jT} R_{t+jT}^{t+jT} + \sum_{\tau=t+jT}^{t+(j+1)T-1} (W_\tau L_\tau^{t+jT} - C_\tau^{t+jT}) R_\tau^{t+jt}. \tag{1b}$$

Given the functions $V_{t+jT}(A_{t+jT})$, one can identify the intergenerational hypothesis with the household maximization problem

$$V_t(A_t) = \max_{(\mathbf{Z}_t, B_{t+T})} U_t[\mathbf{Z}_t, V_{t+T}(B_{t+T}), V_{t+2T}(A_{t+2T}), \ldots, V_{t+kT}(A_{t+kT})] \tag{5}$$

subject to the budget constraint (1b). I shall now define an equilibrium concept that corresponds to this optimization problem.

An *intergenerational equilibrium* consists of a sequence of strategies $(\mathbf{Z}_t^*, B_{t+T}^*)$ and indirect utility functions $V_{t+jT}(\cdot)$ such that, for $t = mT$ (m integers),

(i) $V_t(A_t^*) = U_t[\mathbf{Z}_t^*, V_{t+T}(B_{t+T}^*), V_{t+2T}(A_{t+2T}^*), \ldots, V_{t+kT}(A_{t+kT}^*)]$

$$\text{(ii)}\quad B^*_{t+T} = A^*_t R^t_t + \sum_{\tau=t}^{t+T-1} (W_\tau L^{*t}_\tau - C^{*t}_\tau) R^t_\tau$$

$$\text{(iii)}\quad A^*_{t+(j+1)T} = A^*_{t+jT} R^{t+jT}_{t+jT} + \\ + \sum_{\tau=t+jT}^{t+(j+1)T-1} [W_\tau L^{*(t+jT)}_\tau - C^{*(t+jT)}] R^{t+jT}_\tau .$$

A useful insight may be gained by defining $(\hat{C}^t, \hat{L}^t)$ to be the optimal solution, by generation t, of maximizing $\hat{U}_t(C^t, L^t)$ subject to the infinite horizon budget constraint

$$A_t = \sum_{j=0}^{\infty} \sum_{\tau=t+jT}^{t+(j+1)T-1} \frac{C^{t+jT}_\tau - W_\tau L^{t+jT}_\tau}{\prod_{x=t}^{\tau} (1+r_x)} . \tag{7}$$

Here, members of generation t select an optimal plan for themselves and for all future generations. The difference between the equilibrium vectors (C^{*t}, L^{*t}) and the optimal solution – from the point of view of t – is what generation t perceives to be the 'loss' arising from the fact that members of t cannot control the consumption levels of their children. Now, we shall say that an equilibrium is *generationally consistent* (in short, *consistent*) if $(C^{*t}, L^{*t}) = (\hat{C}^t, \hat{L}^t)$ for all t. It is said to be *generationally inconsistent* (in short, *inconsistent*) if, for some t, $(C^{*t}, L^{*t}) \neq (\hat{C}^t, \hat{L}^t)$. A consistent equilibrium entails no essential intergenerational conflict and is reduced to a simple maximization, by any generation, on behalf of all future generations. I mention without proof the following two examples that have been used in the literature. In the case of a utility function such as

$$u_t = U_t(\mathbf{C}_t, \mathbf{L}_t, u_{t+1}) \tag{8a}$$

all Nash equilibria are consistent, while in case of a utility function such as

$$u_t = U_t(\mathbf{C}_t, \mathbf{L}_t, \mathbf{C}_{t+T}, \mathbf{L}_{t+T}) \tag{8b}$$

all Nash equilibria are inconsistent. In (8b) one assumes that a bequest by generation t is desired only to the extent that it results in consumption of the immediate children.

I remark that intergenerational equilibria have received extensive attention in recent years. Phelps and Pollak (1968), Phelps (1975),

Peleg and Yaari (1973), Kohlberg (1976) and Goldman (1980) are concerned with existence and multiplicity of equilibria. Lane and Mitra (1981) examine the efficiency properties of an economy without a starting date. Loury (1981) examines the equilibrium transfer of human capital in a consistent equilibrium, and Sheshinski and Wise (1981) examine optimal social security under similar conditions. Bernheim and Ray (1983) provide an existence proof for the inconsistent case induced by the utility function (8b); their proof explains a particularly disturbing example due to Kohlberg (1976).

2 FORWARD-LOOKING CONSUMERS AND THE LIFE-CYCLE HYPOTHESIS

Considering the lifespan as extending over T periods, it should be clear that both the life cycle and the intergenerational hypothesis imply a 'forward-looking' consumer: at time 0 each household selects a lifetim consumption and bequest plan that maximizes lifetime utility. In the case of a consistent equilibrium, consumers may be thought of as maximizing over infinite number of periods. Thus, when Professor King writes his utility function in the questionable form of $U_t(\mathbf{Z}_t, B_t)$, he makes no distinction between bequests to one's own children and donations to charitable institutions, both of which should be viewed as a form of consumption. This is a faulty procedure, since a properly formulated theory of bequest imposes additional restrictions which are not recognized by Professor King. More specifically, if one maximizes the function $U_t(\mathbf{Z}_t, B_t)$ subject to the budget constraint (1b), one obtains the standard $2T$ optimality conditions:

$$\frac{\partial U_t}{\partial C_\tau^t}\Big/\frac{\partial U_t}{\partial B_{t+T}} = R_\tau^t \qquad t \leqslant \tau \leqslant t+T \tag{9a}$$

$$\frac{\partial U_t}{\partial L_\tau^t}\Big/\frac{\partial U_t}{\partial B_{t+T}} = -W_0 R_\tau^t \qquad t \leqslant \tau \leqslant t+T. \tag{9b}$$

Under the intergenerational hypothesis as stated in (5), consumer optimization implies the following similar, $2T$ optimality conditions:

$$\frac{\partial U_t}{\partial C_\tau^t}\Big/\frac{\partial U_t}{\partial V_{t+T}}\frac{\partial V_{t+T}}{\partial B_{t+T}} = R_\tau^t \qquad t \leqslant \tau \leqslant t+T \tag{10a}$$

$$\frac{\partial U_t}{\partial L_\tau^t} \Bigg/ \frac{\partial U_t}{\partial V_{t+T}} \frac{\partial V_{t+T}}{\partial B_{t+T}} = -W_\tau R_\tau^t \qquad t \leqslant \tau \leqslant t+T. \tag{10b}$$

However, from the conditions of Nash equilibrium, and using the envelope theorem, we deduce the additional condition

$$V_t'(A_t) = \sum_{j=1}^{k} \frac{\partial U_t}{\partial V_{t+jT}} V_{t+jT}'(A_{t+jT}) R_{t+(j-1)T}^{t+(j-1)T}. \tag{11}$$

This is the additional restriction on the data that is implied by the intergenerational hypothesis. In the case $k = 1$ condition (11) takes the more transparent form

$$\frac{V_t'(A_t)}{V_{t+T}'(A_{t+T})} = \frac{\partial U_t}{\partial V_{t+T}} \prod_{\tau=t}^{t+T} (1+r_\tau). \tag{11a}$$

I note that, mechanically speaking, one may think of the utility function in (5) as depending upon B_{t+T} and to that extent it looks similar to (1a). However, this is misleading, since in an intergenerational equilibrium generation t selects $\mathbf{Z}_t$ and B_{t+T} in response to what they expect subsequent generations to do. Thus, for example, future interest rates and future wage rates, which influence future generations, also influence the choices made by generation t. This optimality is embodied in condition (11) and is absent from the life-cycle hypothesis. For this reason I suggest that the only meaningful way of writing the utility function under the life-cycle hypothesis is simply

$$U[(C_1, C_2, C_3, \ldots, C_T), (L_1, L_2, \ldots, L_T)] \tag{12}$$

where $(C_1, C_2, \ldots, C_T)$ is a vector of lifetime consumptions. Among the components of C_τ there may be some items like charitable contributions, which enhance the welfare of the donor but imply no intergenerational restrictions on behavior. It is interesting that, when he discusses the wealth profile of consumers under the life-cycle model, Professor King adopts the utility function (12) (without bequest) as a basis for the discussion.

This leads me to the conclusion that, contrary to Professor King's characterization of the debate between a myopic Keynesian model and a forward-looking, life-cycle model, we have at hand at least three different models of behavior. Professor King reviews extensively the debate between the Keynesian and the life-cycle models, but after concluding (in section 2) that the empirical tests of the life-cycle model based on his equation (2.16) were not satisfactory, he turns to the examination of the age–wealth profile. However, examination of this profile is one important way of testing the life cycle against the intergenerational hypothesis rather than the Keynesian model. Professor King's review shows that either accumulation or slow decumulation at old age is in conflict with the life-cycle hypothesis. His argument regarding the demand for wealth at old age as a form of insurance against the stochastic date of death is totally unsatisfactory. Had the demand for such insurance been extensive, we would expect to see older people turning in their wealth in exchange for annuities; the evidence seems to be rather clear that there is very little private demand for this form of insurance.

This discussion brings up the fact that the debate between the life-cycle and the intergenerational hypotheses has been as heated as the one between the Keynesian and the life-cycle models. Moreover, the policy implications of this debate are rather drastic with respect to the effects of such social institutions as social security, corporate pensions and the public debt on household consumption. This debate, which has taken place over the last ten years, received no treatment in Professor King's exposition. Since it is my view that this material is crucial for our evaluation of the state of the science in this field, I will undertake to review the state of the evidence.

3 THE EXTENDED FAMILY AND THE INTERGENERATIONAL HYPOTHESIS

The economics and sociology of the extended family are not a heavily studied subject by economists who are interested in the social security system. Yet it is this area in which the system has had its most dramatic and visible effects. In the time before social security, the extended family provided the framework for the intergenerational equilibrium in which income security was granted to the elderly and was to be provided by the young. Equally so, the equilibrium specified the intergenerational transfers of capital from the old to the young. (On the family insurance see also Kotlikoff and Spivak, 1981.) The emergence of the institution of social security removed significant components of the private insurance contract from the realm of the family and placed it in the public domain. Both the compulsory nature of social security and the fact that the provision of the insurance was taken over by the public sector permanently changed the extended family. This change is profound, and we need to examine it a bit closer.

Within the traditional extended family, which still exists in many parts of the world, an age-dependent division of labor exists in which children, adults and the elderly participate and are compensated. Members of the family often live in close proximity and very frequently share the same dwelling. With the limited availability of schooling, the elderly often fulfilled an important function of education and child care. Naturally, the compensation to any member is not equated to his contribution *at that time*, but reflects the earlier defined intergenerational equilibrium which species the obligations and compensations of each member. As formulated by Barro (1974, 1978), the intergenerational hypothesis predicts that any action by the social security system will be neutralized by the private transfer system, and thus social security should be viewed as nothing but a mechanical rearrangement of the resources used by the underlying private intergenerational system. It then follows that social security should have absolutely no effect on any dimension of the traditional structure of the extended family, the division of labor within it, the location of its members, the life-style of the elderly, etc.

In my opinion the most important case against the intergenerational hypothesis is the ample evidence that social security has had a profound influence on the relationship between young and old in our society, on the sense of self-esteem of the elderly, on the retirement age, on the mobility of the aged and on such diverse phenomena as the consumption pattern, nutrition and health care of the aged as well as the social interaction among the elderly in our society.

4 SOCIAL SECURITY AND LIFE-CYCLE SAVINGS: THE EVIDENCE

I will review the evidence gathered using aggregate time-series data and cross-section data, but will not examine the cross-country comparisons.

The time-series evidence

Although interest in social security has been active for a long time, there is little doubt that it was Feldstein's (1974) seminal paper that generated the first widespread scientific debate of the issue. His analysis was based on an aggregate time-series analysis in which an aggregate, Ando–Modigliani (1963)-type life-cycle savings function was formulated. The estimates of this equation lead to the conclusion that the net unfunded benefits of the social security system have, in fact, had a strong negative effect on the aggregate level of private savings. In attempting to implement the rational forecasts of the intergenerational hypothesis, Barro (1978) changed the specifications of Feldstein's equation to introduce variables that would reflect such future tax forecasts. Barro showed that after introducing these small changes the effect estimated by Feldstein disappeared. Feldstein's reply (1978) to Barro was followed by a discovery by Leimer and Lesnoy (1982) that the original Feldstein paper contained serious computational errors. These discoveries led to an extensive examination by Feldstein (1980, 1982) and Lesnoy and Leimer (1981) of alternative specifications of the model, as well as different measures of social security wealth and the period of estimation.

I believe that the professional concensus at this time holds that Feldstein's original claims have not been substantiated. In addition, and perhaps more important, it is the common view that the aggregate time-series data do not contain adequate information about the effect of social security on savings, and that the aggregate time-series methodology is insufficiently fine-tuned to exploit the little information available in the data. Given this conclusion, there is little hope for important results from aggregate time-series analysis.

As for the substantive issue of the two competing hypotheses, the rejection of the life-cycle hypothesis and its conclusions as formulated by Feldstein should not necessarily be taken as a substantiation of the intergenerational hypothesis, since other hypotheses may explain the data.

The cross-section evidence

I start by noting that all cross-section studies face serious methodological difficulties. I shall briefly review some of them. First are the limited micro-data files that are avilable to estimate the parameters of either a life-cycle model or a family optimization model based on the intergenerational hypothesis. Each data base has some crucial component missing; none has an adequately long history of family labor and private intergenerational transfers. No set of data has a complete record of household assets that include social security entitlements and private pensions wealth. Second, most studies use data at a single point in time and treat social security wealth as an exogenous variable. The methodological defect of this approach is the simple fact that, in a fully dynamic model with correct forecasts of future variables, social security wealth is an endogenous variable, and hence an estimation based on a point in time treating social security wealth as exogenous is likely to lead to biased estimates. This point was demonstrated in a simulation model by Auerbach and Kotlikoff (1981). A constructive interpretation of the point-in-time cross-section models would view them as representing updating models with errors in forecasts: at any moment of time, past variables are taken to be exogenous and an updated decision rule is adopted. One must keep in mind that in such a case the interpretation of cross-section results is rather subtle.

A third methodological difficulty was raised by Barro (1978: 36fn). It relates to the interpretation of a negative coefficient of social security wealth in a cross-section study. Barro claims that the response of each family depends upon its perception of how the social security deficit will affect its own budget equation, in the intergenerational sense, which includes future taxes and benefits to all subsequent generations. Barro assumes that all households have identically the same view of the future. Moreover, if the average *net* social security wealth of family j is ssw_j, then the family expects that the future burden of social security taxes on subsequent generations will amount to the mean value, ssw. Barro then concludes that the differences $(ssw_j - ssw)$ constitute true permanent windfall gains or losses to the members of the present generation. This implies that a negative coefficient of a social security wealth variable does not test the intergenerational hypothesis but rather reflects the negative income effect of a windfall on savings – a result well known from the study of the consumption function.

Turning now to the studies available, I remark that the number of cross-section studies in this area of research has been growing rapidly.

A sample of such studies would include Munnell (1976), Feldstein and Pellechio (1979), Kotlikoff (1979), Blinder, Gordon and Wise (1980), Kurz (1981, 1984), King and Dicks-Mireaux (1982), David and Menchik (1982b) and Auerbach and Kotlikoff (1981). Keeping in mind the methodological problems stated above, I think that the most important conclusion that is drawn by almost all the studies is that the life-cycle hypothesis does not provide an adequate framework to explain the data of household accumulation, and to that extent it does not, by itself, provide a satisfactory basis for a theory of savings. Similarly, in almost all studies the estimated effects of social security wealth on personal savings appear to be negative and sometimes statistically significantly different from zero. However, it is universally much smaller than would be anticipated under the life-cycle hypothesis.

Social security and savings after retirement

In section 6 below I shall refer to some important studies of the age–wealth profile which provide additional tests of the life-cycle hypothesis. This is also a central point in Professor King's review. At this point I mention only that these studies provide ample evidence that extensive saving does take place after retirement, and thus capital accumulation continues even during a period in which, according to the life-cycle hypothesis, rapid decumulation should take place. This phenomenon is supported by some micro-cross-section data files as well. Of particular interest is the study by David and Menchik (1984b), which uses a sample of Wisconsin males born between 1890 and 1899. The authors obtained the income tax records as well as the social security records and matched them with the probate court records. This sample is unusual in that it contains a large fraction of persons who never became eligible for social security, and for this reason an adequate exogenous variability in social security entitlement is available in the data. Although the sample is restricted to a specific age group in Wisconsin, the available data are very rich.

David and Menchik present two clear conclusions. First, no decumulation is detected after retirement, and, although statistically insignificant, the effects of age on accumulation remains positive, indicating the continuation of accumulation after retirement. Second, social security has a positive but statistically insignificant effect on accumulation. In addition, the authors estimate that an increase in the present value of social security wealth has the effect of *increasing the discounted value of bequest*, although this effect is neither very strong nor statistically significant. These conclusions contradict both the life-cycle and the intergenerational hypotheses: the life-cycle hypothesis is violated since no decumulation takes place and social security wealth does not appear as a substitute for private accumulation; the intergenerational hypothesis is not upheld since social security eligibility should have a significantly positive effect on bequest and no such effect could be established.

5 THE INTERGENERATIONAL HYPOTHESIS: THE EVIDENCE

Apart from Barro's own aggregate formulation of the intergenerational hypothesis, almost no attempt was made to test these ideas directly on the micro-level. I have already reviewed the work of David and Menchik (1984b) and in section 6 below I evaluate the significance of the rate of decumulation of assets at old age to the bequest motive. I shall now briefly report the results of a direct test that I have recently conducted (Kurz, 1984).

In 1979 President Carter's Commission on Pension Policy drew a random sample of US households to develop a data base for the Commission's work. The file contained extensive information on work, wage rate, asset holding, private pension asset holdings and current income. Also, the file was merged with the social security record, so that a social security wealth variable was created. In addition, a section of the questionnaire was devoted to private transfers that were made by the family to persons outside the household and to private transfers received from persons outside the household. The questionnaire listed 14 ways in which transfers could have been made. This included direct cash payments, contributions toward a specified expenditure such as buying a durable good, or transfer in kind such as a gift of stocks or free use of real property. These were then aggregated to obtain the amounts 'received' and 'given' by each household in the sample during an eight-month period in 1979. When projected to the population, I estimated that the amount of private transfers – excluding transfers within the household and excluding inheritances – amounted in 1979 to $63 billion for the entire United States.

The availability of separate data on 'receiving' and 'giving' lead to an indirect test of the intergenerational hypothesis. The idea of this test is based on the fact that, when the full optimality conditions are written out, a decision function called 'net transfers' at time t denoted by $T(t)$ is written

$$T = \psi(\cdot) + \epsilon \tag{12}$$

where $\psi(\cdot)$ is a function induced by the optimization and ϵ is a random disturbance. Note, however, that

$$T = G - R \tag{13}$$

where G is the amount the family gave to others while R is the amount the family received from others. Using separately the data on amounts 'given' and amounts 'received,' one can develop two non-linear estimates of the parameters of (12), and a test of the equality of these estimates is an indirect test of the intergenerational hypothesis. The conclusion of this test amounted to the rejection of the hypothesis. With this analysis one may also ask the following question: Suppose a $1 increment in social security wealth were uniformly distributed over all the households in the society: by how much would private intergenerational transfers be reduced? Omitting technical details, I can report that, on the basis of the reported models, I estimated the reduction in intergenerational transfers to be 19 cents. This is obviously a first approximation, and much more research is needed to substantiate it. My main conclusion is that some intergenerational forces are clearly operating, but not necessarily as generally and as society-wide as proposed by the intergenerational hypothesis.

6 UNDERSTANDING THE MECHANISM FOR THE INTERGENERATIONAL TRANSFERS OF CAPITAL

How large is the life-cycle capital stock?

Perhaps the most decisive attack on the life-cycle theory of savings came from the direct examination of the wealth–age profile itself. Studies that focused on this issue did not suffer from the various methodological difficulties reviewed earlier, and for this reason their conclusions cannot be lightly dismissed.

Some studies concentrated mainly on the observation that wealth, even after retirement, often continues to rise with age. These studies include Lydall (1955), Atkinson (1971), Shorrocks (1975), Atkinson and Harrison (1978), Brittain (1978), Diamond and Hausman (1983), Menchik (1979), Mirer (1979) and David and Menchik (1984a, 1984b). A recent study by King and Dicks-Mireaux (1982) shows that, although total wealth may be rising with age, the *ratio* of wealth to permanent income (denoted W/Y_p) tends to exhibit a hump-shaped age profile. This same conclusion is repeated in the simulation model presented by Professor King in his review. Both Professors King and Dicks-Mireaux (1982) indicate that the ratio W/Y_p remains far higher than would be predicted by a life-cycle model of savings. It appears to me that the concern with the 'hump-shaped' profile of W/Y_p is misplaced, since this ratio lacks significance. Why not consider $W/\log(Y_p)$, which declines more slowly than W/Y_p, or $W/(Y_p)^2$, which declines more quickly? All the studies cited attempt to express the rather direct proposition that, if you take a *specific* family and examine its age–wealth profile, then for the families with most of the wealth in our society the typical profile either continues to rise after retirement or declines at a much slower rate than that predicted by the life-cycle hypothesis.

Now, the studies cited above did not attempt to evaluate the *quantitative* importance of life-cycle considerations in family savings. The three studies of White (1978), Darby (1979) and Kotlikoff and Summers (1980) estimated directly the fraction of US total wealth that can be explained by life-cycle considerations. White (1978) uses a simulation model to estimate this fraction to be at most 60 per cent, while Darby (1979) finds this ratio to be between 13 and 19 per cent. In a most extensive study Kotlikoff and Summers (1980) establish this ratio to be about 20 per cent. In estimating the life-cycle capital stock under alternate assumptions, they demonstrate that this percentage is a rather robust upper bound to the true ratio (note, however, a recent criticism by Modigliani, 1983).

Formal components of intergenerational transfers

With the quantitative importance of life-cycle savings reduced to a small fraction of the total, our focus necessarily shifts to the alternative methods by which the privately owned non-human capital changes hands from generation to generation.

If the total privately owned non-human US capital in 1982 was around \$9 trillion (\$9 × 10^{12}), then during that year some \$300 billion had to move from older to younger hands in order to enable the entire stock to move from generation to generation over time. If about 20 per cent of the stock is due to life-cycle considerations, then \$60 billion was purchased by the young from the old and paid for by their savings. On the other hand, most studies evaluating life insurance and formal bequests would not predict more than 30 per cent of the annual transfer to take this form. This component would then account for about \$90 billion in 1982. We can add to this the sum of about \$30 billion (about 10 per cent), which is an estimated upper bound on the amount of the parents' cash contributions to their children's formal trust accounts (since this sum includes *both* contributions to trust accounts and contributions towards the cost of their children's college education). This will bring the total explained to no more than \$180 billion, which is 60 per cent of the total. This means that at least 40 per cent of the total annual transfers from generation to generation are not explained by the formal structure discussed here.

The 1979 data of the President's Commission on Pension Policy, which I cited earlier, provided some details on the relationship between each giver and receiver of private transfers. These data reveal that, apart from the conventional intergenerational transfers between children and parents, extensive intergenerational transfers occur both within and outside the extended family. On the one hand, we find transfers between such members as aunts and nieces or among siblings where the givers are, on the average, eight years older than the receivers. However, we also find extensive amounts of transfers between members of the extended family and individuals outside the family, such as 'friends' and 'other persons.' A 1967 probate data file used by Paul Menchik and Martin David (cited in Kotlikoff and Summers, 1980) reveals the following facts:

(1) Males who were married at the time of their death left only 10 per cent of their estates to their children.
(2) Females who were married at the time of their death left only 19 per cent of their estates to their children.

(3) The proportion left to grandchildren and other young *relatives* is unclear but probably does not exceed 2 per cent for males and 4 per cent for females.
(4) For all single decedents, the percentages left to the children was 32 per cent for males and 37 per cent for females. Unfortunately, these numbers do not correct for those decedents who did not have children.

These figures highlight the fact that extensive amounts of private transfers from older to younger people take place via bequests that are not provided to members of the family.

Finally, although accurate data are not available, it appears that over $60 billion a year is currently contributed by Americans to non-profit institutions, and some of this capital does not get consumed but is added to the capital endowment of these institutions. This would provide one more mechanism for the transmission of capital over time.

The main conclusion that one tends to arrive at is that the voluntary transfer of capital from generation to generation takes an extremely complex form with a large multitude of motives. Some individuals indicate strong preference for their children, some prefer their trusted friends, and others contribute to the complex structure of institutions and social causes that they wish to support.

7 POPULATION HETEROGENEITY

In considering the two polar models proposed by the life-cycle and the intergenerational hypotheses, one recognizes that consumption and accumulation would depend upon the nature of the family's preferences with respect to future generations. Contrary to the common practice of assuming that these preferences are uniformly the same in our society, why should a family with five children have the same preferences as a single elderly male without any children? It is also possible that there may be biological reasons for males to have different intergenerational preferences from females. Moreover, as we may recognize the diversity of preferences across the population, the intergenerational preferences are likely to be part of human perception of the future beyond life. Some people may have absolutely no interest in the perpetuation of wealth within their own family and may prefer to donate whatever wealth they have to a specific social objective or charitable organization that they support. Others may demonstrate a total commitment to assist their children in perpetuating the family income. The recognition of this diversity contains the first clue to the view that neither the life-cycle nor the intergenerational hypothesis provides the *universally* correct hypothesis on the basis of which we should formulate the theory of savings.

In a preliminary study (Kurz, 1984) in which I examined this heterogeneity in the context of estimating the accumulation equations of different population groups, it appears that families with a single male head act in accord with the life-cycle hypothesis while families with a single female head tend to act in a way that is closer to the intergenerational hypothesis. Families with two heads act in an intermediate way and therefore support neither hypothesis.

To further highlight the case for heterogeneity, I propose to examine the distribution of savings in our society. Before doing so I remind the reader that family savings tend to be very volatile and its estimates are subject to large variations that are due both to errors in measurement and to variations in concepts used.

Using the 1960–1 survey of Consumer Expenditures and the 1963 Survey of Changes in Family Finances, one can obtain the size distributions shown in table 1. A more comprehensive set of data may be obtained from the 1972–3 Consumer Expenditure Survey, which reported the distribution of net change in family assets. Although this measure has its own limitations, table 2 presents the size distri-

TABLE 1 Size distribution of savings in the USA

1960–1			*1963*		
Percentage of income units (households)		*Percentage of aggregate savings*	*Percentage of income units (households)*		*Percentage of aggregate savings*
Lowest	36.8	−31.6	Lowest	39.4	2.0
Middle	41.1	23.9	Middle	33.3	30.4
Upper	22.2	107.6	Upper	27.3	67.5

Source: Survey of Changes in Family Finances, Federal Reserve Board of Governors, Washington, DC, 1968, table 5, p. 10.

TABLE 2 Size distribution of change in family assets, 1972–3

Annual income range	*Percentage of units*	*Percentage of total increase in assets*
Less than $6999	34.64	0.95
$7000–$14,999	36.32	19.75
Above $15,000	29.04	79.31

bution of this variable. I remark that in 1972–3 families with incomes above $20,000 constituted 14.2 per cent of the total units but generated 56.46 per cent of all increases in family assets!

Recognizing the great volatility in these tables, it is reasonable to conclude that the lowest one-third of the income units in our society do not generate any net savings, the middle one-third of income units generate about 20 per cent of aggregate family savings, while the one-third wealthiest families in our society generate about 80 per cent of aggregate family savings. With the distribution being so skewed, it is perfectly clear that the problem of savings and intergenerational transfers can hardly be the same for the bottom 70 per cent of the families as for the top 30 per cent. It is probable that the Keynesian consumption function will accurately describe the consumption pattern of many low-income families that are subject to various economic constraints. It is also likely that the life-cycle hypothesis will accurately describe the behavior of a large number of family units in the bottom 70 per cent of the income distribution. However, with most of the wealth being owned by a small fraction of the families, who own far more than they would consume during their life-time, the mechanism of the intergenerational transfer of wealth originates in the nature of the wealthy in our society. To hold the view that the wealthy in our society act as predicted by the life-cycle hypothesis is as implausible as the conjecture that all of them are dedicated to their own children and that their own accumulation is only a part of an intergenerational family equilibrium. This leads me to propose that, in the process of accumulating and disposing their capital, the wealthy exhibit an extremely diverse set of preferences.

Professor King and I share the view that population heterogeneity is important. However, Professor King seems to believe that the life-cycle model provides a good approximation for the entire population with the exception of a small group of families with low income and low but positive level of assets. It is my view that there is extensive heterogeneity of preferences across the population. This is the reason why polar hypotheses about behavior, which are assumed to apply uniformly, tend to be rejected by the data. I believe that the challenge of population heterogeneity will lead researchers to abandon the efforts of estimating the parameters of hypothetical utility or demand functions. Instead, research should concentrate on studying the statistical regularities of the stochastic process that result from aggregating over a heterogeneous population. Obviously, we do have a rich prior information about the nature of this heterogeneity.

REFERENCES

Ando, A. and Modigliani, F. (1963), 'The Life-cycle Hypothesis of Saving: Aggregate Implications and Tests,' *American Economic Review*, **53**, 55–84.

Atkinson, A. B. (1971), 'The Distribution of Wealth and the Individual Life Cycle,' *Oxford Economic Papers*, n.s., **23**, 239–54.

Atkinson, A. B. and Harrison, A. J. (1978), *The Distribution of Personal Wealth in Britain*, Cambridge University Press.

Auerbach, A. and Kotlikoff, L. J. (1981), 'An Examination of Empirical Tests of Social Security and Savings,' National Bureau of Economic Research, Working Paper no. 730.

Barro, R. J. (1974), 'Are Government Bonds Net Wealth?' *Journal of Political Economy*, **82**, 1095–117.

Barro, R. J. (1978), *The Impact of Social Security on Private Savings*, American Enterprise Institute, Washington, DC.

Bernheim, B. D. and Ray, D. (1983), 'Altruistic Growth Economics I and II,' Department of Economics, Stanford University (mimeograph).

Blinder, S. A., Gordon, R. H. and Wise, D. E. (1980), 'Social Security, Bequests and the Life Cycle Theory of Savings: Cross-sectional Tests,' National Bureau of Economic Research, Working Paper no. 619.

Brittain, J. (1978), *Inheritance and the Inequality of Material Wealth*, Brookings Institution, Washington, DC.

Darby, M. R. (1979), *The Effects of Social Security on Income and the Capital Stock*, American Enterprise Institute, Washington, DC.

David, M. and Menchik, P. (1984a), 'Distribution of Estate Wealth and Its Relationship to Intergenerational Transfers,' *Papers and Proceedings of the American Statistical Association, Survey Methods Section*, 00, 000–00.

David, M. and Menchik, P. (1984b), 'The Effects of Social Security on Lifetime Wealth Accumulation and Bequests,' *Economica* (forthcoming).

Davies, J. (1982), 'Uncertain Lifetime Consumption and Dissaving in Retirement,' *Journal of Political Economy*, **89**, 561–77.

Diamond, P. A. and Hausman, J. A. (1983), 'Individual Retirement and Savings Behavior,' Department of Economics, Massachusetts Institute of Technology (mimeograph).

Feldstein, M. S. (1974), 'Social Security, Induced Retirement, and Aggregate Capital Accumulation,' *Journal of Political Economy*, **82**, 905–26.

Feldstein, M. S. (1976), 'Social Security and Private Savings: International Evidence in an Extended Life-cycle Model,' in M. Feldstein and R. Inman (eds), *The Economics of Public Services*, International Economics Association Conference volume, Halstead Press, New York.

Feldstein, M. S. (1978), 'Reply,' to R. J. Barro, *On the Impact of Social Security on Private Saving*, American Enterprise Institute, Washington, DC.

Feldstein, M. S. (1980), 'Social Security, Induced Retirement and Aggregate Capital Accumulation: A Correction and Updating,' National Bureau of Economic Research, Working Paper no. 579.

Feldstein, M. S. (1982), 'Social Security and Private Saving: Reply,' *Journal of Political Economy*, **90**, 630–42.

Feldstein, M. S. and Pellechio, A. (1979), 'Social Security and Household Wealth Accumulation: New Microeconomic Evidence,' *Review of Economics and Statistics*, **61**, 361–8.

Friedman, M. (1957), *A Theory of the Consumption Function*, Princeton University Press, Princeton, NJ.

Goldman, S. (1980), 'Consistent Plans,' *Review of Economic Studies*, **47**, 533.

King, M. A. and Dicks-Mireaux, L. D. L. (1982), 'Asset Holdings and the Life Cycle,' *Economic Journal*, **92**, 1–21.

Kohlberg, E. (1976), 'A Model of Economic Growth With Altruism Between Generations,' *Journal of Economic Theory*, **13**, 1–13.

Kotlikoff, L. (1979), 'Testing the Theory of Social Security and Life Cycle Accumulation,' *American Economic Review*, **69**, 396–410.

Kotlikoff, L. J. and Spivak, A. (1981), 'The Family as an Incomplete Annuities Market,' *Journal of Political Economy*, **89**, 372–91.

Kotlikoff, L. J. and Summers, L. (1980), 'The Role of Intergenerational Transfer in Aggregate Capital Accumulation,' National Bureau of Economic Research, Working Paper no. 445.

Kurz, M. (1981), 'The Life-cycle Hypothesis and the Effects of Social Security and Private Pensions on Family Savings,' IMSSS, Technical Report no. 335, Stanford University.

Kurz, M. (1984), 'Capital Accumulation and the Characteristics of Private Intergenerational Transfers,' *Economica*, **51**, 1–22.

Lane, J. and Mitra, T. (1981), 'On Nash Equilibrium Programs of Capital Accumulation under Altruistic Preferences,' *International Economic Review*, **22**, 309–31.

Leimer, D. and Lesnoy, S. (1982), 'Social Security and Private Saving: New Time-series Evidence,' *Journal of Political Economy*, **90**, 606–29.

Lesnoy, S. D. and Leimer, D. R. (1981), 'Social Security and Private Saving: New Time-series Evidence with Alternative Specifications,' Social Security Administration, Working Paper no. 22, Washington, DC.

Loury, G. C. (1981), 'Intergenerational Transfers and the Distribution of Earnings,' *Econometrica*, **49**, 843–64.

Lydall, H. (1955), 'The Life Cycle in Income, Saving and Asset Ownership,' *Econometrica*, **23**, 131–50.

Menchik, P. (1979), 'Intergenerational Transmission of Inequality: An Empirical Study of Wealth Mobility,' *Economica*, **46**, 349–62.

Menchik, P. and David, M. (1983), 'Income Distribution, Lifetime Saving and Bequests,' *American Economic Review*, **73**, 672–90.

Mirer, T. (1979), 'The Wealth–Age Relationship Among the Aged,' *American Economic Review*, **69**, 435–43.

Modigliani, F. (1966), 'The Life-cycle Hypothesis of Savings, the Demand for Wealth, and the Supply of Capital,' *Social Research*, **33**, 160–217.

Modigliani, F. (1983), 'The Life-cycle Hypothesis and National Wealth – A Rehabilitation,' Massachusetts Institute of Technology (mimeograph).

Modigliani, F. and Brumberg, R. (1954), 'Utility Analysis and the Consumption Function,' in K. Kurihara (ed.), *Post-Keynesian Economics*, Rutgers University Press, New Brunswick, NJ.

Munnell, A. H. (1976), 'Private Pensions and Savings: New Evidence,' *Journal of Political Economy*, **84**, 1013–32.

Peleg, B. and Yaari, M. (1973), 'On the Existence of a Consistent Course of Action When Tastes Are Changing,' *Review of Economic Studies*, **40**, 381–401.

Phelps, E. (1975), 'The Indeterminacy of Game-equilibrium Growth in the Absence of An Ethic,' in E. S. Phelps (ed.), *Altruism Morality and Economic Theory*, Russell Sage Foundation, New York.

Phelps, E. and Pollak, R. (1968), 'On Second-best National Saving and Game-equilibrium Growth,' *Review of Economic Studies*, **35**, 185–99.

Shesinski, E. and Weiss, Y. (1981), 'Uncertainty and Optimal Social Security Systems', *Quarterly Journal of Economics*, **95**, 191–206.

Shorrocks, A. F. (1975), 'The Age–Wealth Relationship: A Cross-section and Cohort Analysis,' *Review of Economics and Statistics*, **57**, 155–63.

White, B. (1978), 'Empirical Tests of the Life-cycle Hypothesis,' *American Economic Review*, **68**, 547–60.

5

Fix-Price Models
A Survey of Recent Empirical Work

JEAN-JACQUES LAFFONT

1 INTRODUCTION

The bibliography of quantity rationing and disequilibrium models that Richard Quandt regularly actualizes and kindly circulates now comprises more than 250 items. However, very many economists, especially in the United States, dismiss this literature as irrelevant. Their basic criticism can be borrowed from Barro's comment of a paper by Muellbauer and Winter in the *European Economic Review* (1980): 'The disequilibrium analysis invariably relies at crucial points on unexplained market failures.... Typically, there are arbitrary restrictions on the adjustment of prices to clear markets.'

Faced with unexplained price rigidities, several attitudes are possible.

(1) The first one, exemplified by Barro, is to say that serious macroeconomic policy cannot be designed to cure unexplained market failures, and to ignore fix-price theory.
(2) The second one, exemplified by Benassy, is to say that prices are the result of complex socioeconomic conflicts that must be taken as given for the design of short-run macroeconomic policy.
(3) The third attitude is represented by Solow's 1979 presidential address to the American Economic Association. Solow sees half a dozen possible reasons why wages may not be flexible. Economic theory must develop models to explain these rigidities. Policy prescriptions must be worked out case by case.

If we take Solow's point of view, the basic question is as follows. When the reasons for price rigidities and the dynamics of these price rigidities will be better understood, what will be left of the macro-policy derived from current fix-price models? This question cannot be answered today.

Let me give two examples that point towards opposite directions. The goal of the theory of implicit labor contracts has been to explain why, when faced with an unexpected shock, firms will adjust quantities rather than wages. The basic idea is that firms, and not insurance companies, offer to workers insurance against wage variations because they are able to monitor their effort. In the most sophisticated versions, where asymmetric information is introduced, unemployment occurs in some states of nature for incentive-compatibility reasons. However, the demand for labor cannot be viewed as resulting from the maximization of profit at fixed prices. Fix-price theory results in a mis-specification of the model. On the contrary, the formalization of trade unions' behavior leads to wage rigidities well in the tradition of fix-price theory.

The development of general equilibrium fix-price models is now ten years old, and many surveys have already synthesized this literature. The notion of equilibrium, the existence of equilibrium and the various kinds of inefficiencies it entails are now well understood (see Grandmont, 1977; Drazen, 1980; Silvestre, 1982; Benassy, 1982). Also, it is too soon to predict the outcome of the various very recent efforts made to explain price rigidities and the interaction of macroeconomic policy with these endogenous price rigidities. I believe that this will be an important part of the research of the next ten years. Contrary to the first fix-price models using a temporary equilibrium framework, rational expectations will be a major ingredient of these studies (e.g. Fisher, 1977; Phelps and Taylor, 1977). It is likely that a more detailed theory of the firm under uncertainty will also be needed.

In this paper, I will take a very applied point of view. I will describe the recent empirical work carried out within the fix-price equilibrium setting to question the fix-price paradigm with respect to Aumann's view (chapter 1 above) that 'Scientific theories must be judged by how well they enable us to organize and understand our observations.' Since Quandt (1982) has surveyed the development of the econometric methods dealing with the particular nonlinear models (piecewise linear in general) generated by fix-price models, I will be only marginally concerned with statistical methods.

My paper is organized in two parts. In the following section I present the canonical fix-price macro-model used in the various macroeconometric estimations performed on Western Europe data. I do not cover applications to Eastern Europe because they raise special issues (see for example Portes, Quandt, Winter and Yeo, 1982) and because Professor Janos Kornai will be giving his latest views on this matter. In section 3 I review what recent fix-price theory has to offer to overcome the weaknesses of these first macro-estimations and I give some preliminary results on a micro-approach. In appendices, I discuss some attempts at explaining price rigidities and some developments in public economics with price rigidities.

2 THE EMPIRICAL IMPLEMENTATION OF FIX-PRICE MACROECONOMICS

To discuss macroeconomic policy in a world of rigid prices, the concept of fix-price equilibrium has been used in a prototype model with three commodities (consumption good, labor and money) and three agents (a consumer, a producer and the government). Gathering early contributions by Patinkin (1965), Clower (1965) and others, this elegant and pedagogical model has been developed successively by Barro and Grossman (1971), Benassy (1973) and Malinvaud (1977). The main advantage of this model is to enable a discussion of the Keynesian and classical viewpoints on unemployment in a unified framework. Little attention has been paid to aggregation issues, and the ambitious project of providing microeconomic foundations to macroeconomics still awaits a convincing aggregation theory.

Gourieroux, Laffont and Monfort (1980a) and Ito (1980a) have provided the econometric methods needed for the estimation of disequilibrium macroeconomic models. In the last four years several empirical implementations of these methods have been carried out. For empirical purposes, the need for opening the economy and the desire to reproduce the short-run productivity cycle (Okun's Law) have led the authors to slightly complicate the basic model. On the contrary, a simplification has been achieved by suppressing the spillover effect from the goods market to the labor market for the consumer. In the following subsection I describe the basic structure common to all the models that have been estimated. I then provide a precise comparison of the details of the different models and a discussion of the main achievements performed by the authors in this first wave of empirical work.

The prototype model used for empirical work[1]

Let us first describe the notional behavior of the agents on the labor market and on the goods market (we can ignore the money market because of Walras' Law).

Labor does not enter the utility function of the consumer so that the notional (Walrasian) supply of labor is exogenous:

$$L^s = L^*. \tag{1}$$

The notional consumption demand for the good is determined by the program

$$\max U\left(C, \frac{M}{p}\right)$$

$$\text{s.t.} \quad pC + M = wL^* + M_{-1} \tag{2}$$

where C is real consumption
M is money holdings during the period
M_{-1} is money holdings during the last period
w is the wage rate
p is the price level of the commodity.

Program (2) leads to a consumption demand function

$$C = C\left(\frac{M_{-1} + wL^*}{p}\right) \tag{3}$$

which is assumed to be increasing and differentiable. Moreover, the marginal propensity to consume is less than one: $\partial C/\partial X < 1$.

At the current date, capital, K, is exogenous and the notional behavior of the firm is determined by

$$\max p(Y - wL)$$

$$\text{s.t.} \quad Y = F(K, L) \tag{4}$$

where Y is the level of production and the production function $F(K, \cdot)$ is differentiable increasing and concave with the Inada conditions fulfilled.

Expression (4) leads to the Walrasian demand for labor

$$L^d = L(w/p, K)$$

and to the Walrasian supply of good $Y^s = Y(w/p, K)$.

Exports, X, government expenditure, G, investment, I, and inventories variations, ΔS, are exogenous. Let $EX = X + G + I + \Delta S$, the exogenous part of demand. 'Normal imports' are a function of the level of domestic activity $Im(Y)$. Moreover, when the demand for a domestically produced good is constrained, imports are substituted for it. Let ΔI_m denote in that case these additional imports.

These assumptions generate three regimes with a unique solution for each price vector (w, p).

Regime 1: Keynesian unemployment (KU)

The consumer is constrained on the labor market. Let L be the quantity of labor he sells; his consumption demand is then

$$C = C\left(\frac{M_{-1} + wL}{p}\right) \tag{5}$$

Total demand is $Y^d = C + EX - Im(Y)$. The producer is constrained on the goods market:

$$\begin{aligned} Y &= Y^d \\ L &= L^d = F^{-1}(Y, K). \end{aligned} \tag{6}$$

Substituting (6) in (5) yields the consumption function

$$C = C\left[\frac{M_{-1} + wF^{-1}(Y, K)}{p}\right].$$

The level of activitity is determined by the familiar equation

$$Y = C\left[\frac{M_{-1} + wF^{-1}(Y, K)}{p}\right] + EX - Im(Y) \tag{7}$$

Let us rewrite (7) as

$$Y = \psi(Y) \tag{8}$$

$$\frac{d\psi(Y)}{dY} = \left(\frac{w}{p}\frac{\partial C}{\partial X}\right)\left(\frac{1}{dF/dL}\right) - \frac{dIm}{dY}.$$

Since the producer is constrained on the goods market, $dF/dL \geqslant w/p$ and

$$\frac{d\psi(Y)}{dY} \leqslant \frac{\partial C}{\partial X} - \frac{dIm}{dY} < 1.$$

Consequently (7) has a unique solution denoted $\tilde{Y}(M_{-1}, K, w, p, EX)$ if the intersection of Y and $\psi(Y)$ occurs at $Y \leqslant F(L^*, K)$, which gives an upper limit to the value of w/p, namely $\bar{w}/\bar{p}$. Unemployment is defined by

$$U = L^* - F^{-1}[\tilde{Y}(M_{-1}, K, w, p, EX), K]. \tag{9}$$

The values of the exogenous variables for which this regime is valid are defined by the inequalities

$$Y^s\left(\frac{w}{p}, K\right) \geqslant \tilde{Y}(M_{-1}, K, w, p, EX) \tag{10}$$

$$F(L^*, K) \geqslant \tilde{Y}(M_{-1}, K, w, p, EX). \tag{11}$$

Expression (10) expresses excess supply of good and (11) is derived from the definition of excess supply of labor, $L^* \geqslant F^{-1}[\tilde{Y}(M_{-1}, K, w, p, EX), K]$.

Let $(w/p)^*$ denote the real wage such that

$$Y^s[(w/p)^*, K] = F(L^*, K),$$

i.e., the real wage that leads to full employment for the notional behavior of the firm.

If $(w/p) > (w/p)^*$, $Y^s(w/p, K) < F(L^*, K)$ and (10) is binding to define the relevant region. The slope in the (w, p) space of the equation $Y^s(w/p, K) = \tilde{Y}(M_{-1}, K, w, p, EX)$ is obtained from the equation

$$Y^s\left(\frac{w}{p}, K\right) = C\left\{\frac{M_{-1} + wF^{-1}[Y^s(w/p, K), K]}{p}\right.$$
$$\left. + EX - Im\left[Y^s\left(\frac{w}{p}, K\right)\right]\right.$$

yielding (with $\rho = w/p$)

$$\frac{dw}{dp} = \frac{w}{p}\left\{1 + \frac{M_{-1}}{w}\left[1 \Big/ \left(L^s - \frac{\frac{\partial Y^s}{\partial \rho}\left(1 - \frac{\partial C}{\partial X} + \frac{dIm}{dY}\right)}{\partial C/\partial X}\right)\right]\right\} > 0.$$

This inequality shows that $dw/dp \rightarrow (\bar{w}/p)$ as w increases.

If $w/p < (w/p)^*$, $Y^s(w/p, K) > F(L^*, K)$ and (11) is binding to define the relevant region. The slope, in the (w, p) space, of the curve defined by $F(L^*, K) = \tilde{Y}(M_{-1}, K, w, p, EX)$ is

$$\frac{dw}{dp} = \frac{w}{p}\left(1 + \frac{M_{-1}}{w}\frac{1}{L^*}\right)$$

which is clearly larger than the slope of the curve defined for $w/p > (w/p)^*$. This yields the region represented in figure 5.1.

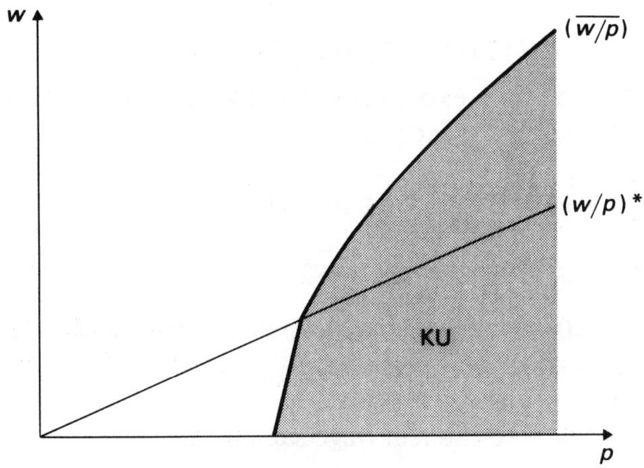

FIGURE 5.1

Regime 2: Classical unemployment (CU)

The firm is not constrained in either market. Then

$$Y = Y^s\left(\frac{w}{p}, K\right)$$

and

$$L = L^d\left(\frac{w}{p}, K\right).$$

Total demand,

$$Y^d = C\left[\frac{M_{-1} + wL^d(w/p, K)}{p}\right] + EX - Im\left[Y^s\left(\frac{w}{p}, K\right)\right]$$

is larger than supply, inducing additional imports:

$$\Delta Im = Y^d - Y.$$

Unemployment is $U = L^* - L^d(w/p, K)$. This case is defined by

$$Y^s\left(\frac{w}{p}, K\right) \leqslant \tilde{Y}(M_{-1}, K, w, p, EX) \tag{12}$$

and

$$F(L^*, K) \geqslant Y^s\left(\frac{w}{p}, K\right). \tag{13}$$

The curve $Y^s(w/p, K) = \tilde{Y}(M_{-1}, K, w, p, EX)$ has been already drawn. (13) is equivalent to $w/p > (w/p)^*$, hence the region depicted in figure 5.2.

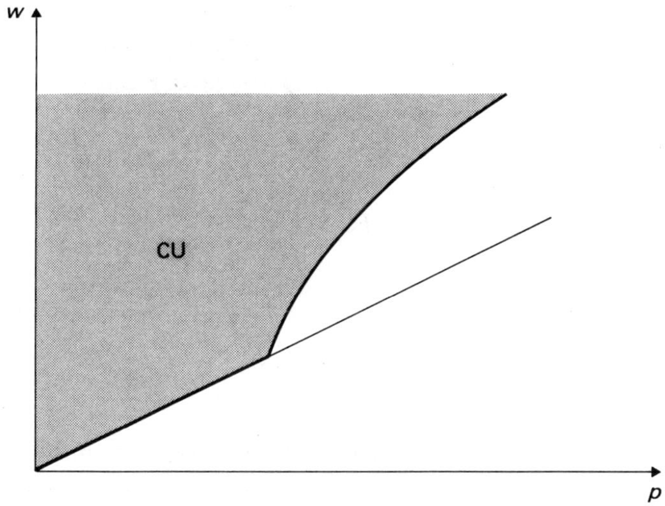

FIGURE 5.2

Regime 3: Repressed inflation (RI)

The consumer is not constrained on the labor market; there is excess demand for the domestically produced goods but imports complete demand:

$$L = L^*$$

$$Y = F(L^*, K)$$

$$\Delta Im = C\left(\frac{M_{-1} + wL^*}{p}\right) + EX - Im[F(L^*, K)] - F(L^*, K).$$

This region is defined by

$$F(L^*, K) \leqslant \tilde{Y}(M_{-1}, K, w, p, EX) \tag{14}$$

$$F(L^*, K) \leqslant Y^s\left(\frac{w}{p}, K\right) \tag{15}$$

which enables us to complete figure 5.3.

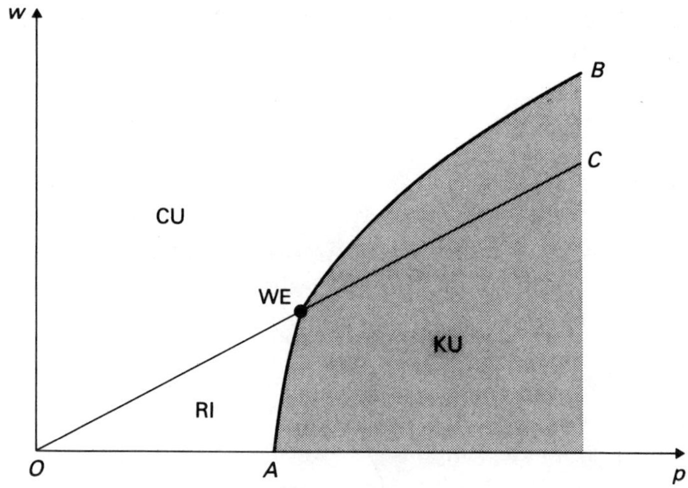

FIGURE 5.3

Any price vector to the left of the curve AB, i.e. in the repressed inflation and classical unemployment regions, leads to a deterioration of the balance of trade. There is unemployment everywhere except in the repressed inflation region; above OC, the real wage is higher than the Walrasian wage. The classical unemployment region is characterized by real wages that are always larger than the Walrasian real wage. On the contrary, the Keynesian region admits real wages that can be either larger or smaller than the Walrasian real wage.

Also, this explicit construction has shown the existence and the uniqueness of equilibrium. Uniqueness will be crucial for econometric analysis to be able to write a well defined likelihood function of the model.

A comparison of four main empirical works

I discuss the main issues dealt with by four empirical papers and conclude this section with a table summarizing the comparison of their models.

Okun's Law

A major empirical findings, known as Okun's Law, is the procyclical pattern of average labor productivity. This empirical phenomenon cannot be made consistent with the model developed above, in which firms' production vectors always belong to a production function with decreasing returns to scale. The common explanation of this empirical regularity is labor hoarding, arising from the high costs of adjustment for labor inputs which make labor a quasi-fixed factor of production.

Kooiman and Kloek (1980) and Sneessens (1980) recognize the problem but have rather *ad hoc* treatments. Sneessens introduces, in periods of decreasing employment only, an adjustment of labor input that sets the firm out of its production function. Arguing the need for a tractable likelihood function, Kooiman and Kloek (1980) introduce linear spillover effects, i.e. effective behavioral functions not derived from their specifications, which imply the possibility of being out of the production function and respecting Okun's Law.

Artus *et al.* (1982) introduce adjustment costs for both labor and output directly into the profit function:

$$\pi(Y, K, L) = pY - wL - C_1 wL_{-1}\left[\frac{L}{L_{-1}} - 1\right]^2 - C_2 pF(K, L)\max\left[\frac{Y}{F(K, L)} - 1, 0\right]^2 \qquad (16)$$

and allow a production vector outside the production function. A consequence of this better formulation, still fairly *ad hoc*, is to imply the possibility of a fourth regime,[2] called underconsumption (UC), in which firms are rationed simultaneously in both markets. This fourth regime is not empirically very significant and the main advantage of (16) is to lead to adjustment rules for labor and notional demands for output which depend on two parameters only, C_1 and C_2.

A major lesson to draw from this work is the need for a better analysis of labor hoarding from a theoretical point of view. In particular, the types of labor contracts that emerge from the social labor–employers bargaining within country-specific social customs and law systems will be a major determinant of this behavior. The empirical work of Boyer and Mistral (1982) shows that the cross-countries differences in the adjustment of labor following macro-shocks such as oil price rises are very great.

Frictional unemployment

The sum of unemployment data and employment data equals labor supply plus frictional unemployment minus discouraged workers. It is crucial to have a theory of frictional unemployment and of the discouraged worker effect to be able to exhibit regimes in which there is excess demand for labor.

The procedure initiated by Kooiman and Kloek (1980) and followed by Artus *et al.* (1982) is to define labor supply (and therefore also frictional unemployment) as a simple function of employment plus unemployment data which is linear in time. This is a rather primitive theory of frictional unemployment which clearly should be improved. The estimation of the model yields a decompositon of unemployment into voluntary and involuntary unemployment. For example, Artus *et al.* (1982) obtain for 1978 in France 671,000 involuntarily unemployed workers out of a registered unemployment population of 1,238,000.

The discouraged worker effect is not taken into account. Eaton and Quandt (1980) have shown how it is possible to formalize this effect. Their microeconomic theory leads to the introduction of the probability of unemployment as an explanatory variable in the labor supply function. Through a maximum likelihood estimation performed for the American labor market, they have concluded that it is a significant effect.

An important consideration that is not adequately dealt with is the problem of immigrants, with all the unobservable components it carries. (Vilares, 1981, treats the question of emigrants from Portugal.)

The debate about the min-condition

Following Fair and Jaffee (1972) and the fix-price theory literature, Gourieroux *et al.* (1980a) and Ito (1980a) have assumed efficiency of the rationing schemes yielding a specification of the type

$$Y = \min(\tilde{S}, \tilde{D}) \tag{17}$$

where the exchanged quantity is the minimum of supply and demand that are stochastic.

At the microeconomic level, this voluntary trade and efficiency assumption is perfectly all right. Of course it is more debatable at the macroeconomic level at which it has been assumed. Following Muellbauer (1978), one can argue that rationing occurs in micro-markets and that efficiency of the rationing scheme is not obtained at the macro-level. To go from this interesting observation to a less *ad hoc* structural form we must start from a microeconomic formulation and model the inefficiency of the rationing scheme (see pp. 349–50 below).

Another criticism of (17) in a simultaneous equation system is the complexity of the likelihood function it generates. Sneessens (1980) has suggested using the simplification provided by the specification

$$Y = \min(S, D) + \epsilon \tag{18}$$

where supply and demand are not stochastic. Despite attempts to show that it is a better formulation than (17) (see also the paper by Richard, 1980), I consider (18) to be weak from a modelling point of view, because I cannot expect a micro-theory to lead to an aggregation that justifies the use of certainty equivalents in (18), D playing the role of ED^j and S the role of ES^j where j denotes the representative jth market. The argument of simplicity used is not decisive either; as shown by Kooiman and Kloek (1980) and Artus *et al.* (1982), the estimation of a model using the formulation (17) is quite possible.

The coherency constraints

Disequilibrium theory generates models with several regimes; even if they are linearized in each regime, these models are highly nonlinear, and for econometric purposes the question of a well defined reduced form appears. This solvability or coherency question raised by Quandt (1978) has been quite generally solved for piecewise general models in Gourieroux *et al.* (1980b) and in the special case of disequilibrium models in Gourieroux *et al.* (1980a) and Ito (1980a).

Consider a piecewise linear model defined by

$$y = A^i X + \epsilon^i \qquad i = 1, \dots, n \tag{19}$$

where y is the vector of endogenous variables, X the vector of exogenous variables and ϵ^i a vector of errors. The reduced form $y = A^i X + \epsilon^i$ is valid in a cone C^i of the space of endogenous variables. When the

C^i are cones originating in 0, are disjoints, and cover the whole space of endogenous variables, and if the mapping

$$\sum_{i=1}^{n} A^i \, 1_{C^i}$$

is continuous,[3] the system (19) associates to any vector of errors and exogenous variables a unique vector of endogenous variables if and only if the determinants $\det A^i$ are of the same sign. This condition yields for disequilibrium models constraints on the products of spillover coefficients. An example of such a relation reduces in some cases to the fact that the marginal propensity to consume is less than one. Some such constraints are guaranteed by convexity assumptions; others, which involve parameters of both the producer and the consumer, cannot be derived from the usual assumptions.

Kooiman and Kloek (1980) have imposed the coherency conditions in their analysis; to obtain manageable likelihood functions they have specified linear spillover effects which are not derived from their notional specifications.

When the model is not linear, the question of uniqueness is more difficult. Laroque (1978) has proved local uniqueness around the Walrasian equilibrium for the Drèze equilibrium with uniform rationing. Schultz (1983) proves a global uniqueness result for the Benassy equilibrium.

Artus *et al.* (1982) have sophisticated the basic prototype model to the point where the coherency problem cannot be solved analytically. Simulations suggest uniqueness of the solution for 'reasonable' values of the parameters, but the difficulty is not clearly solved.

Vilares (1981) solves the coherency question in the following way. Firms base their behavior on *anticipated* demand denoted Y^a. The prototype model can then be simplified into

$$Y = \min\left[F(L^*, K),\ Y^s\left(\frac{w}{p}, K\right),\ Y^a\right] \tag{20}$$

$$L = F^{-1}(Y, K) \tag{21}$$

$$U = L^* - F^{-1}(Y, K). \tag{22}$$

If $F(L^*, K)$ is minimal in (20), full employment is achieved, and there is excess demand for labor and (anticipated) excess demand for the good (repressed inflation). If $Y^s(w/p, K)$ is minimal in (20), there exist (anticipated) excess demand for goods and excess supply for labor (classical unemployment). If Y^a is minimal, there is excess supply of goods and excess supply of labor (Keynesian unemployment).

The combination of the lack of spillover effect from the goods market to the labor market for the consumer, and the fact that firms base their behavior on anticipated demand not on effective demand, yields basically a recursive two-equation model in which the uniqueness question is trivially solved, and can be estimated with single-equation techniques. Moreover, the min condition of (20) is replaced by a smoothening suggested by Ginsburgh, Tischler and Zang (1980), which yields a differentiable likelihood function.

This great simplification is due to the fact that all further feedbacks are absorbed by foreign trade. However, this makes sense only if they induce no structural imbalance of foreign trade.

To conclude this part, I have summarized the main features of the four empirical estimations of fix-price general equilibrium models in table 5.1.

3 THE THEORY BEYOND THE PROTOTYPE MODEL

It is plain that much remains to be done before fix-price theory translates itself into usable macroeconomic models. I discuss now what theory has to offer to solve the main weaknesses of the models described above.

Inventories

A great weakness of the empirical work presented above is the treatment of inventories as an exogenous variable in models, where, by the logic of fix-price equilibria, they are playing an important role as a buffer stock.

Little work is available on the treatment of inventories in disequilibrium models. Malinvaud (1977) and Muellbauer and Portes (1978) (see also Böhm, 1981b) have observed that the introduction of inventories, which play for the firm somewhat the same role as money for the consumer, may lead to a fourth regime in which the firm is constrained on both markets. Muellbauer and Portes show, under the assumption of expectations about next period that agents

TABLE 5.1 Main differences of the four macro-models

Kooiman–Kloek	*Artus–Laroque–Michel*	*Sneessens*	*Vilares*
Annual data, the Netherlands, 1952–78	Quarterly data, France, 1963–78	Annual data, Belgium, 1953–78	Annual data, France, 1952–78; Portugal, 1953–79
GLM–Ito specification; coherency ensured by linear spillover effects; maximum likelihood estimation*	GLM–Ito specification; coherency checked numerically for some range of values for parameters; maximum likelihood estimation	Ginsburgh–Tischler–Zang specification; single-equation estimation technique	Ginsburgh–Tischler–Zang specification; single-equation estimation technique; model made recursive by replacing the endogenous variable demand by the exogenous expected demand
Four regimes	Four regimes	Three regimes	Three regimes
Clay–Clay vintage technology (Den Hartog–Tjan)	Cobb–Douglas production function with technical progress + explicit formulation of adjustment costs of labor and output	Cobb–Douglas production function with technical progress for the long run + little substitution possible in the short run	Clay–Clay vintage technology; slow adjustment of labor

Frictional unemployment is a linear function of (employed + registered unemployed)	(cf. Kooiman–Kloek)	Supply of labor is a constant fraction of exogenous labor force (employed + registered unemployed)	Rosen–Quandt formulation of labor supply + treatment of emigrants for Portugal
Hendry–von Ungern–Sternberg consumption function	Borrowed from French quarterly model		Hendry–von Ungern–Sternberg consumption function
When demand is constrained, some rationing of exports and consumption; then imports complete demand	(cf. Kooiman–Kloek)	Imports complete demand when excess demand; exports exogenous	Imports complete demand when excess demand; some rationing of exports when close to full capacity
Difficulties in the optimization of the likelihood function are reported (multiple maxima); only model not to attribute 1975–8 to Keynesian unemployment regime	Compute the temporary competitive equilibrium		Comparison of results with Insee Business surveys for France

* However, the likelihood function is not quite correct because income is treated as exogenous.

are not rationed, how inventory behavior affects labor demand and goods supply in the different regimes. However, this choice of expectations is not compatible with a rigidity of prices lasting over long periods.

Honkapohja and Ito (1980) have studied the dynamic behavior of inventories with fixed prices, showing the role of the different regimes in the evolution of inventories. Simonovits (1981) has modified their analysis using naive expectations rather than rational expectations. Böhm (1981a) has shown that, for Walrasian prices, after a shock on money balances and inventories the dynamic evolution of money balances and inventories is stable and returns to a Walrasian equilibrium. Moreover, the classical unemployment region and part of the underconsumption region are left in finite time. Let me consider for a while a slightly different model studied in detail by Monier (1983).

Let us consider a dynamic specification of the basic three-commodity model. This is a two-period model in which all agents anticipate that the Walrasian equilibrium will hold next period. The producer now maximizes expected real money holdings of next period. His first-period indirect utility function is

$$\left(\frac{M_t^p}{p_t}\right)^a (i_t)^b$$

where M_t^p is his nominal money holdings and i_t is his inventory level in the current period t. His technology exhibits decreasing returns to scale, taken to be

$$Q_t = L_t^{\frac{1}{2}}$$

where L_t is the labor input and Q_t is the production level in period t.

Let Y_t denote sales, and k a tax rate on his money holdings of last period. Since profits are not distributed, in the long run stationary equilibrium all profits are taxed in this way. The producer's maximization program is then

$$\max \left(\frac{M_t^p}{p_t}\right)^a (i_t)^b$$

$$\text{s.t. } Q_t \leqslant L_t^{\frac{1}{2}}.$$

$$M_t^p + w_t L_t \leqslant p_t Y_t + (1-k)\, M_{t-1}^p.$$

$$Y_t + i_t \leqslant Q_t + i_{t-1}.$$

The consumer has an indirect utility function

$$C_t^2(L_0 - L_t)\frac{M_t^c}{p_t}$$

where $L_0 - L_t$ is his leisure
C_t his consumption in commodity
M_t^c his nominal money holdings in period t

His maximization program is:

$$\max C_t^2(L_0 - L_t)\frac{M_t^c}{p_t}$$

$$\text{s.t. } p_t C_t + M_t^c \leqslant w_t L_t + M_{t-1}^c.$$

Let M be the money supply. The stationary Walrasian equilibrium is characterized by

$$w = \frac{3kM}{(2+k)L_0};\ p = \frac{2kM}{2+k}\sqrt{(6/L_0)};\ M^p = \frac{2M}{2+k};\ M^c = \frac{kM}{2+k}$$

$$i = \frac{b}{ak}\sqrt{(L_0/6)};\ L = \tfrac{2}{3}L_0;\ C = \sqrt{(L_0/6)};\ Q = Y = \sqrt{\tfrac{2}{3}}L_0.$$

If prices are fixed at these long-run Walrasian levels, the dynamics of money holdings and inventories can be described by figure 5.4.

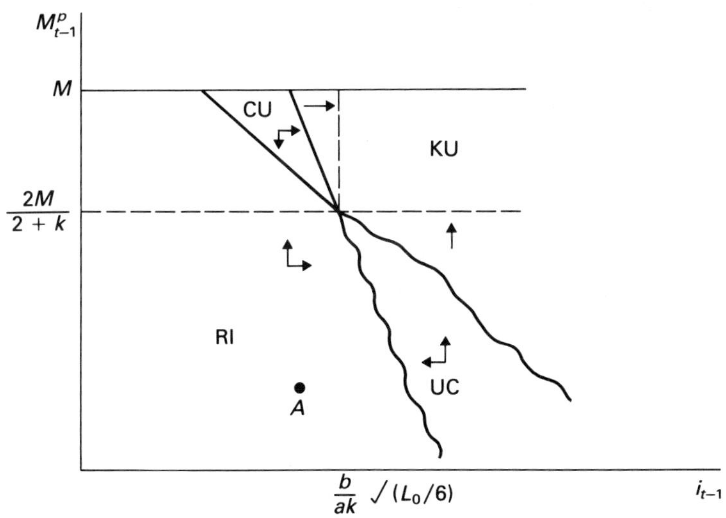

FIGURE 5.4

The Walrasian long-run equilibrium is locally stable; this can be shown analytically for the three regions CU, UC and RI, and by simulation for KU. There is no other stable stationary point, but there is an unstable point in the RI region. Moreover, if we start too far from the equilibrium, the model diverges (these conclusions parallel those obtained by Böhm, 1981a).

A complete study of inventory dynamics necessarily becomes complicated by the need for a price dynamics; however, the above results suggest that the price dynamics will not be seriously disturbed by the inventories–money holdings dynamics.

Inventories play a major role in the dynamics of disequilibrium models. Moreover, they provide observable variables related to disequilibrium phenomena and should facilitate the identification of the various regimes. Green and Laffont (1981) have shown, in a linearized version of the four-regime Muellbauer–Portes model, how the dynamic equations describing the evolution of inventories may lead to a new test of equilibrium theory. Their study is contingent on a theory of price dynamics that can be described as follows. At the beginning of each period prices are set at the levels that equate expected demand and expected supply on both markets. Then, shocks occur; these prices are no longer Walrasian, and a fixed-price equilibrium takes place. Note that this dynamics has the advantage of being compatible with (equilibrium) long-run expectations.

Let me show in a simplified case how the test proceeds. The inventory equation is

$$S_{t+1} = A_0 + A_1 S_t + B_1 \epsilon_t \qquad \text{if Keynesian unemployment, i.e. if } \epsilon_t > 0$$

$$S_{t+1} = A_0 + A_1 S_t + B_2 \epsilon_t \qquad \text{if repressed inflation, i.e. if } \epsilon_t < 0.$$

The equilibrium hypothesis amounts to $B_1 = B_2$, which can be tested by the maximum likelihood ratio test. With quarterly data for 1970–8 (USA), Ducos *et al.* (1982) have rejected the equilibrium hypothesis.[4]

Price dynamics

Fix-price theory claims that a valid representation of our economies is obtained by assuming that prices are rigid during a period and then are adjusted at the beginning of next period. We will distinguish three types of price dynamics.

Backward-looking dynamics

One approach to defining the price dynamics is to assume that prices change according to the size of past net effective demand. In such a model, Honkapohja (1979) shows that quasi-equilibria (in which all real variables are constant) may exist in the Keynesian regime (where they are deflationary) and in the repressed inflation regime (where they are inflationary). Intuitively, these regimes exhibit excess supply on both markets or excess demand on both markets, so that the price–wage dynamics may be such that the real wage remains constant and different from the Walrasian level. Moreover, the government has a constant policy of a given level of real public expenditures which leads to a monetary policy neutralizing the wealth effect.

A number of technical difficulties arise in this approach. First, there are several notions of effective demand and there is no decisive argument in favor of any notion. Moreover, the right-hand side of the dynamic equations describing the evolution of prices is not continuous or not differentiable across the boundaries defining the various regimes. In the case of three commodity exchange economies, Veendorp (1975) and Laroque (1981) have exhibited sufficient conditions that yield convergence toward the competitive equilibrium despite these discontinuities, but this result has not been generalized. Honkapohja and Ito (1983) have suggested a different approach based on the concept of Filippov solution to a differential equation with discontinuous right-hand side. Finally, Laroque (1981) has proposed to make the price dynamics dependent on the Lagrange multiplier associated with the quantity constraints arising in a fixed-price equilibrium.

Forward-looking dynamics

One possibility is to assume that agents are price-setters and fix prices for next period on the basis of their expectations. Then, according to the true values of the parameters and (or) the values of the shocks in the economy, a fix-price equilibrium of one type or another takes place. Benassy (1978) has studied a sequence of fix-price equilibria in which, at the beginning of each period, the wage is set by workers and the price of the good is set by firms. The results depend of course on the assumptions about the government's economic policy (in his model, money creation is endogenous and attempts to stop unemployment). With a simulation, he shows that a Phillips curve describing the trade-off between involuntary unemploy- and inflation is generated (see also Grandmont and Laroque, 1976). Another forward-looking scheme consists in equating expected demand and expected supply as in Green and Laffont (1981).

Staggered contracts

Taylor (1980) has proposed a model in which, at each period, a subset of firms sets its prices for a number of periods. The firm takes into account past prices (set by other firms) which will remain valid for some time, and also its expectation about the prices that other firms will set in the future. The resulting pricing scheme is both forward- and backward-looking; its main advantage is to introduce some serial correlation of unemployment contrary to rational expectations pure forward-looking schemes. However, the analysis is restricted to the Keynesian regime.

Investment and growth

Malinvaud (1980) has offered the first study of the dynamics of fixed-price equilibria which describes the interaction of the dynamics of prices and the dynamics of investment. In particular, he shows that classical unemployment is a transient region while the Keynesian region may have stationary states with a constantly decreasing price level. The wealth effect is there exactly compensated by the dissaving that low incomes generate.[5] This result illustrates clearly the fact that downward price flexibility does not suffice to leave the Keynesian depression.

As stated by Malinvaud himself (1980: p. 58), 'this formulation is definitely weak with respect to the rational reaction of agents to a durable change of their environment. This remark concerns saving and investment behavior as well as revisions in the price level or in the real wage level.'

This weakness is general in the whole literature on growth in a disequilibrium framework. One reason is as follows. If investment behavior is based on microeconomics restrictions, one faces the need for differentiating investment functions according to the regime occurring and according to expectations. Then the number of cases to consider becomes unmanageable. The simplifications that lead to a unique functional form for the investment equation are rather *ad hoc*; the analysis can proceed, but one does not escape a feeling of *ad hoc*kery, and one loses the micro-foundations of macroeconomics that disequilibrium fixed-price theory is supposed to provide (see Ito, 1982; Picard, 1979; Autume, 1981; Laussel, 1980; Fourgeaud and Michel, 1980) for such studies, which clearly show how, in an economy with fairly myopic agents, the interaction of disequilibrium dynamics and various economic policies may influence the long-run behavior of the economy.

On aggregation

In an important paper Muellbauer (1978) has drawn attention to the careless aggregation procedure implicit in the macro-three-commodities approach. Markets – labor markets in particular – are isolated from each other; some can be in an excess-demand regime while others are in an excess-supply regime. In aggregate, unemployment and unfilled vacancies can coexist. Since both variables are observable, Muellbauer finds useful to develop a functional form that incorporates these 'tension' variables.

Consider the jth labor market; supply is $l^s + \epsilon_j$ and demand $l^d + \eta_j$. The situation on market j is defined by levels of average supply and demand l^s, l^d and by a pair of random variables (ϵ_j, η_j) drawn independently from the same distribution $F(\cdot)$.

Defining $z = l^d - l^s$, excess supply occurs on market j if

$$\theta_j = \epsilon_j - \eta_j > z.$$

With many markets aggregate unemployment and vacancies are

$$U = \iint_{\epsilon - \eta > z} (\epsilon - \eta - z)\, dF(\epsilon, \eta)$$

Moreover, employment can be written

$$\begin{aligned} l &= \iint_{\epsilon - \eta \geqslant z} (l^d + \eta)\, dF(\epsilon, \eta) + \iint_{\epsilon - \eta \leqslant z} (l^s + \epsilon)\, dF(\epsilon, \eta) \\ &= \iint (l^d + \eta)\, dF(\epsilon, \eta) + \iint_{\epsilon - \eta \leqslant z} (l^s + \epsilon - l^d - \eta)\, dF(\epsilon, \eta) \\ &= l^d - V. \end{aligned}$$

Or, similarly,

$$l = l^s - U.$$

Unemployment and vacancies are nonlinear functions of average excess demand z:

$$U = \Psi(z) \qquad V = \xi(z)$$

and $l = l^d - \xi(z) = l^s - \Psi(z)$ is a formulation different from the one derived from the macro-approach, $l = \min(l^d, l^s)$.

Spillover effects from the labor market to the goods market occur simultaneously for the producers and the consumers since some producers are constrained (vacancies) and some consumers are constrained (unemployment). Aggregate supply is:

$$Y = Y^s(w, p) - \alpha V.$$

Consumption demand is:

$$C = C(w, p) - \beta U.$$

These results provide the beginning of a rationalization for the use of tension variables in traditional macroeconomic models. (For empirical implementation of this approach see the studies of Kooiman and Kloek, 1979, for the Dutch labor market and Muellbauer and Winter (1980) for labor market and exports in British manufacturing.)

The weak point of this formalization is the arbitrary choice of the distribution $F(\cdot)$. Further progress requires a modelling of the evolution of $F(\cdot)$; otherwise not much is gained compared with an *ad hoc* formulation which, recognizing the lack of efficiency of the rationing scheme, considers that the exchanged quantity is a nonlinear function of supply and demand (see figure 5.5). This *ad hoc* point of view has been adopted by Spencer (1975) in a one-market empirical study and by Broer and Siebrand (1979) in a simultaneous analysis of the product market and the labor market.

Note also that the discrete switching approach can be easily interpreted in a very similar way:

$$Y = \min(D, S)$$

$$Y = \min(ED + \epsilon, ES + \eta)$$

and

$$EY = E\min(ED + \epsilon, ES + \eta) < \min(ED, ES)$$

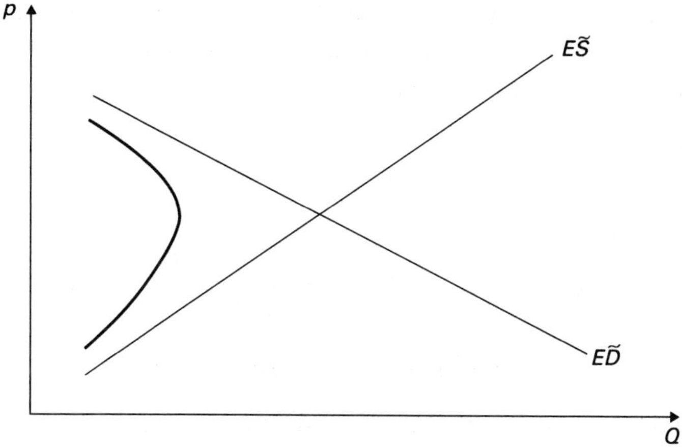

FIGURE 5.5

from Jensen's inequality

$$Y = EY + u$$

and EY is a nonlinear curve such as the one represented in figure 5.5.

A great potential of this more disaggregated view is the ability to determine the relative shares of classical and Keynesian unemployment. For policy purposes it is also important to be able to explain why a given sector is in one type of unemployment or the other.

A micro-approach

Let me consider a simple disaggregated model in the spirit of Muellbauer (1978) and Malinvaud (1981). The production function of firm i at date t is

$$y_{it} = f_i(l_{it}, k_{it})$$

where l_{it} is the labor input and k_{it} is the capital input.

Let $\bar{y}_{it}$ be the efficient production level given the price system. This level depends on individual characteristics of the firm a_i, on the local wage level it faces on the local labour market w_{it}, on the average wage level in the economy $\bar{w}_t$, and on exogenous variables z_t:

$$\bar{y}_{it} = a_i - bw_{it} + c_i z_t + d_i \bar{w}_t.$$

Let $\hat{y}_{it}$ the production level of firm i that would lead to full employment on its local labor market. This level is considered as exogenous in the analysis. Let

$$\hat{y}_t = \sum_i \hat{y}_{it}.$$

Then

$$\sum_i (y_{it} - \hat{y}_{it}) = \sum_i a_i - b \sum_i w_{it} + (\sum_i c_i)\, z_t + (\sum_i d_i)\, \bar{w}_t - \sum_i \hat{y}_{it}$$

$$= A - bn\bar{w}_t + Cz_t + D\bar{w}_t - \hat{y}_t$$

where n is the number of firms. For firm i, we can write

$$\bar{y}_{it} - \hat{y}_{it} = \frac{1}{n} \sum_j (\bar{y}_{jt} - \hat{y}_{jt}) + \epsilon_{it}$$

$$= \frac{A}{n} + \left(\frac{D}{n} - b\right) \bar{w}_t + \frac{C}{n} z_t - \frac{\hat{y}_t}{n} + \epsilon_{it}$$

with

$$\epsilon_{it} = a_i - \frac{A}{n} - b(w_{it} - \bar{w}_t) + \left(c_i - \frac{C}{n}\right) z_t$$

$$+ \left(d_i - \frac{D}{n}\right) \bar{w}_t - \left(\hat{y}_{it} - \frac{\hat{y}_t}{n}\right).$$

We obtain an equation that explains the variable $(\bar{y}_{it} - \hat{y}_{it})$ for firm i with macroeconomic variables and with a random personalized effect. When possible, these individual effects must be explained. For example, the difference between the local real wage and the real wage of the economy can be explained by forecasting errors of demand as

$$w_{it} - \bar{w}_t = h(e_{ity} - \bar{e}_{ty}) + \xi_{it}$$

where e_{ity} is the forecasting error made by firm i and $\bar{e}_{ty}$ is the mean of these errors; ξ_{it} is a zero mean random variable.

Leaving the unexplained individual deviations in the variance of the error, we obtain an equation that can be estimated on individual data:

$$\bar{y}_{it} - \hat{y}_{it} = \mathbf{a} + \mathbf{b}\bar{w}_t + \mathbf{c}z_t + h(e_{ity} - \bar{e}_{ty}) + \tilde{\epsilon}_{it}. \tag{23}$$

Similarly, we obtain an equation explaining the deviation for firm i between anticipated demand and its full-employment production level:

$$d_{it}^a - \hat{y}_{it} = \alpha + \beta g_t + \gamma \bar{w}_t + \delta x_t + k(e_{ity} - \bar{e}_{ty}) + \tilde{\eta}_{it}. \tag{24}$$

Rather than estimating directly these equations (23), (24), we obtain the probability of each regime with the following classification.

	$\hat{y}_{it} > inf(d_{it}^a, \bar{y}_{it})$	$\hat{y}_{it} < inf(d_{it}^a, \bar{y}_{it})$[6]
$d_{it}^a < \bar{y}_{it}$	KU	UC
$d_{it}^a > \bar{y}_{it}$	CU	RI

The probability of each regime is then obtained as:

$$\begin{aligned}
\Pr(\text{KU}) &= \Pr[d_{it}^a - y_{it} < 0 \text{ and } d_{it}^a - \hat{y}_{it} < 0] \\
&= \Pr[(d_{it}^a - \hat{y}_{it}) + (\hat{y}_{it} - \bar{y}_{it}) < 0 \text{ and } d_{it}^a - \hat{y}_{it} < 0] \\
\Pr(\text{UC}) &= \Pr[(d_{it}^a - \hat{y}_{it}) + (\hat{y}_{it} - \bar{y}_{it}) < 0 \text{ and } d_{it}^a - \hat{y}_{it} > 0] \\
\Pr(\text{CU}) &= \Pr[(d_{it}^a - \hat{y}_{it}) + (\hat{y}_{it} - \bar{y}_{it}) > 0 \text{ and } \bar{y}_{it} - \hat{y}_{it} < 0] \\
\Pr(\text{RI}) &= \Pr[(d_{it}^a - \hat{y}_{it}) + (\hat{y}_{it} - \bar{y}_{it}) > 0 \text{ and } \bar{y}_{it} - \hat{y}_{it} > 0]
\end{aligned}$$

From (23), (24), these probabilities are nonlinear functions of the variables we have singled out – public expenditures, wage levels, individual forecasting errors. The qualitative variable, representing the regime in which a firm is operating, has a probability law that depends on all these variables. Finally, if the random variables $\tilde{\epsilon}_{it}$, $\tilde{\eta}_{it}$ are autocorrelated, we must introduce the regime of period $(t-1)$ in the explanation of firm's i's regime in period t.

We borrow from Bouissou, Laffont and Vuong (1983) some empirical results obtained from the INSEE's quarterly business survey. In this survey firms are asked questions about their constraints. With the view that each firm has its local product market and its local labor market, it is possible to use their answers to allocate each firm to one of the four regimes. One question is: 'If you received more orders, could you produce more with your actual capacities?' If the firm answers yes, we presume that there is excess supply; if the firm answers no, we presume that there is excess demand.

Another question is: 'Do you now have difficulties in recruiting?' If the firm answers yes, we presume that there is excess demand on its local labor market; if the firm answers no, we presume that there is excess supply.

There are some problems with the interpretations to these answers; however, various alternative ways of using the answers do not change the qualitative features of the results given in table 5.2.

These results can be compared with table 5.3's *ex post* probabilities of the different regimes obtained by Artus, Laroque and Michel (1982). The two major features of the latter results are a great jump

TABLE 5.2 Proportions of firms in various regimes

Date	*No. of firms*	*KU*	*UC*	*CU*	*RI*
Jun 1974	1649	34.14	20.86	23.35	21.65
Nov 1974	1326	54.38	14.40	20.59	10.63
Mar 1975	1537	70.46	9.11	13.66	6.77
Jun 1975	1688	74.76	7.82	12.15	5.27
Nov 1975	1698	73.50	7.18	12.84	6.48
Mar 1976	1702	68.51	9.64	13.51	8.34
Jun 976	1696	59.49	12.26	17.40	10.85
Nov 1976	1704	61.33	11.97	16.78	9.92
Mar 1977	1793	63.97	9.65	18.01	8.37
Jun 1977	1787	65.53	8.62	17.85	8.00
Nov 1977	1942	67.92	8.75	15.86	7.47
Mar 1978	1856	69.07	8.94	16.06	5.93
Jun 1978	1914	65.89	9.56	17.50	7.05
Oct 1978	1669	67.47	7.91	18.09	6.53
Jan 1979	1930	67.36	7.93	18.55	6.16
Mar 1979	1882	66.79	7.22	20.46	5.53
Jun 1979	1869	61.64	7.87	23.27	7.22
Oct 1979	1890	59.74	8.20	24.34	7.72
Jan 1980	1839	62.10	8.05	23.00	6.85
Mar 1980	1929	59.67	7.83	24.83	7.67
Jun 1980	1869	61.26	7.92	23.06	7.76
Oct 1980	1875	70.67	6.83	17.28	5.22
Jan 1981	1701	75.49	6.05	15.11	3.35
Mar 1981	1605	77.63	4.73	14.46	3.18
Jun 1981	1554	77.54	5.15	14.41	2.90
Oct 1981	1656	76.39	5.13	15.22	3.26
Jan 1982	1699	76.16	3.88	16.07	3.89
Mar 1982	1635	74.56	5.20	16.02	4.22
Jun 1982	1555	71.45	5.40	17.56	5.59

TABLE 5.3 *Ex post* probabilities of regimes

Quarter	*KU*	*RI*	*CC*	*UC*
1974(1)	2	39	57*	2
1974(2)	0	51*	49	0
1974(3)	0	15	85*	0
1974(4)	100*	0	0	0
1975(1)	100*	0	0	0
1975(2)	100*	0	0	0
1975(3)	100*	0	0	0
1975(4)	100*	0	0	0
1976(1)	100*	0	0	0
1976(2)	100*	0	0	0
1976(3)	100*	0	0	0
1976(4)	95*	0	5	0
1977(1)	97*	0	3	0
1977(2)	100*	0	0	0
1977(3)	100*	0	0	0
1977(4)	100*	0	0	0
1978(1)	99*	0	1	0
1978(2)	78*	0	22	0
1978(3)	98*	0	2	0
1978(4)	80*	0	20	0

Source: Artus, Laroque and Michel (1982).

in Keynesian unemployment at the end of 1974 and then the domination of the Keynesian unemployment regime.

During this period two important attempts have been made to decrease unemployment with classical Keynesian policies: the Chirac experiment (June 1975, June 1976) and the Mauroy experiment (June 1981, June 1982). Both share the same features, a strong decline of the proportion of firms in the KU regime, with an increase in all other regimes. The Mauroy experiment appears less effective, with a stronger relative increase of the proportion of firms in the CU regime; it is not surprising given that, in the Mauroy experiment, the low real wages have been increased substantially. Note also the dynamics after the Chirac experiment; the proportion of firms in the Keynesian regime increases again, but the proportion of firms in the classical unemployment regime continues to increase.

One can then attempt to explain the dynamic evolution of the qualitative variable IR (index of regime) defined as

$$\text{IR} = 1 \longleftrightarrow \text{KU}$$

$$\text{IR} = 2 \longleftrightarrow \text{UC}$$

$$\text{IR} = 3 \longleftrightarrow \text{CU}$$

$$\text{IR} = 4 \longleftrightarrow \text{RI}$$

Let us denote MSD the relative prediction error in forecasting demand; IGT the total public expenditures; IGS the sectorial public expenditures; ISB the sectorial cost of labor; ISN the national wage level in terms of commodities, an index of purchasing power. All these variables are qualitative dichotomic variables; we have transformed quantitative variables into qualitative variables by looking at deviations from linear trends. We observed that a majority of firms predict demand well so that MSD is a qualitative variable expressing the absolute and not only relative prediction error. Finally, a number following a variable, for example IGS k, denotes that the variable is lagged by k periods.

I give below a few representative results. These should be read as follows. When UTP (upper tail probability) is larger than 10 per cent, it means that the current model has been accepted against an unconstrained model by a likelihood ratio test at the level 10 per cent. The number below a variable expresses the result of a significance test (by the likelihood ratio test). If the number if less than 5 it means that the suppression of the effect is rejected at the 5 per cent level. When an effect is significant, we have given the signs of the effect on the different components of IRO (+, +, −, 0) means that a large value for the qualitative variable increases the probabilities of being in regimes 1 and 2, decreases the probability of being in regime 3 and has no effect on the probability of being in regime 4.

Intermediary goods

IR:	IR1	MSD	IGT	IGT1	IGT2	IGT3
	0.0	0.0	20	5	1	10
		(+,+,−,−)		(0,−,0,0)	(−,0,+,0)	

UTP 21.2%

Professional equipment

IR:	IR1	MSD	IGS1	IGS2	IGS3	ISB
	0.0	$0 \cdot 10^{-3}$	24	10	3	$0.1 \cdot 10^{-2}$
		(+,+,–,–)			(–,0,0,0)	(–,0,0,+)

UTP 76.8%

Automobile, transportation

IR:	IR1	IGS1	IGT2	ISN
	0.0	0.7	$0.1 \cdot 10^{-2}$	$0.3 \cdot 10^{-2}$
		(–,0,0,0)	(–,0,0,0)	(–,0,0,0)

UTP 35.7%

Consumption goods

IR:	IR1	MSD	IGT3	ISN
	0.0	$0.7 \cdot 10^{-12}$	0.03	$0.2 \cdot 10^{-7}$
		(+,+,–,–)	(–,–,0,+)	(–,0,0,+)

UTP 17.0%

In all sectors we find that there is an extremely strong autocorrelation of regimes with the right signs (not reported). The error in predicting demand is extremely significant in explaining the regime with all signs as expected except in the automobile–transportation sector, where it is not significant; this might be due to the importance of production on orders in this sector. By an expected sign we mean that, when the firm over-evaluates future demand, it increases the probability of being in an excess demand (of goods) regime.

The fact that increase in public expenditure tends to decrease the probability of the Keynesian unemployment regime is clearly shown with a lag of two to three semesters. This result, however, does not have the stability of the previous ones. The index of purchasing power (ISN) has the right sign when significant. We are unable to exhibit the positive impact of an increase in the sectorial wage level on the probability of being in the classical unemployment regime, but this might be due to the dominance of the Keynesian regime in the sample. When this variable is significant, it plays in fact the same role as a purchasing power variable.

4 CONCLUDING COMMENTS

The competitive Walrasian equilibrium and fixed price equilibria are both theoretical constructs privileging adjustments by prices on the one hand and adjustments by quantities on the other hand. *For the long run*, the competitive equilibrium is a more attractive concept than a fixed-price equilibrium because it does not leave open mutual advantageous transactions.

For the short run, both theories are deficient because we do not have satisfactory theories of pricing behaviors in decentralized economies. To my mind the question then becomes empirical. Is the fix-price paradigm or the flex-price paradigm more useful to explain data and make predictions? I believe that a disaggregated view is in order here: for some markets the competitive flex-price approach is best; for others the monopolistically flex-price approach is best and for still others the fix-price approach is best. The short-run behavior of such an economic system is highly complex, and serious economic theory requires progress on the pricing rules (see for example Eden, 1981; Okun, 1981); this is obvious for the normative point of view, but I believe it is also the case for the short-run descriptive viewpoint.

Meanwhile, as I have tried to show in this paper, fix-price theory enables us to look at data from a different point of view, which might prove to be useful to economic policy of the short run.

APPENDIX 1

Implicit labor contracts

The goal of the theory of implicit labor contracts (Baily, 1974; Gordon, 1974; Azariadis, 1975; Holmström, 1983) has been to explain why, faced with an unexpected shock, firms would rather adjust quantities than wages. The basic assumption is that firms are risk-neutral while workers are risk-averse;[7] the rigidity of wages is the result of the insurance offered by the firm to the worker. Insurance takes place within the firm and not outside under the presumption that outside insurance agencies would face moral hazard problems; the firm does not suffer from this moral hazard because it can monitor effort (see Azariadis, 1979, for a survey). Wages are more rigid than spot prices would be, but employment is also more rigid. If workers have no outside opportunity and work is divisible, no layoff occurs and the marginal productivity of labor is equated to the disutility of effort in each state of nature. If workers have some outside opportunities (like unemployment compensations offered by governmental agencies), and/or if work is not divisible, layoffs may occur, but the workers who are dismissed are as well off as the ones who are kept within the firm. If the governmental unemployment compensations are too low the firm is led to pay workers some unemployment compensation.

The idea here is that the contract between firms and workers should use this outside money offered by the economic system. By not keeping the worker in bad states, it can pay the worker more in good states. This theory does not explain involuntary unemployment because workers are as well off whether employed or not. However, (Azariadis, 1979) suppose that unemployment compensations paid by the government are rather low but are paid to workers only if the firm does not provide any sort of compensation to the worker. It will remain true that the firm and the workers have an interest in exploiting this outside opportunity. In bad states some workers (either randomly selected or according to seniority rules) will be dismissed and, indeed, will be worse off than the ones who remain in the firm. This kind of unemployment is clearly *ex post* involuntary, but it can be termed *ex ante* voluntary because workers accepted a contract in which layoff was predicted is some states of nature. But then, firms may be led for insurance purposes to keep workers beyond the point where marginal productivity equals the opportunity cost (unemployment compensation plus disutility of labor); there is *ex post* inefficient allocation of labor, but there is in fact over-employment in comparison with a Walrasian equilibrium with contingent markets.

This theory explains, at the cost of restrictions on the insurance provisions, involuntary unemployment. However, unlike in a fixed-price model, marginal productivity is not equated to the rigid wage. The demand for labor has a very different form from the one assumed in fixed-price theory. The failure of the implicit labor contract theory to explain differences between marginal productivity of labor and opportunity cost of work without appealing to *ad hoc* imperfect insurance clauses has led to a more sophisticated theory based on asymmetric information.

The workers are assumed to be unable to observe their marginal productivity, but the entrepreneur can. The labor contract cannot be based on the unobservable marginal productivity. Following Calvo and Phelps (1977), most authors have assumed that the only common observable variable is the level of employment. Since wage must now depend on the level of employment, any contract that wishes to have some wage variability must have some variability of employment. Unfortunately, depending on the models, the employment variability may be either of an overemployment type (Green and Kahn, 1983) or of an unemployment type (Azariadis, 1983; Grossman and Hart, 1981). What can be said in general is that there is an *ex post* inefficient allocation of labor, which is necessitated by incentives constraints. Unemployment is not involuntary in the sense that laid-off workers are as well off as employed workers. Hart (1983) has argued that the right model must involve risk-neutral agents and a risk-averse manager. This, indeed, leads to unemployment only as a form of misallocation of labor. The argument is that the firm is run by a manager who has private information with respect to owners, and for incentives purposes his contract will not enable him to diversify his risk. On the contrary, he argues that workers can benefit from insurance and should be risk-neutral. Unfortunately, the same type of reason can be invoked to justify risk aversion on the part of workers; indeed, it was the moral hazard problem between an insurance agency and workers that motivated the implicit contracts between entrepreneurs and workers.

Grossman, Hart and Maskin (1982) have imbedded the implicit labor contract with asymmetric information in a macro-model. The basic tool here can be viewed as comparative statics analysis of the optimal contract. Suppose that, in addition to the unobservable variable, there is another jointly observable variable which is correlated with the first one. The contract can be made contingent on the realizations of this jointly observable variable and depends now on two variables (employment and this jointly observable). The question is, then, to compare the working of the contract for different values of the jointly observable variable. In a model where, for a worker, the observable variable is the economy-wide shock on the physical productivity of labor and the unobservable is the realized shock on the productivity of labor in his own firm, an increase in the observable shock leads to an increased unemployment. The reason is that this increase makes him more uncertain about his own marginal productivity. This calls for greater employment variability in the optimal contract, which, in a Grossman–Hart type of model, means more unemployment. As a consequence of our above remarks, it is clear that, in more general models, the implication would be an increase of the inefficiency on the allocation of labor, not necessarily in the form of unemployment.

APPENDIX 2

Monopolistic behavior

It has often been argued that imperfect competition is a necessary ingredient of Keynesian economics. Can we find there a rationale for persistent price rigidities?

Following Maskin and Polemarchakis (1980), one may wonder if it can be in the interest of a monopolist to use quantity constraints in combination with his choice of prices. If there is no constraint on his choice of prices, quantity constraints are not useful in general, as shown by figure 5.6. Consider a two-commodity economy. Let w be the vector of initial resources of the buyer and (x_1, x_2) his consumption of the two commodities. Let the heavy line in the figure represent a typical offer curve of the buyer. The region that quantity

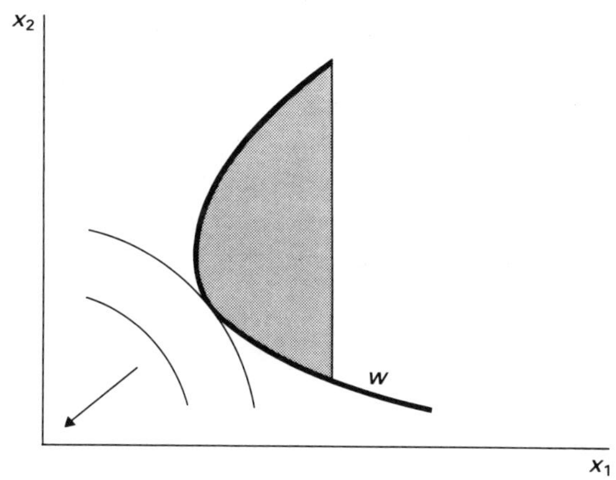

FIGURE 5.6

constraints enable the seller to reach is the shaded area. Since the seller will have a utility function with indifference curves increasing in the south-west direction (think of the Edgeworth box), the optimum is on the offer curve and does not require any rationing.

Various forms of imperfections in the design of the optimal prices may require, as a second-best tool, the use of rationing. The general principle at work here is that, in a second-best world, the additional constraint of rationing may prove to be useful.

APPENDIX 3

Public economics and fixed prices

The importance of unemployment in Europe has raised the question of the appropriate shadow price to use for labor in cost–benefit analysis. More generally, if fixed-price theory is taken seriously, all of public economics can be reconsidered in this light. A number of papers have started exploring these issues in closed economies (Bronsard and Wagneur, 1980; Guesnerie, 1980; Drèze, 1982; and Marchand, Mintz and Pestiau, 1983), as well as in open economies (Picard, 1979); Fourgeaud, Lenclud and Picard, 1983). The criticisms made above are still relevant here, perhaps to a larger extent. It is not clear why taxes cannot be used to disconnect consumption prices and production prices, solving in many cases the problems created by rigid prices (for example in Marchand, Mintz and Pestiau, 1983). This line of work requires a more precise formulation of the price rigidities (such as a detailed specification of indexation rules), as well as a precise dynamic framework recognizing some crucial irreversibilities (important in the European labor markets), in order to study the problem in the right framework. At this point it is too much a very short-run (macroeconomic-type) point of view, not reasonable in my mind for the study of the usual questions of public economics, such as appropriate discount rate, shadow prices, tax rules, etc.

NOTES

1 I benefited from J. M. Grandmont's lecture notes on the Barro–Grossman model.

2 Malinvaud (1977) and Muellbauer and Portes (1978) recognized the possibility of a fourth regime because of inventories; Gourieroux *et al.* (1980a) because of money holdings by firms.

3 $1_{C^i}(x) = 1$ if $x \in C^i$, $= 0$ if $x \notin C^i$.

4 Actually, the likelihood ratio test is not appropriate because the likelihood function is not continuous. Another solution is to introduce noise in the equation yielding the allocation between regimes and still use the likelihood ratio test.

5 Neary and Stiglitz (1980) have also made this point in a two-period disequilibrium model with rational expectations.

6 When $\hat{y}_{it} < d^a_{it} < \bar{y}_{it}$, we say that the firm is constrained on both markets on the presumption that it could satisfy a larger demand by drawing on its inventories. However, we attribute the case $d^a_{it} < \hat{y}_{it} < \bar{y}_{it}$ to Keynesian unemployment, although it could sometimes be in the underconsumption regime if the firm produces to increase its inventory.

7 See Kihlstrom and Laffont (1983) for a model of labor contracts with endogenous determination of who is a worker and who is an entrepreneur.

REFERENCES

Artus, P., Laroque, G. and Michel, P. (1982), 'Estimation d'un modèle macroéconomique trimestriel avec rationnements,' Working Paper, INSEE, Paris.

Autume, A. D. (1981), 'Un modèle cohérent de croissance en déséquilibre,' Conjoncture et Analyse des Déséquilibres, University of Paris I.

Azariadis, C. (1975), 'Implicit Contracts and Unemployment Equilibria,' *Journal of Political Economy*, **83**, 1183–202.

Azariadis, C. (1979), 'Implicit Contracts and Related Topics: A Survey,' University of Pennsylvania (mimeograph).

Azariadis, C. (1983), 'Employment with Asymmetric Information,' *Quarterly Journal of Economics*, Supplement, **98**, 157–72.

Baily, M. N. (1974), 'Wages and Employment under Uncertain Demand,' *Review of Economic Studies*, **41**, 27–50.

Barro, R. J. and Grossman, H. I. (1971), 'A General Disequilibrium Model of Income and Employment,' *American Economic Review*, **61**, 82–93.

Benassy, J. P. (1973), 'Disequilibrium Theory,' PhD dissertation, University of California.

Benassy, J. P. (1978), 'A Neo Keynesian Model of Price and Quantity Determination in Disequilibrium,' in G. Schwödiauer (ed.), *Equilibrium and Disequilibrium in Economic Theory*, Reidel, Boston.

Benassy, J. P. (1982), *The Economics of Disequilibrium*, Academic Press, New York.

Böhm, V. (1981a), 'Inventories and Money Balances in a Dynamic Model with Rationing,' CARESS Working Paper no. 8115, University of Pennsylvania.

Böhm, V. (1981b), *Preise, Löhne und Beschäftigung*, J. C. B. Mohr, Tübingen.

Bouissou, M. B., Laffont, J. J. and Vuong, Q. (1983), 'Econométrie du déséquilibre sur donnés microéconomiques,' GREMAQ Discussion Paper no. 83, University of Toulouse.

Boyer, M. and Mistral, J. (1982), 'Accumulation, inflation, crise,' chapter 6, Presses Universitaires de France, Paris.

Broer, D. P. and Siebrand, J. C. (1979), 'A Simultaneous Disequilibrium Analysis of Product Market and Labor Market,' Discussion Paper no. 781316, Erasmus University, Rotterdam.

Bronsard, C. and Wagneur, E. (1980), 'Second rang et déséquilibre,' Cahier no. 8041, University of Montréal.

Calvo, G. and Phelps, E. S. (1977), 'Employment-contingent Wage Contracts,' *Journal of Monetary Economics*, supplement, 160–8.

Clower, R. W. (1965), 'The Keynesian Counter-revolution: A Theoretical Appraisal,' in F. M. Hahn and F. Brechling (eds), *The Theory of Interest Rates*, Macmillan, London.

Drazen, A. (1980), 'Recent Developments in Macroeconomic Disequilibrium Theory,' *Econometrica*, **48**, 283–306.

Drèze, J. (1982), 'Second-best Analysis with Markets in Disequilibrium: Public Sector Pricing in a Keynesian Regime,' CORE Discussion Paper no. 8216, University of Louvain-La-Neuve.

Ducos, G., Green, J. and Laffont, J. J. (1982), 'A Test of the Equilibrium Hypothesis Based on Inventories,' *European Economic Review*, **17**, 209–19.

Eaton, J. and Quandt, R. E. (1980), 'A Quasi-Walrasian Model of Rationing and Labor Supply: Theory and Estimation,' Econometric Research Program, Research memo no. 251, Princeton University.

Eden, B. (1981), 'Toward a Theory of Competitive Price Adjustment,' *Review of Economic Studies*, **58**, 199–216.

Fair, R. C. and Jaffee, K. M. (1972), 'Methods of Estimation of Markets in Disequilibrium: A Further Study,' *Econometrica*, **42**, 177–90.

Fisher, S. (1977), 'Long-term Contracts, Rational Expectations, and the Optimal Money Supply Rule,' *Journal of Political Economy*, **85**, 191–205.

Fourgeaud, C., Lenclud, B. and Picard, P. (1983), 'Calcul économique, prix fictifs et contrainte extérieure,' CEPREMAP, Paris.

Fourgeaud, C. and Michel, P. (1980), 'Dynamic Analysis of Disequilibrium,' CEPREMAP, Paris.

Ginsburgh, V., Tishler, A. and Zang, I. (1980), 'Alternative Estimation Methods for Two Regime Models,' *European Economic Review*, **13**, 207–28.

Gordon, D. F. (1974), 'A Neoclassical Theory of Keynesian Unemployment,' *Economic Inquiry*, **12**, 431–59.

Gourieroux, C., Laffont, J. J. and Monfort, A. (1980a), 'Disequilibrium Econometrics in Simultaneous Equation Systems,' *Econometrica*, **48**, 75–96.

Gourieroux, C., Laffont, J. J. and Monfort, A. (1980b), 'Coherency Conditions in Simultaneous Linear Equations Models with Endogenous Switching Regimes,' *Econometrica*, **48**, 75–96.

Grandmont, J. M. (1977), 'The Logic of the Fix-price Method,' *Scandinavian Journal of Economics*, **79**, 169–86.

Grandmont, J. M. and Laroque, G. (1976), 'On Temporary Keynesian Equilibria,' *Review of Economic Studies*, **43**, 53–67.

Green, J. and Kahn, C. (1984), 'Wage Employment Contracts,' *Quarterly Journal of Economics*, Supplement, **98**, 173–87.

Green, J. and Laffont, J. J. (1981), 'Disequilibrium Dynamics with Inventories and Anticipatory Price-setting,' *European Economic Review*, **16**, 199–221.

Grossman, S. and Hart, O. (1981), 'Implicit Contracts, Moral Hazard, and Unemployment,' *American Economic Review*, **71**, 301–7.

Grossman, S., Hart, O. and Maskin, E. (1982), 'Unemployment with Observable Aggregate Shocks,' National Bureau of Economic Research Working Paper no. 975.

Guesnerie, R. (1980), 'Analyse microéconomique normative du modèle keynésian élémentaire,' CEPREMAP (mimeograph).

Hart, O. (1983), 'Optimal Labor Contracts under Asymmetric Information: An Introduction,' *Review of Economic Studies*, **50**, 3–35.

Holmström, B. (1983), 'Equilibrium Long-term Contracts,' *Quarterly Journal of Economics*, Supplement, **98**, 23–54.

Honkapohja, S. (1979), 'On the Dynamics of Disequilibria in a Macro-model with Flexible Wages and Prices,' in M. Aoki and A. Marzollo (eds), *New Trends in Dynamic System Theory and Economics*, Academic Press, New York.

Honkapohja, S. and Ito, I. (1980), 'Inventory Dynamics in a Simple Disequilibrium Macroeconomic Model,' *Scandinavian Journal of Economics*, **82**, 184–98.

Honkapohja, S. and Ito, T. (1983), 'Stability with Regime-switching,' *Journal of Economic Theory*, **29**, 22–48.

Ito, T. (1980a), 'Methods of Estimation for Multimarket Disequilibrium Models,' *Econometrica*, **48**, 97–126.

Ito, T. (1980b), 'Disequilibrium Growth Theory,' *Journal of Economic Theory*, **23**, 380–409.

Kihlstrom, R. and Laffont, J. J. (1984), 'Implicit Labor Contracts and Free Entry,' *Quarterly Journal of Economics*, Supplement, **98**, 55–105.

Kooiman, P. and Kloek, T. (1979), 'Aggregation of Micro-markets in Disequilibrium,' Erasmus University, Rotterdam (mimeograph).

Kooiman, P. and Kloek, I. (1980), 'An Aggregate Two-market Disequilibrium Model with Foreign Trade,' Erasmus University, Rotterdam (mimeograph).

Laroque, G. (1978), 'The Fixed-price Equilibria: Some Results in Local Comparative Statics,' *Econometrica*, **46**, 1127–59.

Laroque, G. (1981), 'A Comment on "Stable Spillovers among Substitutes",' *Review of Economics Studies*, **48**, 355–61.

Laussel, D. (1980), 'Disequilibrium Growth Paths,' Université Aix-Marseille II (mimeograph).

Malinvaud, E. (1977), *The Theory of Unemployment Reconsidered*, Basil Blackwell, Oxford.

Malinvaud, E. (1980), *Profitability and Unemployment*, Cambridge University Press.

Malinvaud, E. (1981), 'Econometric Implications of Macro-disequilibrium Theory,' INSEE Working Paper no. 8114, Paris (mimeograph).

Marchand, M., Mintz, J. and Pestiau, P. (1983), 'Public Production and Shadow Pricing in a Model of Disequilibrium in Labor and Capital Markets,' University of Louvain-La-Neuve (mimeograph).

Maskin, E. and Polemarchakis, H. M. (1980), 'Rational Quantity Rationing,' Columbia University Discussion Paper no. 78.

Monier, S. (1983), 'Dynamique du déséquilibre,' third-year thesis, University of Toulouse.

Muellbauer, J. (1978), 'Macrotheory vs. Macroeconometrics: The Treatment of Disequilibrium in Macro-models,' Birbeck College, London, Discussion paper no. 29.

Muellbauer, J. and Portes, R. (1978), 'Macroeconomic Models with Quantity Rationing,' *Economic Journal*, **88**, 788–821.

Muellbauer, J. and Winter, D. (1980), 'Unemployment, Employment and Exports in British Manufacturing or Non-clearing-markets Approach,' *European Economic Review*, **13**, 383–409.

Neary, J. P. and Stiglitz, J. (1980), 'Towards a Reconstruction of Keynesian Economics: Expectations and Constrained Equilibria,' *Quarterly Journal of Economics*, Supplement, **98**, 199–228.

Okun, A. (1981), *Prices and Quantities: A Macroeconomic Analysis*, Brookings Institution, Washington, DC.

Patinkin, D. (1965), *Money, Interest and Prices*, Harper and Row, New York.

Phelps, E. and Taylor, J. (1977), 'Stabilizing Powers of Monetary Policy under Rational Expectations,' *Journal of Political Economy*, **85**, 163–90.

Picard, P. (1979), 'Dynamics of Temporary Equilibrium in a Macroeconomic Model,' University of Paris I (mimeograph).

Portes, R., Quandt, R., Winter, D. and Yeo, S. (1982), 'Macroeconomic Planning and Disequilibrium: Some Preliminary Results for Poland, 1955–1980,' Birbeck College, London.

Quandt, R. (1978), 'Maximum Likelihood Estimation of Disequilibrium Models,' *Pioneering Economics*, Padua, pp. 865–96.

Quandt, R. (1982), 'Econometric Disequilibrium Models,' *Econometric Reviews*, **1**, 1–63.

Richard, J. F. (1980), 'C-type Distributions and Disequilibrium Models,' University of Louvain (mimeograph).

Schultz, N. (1983), 'On the Global Uniqueness of Fix-price Equilibria,' *Econometrica*, **51**, 47–68.

Silvestre, J. (1982), 'Fix-price Analysis in Exchange Economies,' *Journal of Economic Theory*, **26**, 28–58.

Simonovits, A. (1981), 'Buffer Stocks and Naive Expectations in a Non-Walrasian Dynamic Macro-Model,' Hungarian Academy of Sciences (mimeograph).

Sneessens, H. (1980), 'Theory and Estimation of Macroeconomic Rationing Models,' PhD dissertation, University of Louvain.

Spencer, P. D. (1975), 'A Disequilibrium Model of Personal Sector Bank Advances, 1964–1974: Some Preliminary Results,' Working Paper, HM Treasury.

Taylor, J. B. (1980), 'Aggregate Dynamics and Staggered Contracts,' *Journal of Political Economy*, **88**, 1–23.

Vilares, M. J. (1981), 'Macroeconomic Model with Structural Change and Disequilibrium,' Porto (mimeograph).

Veendorp, E. C. H. (1975), 'Stable Spill-overs among Substitutes,' *Review of Economic Studies*, **52**, 445–56.

Comment

FRANK H. HAHN

Jean-Jacques Laffont is a jewel in the crown of economic theory, and he has, as expected, written a clear and crisp paper. None the less, I rather regret that on this occasion he was more intent on adorning the leaden crown of econometrics. The theoretical foundation of 'fix-price' models are so insecure that, should their economic investigation yield results judged as 'very encouraging', one would be sorely puzzled. Simple models with *ad hoc* assumption may serve the theorist well in isolating particular qualitative insight: why they should perform well econometrically is to me mysterious. In any case, in the present instance the question put to innocent French businessmen and the interpretations put on their answers fortunately leave much scope for doubting the encouraging nature of the result.

It is so clear that it is economic theory that must here be put through its paces, and not estimation, that I make no excuse in following in the sequel both my preferences and such talents as I have.

1 THE SETTING

Laffont reports Benassy as holding the views that 'prices are the result of complex socioeconomic struggles', from which it appears that the *non sequitur* is drawn that prices can (for sufficiently long periods) be taken as given. This may be a mis-reading on my part. In any event, there is no reason why the struggle should not feel the power of the invisible hand. One could also, of course, argue that output and employment are the result of all this complex struggling, and then, since no one seems to understand it, we can shut up shop. So this is an intellectually lazy and not very encouraging route.

At the other extreme, we have the dotty view that economies are at all time in perfectly competitive equilibrium. It is dotty because, even if we believe that agents quickly exploit Pareto-improving moves which they perceive and can exploit, this does not entail the conclusion. It is also dotty because everything that is a matter of controversy and political relevance has been not argued away but axiomatized away. The latest econometric effort by economists of that persuasion postulates an infinitely farsighted, infinitely fast auctioneer who sees to it that transversality conditions are satisfied. It takes all sorts!

The complete and widespread misunderstanding of the intellectual use to which the beautiful and important Arrow–Debreu theory can be put I have discussed rather frequently (e.g. Hahn, 1973), and I shall not repeat the arguments here. For present purposes we note that the practical orthodox (PO), as I shall call the adherents of the dotty views, have imposed a most undesirable nomenclature. A state of the economy that is not in Walrasian equilibrium is called *disequilibrium*, and a price rule that does not instantaneously clear Walrasian market is called *inflexible*. That this nomenclature is sloppy and dangerous can be verified with the greatest ease by reading the journals and listening to politicians.

Since the PO, three-stage least-squares notwithstanding, seem to account for so little that we observe macroeconomically, it was not unnatural that some theorists less easily satisfied or less gullible should seek to modify the axioms. All these theorists had contributed significantly to orthodoxy in the past. It is not surprising that their first attempts should have led them to the other extreme from the PO, namely the postulate of fixed and exogenously given prices. In this they had been preceded, albeit less rigorously, by the Swedes and by Hicks. The interpretation to be put on the resulting model was that it referred to 'the short period'. The further interpretation often put on it is that it formalizes what Keynes proposed. But that is just false and need not detain us.

Even if one accepts the implicit periodization of this approach (so that there are actually intervals in which no price changes), not very much has been gained until one has a theory of a sequence of such short-period equilibria in which prices are not exogenous from period to period. Indeed, one must sympathize with the PO if they do not regard the present fix-price literature as much of a threat. It should also be noted that we cannot easily hand over inter-period price changes to an auctioneer of the usual sort unless we agree that the only long-run equilibrium is Walrasian.

In the following section, however, I outline a model in which the short-period interpretation of fix price theory is inappropriate.

Thus, while no doubt something has been learned from the fix-price model, it is high time to get on. Getting on, I believe, requires us to have price-setting agents, and that in turn is most easily studied in a market environment that is not perfectly competitive. Laffont makes a bow in this direction in his appendices. But in the one of most immediate relevance he reports on some work by Maskin and Polemarchasis which seems to have rediscovered the theory of optimum tariffs. In any case, it will be best to break off here to look at a model.

2 A RATIONAL (QUANTITY) EXPECTATIONS NASH EQUILIBRIUM

An economy consists of m firms producing m differentiated goods. These are all produced by homogeneous labour which is inelastically supplied by n households. Each household can supply one unit of labour. There is also money in the economy. Its stock is constant.

I shall take the production functions of the firms to be stochastic. This need not be interpreted as meaning that technology is stochastic – e.g., there may be inputs imported from abroad with stochastic prices. The special assumption of the model will be that prices and wages must be set before the state of the world is known. I shall be interested in a certain kind of rational expectations Nash equilibria.

The notation is as follows. $p \in R^m_+$, $w \in R^m_+$ are respectively price and wage vectors. To economize in notation I shall let $q = (p, w)$. Also, $q(i)$ is the vector derived from q by deleting the ith component from p and w. The set of the states of nature is S with members s. Then $y(s) \in R^m_+$ is the output vector in state s of the firms and $l(s) \in R^m_+$ is the vector of their labour inputs. The demand vector for goods is $X \in R^m_+$ and is written as $X = \Sigma x_h + g$ where x_h is the vector of household h's demand and g is an exogenously fixed government demand vector.

It will be assumed that each firm sets its price and the wage at which it is willing to hire labour. Further, rather in the tradition of this literature (e.g. Malinvaud, 1978), I assume that profits are all taxed away and that the government levies an identical lump-sum tax $T(s) \gtreqless 0$ on each household so as to keep a balance in each state. The net income of the aggregate of identical households in state s is then

$$W(s) = Wl(s) - nT(s).$$

I shall want to ignore distribution effects between households. This is done most easily by supposing that they are of the Gorman (1953)–Hicks (1939) type. Accordingly, I write

$$\omega(s) = \frac{1}{n} W(s), \quad x = \frac{1}{n} \sum_h x_h, \quad m = \frac{1}{n} \quad m_h, \sum \bar{m} = \frac{1}{n} \sum_h \bar{m}_h$$

where m_h is money stock demanded and $\bar{m}_h$ is money stock held by h. For any s and q the choice of x and m satisfies:

$$\max_{x, m} U(x, m, q)$$

$$\text{s.t.} \quad px + m \leqslant \omega(s) + \bar{m}$$

$$x \leqslant \frac{1}{n} y(s). \tag{1}$$

With U 'well behaved', this has a unique solution. Accordingly, one can write the total demand vector X (suppressing the constants $\bar{m}$, g) as

$$X(s) = X[q, \omega(s), y(s)].$$

The production function of firm i is given by

$$y_i(s) = f_i[l_i(s), s]$$

and it too is 'well behaved'. To find the choice of the firm we require some preliminaries.

Let $k_i(w)$ be the number of firms that set the same wage as does firm i, including in this number firm i itself. Let $L(i, w, s)$ be the total labour employed by firms that have set a higher wage than has i. Define

$$\Gamma_i(w, s) = \lambda_i(w)[n - L(i, w, s)], \text{ where } \lambda_i(w) = k_i^{-1}(w).$$

One thinks of $\Gamma_i(w, s)$ as the maximum amount of labour that firm i can hire given the wage that it has set and the wages set by everyone else. Clearly, $\Gamma_i(w, s)$ may have discontinuities.

For every (q, s) the firm will choose output and employment to solve

$$\max\{p_i f_i[l_i(s), s] - w_i l_i(s)\}$$

$$\text{s.t.} \quad l_i(s) \leqslant \Gamma_i(w, s)$$

$$f_i[l_i(s), s] \leqslant X_i[q, \omega(s), y(i, s)]. \tag{2}$$

I shall suppose that the effect of its own employment on the demand for its own good is small enough to be ignored by the firm. (See Hart, 1982, for some assumptions which make its effect zero.) Let

$$\pi_i\{q_i, q(i), \omega(s), \Gamma_i[w_i, w(i), s], y(i, s), s\} \tag{3}$$

be the profit that results from (2).

Definition 1 An equilibrium in state s relatively to q is $l^*(s)$, $y^*(s)$, $x^*(s)$ such that

(i) $x^*(s)$ solves (1) given $[q, l^*(s), y^*(s)]$
(ii) $[y_i^*(s)]$ solves (2) given $[q, y^*(i, s), l^*(i, s)]$ all i.

I now make a highly non-robust assumption:

$$\text{For every } (q, s) \text{ equilibrium is unique.} \tag{A1}$$

Laffont has cited some literature on this matter and readers are referred to his comments.

Given (A1), I can write (3) as

$$\bar{\pi}_i[q_i, q(i), s]$$

and introduce a second definition.

Definition 2 q^* is a rational (quantity) expectations Nash equilibrium (RENE) if, for all i,

$$E\bar{\pi}_i[q_i^*, q^*(i), s] \geqslant E\bar{\pi}_i[q_i, q^*(i), s].$$

Comments I have not seriously investigated the existence of the two kinds of equilibria defined. The discontinuities in labour rations when relative wages change may turn out to be a serious problem, and one would have to investigate whether a Dasgupta–Maskin (1982) theorem is applicable.

However, while a firm may relax a labour constraint in some states by fixing a higher wage, it is also saddled with this higher wage in states in which the labour constraint is ineffective. It is likely that some not too dreadful conditions on the nature of the state and the production functions will yield existence. Of course, assumption (A1) is another matter altogether, and I do not know how to proceed without it.

I now suppose that these technical matters have been settled. If we assume that the model applied to one period but that there is a stationary distribution of states over periods, then it is plainly possible that q^* will be independent of time. One can be more explicit. Suppose that, by some criterion, various equilibria relatively to (q^*, s) are named *à la* Malinvaud (1978). Then if, say, a 'Keynesian equilibrium' results whenever $s = s_k$, there will be no presumption that 'eventually' prices will change. When the prices were fixed the possibility of a Keynesian outcome was taken into account, and by assumption its occurrence leaves the probability of its recurrence in the future unchanged. Hence in this model prices change only if something new is learned from the sample path.

However, suppose that q^* is such that, for every s, households sell less labour than n and firms just sell what is demanded. Then, since firms set the wage, q^* cannot be on a RENE. Exactly the same is true if at q^* the regime is one of 'suppressed inflation' for every s: q^* does not qualify.

Provided then that (a) prices and wages are set before the state is known, (b) firms set prices and wages, (c) quantity expectations are rational and (d) q^* exists, while the economy cannot permanently be in one of Malinvaud's regimes, it can, at fixed prices, permanently fluctuate between them.

There are two rather obvious remarks to be made.

1 The RENE in general will not be unique.
2 If the government followed a policy that made the available money stock a function of s, this policy will have permanent *real effects* (as well as affecting q^*). Moreover, these effects arise precisely because the monetary policy is known. By stripping the model to two goods it is easy to use the constructions in a delightful anti-Lucas manner.

It does not require special attributes to note the shortcomings in the model of the preceding section. There are no inventories, there is no investment, there is too much information and rationality, and there are no unions or even labour contracts. Setting prices before the state is known also requires justification, although here one can think of many – not many markets are fish markets.

But the purpose of the model was to act as a pointer to what I consider a useful direction, and not as a theory of an economy. That direction is to make prices variables that are endogenous and yet may lead to 'fix-price' phenomena and may lead us to stick to general equilibrium rather than macroeconomics. The model was also constructed to help me with Laffont's paper. He gives his own model (on pp. 351–3). I must confess that its economics is not transparent to me. For instance, take the equation at the bottom of p. 352: Who sets the wage in sector i? Why do sectoral wages but not sectoral prices change when there is an error in the forecast of demand? Then again, what has become of inventories? Although there is capital there is no account of investment (I take it that it is included in x_t in the equation of demand (24)). I am not of course suggesting that this model is in some way less credible than the one that I have presented: rather, it is less transparent. That is the cost of 'estimateable equations'. None the less, it may be that there is a family resemblance between the model of the preceding section and that of Laffont. Wages do for instance change when there have been forecasting mistakes, but they change for 'macro-reasons' as well.

3 SOME COMMENTS

In an appendix Laffont surveys the Theory of Implicit Contracts. The question is whether it can help us in the 'fix-price' story. Clearly, the answer is no if we are concerned, as for instance is Malinvaud, with nominal prices. Contracts at best lead to fixed 'real' wages (*not* product wages). Only the most rudimentary 'macro'-general equilibrium models with contracts are at present available. I have been working on these matters recently and I shall not use a 'Comment' as an excuse for a 'paper'. Instead, I list a number of issues that are perhaps worth discussing.

1 Laffont – in the company of many others – puts on a philosopher's hat when it comes to involuntary unemployment. Thus, he

is convinced that, should an equilibrium contract allow laid-off workers to be worse off than those that are retained, one could not really call the laid-off 'involuntarily' unemployed. After all, they agreed to the contract in the first place! Somewhere concepts of 'free will' and 'free choice' are clouding the economist's mind.

Involuntary unemployment is concerned with a certain kind of inefficiency. It has nothing to do with free will and is a purely technical term. At its simplest it denotes a state in which the market real wage exceeds the shadow wage of workers. The question is: Is such a state reconcilable with some equilibrium? And is it interesting? Suppose that in a properly formulated general equilibrium model with contracts (a) there are several rational expectations equilibria and (b) laid-off workers lose utility. Then clearly it may be possible to Pareto-rank such equilibria (e.g. when there are constant returns to scale), and those with less involuntary unemployment will Pareto-dominate those with more. Nothing philosophical about that!

Moreover, in the crudest macro-models involuntary unemployment is of interest since the effects of policy will be sensitive to its occurrence or non-occurrence. Lastly, if the currently unemployed in Western Europe are not involuntary unemployed some rather serious conclusions would follow. If one is Rawlesian, then anything that happens had our 'initial position' assent and therefore we are 'voluntarily' poor or imprisoned. Not a useful way of thinking.

2 A great deal of excitement has been caused by asymmetric information in implicit contracts. If firms are risk-averse it can lead to equilibrium states in which the workers' shadow wage deviates from its marginal product. With a little ingenuity, one can argue that in fact the marginal product will exceed the shadow wage of laid-off workers. This is first-best inefficient but I see no reason for being interested in first-best efficiency that is not feasible given the information structure. It is of course the case that, with symmetric information but imperfect competition, one gets analogous inefficiencies. But the informational twist ensures that even the marginal revenue product may exceed the shadow wage when there are lay-offs.

If in such an economy there were a lay-off-reducing policy it might be Pareto-improving. By distinguishing between correlated shocks (macro-states) and uncorrelated ones (micro-states), Grossman, Hart and Maskin (1983) have given examples of this sort. These are interesting, but I cannot claim to be convinced of the importance to, say, the current unemployment or to current debates about unemployment policy.

But let me mention my theoretical doubts. Moore (1982) has studied the case where employers cannot observe the worker's 'opportunity utility' in any state but where otherwise information is symmetric. It leads to results opposite to those of Grossman *et al.* If both kinds of asymmetries are present, qualitative results are unobtainable. The Moore asymmetry and the moral hazard it gives rise to is at least as convincing as is that of Grossman and Hart.

The next related point is this. With rational expectations, contracts may be over the working life of the worker. When a worker is laid off the relevant calculations involve $V[\bar{w}(s), t]$, which is the maximum expected utility that the worker can attain starting at date–event pair (s, t) when he is paid the lay-off wage $\bar{w}(s)$. It is hard to see how this can be known to the employer.

Next, the efficiency arguments cannot be seriously considered as long as the postulated production function is $f(l)$ with $f''(l) < 0$. The evidence for this seems non-existent and it leads to theoretical conundrums that Weitzman (1982) has been the latest to notice. If there are some increasing returns the whole story is changed in an obvious and radical way. Is there any reason for postulating $f''(l) < 0$ other than that it fits textbook economics? If one at least writes $f(l, K)$ and postulates constant returns to (L, K), will the story lead to 'under-employment'?

Lastly, the literature of 'efficient contracts' concludes, as Laffont notes, that workers do not care whether they are laid off or not. But this may cause problems with work incentives. When they are modelled, then under certain assumptions this ceases to be true and so, even with symmetric information about states, marginal product and shadow wage can diverge.

3 However, implicit contracts do have one consequence favourable to the fix-price approach: namely, that real wages are determined before the state is known. In particular, with risk-neutral firms and locked-in workers the real wage is independent of state. Since the same is true of workers' utilities, this is not of great interest and certainly not an obvious occasion for policy.

But let us introduce births and deaths, and let the working lives of workers overlap. If contracts always clear the market for new labour, then it is obvious that we may have different contracts for different generations. With rational expectations firms know the new contracts that they can make in each state with the new generations. This will of course affect the contract that the current generation can make in the current state. If there are lay-offs of old workers, then new workers cannot get a contract at all. However, they prefer the contracts under which the old workers are engaged to being jobless. In that sense they are involuntarily unemployed. This whole matter needs proper study.

4 Lastly, I return to the distinction between money, product and real wages. The difference between the latter pair raises possibilities of bankruptcy for an otherwise risk-neutral contracting employer. It will make him act 'as if' he were risk-averse over certain states. Hence, in general workers will not be fully insured. Although some 'indexed' wage contracts are found, why are they so rare? The one example I know of is of seventeenth-century miners whose wage was indexed to the price of coal – the product wage was insured!

The real wage, in the general absence of an ideal price index, is of course another source of purely informational difficulties.

But what is striking is that contract theory does not predict the famous 'downward rigidity of money wages'. I mean no more than that money wages seem to lag behind downward movement of prices. On the contrary, the theory predicts instantaneous adjustment up *and* down. From that point of view, it is not very promising for a French approach to macroeconomics.

4 ENVOY

I end on a sour note. Fix-price theory is a striking example of an attempt to take a short cut. Too much effort has gone into it. Traditional macroeconomic problems have their origins in externalities of a very general and pervasive kind. The textbooks are no help here. It is time we set out on the long and arduous route.

REFERENCES

Dasgupta, P. and Maskin, E. (1982), 'The Existence of Equilibrium in Economic Games, I: Theory', ICERD Discussion Paper no. 54, London School of Economics.

Gorman, W. M. (1953), 'Community Preference Fields', *Econometrica*, **21**, 63–80.

Grossman, S., Hart, O. and Maskin, E. (1983), 'Unemployment with Observable Aggregate Shocks', *Journal of Political Economy*, **91**, 907–28.

Hahn, F. H. (1973), *The Notion of Equilibrium in Economics*, Cambridge University Press.

Hart, O. (1982), 'A Model of Imperfect Competition with Keynesian Features', *Quarterly Journal of Economics*, **97**, 109–38.

Hicks, J. R. (1939), *Value and Capital*, Oxford University Press.

Malinvaud, E. (1978), *The Theory of Unemployment Reconsidered*, Oxford University Press.

Moore, J. (1982), 'Optimal Labour Contracts When Workers Have a Variety of Privately Observed Reservation Wages', Birkbeck College, London (mimeograph).

Weitzman, M. (1982), 'Increasing Returns as The Foundations of Unemployment Theory', *Economic Journal*, **92**, 781–809.

Comment

JÁNOS KORNAI

1 INTRODUCTION

Rather than comment directly on Professor Laffont's survey paper, I would like to offer some complementary material: a brief survey of research concerning Eastern European economies. Appendix 1 comprises a bibliography of 24 books and papers. These writings have much in common; they can be regarded as studies aiming at the fulfillment of the same research program, in other words, as a family of models. I shall try to summarize the common attributes of these 24 studies.

There is, of course, some arbitrariness in determining which studies belong to the 'family' and which are, although related in topics and/or methodology, outside it. Most of the authors are Hungarians, but the delineation does not follow national borders. On the one hand, there are Swedish, American, British and German economists among the authors; on the other hand, there are related Hungarian studies that have not been included in the bibliography.[1] I did not consider as a decisive criterion for the inclusion into this research current whether or not the author declares himself to be a member of this group: the only criterion I have tried to apply is a certain similarity in theoretical foundations and research methodology.

It would be a rewarding exercise to make a detailed comparison between our work and the research program called 'fixed-price models' or 'disequilibrium theory.' There are even a few important papers analyzing Eastern European economies with the theoretical apparatus of the 'disequilibrium school.' (See for example the work of R. Portes and D. Winter in the United Kingdom, and K. Hulyák in Hungary.[2]) Unfortunately, limitations of the length of this comment do not allow such a comparison. In any case, the research program summarized here cannot be regarded as an Eastern European branch of the 'disequilibrium school,' but (for better or for worse) as a distinct, separate area of studies.

2 THE ISSUES

The main common feature of our research work is the *subject* of the study. We are working on positive (descriptive–explanatory) theories only; normative theorizing is postponed to a later, more mature stage. We are focusing on a system characterized by permanent excess demand, or in other words by chronic shortage. The other potential states of the system – the Walrasian state, Keynesian or classical unemployment, etc. – are considered only for the sake of comparison. (For a general description and explanation of chronic shortage see Kornai, 1971, 1980; brief summaries can be found in Hare, 1982, and Burkett, 1983.)

I underline the attribute 'permanent' or 'chronic.' These are systems that did not leave Walrasian equilibrium just temporarily, owing to some random disturbance, external shock or wrong governmental intervention. They do not alternate between 'regimes,' switching from a state of excess supply to a state of excess demand or vice versa. A sellers' market is prevailing permanently. The permanent non-Walrasian state is deeply rooted and systemic. The agents expect that shortage will prevail and their behavior is adjusted to that.

Let me make a brief digression here and comment not only on the topics of the present session, but on the whole proceedings of our symposium. The issue of unemployment has come up several times, but it is regarded usually as a matter of 'policy.' Of course, policy may have some influence on employment, but the roots of the problem go deeper. My conjecture is this: chronic unemployment is systemic in a market economy, based on capitalist private ownership, just as chronic shortage (including chronic labor shortage) is systemic in a centralized economy, based on socialist governmental ownership. This is a dichotomy caused by the institutional framework of the two systems. It does not mean that policy is helpless and never effective – it may influence the degree of unemployment or shortage, respectively. But each system has a genetic 'inclination,' i.e. a 'natural' tendency, to fall into either the first or the second type of non-Walrasian state. Long-lasting, secular full-employment Walrasian equilibrium is not impossible in the paper-world of a theoretical model, but it is highly improbable in reality. I raise this question because, reading Western analyses of the present state of market economies, I get the impression that there is a one-sided excessive interest in short-term macro-instruments. At the same time, theorists do not pay great attention to the long-term institutional–structural aspects of the problem.

After this detour I would like to return to my original subject: the survey of our research work. We have now many models that show the conditions of the existence, uniqueness and stability of a *shortage equilibrium*. (To avoid the terminological confusion around the word 'equilibrium,' we prefer to use the term 'normal shortage' as a synonym to 'shortage equilibrium.') The precise concept of shortage equilibrium is defined separately in each study, according to the specific features of the model. The different definitions have one property in common: the degree of shortage is measured by some indicators (I come back to the problem of measurement later). The system is in shortage equilibrium if the degree of shortage is constant over time. All studies indicated in Appendix 2 as 'theoretical works' offer theorems on the existence of a shortage equilibrium, and many of them also offer uniqueness theorems. Stability is, of course, a more difficult problem. There are stability theorems for *n*-sector Leontief–von Neumann shortage economies in Kornai and Martos (1981), especially in the chapter on stability and destabilization by A. Simonovits. Conditions of stability and instability are shown for a macro-dynamic model of the shortage economy in Kornai and Simonvits (1983). In some papers we have only conjectures concerning stability, supported by simulation (for example Kornai, 1982; Kornai and Weibull, 1978).

The issue of stability leads to the next problem. What kind of information and control mechanisms are able to assure that the system, if deviating from its normal path, i.e. from shortage equilibrium, will return to it? And how fast is the convergence? (For the issues of convergence speed see Simonovits, 1981.) We concentrate on systems where control is based on *non-price signals*.[3] In our micro-models the typical non-price signals are (a) output stocks and the backlog of unfilled orders, affecting the control of production or sale, and (b) input stocks, waiting time or search time, affecting the purchase of factors. In the macro-models the aggregate input and output stock signals[4] may serve similar purposes, and in addition there are some other macro-signals: the degree of tension on the investment goods market or the net balance of payments (see e.g. Lackó, 1980). We have theorems in some of the theoretical papers which prove that different sets of non-price signals are sufficient to assure the stability of shortage equilibrium.

Let me underline that the above listed highly abstract questions are inspired ultimately by the reality of Eastern European economies. We have systems that have been far away from a Walrasian state for decades, in which the conventional market signals do not operate. Nevertheless, these economies are able to survive and to grow, and there are control processes that fulfill the tasks of resource allocation. How does such an economy work? What are the regularities of the behavior of the agents or of the system as a whole? The answers to these questions are rather different from the explanations to be found either in Eastern 'official' textbooks or in the standard texts of Western courses on 'comparative systems.'

Some disaggregated n-sector models are built for the comparison of abstract systems, both with different forms of centralization and decentralization, and with different information structures. The conventional dichotomy contrasts a fully centralized non-price-signal system with a fully decentralized price-signal system. We are particularly interested in a third class of systems, which are decentralized, but in which control is based on non-price signals. One can show that, under certain conditions, such systems are viable and have a stable equilibrium path. We introduce classifications of such systems, and compare them with each other. Under certain conditions a kind of 'equivalence' exists: systems with quite different degrees of centralization–decentralization and information structures may show the same basic properties in their performances (see Bródy,[5] Kornai-Martos, 1981, and Martos, 1979).

Some macro-models are designed for the study of the relationships between growth, efficiency and shortage. It is assumed that an increase of the degree of shortage decreases efficiency in production. There are wasteful *ad hoc* adjustments of technology, forced substitution of desired inputs by inferior ones, quality deterioration arising from rush-work, etc. Conditions of different growth paths are discussed for cases where normal shortage, i.e. shortage equilibrium, prevails, and where the growth rate of production, investment and consumption is either constant or declining over time. The latter situation characterizes the performance of present-day Eastern European economies (see Kornai, 1982, and Kornai and Simonovits, 1983).

A *cyclical phenomenon* – an alternation of acceleration and deceleration of investment and of other economic variables – can be observed in most Eastern European countries. Governmental policy over-reacts to signals, which indicate either increasing tensions on the domestic investment goods market or in export markets, or, the opposite situation, an abnormal increase of slack. (For detailed empirical description and causal explanation see Bródy,[6] Bauer,[7] 1978; Soós, 1975–6; and Kornai, 1980; for econometric modelling see Lackó, 1980; Kyn, Schrettl and Slama, 1979; and Maresse, 1981.)

In many works special attention is paid to the study of the buyers' behavior and demand formation in a chronic shortage economy. If the notional demand for a certain good cannot be satisfied, the buyer will accept a forced substitution, will start searching or will wait. The conventional description of the buyers' *ex ante* behavior (response to price by certain original, notional demand) must be complemented by further attributes of his response to shortage: propensities with regard to forced substitution, to search and to postponement. Shortage equilibrium is accompanied by a normal ratio of forced substitution, normal search time, normal waiting time, etc. (see Kornai and Weibull, 1978; Kapitány, Kornai and Szabó, 1982; Weibull, 1983).

An important special case is the behavior of the state-owned firm in its capacity as a buyer of producer goods or factors. There is a paternalistic relationship between the state and its 'children,' the nationalized firms. The state is always willing to bail out firms in financial trouble, using various means – subsidies, tax exemption, soft credits, etc. Firms expect that survival or even growth is granted almost unconditionally, independently of actual profitability. In my book *Economics of Shortage* (Kornai, 1980) this situation is described in the following way. The state-owned firm in the traditional type of socialist system has a 'soft budget constraint.' This is an allegorical expression to describe the behavior and expectation formation of an overprotected and therefore cost- and risk-indifferent firm. The properties of the conventional demand function, which appear under a regime with a hard budget constraint, do not hold under a regime with a soft budget constraint. The firm is, on the input purchase side, only weakly price-responsive or not price-responsive at all. If the budget is unconstrained, demand becomes unconstrained as well. At most, there is some self-restraint for the sake of face-saving, i.e. to make a better impression on the higher authorities and on public opinion. Demand of the firm for inputs in general – and its 'hunger' for investment resources in particular – is almost insatiable. Even if households' demand is constrained, total demand is almost insatiable, since the demand of public firms is almost unlimited. The latter part of demand spills over to other markets. This is the main institutional explanation of chronic shortage.

At this point I return to the dichotomy discussed earlier. Chronic shortage appears in an economy where the dominant sector has a soft budget constraint. Chronic unemployment is the property of a system in which the dominant sectors have hard budget constraints. Keynesian policies aiming at full employment are usually linked to institutional changes associated with a softening of the budget constraint, in the public sector and – to some extent – in subsidized private enterprises. A paper that describes the above discussion phenomenon in a formal model is Kornai and Weibull (1983). This is a stochastic framework for the analysis of the paternalistic relationship of state and firm and its impact on the behavior of the firm.[8] In most other works we simply assume that the socialist firms' demand behavior is adjusted already to the situation of a 'soft budget constraint.'

A word on semantics. It is not by accident that we call our studies in this field 'non-price models,' instead of talking about 'fixed-price models.' The latter term is justified for a system where the price – even a fixed or, what is more, a false price – has an impact on the price-responsive agent. In contrast to that, in our case[9] the agent – the central planner and the decision-maker of the state-owned firm – is not price-responsive, and must react to other signals.

For the same reason we prefer to call the system a 'shortage economy,' instead of using the term 'repressed inflation.' The latter notion is coined for a fully monetized system, with overblown money supply and prices fixed at too low a level. In contrast to that, the system we have in mind is only semi-monetized, or perhaps more precisely only *pseudo*-monetized.[10] Therefore it is better not to emphasize the monetary aspects of the situation, but rather the most characteristic consequence: the prevailing of chronic shortage.

3 METHODS

The results of research are described partly in 'verbal,' non-mathematical writings, and partly in studies using formal models. Both 'languages' are used side-by-side, sometimes by the same authors. The 'verbal' work is more advanced, covers a much larger set of issues and applies more qualifications. Formalization of the originally verbally stated hypotheses follows with some lag. Econometric analysis is still further behind. I believe that this is the usual sequence of research. In any case, there is not yet (or perhaps there will never be) a model that can be called *the* prototype model of the shortage economy. Instead, we have a large number of imperfect, one-sided models, each of them throwing some light on one or two aspects while neglecting others.

As to the formal models, most of them describe *dynamic systems*, i.e. systems of differential or difference equations. In some papers the apparatus of control theory is used.

Most models are *deterministic*. A few exceptions exist: Kornai and Weibull (1983), offering a stochastic framework for the study of firms' behavior, I. Virag's paper on stochastic non-price control (published only in Hungarian), and the simulation of non-price control of n-sector economies with random disturbances in decision-making (see Kapitány, 1979, 1982).

In most models we do not assume an optimizing behavior of the agents; instead, *other behavioral assumptions* are made. Kornai and Weibull (1983) applies H. Simon's model on satisficing behavior. In many other studies (e.g. in Kornai and Martos, 1981, and in Kornai, 1982) we assume that, by social convention, tradition, routine – and in some cases also by governmental prescriptions – certain *norms* are determined. The norms are self-fulfilling expectations of the decision-makers. In our formal models the norms are given exogenously. There are feedback rules, which describe the decision-makers' responses to the deviation of actual performance from the norm. Finally, in a third subset of our model family, the only behavioral assumption is this: the decision-maker has a certain response function, reflecting his reaction to certain signals.

The various models apply different levels of aggregation. For a brief survey from this point of view see Appendix 2. With aggregation on a macro-level, a difficult methodological problem arises. Under chronic shortage demand is not directly observable, since actual purchase reflects the adjustment to shortage already. Forced substitution absorbs a part of money intended originally to satisfy notional demand. The difficulties in observing demand appear even in a graver form in the dominant sector of the economy, in the sector of state-owned firms, where demand is inclined to run away almost without limit. A further problem: excess demand and excess supply as micro-phenomena may appear simultaneously, owing to the frictions of adjustment. (For modeling the effect of frictions, see Weibull, 1984.) Using a 'net' concept of excess demand (deducting excess supplies from the total of excess demand) on the macro-level, the real purpose of this notion would get lost: it would not express the size of unsatisfied demand.

Under all these circumstances, the concept of macro-excess demand is not operational. Instead of using this conventional term, we are compelled to search for other, more workable, concepts which measure the buyers' dissatisfaction and the overall degree of shortage. Different attempts have been made. For example, we have composed a synthetic shortage index on the macro-level, which is a latent variable of the system, as a function of several manifest, observable partial shortage indicators, like waiting times, forced substitution ratios, search times, etc., observed on the micro-level (see Kornai, 1982). Another approach is to insert various observable macro-indicators (e.g. input and output stocks, net balance of payments, etc.), which in an indirect way reflect the degree of shortage, into the model as explanatory variables.

A final remark. Although the total volume of books and papers listed in Appendix 1, plus the literature not yet published in English, add up to several thousand pages, all of us participating in this work share a common feeling: we are only at the very beginning in fulfilling an ambitious and difficult research program.

APPENDIX 1

Bibliography of works on chronic shortage and non-price control, with special reference to Eastern Europe

The bibliography includes only publications in English. Several further related books and papers in Hungarian are not listed here.

Mimeographed papers not yet published in journals are available on request from the author.

Bauer, T. (1978), 'Investment Cycles in Planned Economies,' *Acta Oeconomica*, **21**, 243–60.

Burkett, J. P. (1983), *Shortage and Control: Non-Neoclassical Perspectives*, University of Rhode Island, Kingston, RI (mimeograph).

Hare, P. (1982), 'Economics of Shortage and Non-Price Control,' *Journal of Comparative Economics*, **6**, 406–25.

Hewett, E. A. (1980), *A Macroeconometric Model of a Centrally Planned Economy with Endogenous Plans: The Hungarian Case*, University of Texas, Austin (mimeograph).

Kapitány, Z. (1979), 'Dynamic Stochastic Simulation of a System Controlled by Stock Signals,' in J. M. L. Janssen, L. F. Pau and A. Straszak (eds), *Models and Decision-Making in National Economies*, North-Holland, Amsterdam.

Kapitány, Zs. (1982), 'Dynamic Stochastic Systems Controlled by Stock and Order Signals,' in A. Chikan (ed.), *The Economics and Management of Inventories*, Elsevier, Amsterdam.

Kapitány, Zs., Kornai, J. and Szabó, J. (1984), Reproduction of Shortage on the Hungarian Car Market, *Soviet Studies*, **36**, 236–56.

Kornai, J. (1971), *Anti-Equilibrium*, North-Holland, Amsterdam.

Kornai, J. (1980), *Economics of Shortage*, North-Holland, Amsterdam.

Kornai, J. (1982), *Growth, Shortage and Efficiency: Yrjo Jahnsson Lectures*, Basil Blackwell/University of California Press, Oxford/Berkeley, and Los Angeles.

Kornai, J. and Martos, B. (1973), 'Autonomous Control of the Economic System,' *Econometrica*, **41**, 509–28.

Kornai, J. and Martos, B. (eds) (1981), *Non-Price Control*, North-Holland, Amsterdam; with contributions of A. Brody, I. Dancs, L. Hunyadi, Zs. Kapitany, J. Kornai, B. Martos, A. Simonovits and J. Sivak.

Kornai, J. and Simonovits, A. (1977), 'Decentralized Control Problems in von Neumann Economies,' *Journal of Economic Theory*, **14**, 44–67.

Kornai, J. and Simonovits, A. (1983), *Investment, Efficiency and Shortage: A Macro-Growth Model*, Institute of Economics, Budapest (mimeograph).

Kornai, J. and Weibull, J. (1978), 'The Normal State of the Market in a Shortage Economy: A Queue Model,' *Scandinavian Journal of Economics*, **80**, 375–98.

Kornai, J. and Weibull, J. (1983), 'Paternalism, Buyers' and Sellers' Market,' *Mathematical Social Sciences*, **6**, 153–69.

Kyn, O., Schrettl, W. and Slama, J. (1979), 'Growth Cycles in Centrally Planned Economies: An Empirical Test,' in O. Kyn and W. Schrettl (eds), *On the Stability of Contemporary Systems*, Vanden Hoeck-Ruprecht, Gottingen.

Lackó, M. (1975), 'Consumer Savings and the Supply Situation,' *Acta Oeconmica*, **15**, 365–84.

Lackó, M. (1980), 'Cumulating and Easing Tensions,' *Acta Oeconomica*, **24**, 357–78.

Maresse, M. (1981), 'The Bureaucratic Response to Economic Fluctuation: An Econometric Investigation of Hungarian Investment Policies,' *Journal of Policy Modeling*, **3**, 221–43.

Martos, B. (1979), 'Comparison of Economic Control Systems,' in J. M. L. Janssen, L. F. Pau and A. Straszak (eds), *Models and Decision-Making in National Economies*, North-Holland, Amsterdam.

Simonovits, A. (1981), 'Maximal Convergence Speed of Decentralized Control,' *Journal of Dynamics and Control*, **3**, 51–64.

Soós, A. (1975–6), 'Causes of Investment Fluctuations,' *Eastern European Economics*, **14**, 25–36.

Weibull, J. (1983), 'A Dynamic Model of Trade Frictions and Disequilibrium in the Housing Market,' *Scandinavian Journal of Economics*, **85**, 373–92.

APPENDIX 2

Survey of models, with regard to topics and aggregation

	Aggregate (macro-) model	*Disaggregate (micro-) model*
Covering the whole economy	Hewett (1980) E* Kornai (1982) T Kornai and Simonvits (1983) T	Kapitány (1979, 1982) T* Kornai and Martos (1973, 1981) T Kornai and Simonovits (1977) T Simonovits (1981) T
Covering a delimited field of the economy (partial models)	*Models of investment cycles* Kyn, Schrettl and Slama (1979) E Lackó (1980) E Maresse (1981) E *Model of households' consumption* Lackó (1980) E	*Partial market with queue* Kornai and Weibull (1978) T *Partial market with queue and search* Weibull (1983) T *Firm's behavior* Kornai and Weibull (1984) T

* T, theoretical model; E, econometric model

NOTES

Financial support from the Institute of Economics, Hungary, and the Alexander von Humboldt Foundation, German Federal Republic, is gratefully acknowledged.

1 It is worth mentioning, however, that all authors from Eastern Europe are Hungarians. There is some work along similar lines in Poland, Czechoslovakia and in the Soviet Union. I have not yet seen their final publications in languages accessible to me. Hopefully, in a few years the list can be enlarged with studies produced in other socialist countries.

2 R. Portes and D. Winter, 'The Supply of Consumption Goods in Centrally Planned Economies,' *Journal of Comparative Economics*, **1**, 1977, 351–65; R. Portes and D. Winter, 'Disequilibrium Estimates for Consumption Goods Markets in Centrally Planned Economies,' *Review of Economic Studies*, **47**, 1980, 137–59; K. Hulyak, 'Disequilibrium Models for Consumption Goods in Hungary,' paper presented at the Ninth International Conference on Applied Econometrics, Budapest, 1982 (mimeograph).

3 There are, however, a few papers that look at the joint effect of price and non-price signals (see e.g. Kornai and Weibull, 1978, and Weibull, 1983). Furthermore, some works make comparisons between abstract systems using price signals and others using non-price signals (see Kornai and Martos, 1981, especially the chapters written by B. Martos, and Martos, 1979).

4 In most cases we apply stock-flow models, distinguishing input and output stocks. The double role of stocks is that they serve both as buffers and as an important source of information.

5 A. Brody, 'Szabalyozasi modellekrol' ('On Control Models'), *Szigma*, **7**, 1974, 93–103. English translation appears in Kornai and Martos (1981).

6 A. Brody, 'Gazdasagi novekedesunk uteme 1924-tol 1965-ig' ('The Economic Growth Rate of Hungary from 1924 to 1965'), *Kozgazdasagi Szemle*, **14**, 1967, 417–31.

7 T. Bauer has written an important book describing and explaining investment cycles of different Eastern European countries, which up to now has been available only in the Hungarian language: T. Bauer, *Tervgazdalkodas, beruhazasok, ciklusok* ('Planning, Investment, Cycles'), Kozgazdasagi es Jogi Konyvkiado, Budapest.

8 There is a large-scale empirical project going on, studying income redistribution over state-owned firms. The research – directed by the author and A. Matits – is using the financial data of all Hungarian firms in the last eight years, applying mathematical–statistical analysis. The first mimeographed report in Hungarian has been published recently. The early results provide ample statistical evidence of the 'softness' of the budget constraints of Hungarian firms.

9 This is, of course, a simplified statement. The firm is not perfectly unresponsive to prices. And what is more important: the household has a hard budget constraint, and therefore is price-responsive in the usual way. For a discussion with more detailed qualifications see Kornai (1980). Some of our exercises in pure theory abstract away households and focus exclusively on the sector of state-owned firms.

10 As a continuation of the former footnote: the system is monetized in the sphere of household purchases, on the labor market, and on the market of goods produced by private producers. In the dominant sector – the sector of state-owned firms – transactions are only seemingly monetized and the firms' decisions are not guided by profitability.

6

Rational Expectations Models in Macroeconomics

JOHN B. TAYLOR

1 THE MOTIVATION FOR A RATIONAL EXPECTATIONS APPROACH

One of the most conspicuous features of macroeconomic fluctuations is the close association between the fluctuations in output and prices over the business cycle. In statistical terms, there is a marked positive correlation between aggregate production and the rate of change in the aggregate price level. The relationship between output and inflation is not a new phenomenon, although it has shifted over time as expectations of inflation have changed. It has appeared with few exceptions in business cycles as far back as data on business cycles exist. It was observed and studied by Irving Fisher, A. C. Pigou, J. M. Keynes and many other economic theorists in the early part of this century, and it received even wider notice after being embodied in a simple econometric equation by A. W. Phillips in 1958. The price–output correlation is usually given a top billing in the 'aggregate supply' chapters of modern macroeconomic textbooks – the term 'aggregate supply' itself connoting a positive association between prices and output. And, of course, particular realizations of the correlation have always been major news events; the recent downside realization – the worldwide recession and the decline in the inflation rate – is certainly no exception.

Many macroeconomic policy recommendations have been based on this price–output correlation. In the 1920s business cycle theorists drew conclusions about stabilization policy from it. Examining data for the United States, Irving Fisher argued that fluctuations in economic activity could be reduced by a macroeconomic policy that simply stabilized the aggregate price level. Noting similar correlations in the United Kingdom, Pigou (1927) argued for a policy of 'preventing prices from rising in booms and falling in depressions' and thereby 'lessening industrial fluctuations.' And in his tract *Monetary Reform*, Keynes (1923) also argued for a policy of price stabilization citing Fisher's evidence in the United States. The causal assumption implicit in such policy recommendations clearly is that price fluctuations are the direct cause of production and employment fluctuations.

Although based on the same Phillips-curve-type correlations, policy recommendations in more recent times have been quite different. In the 1960s many macroeconomists argued that a policy of price stabilization, or a low inflation target, would disrupt production and increase unemployment. Price stabilization proposals have been revived in recent years, but the conclusion that too much price stabilization would reduce output stability is still held by many macroeconomists. Given such wide differences in policy recommendations, all arising from the same statistical correlation, the need for a clear and quantifiable theory to explain and understand this correlation seems obvious.

The development in the early 1970s of rational expectations models in macroeconomics – the subject of this paper – was largely in response to such a need. Of course, economic theories of the Phillips curve had already been the subject of an intensive research effort when rational expectations models were introduced, but there were still some problems with this research. Consider, for example, the research of Edmund Phelps (1967) and Milton Friedman (1968), which showed that there is an important distinction between the long-run and the short-run output–inflation relationship. This distinction is due to expectations. According to the Phelps–Friedman theory, the stimulating effects associated with a steady rise in prices could not last, because firms and workers would eventually expect these movements and adjust their behavior accordingly. The theory is elegant, logically consistent, and indeed empirically accurate in its predictions for the *long-run* inflation–output correlation. The problems with the theory are in its description of the *short-run* correlations between inflation and output, where it relies on adaptive expectations to explain why firms and workers would be slow to adjust their expectations to business cycle conditions.

The adaptive expectations assumption might be a reasonable description of how expectations adjust after a major unprecedented development, but it seems particularly inappropriate as an explanation of a phenomenon that has been observed regularly as part of economic fluctuations for hundreds of years. To the extent that business cycles are recurrent phenomena, the assumption that people form expectations adaptively, learning from scratch about the dynamics of each business cycle as if it were a unique event, does not seem appropriate. Almost all applications of economic theory are based on the assumption that individual beliefs are influenced by experience. There is no reason why macroeconomic applications should be different.

John Muth's (1961) rational expectations assumption seems more satisfactory for recurrent phenomena like business cycles, and primarily for this reason it was used by Robert Lucas in his studies of aggregate supply. With rational expectations, agents have already learned from past experience and utilize all information available to them. Moreover, as Muth showed, the approach can be used in practice to derive explicit testable implications. Because of this advantage in business cycle applications, rational expectations models have been extended beyond their original Phillips curve (or aggregate supply) application to many other areas of macroeconomics, including the key components of aggregate demand and open-economy macroeconomics. Rational expectations models are now the rule rather than the exception in macroeconomic research. They have been used as theories to explain other business cycle regularities, such as the persistence of output and inflation, as well as their co-movements. Econometric estimation, optimal control and nonlinear solution techniques have also been modified so as to be compatible with the rational expectations models. I will review these developments in this paper. However, as I have characterized it, the original, as well as the most controversial, part of rational expectations research has been in macroeconomic models of aggregate supply, and I will concentrate most of my review in this area. The rational expectations approach is not without its own inadequacies, and I will review these in the course of the paper.

Before proceeding, it may be appropriate briefly to review how the research surveyed here relates to other research developments that have implications for macroeconomics. The 'disequilibrium' approach to macroeconomics surveyed by Malinvaud (1978), for example, is concerned with the implications of a fixed (or exogenous) vector of wages and prices rather than with how these wages and prices are determined, or how they fluctuate over the cycle with production and employment. The main motivation is with a rigorous development of the Keynesian consumption function, with spillover effects in a multi-sector model, and with the *level* of unemployment given this wage–price vector. Although there does not appear to be any substantive reason why rational expectations methods could not be fruitfully integrated with these disequilibrium models, this is a technically difficult problem. The work by Green and Honkapohja (1983), Neary and Stiglitz (1979) and Green and Laffont (1981) seems to be moving in this direction. In particular, Green and Laffont's approach to anticipatory price setting is closely related to some of the work I will review in this paper. The technical problems arise because of the difficulties of obtaining closed-form solutions when there are nonlinearities associated with the spillover effects and with the 'min' condition in *stochastic* rational expectations models.

A second development in macroeconomics, which has evolved from work in a number of areas of microeconomics (asymmetric information, search), is concerned with investigating whether the *average* level of unemployment is efficient or not. Papers by Arnott and Stiglitz (1981), Calvo (1979b), Diamond (1982) and Salop (1979) are examples of this type of research and illustrate the wide variety of approaches that have been taken in such investigations. These models give rise to equilibrium (perhaps inefficient) unemployment, but are not directly concerned with the *dynamic co-movements* of inflation and unemployment as are the rational expectations models surveyed here. Peter Diamond (1982) explains the difference in terms of a general research strategy: 'Inflation and unemployment are both such difficult problems to understand, that it is a good strategy to attempt to model each of them separately before worrying about a model that would address both of them at once.' As should already be clear, the rational expectations modelers discussed in this lecture have been worrying about too much, according to this view.

2 ALTERNATIVE RATIONAL EXPECTATIONS MODELS OF AGGREGATE SUPPLY

Robert Lucas introduced rational expectations to the study of aggregate supply in a series of now famous papers (see Lucas, 1972a,

1972b, 1973). As I will describe in more detail later, the introduction of the rational expectations approach requires a very well specified and detailed model. As a result, the Lucas models are much more explicit than earlier models in describing the reasons for the short-run inflation–output relationship. In addition to the rational expectations assumption, they are explicit about assuming perfectly flexible prices and market-clearing at every date. The mechanism generating the inflation–output correlations is information-based; a limitation is placed on the information available to agents in different markets. This explicitness has enormous advantages from the viewpoint of statistical testing, as I will describe later. Moreover, the policy implications of the theory are also very specific. According to the theory, a well-understood monetary policy does not affect real variables. These implications of the model of Lucas were studied and extended by Sargent and Wallace (1975) and Barro (1976), and now by many others. The term 'new classical macroeconomics' is used for these models.

But the Lucas market-clearing type was not the only rational expectations model being explored as a theory to explain the price–output fluctuations and derive policy implications. An alternative rational expectations approach to the problem was taken by Stanley Fischer (1977) and Phelps and Taylor (1977). Although the Fischer and Phelps–Taylor models were at least partially motivated by the policy implications of the Lucas models, other aspects of economic behavior and policy were also explored. Rather than describing price movements using the market-clearing assumptions, these models contain explicit mechanisms to describe how prices (or wages) are determined. The rigidities in these models are due to sticky prices. There is a finite period of time in which a *nominal* wage or price is set and transactions are assumed to take place at that price. Formal wage or price contracts are not necessarily involved; wage-setting customs are sufficient. These models give rise to a quite different mechanism for price and output fluctuations than those introduced by Lucas, and their properties and policy implications are much different. One difference that has attracted much attention is that anticipated and perceived changes in the money supply can affect output and employment.

Despite this apparently fundamental difference, there are similarities between the two approaches. Of course, because of the rational expectations assumption the mathematical techniques are very similar. But there is also a substantive similarity in that wage and price decisions are forward-looking. Decisions are forward-looking if expectations of future events matter for current decisions regardless of how expectations are formed. The prices in the *information-based* market-clearing rational expectations models are obviously forward-looking; but, as I will emphasize in this paper, price and wage decisions in the sticky price models are also forward-looking. The prices in these models are like capital: once in place they are predetermined (at least beyond one market-clearing period under normal conditions), but the way they are set in place depends on future developments such as expected demand conditions and price developments in other markets. Because price and wage-setting is anticipatory, the policy implications of the sticky price rational expectations models are much different from sticky price or wage models without rational expectations.

The terminology used here deserves some comment. I use the term 'information-based' because the models rely on informational restrictions on firm's and worker's perceptions about other markets in the economy. I use the term 'sticky price' rather than 'contract' because the rigidities are not necessarily due to the types of factors considered in the *contract theory* studies such as by Azariadis (1975) and Bailey (1974). The use of the term 'information-based' may be too narrow because the macroeconomics of the sticky-price models are based partly on information arguments.

Information-based models

The information-based models proceed from the simple assumption that the positive relation between aggregate prices and output is due to movements along a *producer's or worker's supply curve*. For this reason, the version of the Phillips curve that has emerged from this research has come to be called the 'Lucas supply curve.' Movements along supply curves can occur only if there is an increase in some *relative* price: for a firm, the output price must rise relative to input prices; for a worker, the wage must rise relative to the price level. Because the phenomenon we wish to explain concerns an increase in the general price level where all prices rise together, it is necessary to impose informational constraints on suppliers about certain prices in the economy. These constraints give rise to a perception of a relative price increase when in reality there is none. Firms are assumed to have difficulty obtaining information about what is going on outside the market in which they are selling. It is here that the models get 'rigged,' as later characterized by Lucas (1981).

An exposition of the model

The best way to see the importance of this theory is to study it in detail. I have found that attempts to summarize it less formally do not give one the same appreciation of its theoretical innovation. With the help of some diagrams and elementary statistics, the rudimentary model developed by Lucas (1973) can be explained rather simply.

We start with a supply curve for a representative firm:

$$y_i = c(p_i - p_i^e) + y_i^f, \qquad i = 1, \ldots, n \tag{1}$$

where y_i is the ith firm's production, p_i is the ith firm's price, and y_i^f is the ith firm's normal level of production. The variable p_i^e is the ith firm's *perception* of the average price level (i.e. the 'general' price level) elsewhere in the economy, and c is a parameter. The general price level should be an indicator of the firm's input costs. (Alternatively, if we think of a worker-supplier, p_i would be the wage and the general price level would be the price index of consumer goods.) Equation (1) states that the firm will produce more if the price of its products rises *relative* to the general price level. Note that, if both p_i and p_i^e rise by the same amount, the firm will not produce more, because the relative price does not change. Hence, equation (1) shows explicitly why a properly specified supply curve will not explain Phillips curve correlations in which the general level of prices (all prices) and production move together. According to (1), a general price rise that is fully perceived by all firms will not affect production, because p_i and p_i^e would move together.

As suggested earlier, the Phillips curve correlations come from confusion on the part of firms about what is happening to the general price level. Suppose that firm i cannot immediately observe the general price level, but that it can still observe its own price. Then, when all prices rise simultaneously, firm i will not know that these other prices are rising. It will see only its own price rise. Hence, it will produce more. If other firms have similar lack of information, this confusion could cause production in the entire economy to increase, because all firms will mistake a general price rise for a rise in their own relative price. Phillips curve correlations will result. Essentially, firms are fooled into producing more.

It should be noted that, if we interpret the 'general price level' as an indicator of the firm's input costs, then the model implies that the firm has less information about its input costs than it does about its own price. If we think of the model as describing a worker supplying labor, then we are assuming that the worker will know more about his own wage than about prices generally. These features of the model have been questioned by some as being unrealistic.

Even if the firm cannot observe the general price level, the observation on its own price might provide useful information about the general price level. At the extreme, if relative prices *never* changed, then the firm would realize that the price of all other goods was increasing whenever its own price went up. Even in a less extreme situation, when price changes *sometimes* represent a relative shift, firms would guess that an increase in their own price might reflect an increase in inflation generally.

The information-processing problem faced by the typical firm i is illustrated in a scatter diagram in figure 6.1. The diagram represents the historical experience of the firm during several fluctuations in its own price and general price level. It is a scatter plot of these historical observations on prices. It plots the general price level p on the vertical axis and the firm's own price on the horizontal axis, both measured relative to the unconditionally expected level of prices $\hat{p}$. By 'unconditional' we mean without knowledge of the firm's own price p_i. This could be a forecast at the start of the year based on some econometric forecasting service. According to the picture, when the firm's price is above normal, the general price level is frequently, but not always, above normal. The deviations of the scatter from the 45° line represent *relative* price changes. Based on this historical experience, and despite the deviations from the 45° line, the firm would be wise to estimate that *some* general increase in prices had occurred whenever it saw its own price higher than normal. The firm could make this estimate by putting a least squares line through the points as shown in the diagram. Clearly, the slope of the least squares line depends on the spread of the scatter of points. As shown in figure 6.2, if the cluster of points are all close to

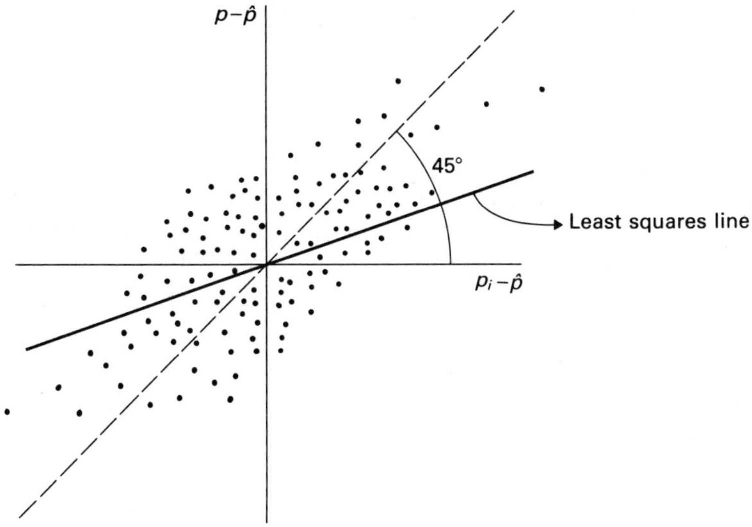

FIGURE 6.1

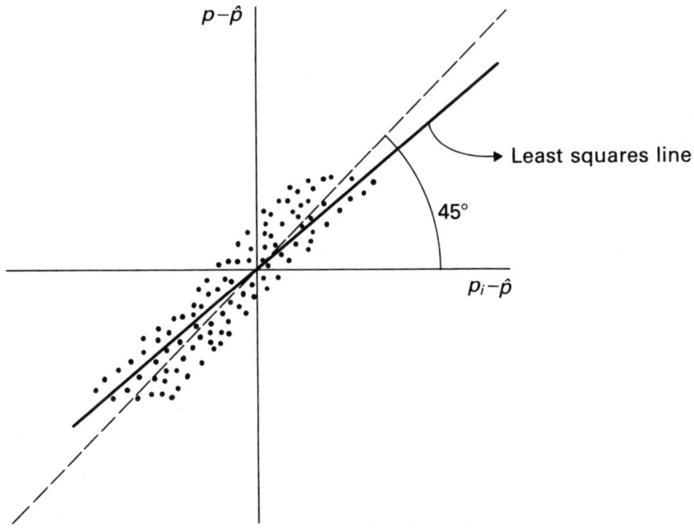

FIGURE 6.2

the 45° line, so that there are only small relative price shifts compared with aggregate price movements, then the slope of the line gets close to 1. As the points spread, representing larger relative price shifts, the slope goes to zero.

Write the least squares regression equation corresponding to the line in figures 6.1 and 6.2 as

$$p-\hat{p} = b(p_i - \hat{p}). \tag{2}$$

Then the scatter diagrams suggest that the coefficient b is between 0 and 1 and is a decreasing function of variability of relative prices (measured by the horizontal spread of the observations from the 45° line), and an increasing function of the variability of the general price level (represented by the vertical spread of the observations along the 45° line).

In fact, the firm is facing an elementary signal extraction problem, and the previous informal description of its behavior can be formalized by assuming that the firm extracts the signals optimally. This can be derived most easily using a bivariate normal model.

The algebraic representation of the individual firm's price p_i relative to the general price level p corresponding to the diagram is given by

$$p_i = p + \epsilon_i, \tag{3}$$

where ϵ_i is an additive relative price shift. This is the horizontal distance between the 45° line and each point in the diagram. In order to derive the slope of the regression line in figures 6.1 and 6.2, it is useful to treat the prices as random variables with a normal distribution. Then the best guess of the aggregate price level p from the viewpoint of firm i can be interpreted formally as the conditional expectation of p given the individual firm's observation on p_i. That is, $p_i^e \equiv E(p \mid p_i)$. If p and p_i are jointly normally distributed, then this expectation can be easily derived from well-known properties of the normal distribution.

Define the mean and variance of p and ϵ_i as $Ep = \hat{p}$, $\operatorname{var} p = \sigma_p^2$, $E\epsilon_i = \hat{\epsilon}$, and $\operatorname{var} \epsilon_i = \sigma_\epsilon^2$. Since ϵ_i represents relative price fluctuations, it is appropriate to assume that these average out to zero for each firm and are uncorrelated with the general price level. That is, $\hat{\epsilon}_i = 0$ and $\operatorname{cov}(p, \epsilon_i) = 0$.

In order to calculate $E(p_i \mid p)$ we need to calculate the mean and variance of p_i and the covariance between p_i and p. From equation (3), the *mean* of p_i is given by

$$Ep_i = \hat{p}, \tag{4}$$

and the *variance* of p_i is given by

$$\begin{aligned} \operatorname{var} p_i &= \operatorname{var} p + \operatorname{var} \epsilon_i \\ &= \sigma_p^2 + \sigma_\epsilon^2. \end{aligned} \tag{5}$$

The covariance between p_i and p is then computed as

$$\begin{aligned} \operatorname{cov}(p_i, p) &= E(p_i - \hat{p})(p - \hat{p}) \\ &= E(p + \epsilon_i - \hat{p})(p - \hat{p}) \\ &= E(p - \hat{p})^2 + E(p - \hat{p})\epsilon_i \\ &= \operatorname{var} p + \operatorname{cov}(p, \epsilon_i) \\ &= \sigma_p^2. \end{aligned} \tag{6}$$

The variables p and p_i are viewed as jointly normally distributed with these means, variances and covariances. From the properties of the normal distribution, the conditional expectation of p given p_i can be computed from the formula:

$$E(p \mid p_i) = Ep + \frac{\operatorname{cov}(p_i, p)}{\operatorname{var} p_i}(p_i - Ep_i). \tag{7}$$

Substituting in the means and variances, this gives

$$p_i^e = \hat{p} + \frac{\sigma_p^2}{\sigma_p^2 + \sigma_\epsilon^2}(p_i - \hat{p}). \tag{8}$$

Comparing equation (8) with equation (2) above, we see that the slope coefficient of the regression line is given by

$$b = \frac{\sigma_p^2}{\sigma_p^2 + \sigma_\epsilon^2}. \tag{9}$$

The term σ_ϵ^2 represents the variability of relative prices. Clearly, as this variability gets larger the slope is reduced. At the extreme case where σ_ϵ^2 is infinite, an increase in the individual firm's own price provides no information about the general price level. These results of the theory are potentially important, for they provide an empirical test.

Substituting equation (8) into (1) results in

$$y_i = c(1-b)(p_i - \hat{p}) + y_i^f. \tag{10}$$

The behavior of output and prices for the economy as a whole can now be obtained by aggregating over all the producers. Note that we avoid a number of aggregation problems by assuming that all firms have identical supply functions. Simple summation then gives the aggregate supply function. The general story is not dependent on their being identical firms, however. Letting the same symbols without subscripts represent the aggregate and summing up results in

$$y = \gamma(p - \hat{p}) + y^f, \tag{11}$$

where $\gamma = c(1-b)n$. This is the Lucas supply function. Another way to write (11) is to put the price level p on the left-hand side and subtract the lagged aggregate price level from both sides. This results in

$$p - p_{-1} = \hat{p} - p_{-1} + \lambda(y - y^f), \tag{12}$$

where $\lambda = \gamma^{-1}$. Equation (12) now has the form of an 'expectations-augmented' Phillips curve.

The relationship between the slope parameter b and the variability of prices can now be interpreted in terms of the slope of the Phillips curve λ. Since λ is an increasing function of b, any increase in the variance of overall prices will increase the slope of the short-run Phillips curve. At the time in which this model was derived, an increased slope represented a 'less favorable' trade-off since it meant that an increase in inflation would result in a smaller stimulus to production and employment. Now, such a slope increase would be 'more favorable,' since it would permit a reduction in inflation with a smaller loss of production and employment. In any case, this prediction of the theory provided one of the earliest tests.

Note how this equation captures both the long-run vertical Phillips curve (an anticipated inflation with $p = \hat{p}$ will result in production at normal levels with $y = y^f$) and the short-run positive correlation noted at the start of the paper (a temporary unanticipated movement in inflation causing $p > \hat{p}$ will result in above normal production). The economic explanation underlying these correlations is that firms or workers are producing more than was expected when the aggregate price level is greater because they think that there is a good chance that their own price has risen.

Policy implications

The policy implications of this information-based model are quite striking. To derive the implications, first introduce a simple aggregate demand equation

$$y = a_0 + a_1(m - p), \tag{13}$$

where m is the log of the money supply. Now, suppose $\hat{m}$ is the 'rational' expectation of the level of m; then the rational forecasts of p and y must satisfy (from (13)) the relationships

$$\hat{y} = a_0 + a_1(\hat{m} - \hat{p}), \tag{14}$$

and (by taking expectations in (11))

$$\hat{p} = \hat{p} + \lambda(\hat{y} - y^f). \tag{15}$$

Equation (15) implies that $\hat{y}$ is equal to y^f, and therefore from (14) we have

$$y^f = a_0 + a_1(\hat{m} - \hat{p}). \tag{16}$$

Now, solve (13) and (16) for p and $\hat{p}$ and substitute (11) to get

$$y - y^f = \frac{a_1 \gamma}{a_1 + \gamma}(m - \hat{m}). \tag{17}$$

The policy implications follow from equation (17): if monetary policy is perfectly anticipated, then $m = \hat{m}$ and output does not deviate from normal levels. Hence, *anticipated* changes in money do not affect real GNP: they affect only the price level. Put differently, only *unanticipated* money $(m - \hat{m})$ affects GNP. This is the central policy ineffectiveness result established in a slightly more elaborate model by Sargent and Wallace (1975), and it forms the basis for tests of the hypothesis by Barro (1977, 1978). Announced (and believed) changes in money can affect prices (and therefore inflation) with no real output effects. Note also that, according to this theory, disinflation would not require any lost output, a possibility investigated by Sargent (1982) in a study of the Eastern European hyperinflations.

These results highlight the importance of distinguishing between anticipated and unanticipated policy in rational expectations analyses. In rational expectations models based on contracts or sticky prices, this distinction is also important, but it is not so extreme.

Empirical evidence

As shown above, the information-based model was designed specifically to explain the long-observed empirical relationship between prices and output over the cycle. In this sense it was successful; it fitted the facts it was designed to explain. But because the model was laid out so explicitly, many other testable implications could be derived, and these have formed the basis of a vast array of statistical tests of the model. In my view this is an important advantage of the information-based model. Were it less explicit – or based on the informal explanations used by many early business cycle theorists – these testable implications could not have been derived, and as a consequence we would know much less about the validity of the model.

The implication that the Phillips curve slope should be positively related to the variability of the overall price level served as the first test of the model conducted by Lucas (1973). Deriving Phillips curve slopes for 20 countries and comparing these with the variability of the overall price level, Lucas found some evidence for the hypothesis, but this was based on two outliers in his sample, Argentina and Paraguay, which had steep Phillips curves (a small γ in the previous notation) and high aggregate price variance. For the other 18 countries, and for the OECD countries, there was little evidence for the hypothesis. If the theory was correct, it seemed to show up only in countries with extremely high inflation variability, outside the realm of experience of many industrial economies.

A second test of the hypotheses was conducted by Sargent (1976), who utilized the fact that only *unanticipated* movements in the price level should affect production. Using various proxies for the expected price level and regressing the unemployment rate on the resulting measure of unanticipated prices (along with lagged values of unemployment), Sargent found evidence of a Lucas-type supply function for the United States during the 1951(I)–1973(III) sample period. The coefficient of $p-\hat{p}$ in the unemployment equation was negative and significant. Fair (1979), using a different estimation procedure, found that the slope coefficients in the supply curve were smaller than Sargent's and insignificant. Moreover, when he lengthened the sample to consider the period through 1977, he found that the coefficient reversed sign and became significant. Hence, the evidence suggests that unanticipated prices do not give the Phillips curve correlation necessary for the Lucas theory. Altonji (1982), using data on wages, obtained similar negative results focusing on the labor supply decision.

One reason for the reverse effect uncovered by Fair might be prevalence of supply shocks as distinct from demand shocks during the 1970s. Supply shocks – if they created movements along a negatively sloped aggregate demand curve in the (p, y) plane – could be responsible for the finding.

In a series of papers, Barro (1977, 1978) attempted to test the theory indirectly by studying the effects of unanticipated money on output (rather than the effects of unanticipated prices). Equation (17) shows how the Lucas theory can be interpreted in this way. The results of this approach were much more dramatic and showed a strong and significantly positive influence of money on real output. Moreover, Barro's results showed that anticipated money had a smaller effect which was frequently statistically insignificant.

Barro obtained measures of anticipated money by using regression methods to estimate a forecasting equation for money. The anticipated money values were taken to be the forecasts of a regression of the change in the growth rate of money (*DM*) on its own lagged values and on two other potential influences of money growth – de-trended federal government expenditures and the unemployment rate. The difference (*DMR*) between the forecasted *DM* and actual *DM* was then taken as a measure of unanticipated money and was in turn regressed on real GNP(y) with a time trend removed. In more recent work, the two-step procedure has been replaced by a joint estimation method but the general idea is the same. Subsequently Small (1979) and Germany and Srivastava (1979) have shown that these results are sensitive to how the forecasts of money are proxied. Since the Barro results appeared to be in such strong agreement with the theory, and because they have been quite influential in the field, it is worth focusing on them.

Figure 6.3 plots the annual data on *DM*, *DMR* and y used by Barro (1978). Although this is a busy chart the plot is quite revealing. Note that the short-run business cycle swings of both actual money (*DM*) and unanticipated money (*DMR*) correspond closely with the movements of real GNP. Both anticipated and unanticipated money seem important. In the period up to 1960 anticipated money seems

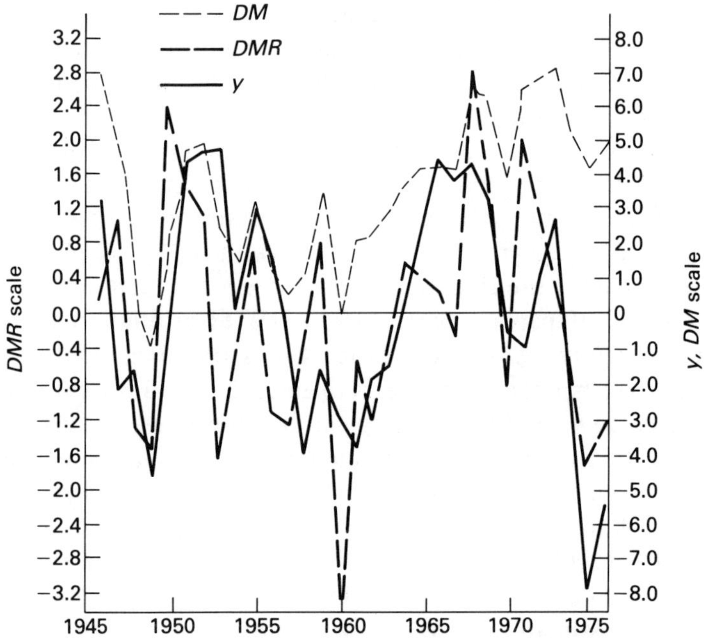

FIGURE 6.3

Source: Barro (1978).

more important. However, the real problem with the actual *DM* series is the secular increase which begins in the early 1960s as inflation began to accelerate. Clearly, anticipated money does not have a chance in a regression that includes both anticipated and unanticipated money, unless one takes out the changed trend. One way to do this would be to measure *DM* in real terms and thereby take out the inflationary trend. Another way would be to use a very long lag distribution. In fact, in recent work Mishkin (1982) has shown that the Barro results change significantly in that unanticipated money becomes relatively less important when the lag distribution in the output equation is increased.

The Barro test procedure was criticized by Fischer (1980a), who argued that, by replacing unanticipated *price* variables, as in the original Lucas model, by unanticipated *money* variables, the method could no longer distinguish between the Lucas model and other rational expectations theories such as the sticky price theories described later in this paper. In any rational expectations model in which there are rigidities that are not permanent, anticipated changes will have smaller real effects than unanticipated changes: adjustments can be made in advance when policy changes are anticipated. In rational expectations models with price rigidities, the anticipated policy variables will have effect, but the effect of unanticipated policy can often be larger. Hence, it is not clear what rational expectations model Barro's results were testing. In fact, the finding that unanticipated *money* has a much larger effect than unanticipated *prices* can be more easily reconciled with sticky price–wage models than with information-based models.

Some more recent empirical work sheds further doubt on the information-based models. Boschen and Grossman (1980) and Barro and Hercowitz (1980) show, using preliminary data on the money supply, that a very small part of the output effects can be caused by 'unperceived' as distinct from 'unanticipated' money. As is clear from the exposition of the Lucas model, if the current money supply or aggregate price level is known (even if it was unanticipated at the start of the period) it would not affect output. But in fact the misperceived part of money seems to be very small.

In addition, work by Hercowitz (1980), Fischer (1981), and Taylor (1981) seems to show that very little of the price *dispersion* in the cross-section can be explained by monetary shocks. At least in recent years the impulse to price movements have come from the supply side (energy, agricultural, and productivity shocks). These findings correspond with the intuitive explanation for the negative movement between prices and output, mentioned above in my discussion of the empirical tests of Fair.

Another approach to testing the information-based models has been to look directly at the intertemporal supply elasticities to determine whether these are at least plausibly high enough to explain the cyclical movements. If the information constraints turned out to be important, contrary to the above empirical results, then examining such elasticities would be a second check on the theory. Unfortunately, the results are very mixed here: Hall (1980) finds a high intertemporal macro labor supply elasticity and gives evidence from micro studies to indicate that the supply elasticities are plausibly high. Altonji (1982) as well as Mankiw, Rotemberg, and Summers (1982) have recently presented tests contrary to this finding. Kydland

and Prescott (1982) have argued that the conventional time separability assumption may be leading to the small supply response, but this has yet to be tested empirically.

Extensions

A number of extensions of the simple information-based model have appeared since Lucas's early work. Barro (1976) developed a considerably more detailed model in which aggregate demand was also derived from individual demand curves (a Lucas demand curve). Barro (1980) also developed a model with an economy-wide capital market in order to examine how information provided in such a market would influence the dynamics and the correlations of the model. Cukierman (1979) generalized the model to allow firms to spend research money in order better to determine economy-wide events. This modification makes the information structure endogenous in a particular way, and Cukierman finds that the general theoretical results are robust to such a change. McCallum and Whitaker (1979) showed that, if a policy variable could react to current events, as in the case of automatic fiscal stabilizers, then it could effectively stabilize real output.

Another type of generalization of the market-clearing information-based model has been investigated by Weiss (1980). In the Weiss model some agents (firms) are informed and some agents (workers) are uninformed. Monetary policy can be used to improve the transmission of information to the uninformed agents. By reacting to economic developments in a particular way, the monetary authorities reveal information about the state of the economy to workers, resulting in an allocation equivalent to that of the fully informed state.

The information-based models were not originally designed to capture the *serial* correlation of output and prices, but only the correlation between these variables. Some of the extensions of these models have been aimed at explaining this serial correlation, without abandoning the basic limited information market-clearing approach. For example, Lucas (1975) added fixed capital to the model to capture these dynamic effects. Blinder and Fischer (1981) included inventories in the model providing another source of serial correlation. Most recently, Kydland and Prescott (1982) have developed a complete model that uses construction lags, which have effects similar to capital stock adjustment costs, to explain serial correlation in a market-clearing model. Sargent (1978b) had earlier stressed adjustment costs as a source of persistence, focusing on firms' adjusting their labor force.

Sticky price models

The crucial difference between the models of aggregate supply described in this section and the information-based models is that prices are 'sticky.' Prices do not instantaneously adjust to clear all markets. In addition to the extensive use of rational expectations, these models also differ from earlier work on sticky wages and prices in that there is more development of the dynamics of price adjustment. Rather than just assuming that prices adjust slowly – as for example by using a simple price adjustment equation – there is an attempt to describe how prices and wages are determined. These models are 'period' models generating discrete-time stochastic difference equations, and my review will be limited to such discrete-time formulations. A continuous-time approach is found in Calvo (1982).

Two different approaches to wage and price determination can be distinguished. One approach, used by Fischer (1977), Gray (1976) and Phelps and Taylor (1977), starts with a set-up in which wages or prices are set at least one period in advance of when they will apply. One can think of this as a contract, in that the price is determined in advance, but there is no presumption that actual contracts are written. The distinguishing feature of this approach is that prices or wages are assumed to be set as if they were *expected to clear markets* during the period in which they will apply. Economic agents are assumed to make conditional forecasts of supply and demand conditions. Actual supply and demand conditions will differ from these forecasts because of unexpected events, such as productivity or monetary shocks. Since the conditional forecasts of demand and supply depend on the price, it is possible to determine the price so that forecasted demand equals forecasted supply; this price is the *expected market-clearing price*. The assumption is that the prices actually set by firms and workers are equal to this expected market-clearing price. When the next period occurs actual demand will not equal actual price because the price level is fixed.

The assumption used in the rational expectations macro-literature has been that the demand side rules the market. This assumes, of course, that there are always sufficient stocks and enough excess productive capacity that the required amount of production is feasible. Because these models are stochastic, there is an advantage to the 'demand is determining' condition in that it preserves linearity, unlike the 'min' condition. Hence it is not necessary to take expectations of nonlinear functions of random variables when finding agents' expectations, and it is primarily for this reason that such an assumption is used. (As I mentioned previously, this technical factor may be one of the reasons why the rational expectations assumption has not yet been explored extensively in the disequilibrium macroeconomic literature.)

This general approach to wage and price determination can obviously be applied in many different ways. In Phelps and Taylor (1977) it is assumed that the aggregate price level is set so that expected total aggregate demand is equal to expected total aggregate supply. Aggregate demand depends negatively on the price level through the usual real balance channel: a higher price level reduces real money supplied and raises real interest rates; expected aggregate supply is assumed always to equal the unconditional average or normal level of supply. Although interest rate determination as well as the dynamics of inventory behavior are modeled explicitly, the basic mechanism can be explained (although at the risk of some oversimplification) using the simple aggregate demand equation (13). If normal or capacity output is equal to the constant y^f (using the same notation as in the previous section), then from (13) the price level that is expected to clear markets in any period is given by

$$p_{-1} = \frac{1}{a_1}(a_0 + a_1\hat{\hat{m}} - y^f). \tag{18}$$

The subscript on the price level in (18) indicates that it was set at the start of the previous period. Equation (18) indicates in a very elementary way how price setting is *anticipatory* in this type of model; *tâtonnement* price adjustment mechanisms do not have this feature. The double circumflex over the money supply is meant to indicate that this was the expectation of the money supply based on information at the *beginning* of the *previous* period (recall that the single circumflex used in the previous section on market-clearing models indicated an expectation based on information at the beginning of the *current* period). This difference is essential to the predictions of the model.

Substituting (18) into (13) results in

$$y = a_1(m - \hat{m}) + y^f. \tag{19}$$

As (19) indicates, output deviates from full-capacity output by the amount that the money supply differs from what was announced at the start of the previous period. Hence, an increase in the money supply that is *announced* and perceived at the start of the current period (after prices for the period have been set) will affect output. It is in this sense that anticipated changes in the money supply can affect output – as long as they are not anticipated for a period longer than the time that prices are sticky. Monetary policy has effect in this model because, by assumption, the monetary authorities have a shorter lead time in their money supply decisions than do firms in their pricing decisions. In the flexible-price market-clearing models this lead time is ruled out by assumption, as a comparison of equation (17) with (19) should make clear. McCallum (1980) has shown how it is possible to rig sticky-price models so that changes in expectations can affect actual prices in a way in which policy-makers cannot exploit this lead time.

The rational expectations models developed by Fischer (1977) and Gray (1976) assume that wages are sticky, permitting prices to be perfectly flexible. Changes in the real wage are the source of output fluctuations. Wage determination in these models is analogous to the price determination in the Phelps–Taylor model. Fischer also assumes that wage-setting is staggered over time, but this does not affect the conclusions of his analysis in any way. Again, anticipated monetary policy can affect real variables only if the monetary authorities can act with less lead time than wage-setters. Casual observation suggests that this time advantage of monetary policy does exist for wage determination, even if it is more questionable for price determination.

An important feature of all these models, which also emerges from the algebra, is that monetary policy is neutral in the long run, even if not in the short run. In fact, output returns to normal after only one period in the model in equation (19), corresponding to the single-period price-setting assumption. Serial correlation of output (more specifically, the autocorrelation function) cannot be longer than the length of the longest contract in these models, unless other sources of persistence are added.

The expected market-clearing approach to wage and price determination is clearly an 'as if' technique, and has many similarities with the market-clearing approach in which wages and prices actually do clear markets. An advantage of this approach is that it preserves *long-run* neutrality properties. This advantage has recently been emphasized by McCallum (1982).

An entirely different approach to modeling how prices are determined in sticky-price rational expectations models is to focus directly on the price decision of individual agents. Consider, for example, a nearly competitive market consisting of n firms in which a firm's unit sales decline slowly if the firm charges a price above the prevailing market price, and increase slowly if the firm charges a price below the market price. In other words, suppose that there are enough substitution possibilities between the products of different firms that the demand for each firm's product depends on the price of that firm measured *relative* to the average price at other firms, but not so many substitution possibilities that the firm's sales are infinitely responsive to any deviation from the market price. Suppose also that firms set their prices at different points in time; that is, that price-setting is staggered or non-synchronized. Let x_t be the price set by firms who set price at time t and suppose that the n firms each set their price every $1/n$ periods. The average price of all firms in the market is then

$$p_t = \frac{1}{n} \sum_{s=1}^{n} x_{t-s+1}. \tag{20}$$

Figure 6.4 illustrates the way in which prices will evolve in a steady inflation when $n = 3$.

What might be a reasonable pricing strategy for firms in such an environment? In the absence of a need for a change in sales, the representative firm would attempt to meet the prevailing price *during* the period when its own price was applicable; that is, during the 'contract' period. Algebraically, this might be captured by assuming that prices are formed using the following equation:

$$x_t = \frac{1}{n} \sum_{s=0}^{n-1} \hat{p}_{t+s}. \tag{21}$$

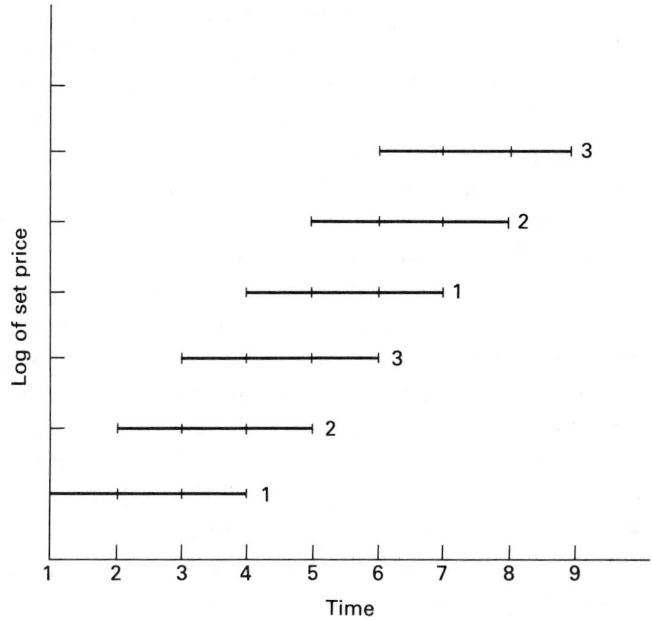

FIGURE 6.4 Price setting by three groups of firms in a steady inflation

In other words, the 'contract' price x_t of the firm is set to equal the expected average price of other firms during the n future periods in which x_t is expected to apply. If the firm found that it was out of equilibrium, then its price decisions would differ from (21). For example, if an increase in sales were desired, the firm would charge a price below the value in (21), and if it wanted to reduce sales it would charge a higher price. A simple way to capture this 'disequilibrium' would be to modify (21) by incorporating a term reflecting the firm's sales relative to normal (desired) levels. That is, equation (21) would become

$$x_t = \frac{1}{n}\sum_{s=0}^{n-1} \hat{p}_{t+s} + \frac{c}{n}\sum_{s=0}^{n-1} (\hat{y}_{it+s} - y_i^f). \tag{22}$$

The pricing equation in (22) is similar to that used in Taylor (1979, 1980a) and Phelps (1978), in the case of either wage determination or price determination. Blanchard (1982), Calvo (1983) and Dornbusch (1982) have also used this general approach. Relative to the *expected* market-clearing pricing approach, this type of price determination has some empirical advantages. The dynamics of the price and output correlation that can emerge from an equation like (22) are much richer than the simple expected market-clearing approach. In fact, it was in response to empirical requirements that this alternative to the expected market-clearing approach was developed. In the early empirical work on sticky-price rational expectations models that was eventually reported in Taylor (1979), it was found that the expected market-clearing approach did not produce enough serial correlation in either output or prices to be empirically realistic. From a technical viewpoint, equations like (22) can produce more realistic price and output behavior because of their lagged dependent variables. Although such lags are not immediately visible in (22), substitution of equation (20) into (22) results in an equation with $(n-1)$ lags in x_t, along with $(n-1)$ leads. The lags arise because of the lasting effect of past price decisions on today's prices. In fact, equation (22) implies both forward-looking and backward-looking behavior.

By adding to equation (22) a model for the determination of actual demand (so that the rational expectations assumption can be used) the following conclusions are easy to derive. First, there is no long-run effect of a steady inflation on the deviations of output from normal levels. (In other words, the long-run Phillips curve is vertical.) This can easily be shown by noting that, if $x_t - x_{t-1} = \mu$ for all t, then $y_{it} = y_i^f$ for all t. Second, anticipated changes in the money supply will affect real output even if the announced lead time is longer than the length of the longest contract. Third, the effect of an anticipated change in monetary policy is quite different from the effect of an unanticipated change.

Empirical tests of the sticky-price models have not yet been as extensive as tests of the information-based models. A comparison of predicted and actual output correlation for the United States reported in Taylor (1980a) indicates that the non-synchronized price (or wage) model captures some of the serial correlation properties. But more detailed tests of the model reported in Taylor (1980b) and Ashenfelter and Card (1982) indicate that there are some problems in matching the exact shape of the lag distributions and the pattern of intertemporal correlation between output and prices. Generalizations of the non-synchronized price determination model to allow for the real-world fact that all contracts do not last the same length of time appear to improve the fit of the models. I am not aware of any published tests of the expected market-clearing pricing models of aggregate supply.

The micro-foundations behind the sticky-price models generally rely on some type of cost of adjustment idea. Barro (1972) and Sheshinski and Weiss (1977) have taken this approach. Because of adjustment costs it is optimal for firms to adjust their prices at discrete intervals; hence, there are periods of time when prices are sticky.

Despite these advances, there is a need for more microeconomic work to be done before we can make policy evaluations using sticky-price models at the same level of rigor as modern welfare economics (optimal taxation, for example). Nevertheless, the policy problems that these models are designed to address are present and important. As further progress on the microeconomic foundations is being made, certain features of these models – for example, the explicit attempt to model and test the price-setting mechanism, the use of the forward-looking expectations assumption, and the focus on policy rules – could provide an important improvement over 'pre-rational expectations' models that have been and are currently used in policy analysis.

3 RATIONAL EXPECTATIONS MODELS OF THE COMPONENTS OF AGGREGATE DEMAND

In discussing the implications of alternative theories of aggregate supply in the previous section, it was necessary to make at least some rudimentary assumptions about aggregate demand. Another area of rational expectations research in macroeconomics has been the development of more detailed models of aggregate demand. In fact, although most rational expectations research in the early 1970s focused on questions relating to aggregate supply, in the late 1970s and early 1980s this emphasis of research has been shifting to the demand side, and especially to consumption and investment. It is impossible to review all the research here, but a brief summary of its highlights might be useful.

Consumption

Rational expectations has generated a renewed interest in the permanent income hypothesis of consumption behavior. Recent literature on the consumption function has emphasized that the permanent income hypothesis places restrictions on the relationship between consumption and current and past income flows. Moreover, these restrictions depend on the time-series properties of income. Sargent (1978a), Hall (1978), Blinder (1981) and Flavin (1981) have estimated models of consumption using the permanent income hypothesis and rational expectations. With few exceptions, the general approach in this research has been to use the traditional permanent income hypothesis, and simply add to it the hypothesis of rational expectations. Early on this approach seemed to work well; in particular, Hall (1978) found broad agreement between the theory and the facts. More recently, however, there have been discrepancies. Using panel data, Hall and Mishkin (1982), for example, found that the permanent income model with rational expectations can be rejected. Findings such as this are likely to lead to modifications of the permanent income hypothesis, perhaps using liquidity constraints; but this is yet a topic for future research.

Investment

It is impossible to do justice here to all the work on investment modeling with rational expectations. Lucas and Prescott (1971) focused on investment behavior in one of the first fully developed rational expectations models under uncertainty, and in a long unpublished paper Lucas (1966) explored a model of firms' investment demand using rational expectations. Most of the research on investment since this early work has been motivated by the problems of the neoclassical model, as pioneered by Jorgenson, which does not deal explicitly with expectations. Implicit in the Jorgenson model is an assumption that the variables influencing investment are permanent and fully anticipated. Recently more complicated expectations effects have been approached empirically by formally modeling the cost of adjusting the capital stock as part of the firm's optimization problem. Sargent (1979) devotes several sections of his text to reporting and further developing this literature. Tobin's (1969) theory of q has been extremely helpful in expectations modeling, because it automatically incorporates future expectations in the value of the firm. The q theory has been studied in a rational expectations context, for example, by Summers (1981) and Hayashi (1982). An alternative to the adjustment cost approach is to incorporate construction (or gestation) times directly into the firm's optimization problem. This has been done by Kydland and Prescott (1982) and by Taylor (1982) in an applied investment policy problem.

Inventory investment models with rational expectations have also been intensively investigated recently. The Blinder and Fischer (1981) study – mentioned earlier as an example of an extension of the information-based models – develops a complete model of inventories using rational expectations assumptions. Blanchard (1983) has designed and estimated a detailed model of automobile inventories with rational expectations.

4 TECHNIQUES FOR ESTIMATION AND POLICY EVALUATION

Macroeconometric techniques have also been developed and modified to handle rational expectations models in macroeconomics. To some extent the pace of development here has lagged behind the substantive theoretical needs, and for this reason many rational expectations models have been given a very simple structure. The most extensive research effort in this area is that exemplified by Hansen and Sargent (1980, 1981), and Chow (1981), whose econometric strategy is to estimate the parameters of utility functions of agents solving maximization problems under rational expectations. A number of applications of this approach are currently under way. An example is the Blanchard (1982b) application previously mentioned. In addition, techniques for solving and estimating general rational expectations models have been developed and experimented with in work by Lipton *et al.* (1982), Fair and Taylor (1983), and Blanchard and Kahn (1980).

As I indicated earlier, policy questions arising from the appropriate interpretation of the Phillips curve correlations have been a major concern of rational expectations research. The general problem of interpreting such time-series correlations for policy questions was generalized and developed into a broad critique of conventional econometric work by Lucas (1976). The Lucas critique has had a profound influence on policy evaluation research in macroeconomics. To date, most of the influence has been to shed doubts on traditional econometric policy studies, but in recent years attempts have been made to deal constructively with the Lucas critique in policy work by using rational expectations explicitly in econometric models. Two of my research studies (Taylor, 1979, 1982) are examples of this, and the research effort by Hansen, Sargent and many others has the general aim of improving existing policy evaluation methods in this way.

An important macroeconomic policy issue that emerged from policy evaluation research in macroeconomics is the time inconsistency issue (see Kydland and Prescott, 1977; Calvo, 1979a; Fischer, 1980b; Barro and Gordon, 1983). Because anticipated as well as actual policy affects the behavior of agents, there is a temptation to use announced policy as an additional policy instrument. Time inconsistency occurs because, once a policy is announced and time has passed, it will generally be optimal to change the policy. The problem is not unique to macroeconomics, and its resolution is likely to come in fully developed theories of reputation and credibility (see Kreps and Wilson, 1980, for example).

5 PROBLEMS WITH RATIONAL EXPECTATIONS IN MACROECONOMICS

I started this paper by regarding rational expectations models in macroeconomics as a needed improvement over previously available methods for studying macroeconomic fluctuations. But rational expectations itself is likely to be modified and improved upon as research in macroeconomics proceeds. There are already a number of problems with rational expectations models that suggest the need for such improvement, at least for the study of certain policy issues.

The question of how agents learn about the economic environment that influences their behavior is rarely addressed in rational expectations research. Bayesian or least-squares learning rules were suggested in macroeconomic research by Taylor (1975) and Friedman (1979). The econometric difficulties in incorporating such learning assumptions in practical work has probably been one reason why these approaches have not had more applications in macroeconomics. The research by Bray (1982) and Blume and Easley (1982) has developed ways to deal with learning in which the behavior of individual agents is modeled explicitly.

Another problem with rational expectations is related to the uniqueness of rational expectations equilibria. Because of the self-fulfilling feature of rational expectations, there is generally a continuum of solutions to rational expectations models. Uniqueness has usually been obtained by assuming stability (i.e. no speculative bubbles) of the paths of expectations of variables, and in most cases this approach works (see Taylor, 1977, for a discussion of cases where it does not work). But the stability assumption itself has not always been motivated adequately, and recent research has attempted to test whether speculative bubbles do exist. Flood and Garber (1980) and Blanchard and Watson (1982) are examples of this type of empirical work.

A third problem with the rational expectations approach is that it implicitly assumes that agents expect that other agents have the same view of the economic environment as they do. In cases where events are recurrent, such as the business cycle phenomena discussed earlier, this assumption seems reasonable. But for the unusual events it should be questioned. Frydman and Phelps (1983) have discussed this problem in detail, and research is beginning to develop practical ways to deal with the problem (see Townsend, 1983, for example).

6 CONCLUDING REMARKS

This paper has concentrated on models of macroeconomic activity that use the rational expectations assumption. The aim has been to examine in some detail the differences between the models, the advantages and disadvantages of alternative models, the empirical support for the models, and their policy implications. The theme has been that there is wide diversity among rational expectations models in macroeconomics, despite their common expectational assumptions and techniques of analysis.

Continuing research on rational expectations models in macroeconomics – both in applications and in modifications of the basic assumption – indicates that it is still a developing field. Its overall contribution to economics will be better evaluated in later surveys with a perspective on these and future developments. At this time, however, it is clear that, despite the empirical shortcomings of the information-based models and the needed improvements in the microeconomic foundations for the sticky-price models, the rational expectations research to date has forced a useful rethinking of many relationships in macroeconomics (including the price–output relation emphasized here). Many of these relationships have been and are being used for policy analysis. Perhaps more importantly, it has also provided a methodology – along with requisite theoretical and empirical techniques – to continue developing an understanding for these relationships with the ultimate aim of sounder policy evaluation.

NOTE

A grant from the National Science Foundation is gratefully acknowledged. I am grateful to Kenneth Arrow, Alan Blinder, Roman Frydman, Seppo Honkapohja, Edmund Phelps, Carl Walsh, and Laurence Weiss for helpful comments.

REFERENCES

Altonji, J. G. (1982), 'The Intertemporal Substitution Model of Labor Market Fluctuations: An Empirical Analysis,' *Review of Economic Studies*, **49**, 783–824.

Arnott, R. and Stiglitz, J. E. (1981), 'Labor Turnover, Wage Structures, and Moral Hazard: The Inefficiency of Competitive Markets,' Economic Research Program Working Paper no. 289, Princeton University.

Ashenfelter, O. and Card, D. (1982), 'Time-series Representations of Economic Variables and Alternative Models of Labor Market,' *Review of Economic Studies*, **49**, 761–82.

Azariadis, C. (1975), 'Implicit Contracts and Underemployment Equilibria,' *Journal of Political Economy*, **83**, 1183–202.

Baily, M. N. (1974), 'Wages and Employment under Uncertain Demand,' *Review of Economic Studies*, **41**, 37–50.

Barro, R. J. (1972), 'A Theory of Monopolistic Price Adjustment,' *Review of Economic Studies*, **39**, 17–26.

Barro, R. J. (1976), 'Rational Expectations and the Role of Monetary Policy,' *Journal of Monetary Economics*, **2**, 1–32.

Barro, R. J. (1977), 'Unanticipated Money Growth and Unemployment in the United States,' *American Economic Review*, **67**, 101–15.

Barro, R. J. (1978), 'Unanticipated Money, Output and the Price Level in the United States,' *Journal of Political Economy*, **86**, 549–80.

Barro, R. J. (1980), 'A Capital Market in an Equilibrium Business Cycle Model,' *Econometrica*, **48**, 1393–417.

Barro, R. J. and Gordon, D. B. (1983), 'A Positive Theory of Inflation in a Natural Rate Model,' *Journal of Political Economy*, **91**, 589–610.

Barro, R. J. and Hercowitz, Z. (1980), 'Money Stock Revisions and Unanticipated Money Growth,' *Journal of Monetary Economics*, **6**, 257–67.

Blanchard, O. J. (1982), 'Price Desynchronization and Price Level Inertia,' NBER Working Paper no. 900.

Blanchard, O. J. (1983), 'The Production and Inventory Behavior of the American Automobile Industry,' *Journal of Political Economy*, **91**, 365–400.

Blanchard, O. J. and Kahn, C. (1980), 'The Solution of Linear Difference Models under Rational Expectations,' *Econometrica*, **48**, 1305–11.

Blanchard, O. J. and Watson, M. (1982), 'Bubbles, Rational Expectations and Financial Markets,' NBER Working Paper no. 945.

Blinder, A. (1981), 'Temporary Income Taxes and Consumer Spending,' *Journal of Political Economy*, **89**, 26–53.

Blinder, A. and Fischer, S. (1981), 'Inventories, Rational Expectations and the Business Cycle,' *Journal of Monetary Economics*, **8**, 277–304.

Blume, L. E. and Easley, D. (1982), 'Learning to be Rational,' *Journal of Economic Theory*, **26**, 340–51.

Boschen, J. F. and Grossman, H. I. (1980), 'Tests of Equilibrium Macroeconomics using Contemporaneous Monetary Data,' *Journal of Monetary Economics*, **10**, 309–33.

Bray, M. (1982), 'Learning, Estimation, and Stability of Rational Expectations,' *Journal of Economic Theory*, **26**, 318–39.

Calvo, G. (1979a), 'On the Time Consistency of Optimal Policy in a Monetary Economy,' *Econometrica*, **46**, 1411–28.

Calvo, G. (1979b), 'Quasi-Walrasian Theories of Unemployment,' *American Economic Review*, Papers and Proceedings, **69**, 102–7.

Calvo, G. (1983), 'Staggered Contracts and Exchange Rate Policy,' in J. A. Frenkel (ed.) *Exchange Rates and International Macroeconomics*, University of Chicago Press.

Chow, G. (1981), 'Estimation and Control of Rational Expectations Models,' *American Economic Review*, Papers and Proceedings, **71**, 211–16.

Cukierman, A. (1979), 'Rational Expectations and the Role of Monetary Policy: A Generalization,' *Journal of Monetary Economics*, **5**, 213–30.

Diamond, P. A. (1982), 'A Search Equilibrium Approach to the Micro Foundations of Macro Models,' Wicksell Lectures.

Dornbusch, R. (1982), 'PPP Rules and Exchange Rate Stability,' *Journal of Political Economy*, **90**, 158–65.

Fair, R. (1979), 'An Analysis of the Accuracy of Four Macroeconomic Models,' *Journal of Political Economy*, **87**, 701–18.

Fair, R. and Taylor, J. B. (1983), 'Solution and Maximum Likelihood Estimation of Nonlinear Dynamic Rational Expectation Models,' *Econometrica*, **51**, 1169–85.

Fischer, S. (1977), 'Long-term Contracts, Rational Expectations, and the Optimal Policy Rule,' *Journal of Political Economy*, **85**, 191–206.

Fischer, S. (1980a), 'On Activist Monetary Policy with Rational Expectations,' in S. Fischer (ed.), *Rational Expectations and Economic Policy*, University of Chicago Press for National Bureau of Economic Research.

Fischer, S. (1980b), 'Dynamic Inconsistency, Cooperation, and the Benevolent Dissembling Government,' *Journal of Economic Dynamics and Control*, **2**, 93–107.

Fischer, S. (1981), 'Towards an Understanding of the Costs of Inflation: II,' in K. Brunner and A. H. Meltzer, *The Costs and Consequences of Inflation*, North-Holland, Amsterdam.

Fisher, I. (1925), *Purchasing Power of Money*, Macmillan, New York.

Flavin, M. (1981), 'The Adjustment of Consumption to Changing Expectations of Inflation,' *Journal of Political Economy*, **89**, 974–1009.

Flood, R. P. and Garber, P. M. (1980), 'Market Fundamentals versus Price-level Bubbles: The First Tests,' *Journal of Political Economy*, **88**, 745–70.

Friedman, B. (1979), 'Optimal Expectations and the Extreme Information Assumptions of "Rational Expectations" Macromodels,' *Journal of Monetary Economics*, **5**, 23–42.

Friedman, M. (1968), 'The Role of Monetary Policy,' *American Economic Review*, **58**, 1–17.

Frydman, R. and Phelps, E. S. (1983), 'Individual Expectations and Aggregate Outcomes: An Introduction to the Problem,' in R. Frydman and E. S. Phelps (eds), *Individual Forecasting and Aggregate Outcomes: 'Rational Expectations' Examined*, Cambridge University Press.

Germany, J. D. and Srivastava, S. (1979), 'Empirical Estimates of Unanticipated Policy Issues in Stability and Identification,' unpublished paper, Princeton University.

Gray, J. A. (1976), 'Wage Indexation: A Macroeconomic Approach,' *Journal of Monetary Economics*, **2**, 221–36.

Green, J. and Honkapohja, S. (1983), 'Variance Minimizing Monetary Policies with Lagged Price Adjustment and Rational Expectations,' *European Economic Review*, **20**, 123–41.

Green, J. and Laffont, J. J. (1981), 'Disequilibrium Dynamics with Inventories and Anticipatory Price-setting,' *European Economic Review*, **16**, 199–223.

Hall, R. E. (1978), 'Stochastic Implications of the Life-Cycle–Permanent Income Hypothesis: Theory and Evidence,' *Journal of Political Economy*, **86**, 971–87.

Hall, R. E. (1980), 'Labor Supply and Aggregate Fluctuations,' *Carnegie-Rochester Conference Series on Public Policy*, **12**, 7–33.

Hall, R. E. and Mishkin, F. S. (1982), 'The Sensitivity of Consumption to Transitory Income: Estimates from Panel Data on Households,' *Econometrica*, **50**, 461–81.

Hansen, L. P. and Sargent, T. J. (1980), 'Formulating and Estimating Dynamic Linear Rational Expectations Models,' *Journal of Economic Dynamics and Control*, **2**, 7–46.

Hansen, L. P. and Sargent, T. J. (1981), 'Linear Rational Expectations Models for Dynamically Interrelated Variables,' in R. E. Lucas and T. J. Sargent (eds), *Rational Expectations and Econometric Practice*, University of Minnesota Press, Minneapolis.

Hayashi, F. (1982), 'Tobin's Marginal q and Average q: A Neoclassical Interpretation,' *Econometrica*, **50**, 213–24.

Hercowitz, Z. (1980), 'Money and Relative Price Dispersion in the United States,' NBER Working Paper no. 433.

Keynes, J. M. (1923), *Monetary Reform*, Macmillan, London.

Kreps, D. M. and Wilson, R. (1980), 'Reputation and Imperfect Information,' *Journal of Economic Theory*, **27**, 253–79.

Kydland, F. and Prescott, E. C. (1977), 'Rules Rather than Discretation: The Inconsistency of Optimal Plans,' *Journal of Political Economy*, **85**, 473–92.

Kydland, F. and Prescott, E. C. (1982), 'Time to Build and Aggregate Fluctuations,' *Econometrica*, **50**, 1345–70.

Lipton, D. *et al.* (1982), 'Multiple Shooting in Rational Expectations Models,' *Econometrica*, **50**, 1329–33.

Lucas, R. E., Jr (1966), 'Optimal Investment with Rational Expectations,' in R. E. Lucas, Jr and T. J. Sargent (1981), *Rational Expectations and Econometric Practice*, University of Minnesota Press, Minneapolis.

Lucas, R. E., Jr (1972a), 'Expectations and the Neutrality of Money,' *Journal of Economic Theory*, **4**, 103–24.

Lucas, R. E., Jr (1972b), 'Econometric Testing of the Natural Rate Hypothesis,' in O. Eckstein (ed.), *The Econometrics of Price Determination*, Board of Governors of the Federal Reserve System, Washington, DC.

Lucas, R. E., Jr (1973), 'Some International Evidence on Output–Inflation Tradeoffs,' *American Economic Review*, **63**, 326–34.

Lucas, R. E., Jr (1975), 'An Equilibrium Model of the Business Cycle,' *Journal of Political Economy*, **83**, 1113–44.

Lucas, R. E., Jr (1976), 'Econometric Policy Evaluation: A Critique,' *Journal of Monetary Economics*, Supplement, 19–46.

Lucas, R. E., Jr (1981), 'Tobin and Monetarism: A Review Article,' *Journal of Economic Literature*, **19**, 558–67.

Lucas, R. E. and Prescott, E. C. (1971), 'Investment under Uncertainty,' *Econometrica*, **39**, 659–81.

Malinvaud, E. (1978), *The Theory of Unemployment Reconsidered*, Basil Blackwell, Oxford.

Mankiw, N. G., Rotemberg, J. J. and Summers, L. H. (1982), 'Intertemporal Substitution in Macroeconomics,' NBER Working Paper no. 898.

McCallum, B. T. (1980), 'Rational Expectations and Macroeconomic Stabilization Policy,' *Journal of Money Credit and Banking*, **12**, 716–46.

McCallum, B. T. (1982), 'Macroeconomics after a Decade of Rational Expectations: Some Critical Issues,' unpublished paper, Carnegie-Mellon University.

McCallum, B. T. and Whitaker, J. K. (1979), 'The Effectiveness of Fiscal Feedback Rules and Automatic Stabilizers under Rational Expectations,' *Journal of Monetary Economics*, **5**, 171–86.

Mishkin, Frederic S. (1982), 'Does Anticipated Monetary Policy Matter? An Econometric Investigation,' *Journal of Political Economy*, **1**, 22–51.

Muth, J. (1961), 'Rational Expectations and the Theory of Price Movements,' *Econometrica*, **29**, 315–35.

Neary, J. P. and Stiglitz, J. E. (1979), 'Towards a Reconstruction of Keynesian Economics: Expectations and Constrained Equilibria,' NBER Working Paper no. 376.

Pigou, A. C. (1927), *Industrial Fluctuations*, Macmillan, London.

Phelps, E. S. (1967), 'Phillips Curves, Expectations of Inflation and Optimal Unemployment Over Time,' *Economica*, **34**, 254–81.

Phelps E. S. (1978), 'Disinflation without Recession: Adaptive Guideposts and Monetary Policy,' *Weltwirtschaftliches Archiv*, **2**.

Phelps, E. S. and Taylor, J. B. (1977), 'Stabilizing Powers of Monetary Policy Under Rational Expectations,' *Journal of Political Economy*, **85**, 163–90.

Phillips, A. W. (1958), 'The Relation between Unemployment and the Rate of Change of Wage Rates in the United Kingdom, 1861–1957,' *Economica*, **25**, 283–99.

Salop, S. C. (1979), 'A Model of the Natural Rate of Unemployment,' *American Economic Review*, **69**, 117–25.

Sargent, T. J. (1976), 'A Classical Macroeconometric Model for the United States,' *Journal of Political Economy*, **84**, 207–38.

Sargent, T. J. (1978a), 'Rational Expectations, Econometric Exogeneity, and Consumption,' *Journal of Political Economy*, **86**, 673–700.

Sargent, T. J. (1978b), 'Estimation of Dynamic Labor Demand Schedules under Rational Expectations,' *Journal of Political Economy*, **86**, 1009–44.

Sargent, T. J. (1979), *Macroeconomic Theory*, Academic Press, New York.

Sargent, T. J. (1982), 'The Ends of Four Big Inflations,' in Robert E. Hall (ed.), *Inflation: Causes and Effects*, University of Chicago Press.

Sargent, T. J. and Wallace, N. (1975), 'Rational Expectations and Optimal Monetary Instrument and the Optimal Money Supply Rule,' *Journal of Political Economy*, **83**, 241–54.

Sheshinski, E. and Weiss, Y. (1977), 'Inflation and the Cost of Price Adjustment,' *Review of Economic Studies*, **44**, 287–304.

Small, D. H. (1979), 'Unanticipated Money Growth and Unemployment in the United States: Comment,' *American Economic Review*, **69**, 996–1003.

Summers, L. H. (1981), 'Taxation and Corporate Investment: A q-Theory Approach,' *Brookings Papers on Economic Activity*, no. 1, 67–127.

Taylor, J. B. (1975), 'Monetary Policy during a Transition to Rational Expectations,' *Journal of Political Economy*, **83**, 1009–21.

Taylor, J. B. (1977), 'Conditions for Unique Solutions in Stochastic Macroeconomic Models with Rational Expectations,' *Econometrica*, **45**, 1377–86.

Taylor, J. B. (1979), 'Estimation and Control of a Macroeconomic Model with Rational Expectations,' *Econometrica*, **47**, 1267–86.

Taylor, J. B. (1980a), 'Aggregate Dynamics and Staggered Contracts,' *Journal of Political Economy*, **88**, 1–23.

Taylor, J. B. (1980b), 'Output and Price Stability: An International Comparison,' *Journal of Economic Dynamics and Control*, 2, 109–32.

Taylor, J. B. (1981), 'On the Relation between the Variability of Inflation and The Average Inflation Rate,' in *Carnegie-Rochester Conference Series on Public Policy*, **15**, 57–86.

Taylor, J. B. (1982), 'The Swedish Investment Funds System as a Stabilization Policy Rule,' *Brookings Papers on Economic Activity*, no. 1, 57–99.

Tobin, J. (1969), 'A General Equilibrium Approach to Monetary Theory,' *Journal of Money Credit and Banking*, **1**, 15–29.

Townsend, R. M. (1983), 'Forecasting the Forecasts of Others,' *Journal of Political Economy*, **91**, 546–88.

Weiss, L. (1980), 'The Role for Active Monetary Policy in a Rational Expectations Model,' *Journal of Political Economy*, **88**, 221–33.

Comment

SEPPO HONKAPOHJA

Let me start by congratulating John Taylor for giving us a comprehensive, broadly based and highly readable guide to the voluminous literature on rational expectations models in macroeconomics. He also succeeds very well in avoiding the polemic approach that sometimes occurs in this literature, and thus the survey incorporates a well balanced evaluation of the major macroeconomic policy implications of the rational expectations approach.

I want to divide my comments into two parts. First, I will make some remarks of more general nature to certain issues taken up in the survey. Second, I will briefly examine a simple prototype of the influential models developed by Taylor himself to focus on some aspects and results that have not been considered previously.

1 GENERAL COMMENTS

At the fundamental level, the controversies in current macroeconomic theory presently concern the question of whether or not the capitalist market economy is best modeled in terms of Walrasian market-clearing. The problems of how expectations are formed seems now less topical, though, as pointed out by Taylor, a number of important, analytical and empirical troubles persist. As surveyed in the paper, and as is evident from many of the recent assessments by different scholars, the information-based or market-clearing models seem to have difficulties in empirical performance, and the broad viewpoint that in some sense markets do not clear and economic agents face quantity constraints appears to survive the rational expectations revolution.[1] But, then, the economics profession is facing the hard problem of how to model the non-Walrasian market behavior.

One approach is provided by the fixed-price or quantity-constrained models, surveyed by Jean-Jacques Laffont, and evaluated by Frank Hahn and Janos Kornai in this volume. I will not expand on them now, but I would like to stress that the fixed-price models taught at least one important lesson, namely that non-clearing markets have significant implications on modeling the behavior of individual agents – the so-called spillover effects, if you like. This general point is valid irrespective of particular modeling details, properties of the rationing mechanisms and the like. The fixed-price models do not incorporate rational expectations – indeed, most of them are of short-run nature – but, as pointed out by Taylor, some attempts at bridging the two approaches have been made. In fact, one can view the contract-based or non-market-clearing rational expectations models as quantity-constrained equilibrium models (compare Taylor, p. 410), about output being determined by demand) which specifically assume away the spillover effects and other such phenomena. In other words, the economy is always in the regime of Keynesian unemployment, in the terminology of the quantity-constrained models. In doing so, the models also tend to abstract from rational expectations of future rationing and their influence on current behavior (intertemporal spillovers), which are known to have quite significant consequences, at least in the context of fixed-price analysis (see, e.g., Hildenbrand and Hildenbrand, 1978; and Neary and Stiglitz, 1983).

On the technical side, incorporating spillover effects of current and future rationing leads to severe mathematical problems, since nonlinearities are bound to occur, even if the model is otherwise linear. (If the 'min' condition is adopted a linear model becomes at least piecewise-linear.) So far these problems seem unsolvable, though a couple of special cases have been treated: if the behavioral relations are linear, but output is determined as the minimum of demand and supply, then the methods of Green and Honkapohja (1983) are available; the other solvable case is that of market-clearing apart from random disturbances, analyzed by Green and Laffont (1981).[2]

This remark seems pertinent irrespective of the specifics of the theory of price determination adopted in the contract-based rational expectations models. It is, of course, at this point that economic theory faces very serious and hard challenges, and where currently a lot of important theoretical research is being carried out. At this point the literature on contract-based or non-market-clearing rational expectations models has taken another shortcut: it simply focuses on consequences and empirical explanatory power of intuitively conceivable price and wage adjustment rules. These formulations can easily be criticized as being either fully *ad hoc* or having at the most some partial justification in terms of 'choice-theoretic behavior' or bounded rationality. The postulated behavior is not necessarily optimal in the environment of the theoretical model. It should also be said that the loose adherence to the postulate that 'all expected gains from trade be realized' is pretty useless unless one is very explicit about the microeconomic detail of the model, but then some hard modelling problems have to be faced. The bold short-cut permits one to obtain results that hopefully give some guidance to what is to be expected from a more thorough scrutiny.

In this literature there exists a wide variety of different models, and we do not get very much guidance about the proper role of monetary policies beyond some general characteristics, since many of the more detailed results are quite sensitive to the structure of the model, especially to the choice of the price and wage determination equations. This is documented in detail by Taylor, but I want to take up a couple of specific points. As Taylor points out, one approach that has been used is to postulate expected or average market-clearing, so that prices are set to equate anticipated demand and supply, and then monetary policy has a stabilization role only when it has some lead time over price setting. In this context Taylor also mentions McCallum's (1980) result showing a particular case of neutrality, when the change in prices in each period depends on lagged excess demand and, with unit coefficient, on the anticipated change in the market-clearing prices. In my view there is no natural lead time for monetary policy in this case, as both it and prices are decided at the start of each period.[3] The McCallum model should more appropriately be included to the other group of models, namely those that directly model pricing decisions.

Many of these models are usefully interpreted as different formulations of the insight, from the expectations-augmented Phillips curve, that two factors are important for price setting decisions: (1) the prevailing average of prices over the relevant time span needs to be guessed, and (2) prices are probably responsive to excess demand or supply for the commodity. In both of these aspects different choices have been made in the literature, which has moreover introduced varying assumptions about the spacing over time of individual pricing decisions. If prices are systematically sluggish, then a conceivable choice for the former is the average of the expected price level in the relevant time span. This is the viewpoint adopted in the influential models by Taylor (1979; 1980a, 1980b), and he supplements it by assuming that individual pricing decisions are staggered over time, and that the relevant excess demand variable is the average of anticipated excess demands over the duration of the price decision. A questionable feature in his models is the fact that, while relative price considerations in pricing decisions appear, the models contain no relative price effects in the demand side, and the excess demand variable in individual price-setting decisions is the aggregate excess demand. In the survey Taylor suggests the disaggregation, but he does not analyze it, and I will briefly do so in the second part of this paper.

As Taylor points out, the rational expectations models with sticky prices typically yield the natural rate property that monetary policy is neutral in the long run, at least under stationarity, and provided its possible influence on the natural rate or steady-state level of output is abstracted away. However, the survey does not sufficiently emphasize that much of the recent debate has concerned neutrality over second moments, and in this respect neutrality fails in these models (there are a few exceptions).

As my last general remark, I would like to stress the significance of the non-uniqueness of equilibria ass a basic issue in rational expectations models. In the following section I will illustrate the phenomenon in the context of a prototype of Taylor's models. The stability argument, mentioned by Taylor, is problematic. It can be used only when justified by the model itself; e.g., the economic agents live for ever. Macroeconomic models are often silent about such features, and the stability assumptions are *ad hoc* and are adopted solely for the purpose of analytical ease.

2 A RE-EXAMINATION OF MODELS À LA TAYLOR

In several important papers John Taylor (1979, 1980a, 1980b) has formulated rational expectations models incorporating sticky wages and prices. The basic idea in Taylor's models is to modify the usual

Phillips curve price adjustment rule incorporating response to excess demand/supply and expected inflation into explicit rigidity of individual prices over several periods with partially overlapping durations, but taking into account forward-looking expectations in price-setting. In the simplest case of prices set for two elementary periods the decision takes into account two aspects. First, one considers what the aggregate price level will be on average over the two periods; second, an attempt is made to correct partially any anticipated discrepancy between demand and productive capacity.

In the earlier papers Taylor has used fully aggregated frameworks, and a very simple prototype of them is the following.

Model I

1 Aggregate demand:

$$y_t = 2a_1(m_t - p_t) + \mu_t$$

2 Definition of price level:

$$p_t = (1/2)\,(x_t + x_{t-1})$$

3 Price setting

$$x_t = (1/2)\,({}_{t-1}\hat{p}_t + {}_{t-1}\hat{p}_{t+1}) + (c/2)\,({}_{t-1}\hat{y}_t + {}_{t-1}\hat{y}_{t+1}) + \epsilon_t$$

4 Monetary accommodation:

$$m_t = \alpha p_t$$

where all variables are in logarithms, and output is measured in deviation form, so that y_t = aggregate demand (= output), p_t = aggregate price level, m_t = money supply, x_t = price set at the start of period t, and ϵ_t and μ_t are white noise disturbances; ${}_{t-1}\hat{y}_t$ denotes rational expectations formed at the beginning of period t of variable y_t, and similarly for other variables.

As I already pointed out, the model sketched in the survey is more disaggregated, and it attempts to capture some consequences of the fact that relative price considerations are present, and they are not constant over time. Since Taylor does not fully develop the generalization, I formulate a symmetric two-period-rigidity, two-sector (or 'island') version.

Model II

1 Aggregate demand for sector i:

$$y_{it} = a_1(m_t - p_t) + a_2(p_t - x_{it}) + \mu_{it}, \qquad i = 1, 2$$

2 Definition of price level:

$$p_t = (1/2)(x_{1t} + x_{2t})$$

3 Price setting equations:

$$x_{1t} = x_{1,t+1} = (1/2)({}_{t-1}\hat{p}_t + {}_{t-1}\hat{p}_{t+1}) + (c/2)({}_{t-1}\hat{y}_{1t} + {}_{t-1}\hat{y}_{2t}) + \epsilon_{1t}$$

$$x_{2,t-1} = x_{2t} = (1/2)({}_{t-2}\hat{\hat{p}}_{t-1} + {}_{t-2}\hat{\hat{p}}_t) + + (c/2)({}_{t-2}\hat{\hat{y}}_{2,t-1} + {}_{t-2}\hat{\hat{y}}_{2t}) + \epsilon_{2,t-1}$$

4 Monetary accommodation:

$$m_t = \alpha p_t$$

Here, subscript $i = 1, 2$ refers to the sector; ${}_{t-1}\hat{y}_{1t}$ denotes rational expectations of y_{1t} formed at the start of period t; and ${}_{t-2}\hat{\hat{y}}_{2t}$ denotes them at the start of $t-1$ and similarly for other variables. Otherwise the notation is the same as in model I. (It should be pointed out that this description is a little bit inexact, as it assumes that sector 1 sets its price at the beginning of the current period t. A symmetric description should be given for periods at which sector 2 sets its price.) Note that demand functions now incorporate the relative price effect. This symmetric formulation of the two sectors in model II facilitates the comparison of the aggregate implications of the two models.

It is a straightforward task to solve the two models. For model II, denote $\mu_t = \mu_{1t} + \mu_{2t}$, $\epsilon_t = \epsilon_{1t}$ or ϵ_{2t} (depending on the occurrence), $y_t = y_{1t} + y_{2t}$, x_t = price set at the start of t. Then the models may be written as follows.

1 Aggregate output:

$$y_t = a_1(\alpha - 1)(x_t + x_{t-1}) + \mu_t$$

2 Equation governing the behavior of x_t:

$$x_t = \beta_i x_{t-1} + \gamma_i \hat{x}_t + \beta_i \hat{x}_{t+1} + \epsilon_t, \qquad \text{for model } i = \text{I, II}.$$

In the second equation β_i and γ_i are parameters which differ for the two models, and they are given by

$$\text{Model I:} \quad \gamma_I = 2\beta_I;\ \beta_I = (1/4)[1+ca_1(\alpha-1)]$$

$$\text{Model II:} \quad \beta_{II} = (1/4)[1+ca_1(\alpha-1)+ca_2]$$

$$\gamma_{II} = (1/2)[1+ca_1(\alpha-1)-ca_2].$$

In this form the models are best analyzed by solving the latter equation, after which the behavior of output is easily determined from the former. Taylor (1980a) gives a method for solving the stationary solutions of the price equation. However, it is worth adopting a more general approach. Using the technique sketched in the Appendix, it may be shown that all solutions in the class of finite ARMA models involving (x_t, ϵ_t) are given by

$$x_t = (\beta_i)^{-1}(1-\gamma_i)\,x_{t-1} - x_{t-2} + \epsilon_t + C\epsilon_{t-1} \tag{A}$$

where C is an arbitrary constant; or

$$x_t = \lambda x_{t-1} + \epsilon_t \tag{B}$$

where λ is a real root of the quadratic equation

$$\lambda^2 + (\beta_i)^{-1}(\gamma_i - 1)\lambda + 1 = 0 \tag{*}$$

(if it exists as a real number). Note that there is a continuum of solutions of type (A) and two, one or no solutions of type (B).

It should be pointed out that this class of solutions can incorporate certain non-stationary processes, but evidently sunspot phenomena are ruled out.[4] We see immediately that solutions of class (A) are not stationary. Inspecting (B), we see that if it is non-empty a stationary solution exists, provided that the quadratic equation has distinct roots, that is, if and only if $|(\beta_i)^{-1}(\gamma_i-1)| > 2$, in view of the symmetry of the quadratic (implying that its roots are reciprocals of each other). Note that then a non-stationary solution of type (B) also exists.

If c, a_1 and $a_2 > 0$, the existence of a stationary solution is guaranteed in both models when $\alpha < 1$. It is straightforward to compare the stationary solution of the disaggregated extension (model II) with that of the aggregated model (model I). It may be shown that if c, a_1 and a_2 are not too large, and if monetary policy accommodates inflation at least to some extent, then the introduction of the relative price effects increases the steady-state variances of output and the price level. The opposite outcome is also *a priori* possible. The effects of varying the structural parameters on the steady state are partly similar, partly different for the two models. Therefore, as a conclusion we see that the systematic disaggregation in the Taylor model leads to some modifications, but it can be critical only in some specific circumstances.

More important is the fact that multiple solutions to the model always exist quite naturally, as there is no explicit reason for stationarity in Taylor's model. Indeed, there are circumstances in which all solutions shown above are non-stationary, a striking example being given by $c = 0$; i.e., expected average excess demand/supply has no effect on the individual price decisions. Since the various solutions (A) and (B) have ARMA forms, it would seem that ARMA modeling techniques are quite useful tools. Thus, a conceivable approach to the problem of multiple solutions and a possible alternative to the use of *a priori* selection criteria (such as stationarity) is an empirical one; let the data 'determine' the value of the multiplicity parameter.[5] However, one may object to this by asking why an economy should 'select' and follow a dynamic path given by a particular time-invariant value of the parameter? In my opinion, the existence of a continuum of solutions to many rational expectations models, whether of 'new classical' or 'Keynesian' variety, is a fundamental unresolved difficulty in this research.

APPENDIX

A class of solutions to the equation

$$p_t = \alpha + \Delta p_{t-1} + \gamma \hat{p}_t + \zeta \hat{p}_{t+1} + v_t \qquad (\%)$$

where α, Δ, γ, ζ are parameters with $\Delta \neq 0$, $\zeta \neq 0$, $\gamma \neq 1$, v_t is white noise, and $\hat{p}_t = E(p_t | I_{t-1})$, $\hat{p}_{t+1} = E(p_{t+1} | I_{t-1})$ with $I_{t-1} = [p_{t-1}, p_{t-2}, \ldots, ; v_{t-1}, v_{t-2}, \ldots,]$.

Proposition For the class of solutions of finite ARMA type, i.e.,

$$p_t = a + A(L) p_{t-1} + v_t + \Lambda(L) v_{t-1} \qquad (*)$$

where $A(L)$ and $\Lambda(L)$ are finite polynomials, all solutions are given by

$$p_t = A + B_1 p_{t-1} + B_2 p_{t-2} + v_t + Cv_{t-1} \tag{I}$$

where $A = -\alpha\zeta^{-1}$, $B_1 = \zeta^{-1}(1-\gamma)$, $B_2 = -\zeta^{-1}\Delta$, and C is arbitrary, and

$$p_t = A + B_1 p_{t-1} + v_t \tag{II}$$

where $\alpha = A[1-\gamma+\zeta(1+B_1)]$, and B_1 is a real root of $\zeta B_1^2 + (\gamma-1)B_1 + \Delta = 0$ (if a real root exists). This result can be proved by appropriately modifying the techniques of G. Evans (1983).

Proof: One first verifies that (I) and (II) give solutions to the equation. Consider then any finite ARMA model (*). Assume that $A(L)$ is of degree $(p-1)$, and $\Lambda(L)$ is of degree $(q-1)$. Rewrite the model as

$$p_t = A + B_1 p_{t-1} + B_2 p_{t-2} + \tilde{A}(L) p_{t-3} + v_t + Cv_{t-1} + \tilde{\Lambda}(L) v_{t-2} \tag{\$}$$

where then $\tilde{A}(L)$ is of degree $(p-3)$, and $\tilde{\Lambda}(L)$ is of degree $(q-3)$. Using ($), one computes the expectations $\hat{p}_t$ and $\hat{p}_{t+1}$, which can be then substituted into the basic equation (%). Subtracting ($) from it gives the identity

$$\begin{aligned} 0 \equiv & [\alpha+\gamma A+\zeta A(1+B_1)-A] + p_{t-1}[\Delta+\gamma B_1+\zeta(B_2+B_1^2)-B_1] \\ & + p_{t-2}[\gamma B_2 + \gamma\tilde{A}(L)L + \zeta B_1 B_2 + \zeta\tilde{A}(L) + \zeta B_1\tilde{A}(L)L \\ & - B_2 - \tilde{A}(L)L] + v_{t-1}[\gamma C + \gamma\tilde{\Lambda}(L)L + \zeta B_1 C + \zeta B_1\tilde{\Lambda}(L)L \\ & + \zeta\tilde{\Lambda}(L) - C - \tilde{\Lambda}(L)L]. \end{aligned}$$

In this expression all the square-bracketed terms must be equal to zero, for otherwise p_t would be ARMA of lower order. Then introduce the notation

$$\tilde{\Lambda}(L) = \sum_{s=0}^{m} \lambda_s L^s,\ \tilde{A}(L) = \sum_{s=0}^{n} a_s L^s, \text{ where } m = q-3, n = p-3.$$

Using the identities mentioned, it follows that

$$\lambda_m = 0,\ \zeta\lambda_s + (\gamma+\zeta B_1-1)\lambda_{s-1} = 0,\ C(\gamma+\zeta B_1-1)+\zeta\lambda_0 = 0.$$

Since $\zeta \neq 0$, it follows that $\tilde{\Lambda}(L) = 0$, irrespective of whether $(\gamma+\zeta B_1-1) = 0$ or not. Moreover, $C(\gamma+\zeta B_1-1) = 0$. Since in the identity the coefficient of p_{t-2} is zero operator, we get

$$a_n = 0,\ \zeta a_s + (\gamma + \zeta B_1 - 1)a_{s-1} = 0,\ B_2(\gamma + \zeta B_1 - 1) + \zeta a_0 = 0.$$

Again, it follows that $\tilde{A}(L) = 0$, and $B_2(\gamma + \zeta B_1 - 1) = 0$.

Consider the case $B_2 = 0$. It is easy to show that $B_1 = -(\gamma - 1)\zeta^{-1}$ is not the root of the quadratic equation obtained from the coefficient of p_{t-1} in the above identity. It follows that type (II) is the solution class. If $B_2 \neq 0$, then it is easy to see that we obtain type (I) solutions.

Remark: Analogous result holds for the solution class

$$p_t = \bar{p} + \sum_{s=0}^{\infty} \pi_s v_{t-s},\ \text{with } \bar{p} \text{ a constant.}$$

NOTES

Financial support from the Jenny and Antti Wihuri Foundation and the Finnish Cultural Foundation is gratefully acknowledged.

1 For example, see the recent evaluations by Grossman (1982) and McCallum (1982).

2 Green and Honkapohja (1983) develop an approximation for the expected value and variance of $\min(x, y)$ for a bivariate normal (x, y) with zero mean, but this approach works only when the model permits the solution of the rational expectations equilibria separately. For that the model should be linear. On the other hand, the Green–Laffont analysis can be consistent, because, given market-clearing apart from stochastic disturbances, no anticipated spillover effects are present.

3 It should be mentioned that in the McCallum model the results concerning monetary policy depend in fact on the structure of the model: compare McCallum (1982).

4 A characterization of all solutions to simple linear rational expectations models has been given in Gourieroux, Laffont and Monfort (1982).

5 Indeed, it is apparent that solutions (B) are related to (A). By multiplying both sides of (B) by $(1 - \lambda L)$, where λ is the other root (not used in (B)) of the polynomial (*), one obtains (A), with a particular value for the free parameter C. Thus, it seems possible to nest (A) and (B).

REFERENCES

Evans, G. (1983), 'Expectational Stability and the Multiple Equilibria Problem in Linear Rational Expectations Models' (mimeograph).

Gourieroux, C., Laffont, J.-J. and Monfort, A. (1982), 'Linear Rational Expectations Models: Analysis of the Solutions,' *Econometrica*, **50**, 409–25.

Green, J. R. and Honkapohja, S. (1983), 'Variance Minimizing Monetary Policies with Lagged Price Adjustment and Rational Expectations,' *European Economic Review*, **20**, 123–41.

Green, J. R. and Laffont, J.-J. (1981), 'Disequilibrium Dynamics with Inventories and Anticipatory Price-Setting,' *European Economic Review*, **16**, 199–221.

Grossman, H. I. (1982), 'The Natural-rate Hypothesis, the Rational Expectations Hypothesis, and the Remarkable Survival of Non-market-clearing Assumptions,' NBER Working Paper no. 1010.

Hildenbrand, K. and Hildenbrand, W. (1978), 'On Keynesian Equilibria with Unemployment and Quantity Rationing,' *Journal of Economic Theory*, **18**, 255–77.

McCallum, B. T. (1980), 'Rational Expectations and Macroeconomic Stabilization Policy: An Overview,' *Journal of Money, Credit, and Banking*, **12**, 716–46.

McCallum, B. T. (1982), 'Macroeconomics After a Decade of Rational Expectations: Some Critical Issues,' NBER Working Paper no. 1050.

Neary, J. P. and Stiglitz, J. E. (1983), 'Towards a Reconstruction of Keynesian Economics: Expectations and Constrained Equilibria,' *Quarterly Journal of Economics*, Supplement, **98**, 199–228.

Taylor, J. B. (1979), 'Estimation and Control of a Macroeconomic Model with Rational Expectations,' *Econometrica*, **47**, 1267–86.

Taylor, J. B. (1980a), 'Aggregate Dynamics and Staggered Contracts,' *Journal of Political Economy*, **88**, 1–23.

Taylor, J. B. (1980b), 'Output and Price Stability: An International Comparison,' *Journal of Economic Dynamics and Control*, **2**, 109–32.

Comment

LAURENCE WEISS

Rational expectations models in macroeconomics may be assessed from a variety of perspectives. Among these are:

(1) as a criticism of the expectations formulation mechanism as embodied in Keynesian econometric models;
(2) as a positive model of actual business cycles;
(3) for giving predictions about how the economy would respond to hypothetical interventions, particularly alternative rules for conducting monetary policy;
(4) as a normative guide to the conduct of policy;
(5) as a methodological commitment to demonstrate how observed aggregate outcomes are the result of individual optimizing behavior;
(6) as a continuation of the longstanding study of whether price signals are sufficient to guide efficient resource allocation in competitive economies.

John Taylor's excellent and lucid survey does an admirable job of addressing the first three sets of issues. Although one may quibble with his assertion of a 'conspicuous' empirically robust link between prices and output known as the 'Phillips curve,'[1] Taylor's emphasis on 'the policy ineffectiveness' debate accurately reflects the major research interest in the field. Few theoretical propositions in economics have received as much scrutiny and caused as much commotion as the idea that anticipated policy doesn't matter, and unanticipated policy can only make matters worse. Doubtless this debate, like earlier controversies, serves a useful pedagogical purpose. However, it has overshadowed what I believe to be the more valuable contribution of rational expectations models which relates to the last three issues above.

Rational expectations models have advanced the idea that macroeconomics is a branch of applied general equilibrium analysis and have greatly enhanced our theoretical understanding of the price system. Business cycles, particularly at their trough, certainly appear to be non-optimal. Reconciling this appearance with the strong efficiency properties of the price system, formally articulated in Arrow–Debreu models of general equilibrium, has been a longstanding challenge to economic theorists. A related research program has been to integrate accepted price theory with the appearance that 'money matters' for determining aggregate real variables.[2] Lucas's important (1972) article showed how both of these tasks might be accomplished. Lucas modified the Arrow–Debreu construct in two distinct ways. First, rather than positing a complete set of atemporal contingent claim markets, Lucas revived the earlier notion suggested by Hicks (1939) that agents transact in a sequence of spot markets in which current-period choices depend on agents' expectations of future spot prices. The second, more novel, feature of his approach was to assume that agents have asymmetric information and utilize observed price signals as imperfect summaries of other agents' information. In this framework 'money' could have real consequences because agents react to observed money prices which could be misleading indicators of the relevant relative price variable. By reacting to these possibly misleading signals, Lucas showed how *ex post* inefficient outcomes were compatible with *ex ante* optimal individual decisions. Rational expectations models are models of 'rational mistakes,' and suggest that business cycles are a manifestation of these regrettable, but comprehensible, decisions. Given this commitment to unify aggregate economic analysis with the theory of optimizing individual behavior, the assumption that agents' expectations are rational appears no more problematic, or falsifiable, than the assumption that agents maximize expected utility.

By focusing on the informational role of prices, rational expectations macro-models obviously have been influenced by, and contributed to, the extensive finance literature on 'the efficient market hypothesis.' This line of work was aimed primarily at showing empirically that security prices have the martingale property. The theoretical support for this hypothesis was that competitive traders would exploit the information in past stock prices such that, in equilibrium, this information was economically useless. The Lucas

(1972) article made analytically precise the idea that prices simultaneously are determined by, and determine, people's available information. To achieve this, Lucas utilized the apparatus in Muth (1961), which introduced the idea that in repeated stochastic settings the Marshallian equilibrium concept could be reinterpreted as a function mapping exogenous disturbances to market-determined prices and quantities. By extending this apparatus to situations in which traders have diverse private information, Lucas showed how the information flows both ways between agents and prices, and how prices could be more informative than any single agents' private information. A key insight of this formalization, not universally appreciated, was to show that this process did not necessarily have the strong efficiency properties portrayed in earlier, mostly verbal, developments. The connection between the equilibrium concept employed by Lucas and the earlier work in finnce was made explicit in Grossman (1975). In that paper, necessary and sufficient conditions were found for the price system to substitute for a direct exchange of agents' diverse information and thus to yield an allocation equivalent to that of a benevolent, omniscient social planner. Thus, rational expectations models have been instrumental for understanding the role of security prices to aggregate and convey information among diverse agents. Clearly, this line of research has implications for contexts beyond business cycle theory.

Much of my own research has been to show how asymmetric information in monetary sequence economies could have macroeconomic consequences beyond those considered in the original Lucas article. I developed a model in which exogenous (but rational) changes in the perceived profitability of new investment, a type of private sector instability emphasized by earlier theories, could generate undesirable fluctuations when these shocks were not universally perceived (Weiss, 1980). That analysis showed that 'policy' could have real and possibly beneficial effects through channels not considered by earlier theories, and thus that 'the policy ineffectiveness proposition' was of more limited applicability than had been previously thought. In Grossman and Weiss (1982), it was shown that asymmetric information about *ex ante* real interest rates could generate non-optimal fluctuations even when all current-period commodity prices and market-clearing nominal interest rates are directly observable. These analyses illustrate that problems of 'information' and 'signal extraction' are not figments of any one particular model, but a mode of analysis with wide applicability.

Existing contract-based monetary rational expectations models, of the type formulated by Taylor, have very different antecedents and motivations from the information-based models outlined above. If the term 'contract' is defined as a voluntary assent to deliver something in the future, perhaps conditional on some event, in return for some consideration, then the Arrow–Debreu model is a contract model par excellence. Thus the existence of contracts *per se* in no way vitiates the usefulness of that approach. However, not all feasible efficient allocations may be represented as outcomes of Arrow–Debreu economies. As is well understood (Arrow, 1971), the applicability of that analysis is limited to situations in which both parties can verify the occurrence of the event that dictates some specific performance. When agents have asymmetric information about some action or event of mutual interest, we would expect competitive analysis to be non-applicable and would have to seek elsewhere for a positive theory. If we interpret the word 'contract' to be exchanges that differ from trades where agents choose quantities at market-clearing prices because of asymmetric information, then 'contract theory' is an important departure from Arrow–Debreu models. Yet, the contract models of Taylor are not motivated by these considerations. Indeed, Taylor draws a sharp distinction between rational expectations models based on 'asymmetric information' and those based on 'contracts.'[3]

Taylor's model differs from the predictions of an Arrow–Debreu economy and yields a non-trivial role for policy not because agents contract in advance, but because of apparently non-optimal failure to index wage payments s to exogenous data. I say 'apparently' because the nature of the joint decision problem faced by the parties to this agreement is not fully articulated. Theoretical short-cuts are common in most branches of applied economics, and in macroeconomics the tradition is well entrenched. At the core of traditional Keynesian analysis is the idea that the labor market is somehow different, and that to explain observed outcomes we need to abandon optimizing behavior in favor of 'special assumptions' about the wage process, as Modigliani called them in his classic (1944) article. These assumptions implicate nominal wage stickiness as the source of fluctuations. Contract-based rational expectations models show that such 'special assumptions' can, in a formal sense, be made compatible with the rational expectations hypothesis, but I have never understood fully why one should attempt this demonstration. If one is willing to posit 'reasonable' descriptions of how wages and prices are determined without reference to an explicit optimizing justification, then why not simply assert that expectations can be similarly modeled? What is gained by substituting rational expectations for an alternative behavioral hypothesis? Surely, there is no direct evidence that expectations are more sensitive to changes in policy than is wage and price-setting behavior.

The answer provided by Taylor, with which I have some sympathy, is that these models make consistent various long-run neutrality propositions, about which there is widespread consensus, with a theory of short-run fluctuations, about which economists tend to be more eclectic. In this aspect the models represent a theoretical advance over earlier Keynesian theories. But the disenchantment with Keynesian models, within both the economics profession and the public at large, did not rest on this fine theoretical distinction. Rather, it rested on the failure of this theory to account for observed outcomes and for yielding misleading policy advice. Perhaps contract-based models have remedied these shortcomings, but I am skeptical. In what ways do these models make better contact with the data than earlier Keynesian models? Is there any evidence that the over-identifying restrictions implied by these theories are consistent with the data? Absent this type of empirical support, what reason is there to believe that contract-based models yield better forecasts of how the economy would respond to alternative policies than large-scale Keynesian econometric models?

My own view is that emphasis on the wage–employment bargain for understanding aggregate fluctuations has been misplaced. This is not to deny that there are many sound theoretical reasons for modeling the labor market different from, say, the market for applies. Rather, it stems from the empirical observation that observed co-movements between nominal wages, commodity prices, money and output, at least in the postwar US data, do not highlight these distinctions.[4]

What, then, have the information-based models accomplished? Can they claim any empirical success? Taylor's paper is a bit contradictory on this issue. At one point he says this model was 'successful' insofar as it 'fitted the facts it was designed to explain.' However, he goes on to write 'the evidence suggests that unanticipated prices do not give the Phillips curve correlation necessary for the Lucas theory.' He attempts to exonerate this failure by invoking 'supply shocks,' a term not precisely defined. While it is sometimes comforting to give names to unexplained components of observed outcomes, I find the evidence on price surprises and output compelling. If the Lucas model is to be judged as an empirically convincing model of actual business cycles, then, like the Keynesian theory it was designed to supplant, it must be judged a failure.

However, the information-based models can claim some more limited successes. Fama (1975) has shown that nominal interest rates use useful predictors of future inflation. Subsequent research has confirmed this finding and found also that the information contained in nominal interest rates is not made redundant by other observable aggregate data.[5] This latter finding clearly supports the proposition that market prices aggregate diverse information, a key insight of asymmetric rational expectations models. Similarly, Sims (1980) has shown that nominal interest rates help to predict output. In Litterman and Weiss (1982) we interpret this evidence as being most consistent with a non-monetary theory of output in which new information about future output is first reflected in market-clearing nominal rates.

One of the more interesting areas of empirical rational expectations work has been to assess if asset prices are 'too' volatile to be compatible with the rational expectations hypothesis (e.g., Shiller, 1981). This work is not cited in Taylor's survey, perhaps because its relevance to macroeconomics has not been made explicit. Yet I believe it has strong implications for aggregate economic activity. In a recent paper (Scheinkman and Weiss, 1983) we have shown how the inability to insure against idiosyncratic labor productivity disturbance can give rise to both aggregate fluctuations and apparently 'excessive' asset price volatility. This work points to a number of new directions for equilibrium business cycle research. First, it emphasizes how real, sectoral shifts might be an important source of aggregate fluctuations, a point that has received some empirical support in Lilien (1982). Second, it suggests that departures from the presumptive norm of frictionless, complete-information capital markets may be important for understanding aggregate outcomes, a point with a long tradition but not subject to much analytic developments. Third, it downplays the role of money and monetary policy for affecting real outcomes.

It is clear that rational expectations models have taught us a great deal. Much of what it has yielded is disquieting, both for pointing out defects in previous theories and for challenging the idea that economics can yield operational useful methods for improving the performance of competitive economies. Indeed, the rational expectations approach has revived the debate on whether business cycles are a social problem at all, in the sense of being correctable by some extra-market solution. We are still very far away from a resolution to this debate. It is clear that we have not exhausted the implications of maximizing behavior for aggregate outcomes. I feel strongly that, if we develop a successful model of business cycles, it will be of this type.

NOTES

1 For example, Barro (1983) concludes: 'There is no stable relation between the unemployment rate – or real economic activity more generally – and the growth rates of wages, prices or money.' He reports no significant correlation between these two variables in either interwar UK data, or postwar US data. A weak, positive association is found in postwar UK data.

2 The support that 'money matters' empirically was made in Freidman and Schwartz (1963). A more controversial demonstration of this proposition is in Sims (1972). However, this evidence is far from overwhelming (see Litterman and Weiss, 1982).

3 A similar sort of critique of the 'micro-foundations' of macroeconomic contract models is found in Harris and Hölmstrom (1983).

4 For example, in my own exploratory (unpublished) work with Bob Litterman (Litterman and Weiss, 1982), we were unable to find any predictive content in either average nominal wages or first-year contract wage increases for either prices or output beyond that contained in other aggregate series.

5 For example, Shiller (1980) writes (p. 148): 'We thus concur with Fama that his results and the results of his critics do suggest that most of the variation in nominal short rates can be attributed to inflationary expectations. Fama's results must give pause to those who believe that inflationary expectations are highly sluggish or follow a trend and that medium-run movements in short-term interest rates are movements in *ex ante* real rates.'

REFERENCES

Arrow, K. J. (1971), 'Insurance Risk and Resource Allocation,' in K. J. Arrow, *Essays in the Theory of Risk Bearing*, Markham, Chicago.

Barro, R. (1983), *Macroeconomics*, John Wiley, New York.

Fama, E. F. (1975), 'Short-term Interest Rates as Predictors of Inflation,' *American Economic Review*, **65**, 269–82.

Freidman, M. and Schwartz, A. (1963), *A Monetary History of the United States 1867–1960*, Princeton University Press.

Grossman, S. (1975), 'On the Efficiency of Competitive Stock Markets,' *Journal of Finance*, **31**, 573–85.

Grossman, S. and Weiss, L. (1982), 'Heterogenous Information and the Theory of the Business Cycle,' *Journal of Political Economy*, **90**, 699–728.

Harris, N. and Holmström, B. (1983), 'Macroeconomic Developments and Macroeconomics,' *American Economic Review*, **73**, 223–8.

Hicks, J. R. (1939), *Value and Capital*, Oxford University Press, New York.

Lilien, D. (1982), 'Sectoral Shifts and Cyclical Unemployment,' *Journal of Political Economy*, **90**, 777–94.

Litterman, R. and Weiss, L. (1982), 'Money, Real Interest Rates and Output – A Reinterpretation of Postwar US Data,' *Econometrica*, forthcoming.

Lucas, R. (1972), 'Expectations and the Neutrality of Money,' *Journal of Economic Theory*, **4**, 103–24.

Modigliani, F. (1944), 'Liquidity Preference and the Theory of Interest and Money,' *Econometrica*, **12**, 45–88.

Muth, T. F. (1961), 'Rational Expectations and the Theory of Price Movements,' *Econometrica*, **29**, 315–35.

Scheinkman, J. and Weiss, L. (1983), 'Borrowing Constraints and Aggregate Economic Behavior,' *Econometrica*, forthcoming.

Shiller, R. (1980), 'Can the Fed Control Real Interest Rates?' in S. Fisher (ed.), *Rational Expectations and Economic Policy*, University of Chicago Press for NBER, pp. 117–69.

Shiller, R. (1981), 'On the Use of Volatility Measures for Assessing Market Efficiency,' *Journal of Finance*, **36**, 291–304.

Sims, C. (1972), 'Money, Income and Causality,' *American Economic Review*, **62**, 540–52.

Sims, C. (1980), 'Comparison of Interwar and Postwar Business Cycles: Monetarism Reconsidered,' *American Economic Review*, **70**, 250–7.

Weiss, L. (1980), 'The Role for Active Monetary Policy in a Rational Expectations Model,' *Journal of Political Economy*, **88**, 221–33.

Contributors

Kenneth J. Arrow is Joan Kenney Professor of Economics at Stanford University. He was awarded the Nobel Prize for Economic Sciences in 1972.

Robert J. Aumann is Professor in the Department of Mathematics at the Hebrew University, Jerusalem.

Peter A. Diamond is Professor of Economics at the Massachusetts Institute of Technology, where he has taught since 1966.

Jean Jaskold Gabszewicz is Professor of Economics at the Catholic University of Louvain in Belgium. He is President of the Center for Operations Research and Econometrics (CORE).

Jerry R. Green is Professor of Economics and Chairman of the Economics Department at Harvard University, where he has taught since 1970. His work concerns the economics of information, taxation and related problems in public and corporate finance.

Frank Hahn is Professor of Economics at the University of Cambridge and a Fellow of Churchill College. He is a Fellow of the British Academy and an ex-President of the Econometric Society.

Oliver Hart is Professor of Economics at the London School of Economics. He is a former managing editor of the *Review of Economic Studies* and a Fellow of the Econometric Society.

Bengt Holmström is Professor of Economics and Organization at Yale University. He is a Fellow of the Econometric Society and an associate editor of *Econometrica*, *Review of Economic Studies*, and *Journal of Economic Theory*.

Seppo Honkapohja is Scientific Director of the Yrjö Jahnsson Foundation. He teaches at the University of Helsinki and has been editor of the *Scandinavian Journal of Economics* since 1984.

Mervyn King is Professor of Economics at the London School of Economics.

János Kornai is Professor of Economics at the Karl Marx University of Economics at Budapest, and the author of numerous books and papers.

Mordecai Kurz is Professor of Economics and Director of Economics at the Institute for Mathematical Studies in the Social Sciences, Stanford University.

Jean-Jacques Laffont is Professor of Economics at the University of Toulouse, France. He is a member of the Council of the Econometric Society and associate editor of several scientific journals.

John G. Riley was a member of the Faculty of Boston College 1971–3 and since then of UCLA. His primary research area is the economics of uncertainty and information. He is co-editor of the *American Economic Review*.

Reinhard Selten was Professor of Economics at the Free University of Berlin until 1972, at the University of Bielefeld until 1984 and since then at the University of Bonn.

Martin Shubik is Seymour H. Knox Professor of Mathematical Institutional Economics at Yale University. He is a Fellow of the Econometric Society and the World Academy of Arts and Sciences, and has been consultant to many major corporations and government agencies. He is the author of many books and articles and has specialized primarily in strategic analysis.

Hugo Sonnenschein has been Professor of Economics at Princeton University since 1976. He has been awarded fellowships by the Guggenheim Foundation, the Ford Foundation, and the Social Science Research Council. He is a Fellow of the Econometric Society and the American Academy of Arts and Science. From 1977 to 1984 he was the editor of *Econometrica*.

John B. Taylor is Professor of Economics, Stanford University. He has been a Research Associate at the National Bureau of Economic Research since 1984 and co-editor of *American Economic Review*.

Laurence Weiss is Professor in the Department of Economics, University of Chicago.

Author Index

Subject Index